SALTWATER FLY FISHING

From Maine to Texas

Edited by Don Phillips

SALTWATER FLY FISHING
From Maine to Texas

Local Guides Describe 43 of the Best Shallow-Water Destinations and the Fly Patterns that Work for Them

Edited by Don Phillips

Frank Amato
PORTLAND

About the Author

Don Phillips was born in Chattanooga, Tennessee in 1933, but he was brought up in Springfield, Massachusetts and spent his working life in north-central Connecticut. He is married to Dee, his wife of fifteen years, and has four children and ten grandchildren.

Don graduated from Technical High School in Springfield, and went on to receive a Bachelor of Science degree in Mechanical Engineering from the University of Massachusetts and a Master of Science degree in Business Management from the Hartford Graduate Center.

He worked for the Hamilton Standard division of United Technologies Corporation for over thirty-three years, holding various positions in Engineering, Marketing, Planning and Administration. While still working full time, he designed and developed the world's first fly-rod made from boron fibers, and went on to form his own company, producing over 700 rods and blanks under the FlyCraft® label. He received two U.S. patents related to composite material fly-rod design.

Don has written many feature articles for most of the major fly-fishing magazines and he is an FFF-Certified Casting Instructor.

Retired since 1989, Don lives on Marco Island, Florida, where he fishes, golfs, writes, and travels extensively.

Softbound ISBN: 1-57188-252-9; Hardbound ISBN: 1-57188-254-5

Frank Amato Publications, Inc.
P.O. Box 82112, Portland, Oregon 97282
(503) 653-8108
Printed in Singapore

1 3 5 7 9 10 8 6 4 2

Table of Contents

Foreword
By Lou Tabory

I first met Don Phillips when he tossed a skinny fly-rod in my hands and said "Try it." Don was one of the early pioneers developing fly rods from boron and graphite fibers. The rods had a different feel and they took several years to become popular; but the rest is history.

Now, Don again has created something unique, a book that helps anglers find new places to fish. This book is not meant to teach you to fly-fish in the sea or to give you every secret fishing spot within a destination area. What it does accomplish is to provide fly-fishers with a good starting point so that they can try different areas with less effort. Finding good fishing spots in salt water takes time and effort. Many novices become completely lost when trying new locations. Most freshman anglers should hire a guide when fishing a new area, or at least get help from a local tackle shop.

The more-skilled anglers know how to read the water and find the conditions that offer hot fishing but, even then, learning a new spot takes some work. Having a reference guide to consult gives even the experienced fly-fisher some insight into the fishery. I tell my students "Learn several spots well and then keep learning other places so you can broaden your knowledge." When fishing new waters it helps to have confidence so you can be prepared. It is important to have some background when you travel, such as knowing the type of forage fish and game fish you can expect to find at different times of the year. And it is very helpful to know what flies to bring and their sizes, what tackle and line types work best, and what is the best time of year to plan a fishing trip. There is important information contained in this book that will help anglers enjoy fishing many popular areas from Maine to Texas.

The other value I found in this book is reading about places in new locations that I have never fished. It generated curiosity in my fishing juices that makes me want to travel to different locations along the Gulf coast and to the east coast of Florida. And I know that on those trips the contacts listed and information provided in this book will help both my planning and my fishing.

Introduction and Summary
By Don Phillips

To those of us who live near the salt, it has been obvious that the popularity of saltwater fly-fishing has skyrocketed over the past 10 to 15 years. In the late 1980s, I would hardly ever see a flats skiff in the waters around my hometown of Marco Island, Florida, and when I did it was invariably piloted by a local fishing guide working the waters with his spin- or bait-fishing clients. I could easily go out fishing for a dozen days before seeing anyone who was fly-fishing. When fly-fishers were seen, they were usually in a bass or jon boat like mine. We reveled in our ability to get way back into the shallow mangrove bays, but often paid the price by taking on water and a rough ride when we had to go out in the Gulf to access our favorite haunts. Today, our bays and creeks are often visited by modern flats skiffs and it's not uncommon to see a half dozen fly-fishers during a day's outing. And friends in Massachusetts, Connecticut and Texas have reported the same extent of growth in the popularity of fly-fishing.

Over this 10- to 15-year period, Collier County in southwest Florida has seen an explosion in the number of fly shops and skilled fly-fishing guides, and the introduction of two fly-fishing clubs having a combined membership totaling nearly 200. Nationally, two new magazines specializing in saltwater fly-fishing have been introduced and the half dozen general fly-fishing magazines have substantially increased their coverage of the salt. Even the high-circulation sporting magazines like *Field & Stream, Outdoor Life, Florida Sportsman, Saltwater Sportsman* have jumped into the fray and increased their feature content of saltwater fly-fishing.

Why is saltwater fly-fishing growing so rapidly? Well, first of all the larger market of fly-fishing is still growing, no doubt partially due to our country's expanding economy and the accompanying rise in discretionary income. Along with the growth of the overall fly-fishing market, the increased pressures on freshwater resources have surely persuaded some fly-fishers to cast their flies into the salt waters. It's becoming increasingly difficult to experience the joys of freshwater fly-fishing without being crowded or otherwise exposed to the negative impacts of man on his environment. Sure, one can always get away to places where one can fly-fish in solitude; the problem is that these freshwater places are increasingly fewer and more distant. The best places are seldom private, or at least not for long.

Our coastal waters are of course also subjected to increasing pressures, but not yet to the extent of freshwater streams, rivers and lakes. The casual observer may see the saltwater fishing playing field as a few thousand miles of shoreline, but those who have gotten their feet wet appreciate that the coastal shoreline is literally the tip of the iceberg. The beaches and their near-shore flats and structure are gratefully augmented by inshore bays, flats, creeks, canals, estuaries, marshes and rivers wherein tidal influence can extend many miles upstream. The saltwater fly-fisher's playground is thus a huge area that as a whole has only been nominally impacted by fishing pressure. And, recent restrictions on commercial fishing have increased the health of our inshore gamefish populations. Let's just hope that the outlook remains positive ten or twenty years from now.

Saltwater fly-fishing has been a recognized pastime for well over 100 years, and yet it is still an exciting new frontier whose challenges are increasingly attractive to many fly-fishers. And, nowadays, the technology of fly-fishing equipment and the profusion of how-to literature is very helpful in enabling the average fly-fisher to meet the special challenges of the salt. Lightweight multi-piece rods, corrosion-resistant high-performance reels, slippery long-life lines and innovative flies made from both natural and man-made materials have been very influential in helping fly-fishers to be successful in salt water. While appreciating the benefits of technology and knowledge, it's very easy to admire the accomplishments of Henshall, Brooks, Albright and others who pioneered our sport with relatively crude equipment and a sparse base of knowledge.

There are certainly many skills which can be effectively transferred from freshwater to saltwater fly-fishing. Nevertheless, it's a different ball game that can be very intimidating to the novice. In general, saltwater game fish are larger, stronger and faster than their freshwater cousins. These characteristics will often mean that getting the fish on the hook is just part of the challenge to a fly-fisher's skill. The process of fighting and landing the fish can be a formidable test of one's strength and skill. However, it is this writer's opinion that the most difficult challenges still lie in first locating and then enticing the fish to impale itself on the sharp end of your fly.

When I used to fly-fish my favorite streams and rivers in the Northeast and in the Rocky Mountains, the process of locating the fish was usually rather routine. Past experience usually led me to familiar locations where, day after day and year after year, trout were finning and feeding. Even in unfamiliar waters, these generic places can still be located where water depth, current speed, structure, etc. fit recognizable criteria. Locating the game fish in salt water is much more complicated. First of all, your target game fish might literally be hundreds of miles distant from where you last saw them months ago. Striped bass, bluefish, bonito, false albacore and tarpon all migrate very long distances as they proceed through their annual life cycle. Even if it's time for a species to be "in the neighborhood", their specific location may be difficult to determine.

In general, the location of a particular species will depend upon its level of comfort, the availability of food, the proximity of larger predators and the timing of the various stages of its spawning cycle. Water depth, current speed, water salinity, and water temperature are all additional factors which will influence where the fish are most likely to be located. And, of course, most species are different in their spawning cycles, tolerance to water temperature, prey preferences, etc. It is thus a most complicated equation which determines where any given gamefish species will be on any given day or even hour of the day. This is the fundamental reason why the skill of the professional fishing guide can be the dominant factor in determining whether or not the fly-fisher will be successful. The professional guide who works a given area for weeks and months at a time has the benefit of knowing where the fish are each day, day after day. Yesterday's action is almost always the best starting point for today's adventure.

Even after locating the fish, there remains the challenge of casting the fly to it and retrieving it in a manner that will get its attention and provoke it into inhaling your offering of fur and feathers. Casting is a fly-fishing skill that is readily transferred from fresh to salt water, but the level of required skill is an order of magnitude more demanding. The required fly-fishing equipment will also be different. The casts usually need to be longer and will sometimes have to be delivered within a few seconds. And, to match the local prey, the flies are larger and more wind-resistant, making them more difficult to deliver. Just to make things even more difficult, the target is sometimes moving in random directions and the wind is usually blowing enough to challenge your attempts at both distance and accuracy. Nevertheless, the fly-fisher who is willing to do his or her homework and put in the necessary practice time can overcome these hurdles and become an accomplished saltwater fly-caster.

Once the fly has been delivered to the correct location, its subsequent movement can make the difference between success and failure. As with their freshwater cousins, different saltwater prey behave in different ways and the same species will behave differently under varying circumstances. Shrimp and crab tumble in a strong current not unlike mayfly nymphs in a trout stream, suggesting the need for a drag-free drift. They will however behave in much different ways when confronted by a predator or when just going about their usual business on the grass flats. Baitfish exhibit similar differences in motion behavior under varying circumstances.

Selection of the right fly can also be important to success in saltwater fly-fishing. The bonefish of the Florida Keys are very selective when it comes to fly pattern; like the brown trout of heavily fished spring creeks. Snook in particular can be very selective, especially in clear, shallow water along the beaches. Of course, at the other end of the scale, a school of bluefish or striped bass blitzing a pod of bay anchovies will seldom exhibit selectivity while competitively participating in this feeding frenzy. And so, "matching the hatch" is sometimes important, but not always.

Summarizing the last several paragraphs, catching saltwater fish on a fly requires several elements of success: 1) Go to the right destination at the right time of the year, 2) Be at the right place at the right tidal stage, 3) Be equipped with the appropriate fly-fishing equipment, 4) Select the proper fly, 5) Make a good cast to the fish, 6) Retrieve the fly in an appropriate manner, 7) Set the hook at the time of the strike and 8) Fight the fish and bring him to hand. These eight elements make up the subject matter of the many books and magazine articles that have been written on saltwater fly-fishing. This book focuses on the first four of these eight elements.

Although the personal research required for me to write this book would be immensely pleasurable, covering the geographic scope of "Maine to Texas" would not be practical from a time or a financial viewpoint. At least, not to cover the level of detail intended. My solution to this problem was to use the literature and personal contacts to identify a wide range of good saltwater destinations and to then select a local, knowledgeable, professional guide to author a chapter on each destination. Recognizing the difficulty of getting similar coverage from dozens of guides with varying backgrounds, I spent considerable time in preparing a specification defining the content of the chapters, their length and the format of the common charts. This approach risked the possibility of a boring read, because of the repetitive nature of the content of each chapter. This risk was worth taking, however, since this book is really a reference handbook for fishing destinations and not likely to be read cover-to-cover, in chapter sequence. As it turned out, there is sufficient variability in the writing style of the guides to prevent the impression of a series of cloned chapters. I am immensely grateful to each of the 43 guides who, without compensation, agreed to work with me in the preparation of this book. Each of them had to take considerable time out from their demanding work schedules to put their local knowledge down on paper.

In this book, each chapter covers a specific shallow-water destination and describes the local geography in sufficient detail to permit a visiting fly-fisher to get a feel for the area. Major roads are identified, as are areas for lodging, meals, and rental of boats, canoes or kayaks. Access areas are identified for those striking out on their own, and guides and fly shops are identified to assist the fly-fisher in advanced planning. Recommended tackle is described for the various types of fly-fishing that will be encountered. Most important, the specific gamefish targets for the area are identified, together with their typical size ranges and the extent that they are likely to be available for each month of the year. Similarly, the most important prey are identified, their typical size ranges and the extent that they are likely to be available by month. Local prey names have been used in these charts, even though there is some inconsistency at times in the terminology used at various destinations. For both game fish and prey, availability is numerically rated from 0 to 5, so a brief glance at the charts conveys a lot of information to help predict the expected opportunities for a particular trip date. Finally, each prey species is linked to one or more fly patterns which our author-guides have found to be productive when these prey are active. The recipes for each of these more than 260 fly patterns are provided in the Appendix, so that fly tiers can prepare for their trips with a suitable arsenal of flies. Each guide was also requested to identify his one favorite fly and to send a replica to me. These flies are depicted in the color plate section of this book, to again assist the fly tier in constructing faithful copies.

Although the specific nature of this book's content might suggest that the catching of fish with a fly is simply a case of following programmed instructions (a+b+c+d+e = fish), those experienced in such matters will readily appreciate that these data are intended to simply lead the fly-fisher in the right direction.

An overall perspective of gamefish availability can be seen from the chart on page 9, which was prepared from the information on the charts in the chapters. The numbers in this chart are the highest numbers of availability for any destination in each of the coastal states, regardless of the months of highest availability. The game fish were separated into

Gamefish Species	*Extent of Gamefish Availability, by State													
	ME	MA	RI	CT	NY	NJ	MD	NC	SC	GA	FL	AL	LA	TX
Bluefish	3	5	5	5	5	5	5	5	5	5	5	5	5	
Bonito		5	5	3	4	4	5							5
False Albacore		5	5	5	5	5	5							
Striped Bass	5	5	5	5	5	5	5	5						5
Weakfish		3	3	5	5	4								
Flounder					3	5			5	5			5	5
Spanish Mackerel			5		1	4	5	5	5	5	5			5
Black Drum											4		5	5
Cobia						3					5	5	4	3
Jack Crevalle								5	5		5		5	5
Ladyfish						4		5	5	5	5			5
Pompano						4					5	5		
Redfish							3	5	5	5	5	5	5	5
Sheepshead													4	5
Snook											5			4
Sp. Seatrout							5	5	5	5	5	5	5	5
Tarpon											5	5	4	5
Tripletail											5	4	5	4
Barracuda											4			
Bonefish											5			
Permit											5			
Snapper											5	5		

*1=Scarce, 2=Spotty, 3=Available, 4=Readily Available, 5=Widely Available

Prey Species	*Extent of Prey Availability, by State													
	ME	MA	RI	CT	NY	NJ	MD	NC	SC	GA	FL	AL	LA	TX
Butterfish		5		4	3									
Eels	5	5			4		5							
Sand Eels	5	5	5	5	5	5								
Silversides/Spearing	5	5	5	5	5	5	5							
Squid		5		3	3									
Alewives/Herring	5	5	5	3	3	4	4	5			5	5		
Anchovies		5	5	5	5	5	5				5	5	5	4
Crabs	5	5	3	3	4	5	5	5	5	3	5		5	5
Croakers								4						5
Bunker/Menhaden		5	5	5	4	5	5	5	5	3	5	5	5	5
Killifish		3	5					5	5	3	5			5
Shad	5			3							5			5
Shrimp	5	3	3	3	4	5	4	5	5	3	5		5	5
Worms		2	5	3	3	5	5				4			4
Ballyhoo											4			4
Glass Minnows								5	4		5	5	5	5
Mullet							5	5	5	3	5	5	5	5
Needlefish											5			4
Pilchards											5			
Pinfish								5			5			4
Sand Fleas											5			
Sardines											5			4

*1=Scarce, 2=Spotty, 3=Available, 4=Readily Available, 5=Widely Available

four groups. The first group of five are those game fish that are generally associated with the cooler waters of the northeastern coastal states, the second group of two cover a rather broad range from Connecticut to Texas, the third group of eleven are those which are usually considered to be warmwater species, and the last group of four species are uniquely associated with the sub-tropical regions of Florida. Although this chart tends to raise more questions than it answers, I believe that it has some utility in demonstrating the very large number of gamefish species that we pursue, and the wide range of their dispersal. And this chart is actually understated, since many pelagic, anadromous and bottom-dwelling species which often are caught by coastal fly-fishers were intentionally omitted in the interests of brevity.

Similarly, the Prey Availability Chart reflects the large number of prey which we attempt to imitate with our flies, and the extent to which they are available in our eastern coastal states. And, again, many less-common prey like lobsters and juvenile game fish were omitted to simplify the chart.

The large number of prey species represents a formidable database of models for fly-tying and, indeed, thousands of saltwater fly patterns have been developed for these prey over the years. The Appendix describes the recipes for all of the 260+ fly patterns listed on the prey charts of the 43 destination chapters. Even though this is just a modest sampling of the successful fly patterns used from Maine to Texas, it's a large enough sample to illustrate some of the common characteristics of productive fly patterns. One interesting aspect of these patterns is the extent to which a few of them have been adopted by many guides along the whole coastline. This is illustrated in the table at right, prepared by summarizing the number of times that a fly pattern (or a minor variation thereof) was specified in the right-hand column of the chapters' prey charts. I've listed only those patterns which have been mentioned four or more times.

This table shows that a few innovative fly-tiers have developed basic tying concepts that have proven to be successful far beyond the scope of the original applications.

I am most grateful to Lou Tabory for agreeing to write the foreword for this book. I first met Lou back in the late 1970s when we both lived in Connecticut. I was literally mesmerized by his casting skills, as demonstrated during various fly-fishing expositions and programs. Since then, his considerable saltwater fly-fishing knowledge and writing skills have also received wide recognition. But, most important, Lou is one of the nicest guys in our field, and I'm honored to be sharing these pages with him.

Fly Pattern Name	No. Of Citations*	Pattern Originator
Clouser Deep Minnow	78	Bob Clouser
Lefty's Deceiver	64	Lefty Kreh
Del Brown's Permit Fly (Merkin)	19	Del Brown
Surf Candy	8	Bob Popovics
Woolhead Mullet	7	Unknown
Bendback	6	Chico Fernandez
Seaducer	6	Chico Fernandez
Ultra Shrimp	6	Bob Popovics
Tabory's Slab Side	5	Lou Tabory
Epoxy Baitfish	5	Glenn Mikkleson
Crazy Charlie	4	Bob Nauheim
Grocery Fly	4	Brock Apfel

*No. of times specified in prey charts by guides other than the originator.

The Northeast

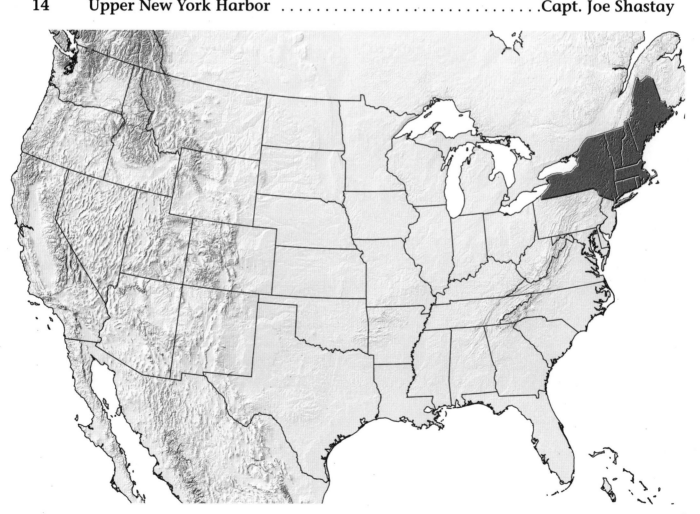

Chapter 1: Kennebec River and Eastern Casco Bay

by Capt. Doug Jowett

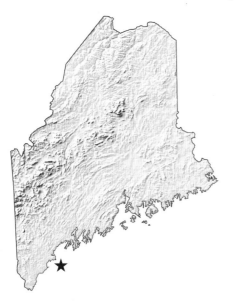

The striped bass fly-fishing in Maine's Kennebec River and Casco Bay has been often described as "World Class". This description is justified, since these waters provide outstanding striped bass angling for the fly-fisher from May into October. Casco Bay is a large area encompassing the Portland, Maine vicinity to the village of Phippsburg to the east. Dozens of islands dot the bay to provide for outstanding habitat for feeding stripers. The waters are rich with both structure and bait.

The entrance of the "mighty" Kennebec River is located east of Phippsburg at the famed Wood and Seguin islands, both of which have lighthouses. The river then winds inland with a tidal push of 42 miles to Augusta, Maine. These waters are so rich in habitat and feed, that almost any location will hold stripers but some spots are always more prolific than other feeding areas. Like most striped bass fishing waters, heavy current flowing over or around structure will fish the best.

On the eastern side of Casco Bay, there is a little river called the Royal that flows out into the Bay and splits into several small channels as it finds its way to the open ocean.

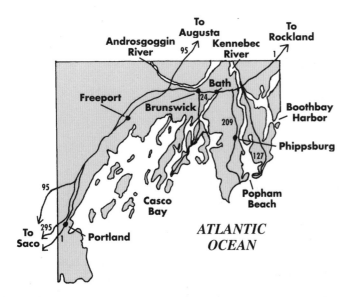

The channels around Cousins Island and the channel to Lanes Island and the eastern shore in South Freeport are very productive areas to fish. There is an area called Pound of Tea at the entrance of Freeport Harbor that holds big fish regularly. When fishing the numerous islands of Casco Bay, one should concentrate on the south side (ocean facing) where there is considerable turbulence created by moving tides. The outer island fishing can be the most productive for large fish but it is also the most dangerous.

From South Freeport east to Phippsburg, there are numerous points facing the open Atlantic Ocean that hold fish all season long. Places like Mere Point, Ash Point, Land's End, West Cundy Point and Small Point are all names often found in striper anglers' log books. All are rocky points that create wonderful holding waters for stripers. Inside all these points, up inside as we say in Maine, you will find tidal flats that regularly attract schools of striped bass on most tides. Keep in mind that these flats drain completely dry at low tide and will have as much as eight feet of water during high tide. Clam and worm diggers work the flats daily, creating a natural chum-line when the water comes back in. This chum always attracts stripers that must be approached with stealth in the shallow water. Flats fishing will be productive with small shrimp patterns, crab patterns, lobster patterns and various herring patterns; all fished close to the bottom with clear-intermediate fly lines. In mid-summer, both small and large popper flies will get the stripers' attention. A particularly good pattern is the popular Gartside Gurgle Bug.

From Small Point, heading east to the Kennebec River, you enter one of the "world series" locations of striper territory. The entrance of the river on the west side is guarded by extensive beach areas extending up the river a half mile to Fort Popham. Here, the mix of current, structure and bait provide a Nirvana for striper anglers. This is one of the more accessible public areas for striped bass anglers that regularly provides quality sport. There is no vehicle access allowed on any Maine beach.

From Fort Popham, upriver 42 miles to Augusta, there exists a potpourri of fishing opportunities from small flats to dangerous ledges to numerous humps. One famous spot is "The Hump" at Green Point on the east side of the Kennebec. This tiny area is situated perfectly for feeding fish that wait for bait to be washed by their positions. The area is so small that only one boat at a time can drift through it. Boats will line up hoping for the opportunity to try their luck. You can spend hours at this location trying to make just the right presentation of a large Grocery Fly, to attract the large fish that stage in this area. Many anglers have been known to spend an entire day fishing the Hump while fish come and go during outgoing and incoming tides. The river itself is so big and productive that it deserves a small book of its own to cover all the potential. It is very accessi-

Species	Typical Size - inches	J	F	M	A	M	J	J	A	S	O	N	D
Striped Bass	12 - 40				1	4	5	5	5	5	5	2	1
Bluefish	12 - 30						2	2	3	2			

1=Scarce, 2=Spotty, 3=Available, 4=Readily Available, 5=Widely Available

ble by boat but has limited accessibility by land. The areas most accessible by land are the numerous bridges and the public parks in Bath, Hallowell, Gardner and Augusta.

A few miles east of the mouth of the Kennebec River is Reed State Park, a vast, sandy beach where the Little River dumps into the ocean. The entire public beach is storied water for beach, striped bass angling.

I recommend the use of 9-foot, 10-weight fly rods that can handle heavy, 450-grain shooting heads, clear intermediate lines and weight-forward floating lines. Fishing for larger striped bass is accomplished using the heavy shooting heads with large Grocery Flys. Schoolie striped bass to 30 inches will take many different types of flies fished on clear, intermediate or floating lines. Chartruese and white Clousers, Deceivers and Half and Halfs tied on 1/0 to 5/0 hooks will produce all season. The forage fish that striped bass chase in Maine's mid-coast area include fin-fish such as herring, mackerel, harbor pollock, shad, spearing, smelt, sand eels and American eels. Crustacean prey include shrimp, crabs and lobsters. Brown crab patterns with 2/0 to 5/0 hooks also work well on the flats. Small shrimp patterns tied on 2 to 1/0 hooks are sometimes the only fly that will produce during hot summer days. Hard-bodied epoxy flies in sizes 1 to 2/0 representing spearing and sand eels will work well when fished in sandy beach areas.

The land area between Portland and Bath consists of many popular tourist destinations. Accordingly there is no shortage of restaurants of all types and overnight accommodations include everything from campgrounds to five-star inns and hotels. Early bookings are always necessary. Boat rentals are scarce, but canoe and kayak rentals are readily available. The enclosed tables list fly-fishing guides and fly shops in this local area.

Guides (Capt.)	Phone/Fax	Email Address
John Ford	207-471-5858	captjohn@mainesaltwater.com
Doug Jowett	207-725-4573	djowett@gwi.net
Dave Pecci	207-442-8581	dave@obsessioncharters.com
Tim Rafford	207-829-4578	trafford@gwi.net
Jerry Sullivan	207-833-5447	flyfishing@maine.com
Robin Thayer	207-737-4695	pmo@agate.net
Harvey Wheeler	207-829-5485	cptwheeler@aol.com

Eldridge Brothers Fly Shop
PO Box 69, US Route 1
Neddick, ME 0309297
207-363-9269

Kennebec Angler
Commercial St.
Bath, ME 04530
207-442-8239

Kittery Trading Post
301 Route 1, Kittery, ME 03904
Contact: Chris Henson
207-439-2700

L.L. Bean Inc.
Main St. Freeport, ME 04033
Contact: Fly Fishing Hotline
800-347-4552

Port Fly Shop
176B Port Rd.
Kennebunkport, ME 04043

The Tackle Shop
61 India St., Portland, ME 04101
207-773-3474
207-967-5889

Captain Doug Jowett is a full-time striped bass and false albacore guide in Maine and on Cape Cod who has taught fly-fishing for L.L. Bean, is a pro staffer for Diamondback Fly Rods and founder of the Atlantic Canada fly-fishing Institute. Doug's writings are found in national magazines, regional publications, several newspapers and four books. He caught his first fly rod striped bass in 1962.

Most Common Prey	Typical Size (inches)	Usual Months of Availability*												Typical Matching Fly Patterns**
		J	F	M	A	M	J	J	A	S	O	N	D	
American Eels	6 - 30				1	1	3	5	5	4	2	2	2	Keel Eel
Crabs	1 - 3					1	4	5	5	5	4	1	1	Tarpon Crab
Harbor Pollack - Juvenile	2 - 12						3	5	5	5	3	1	1	Grocery Fly (B)
Herring	6 - 10	1	1	1	2	4	5	4	2	2	2	1	1	Grocery Fly (A)
Herring - Juvenile	1 - 2							4	4	3	3	3	3	Lefty's Deceiver (D)
Lobster	4				1	4	5	5	5	5	4	4	1	Lobster Fly
Mackerel	5 - 16					1	3	4	4	3	2	1	1	Lefty's Deceiver (E)
Rainbow Smelt	2 - 6				1	2	2	3	5	4	3	1	1	Lefty's Deceiver (F)
Sandeels	1 - 6					1	3	5	5	4	3	1	1	Stick Candy
Shad	10 - 12				2	4	4	1	1	1				Grocery Fly (A)
Shad - Juvenile	1 - 3							5	4	2	2	2	1	Lefty's Deceiver (D)
Shrimp	1 - 3					3	4	5	5	5	3	1	1	Ultra Shrimp
Spearing	1 - 2					1	4	5	5	5	4	2	1	Surf Candy

*1=Scarce, 2=Spotty, 3=Available, 4=Readily Available, 5=Widely Available • ** Pattern Recipe in Appendix A.

Chapter 2: Plum Island and Cape Ann

By Capt. Barry J. Clemson

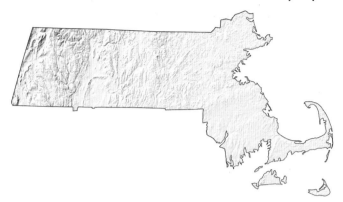

Plum Island has long been recognized as one of the most pristine estuary habitats in the northeastern United States. Plum Island Sound is the center of 20,000 acres of salt marsh between Cape Ann and the New Hampshire state border. The area is well known for its anadromous fish runs, for its finfish spawning habitat, and as an important migratory stop for birds using the Atlantic Flyway. Most of the Sound is included within the boundaries of the Parker River National Wildlife Refuge. The Sound is located only 27 miles from the city of Boston; its average tidal range is 9 feet.

Boat access to the north of Plum Island, near the mouth of the Merrimack River, is by way of a paved ramp at Salisbury State Park. Other launching ramps are also available on the Merrimack River. During high tide, boats can move from the Merrimack River to the north end of Plum Island Sound by passing through the Plum Island River. At lower tides, boats must exit the mouth of the Merrimack and proceed south along the beachfront to the Ipswich area. Boaters should be cautious about traversing the Merrimack River mouth; it can be dangerous, especially during outgoing tides with a strong wind from the east. Access to the south end of the Sound can also be obtained via boat ramps on the Rowley River and at the Ipswich River town landing. These departure points will provide access to prime fishing areas, but local knowledge is recommended because of the many shallow areas at low tide.

Plum Island/Cape Ann consists of an exceptionally large number of fishing areas and offers many different types of fly-fishing experiences. Regardless of the conditions of tide, wind or weather, there are bound to be accessible areas worth targeting. In the spring, striped bass migrate into the estuaries, traveling up the rivers and creeks in search of the warm water and prey provided by the shallow mud flats. Water temperatures can rise 10 to 15 degrees from the ocean to the estuaries and 65-70 degrees F. seems to be a good temperature range for fish activity and feeding. In the summer, the stripers will move out of the back creeks, to the river mouths and to Plum Island Sound and the Atlantic Ocean, to reach the cooler water temperatures.

At times, large schools of fish will be feeding on the surface. With the simultaneous activities of baitfish jumping, stripers swirling and birds diving, the excitement can easily give the fly-fisher a bad case of striper fever. At these times, it's not uncommon for anglers to land 50 fish within a single morning. Sometimes, poppers are the best prey imitations, while at other times a deep-diving Clouser Minnow will be more productive. As shown on the included prey chart, our game fish enjoy a varied diet and will feast on a wide range of food from krill to lobster. Matching the fly to the prey size and profile seems to result in more hookups than simply focusing on fly color. The odds will also increase in your favor if your stripping technique results in the fly matching the movement of the prey species. The best times to fish are at pre-dawn, dusk, at night and on foggy, cloudy or rainy days.

The fishing areas of Plum Island and Cape Ann can be divided into three different categories. First, the sandy beaches of Plum Island; Crane's Beach and Coffin's Beach are fly-fishers' delights because of the beautiful and uncrowded surroundings. Sight-fishing for stripers in the surf is quite productive from mid-summer and into the fall, either by wading or from a boat. Large schools of fish can be found along the miles of beaches during the striped bass spring and fall migrations.

The coastal areas of Cape Ann and vicinity are a hallmark of the New England coastline and they include imposing rock outcroppings, ledges and cliffs, especially along the north coast of Cape Ann. Precise casting is required into the whitewater surge just inches from the rock for success. Fishing in these areas can be successful both from the rocks or from a boat. Although not an optimum time for striper fishing, hookups can be gotten at mid-day in the bright sun. Keep a particular lookout for rocky points with good current flow. Larger fish can often be found holding in 10 to 20 feet of water, just off these points.

The estuaries of Plum Island Sound, the Essex River basin and adjacent rivers and creeks offer calmer water to drift and cast flies to sod banks, mussel beds, tidal rips,

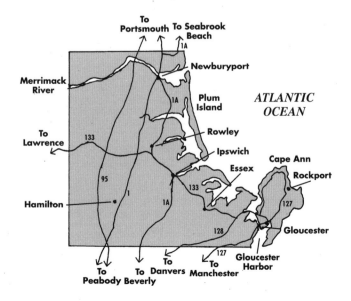

Species	Typical Size - Pounds	J	F	M	A	M	J	J	A	S	O	N	D
Bluefish	1 - 15						1	2	4	5	5	4	2
Bluefin Tuna	15 - 900						1	3	4	5	5	5	3
Striped Bass	1 - 25				2	5	5	5	5	5	5	4	3

1=Scarce, 2=Spotty, 3=Available, 4=Readily Available, 5=Widely Available

marsh grass, deep holes and clam beds. The latter areas are particularly good where clammers have been at work; the stripers love to feed on broken clams and the beds produce a natural chum line to attract schools of fish to the flats.

For the shorebound angler, Joppa Flats off the southern side of the mouth of the Merrimack River is a great place to fish early in the season. Another good spot is Plum Island Point, near the northern tip of the Island. The boat docks, rips and jetties of this area are also worth trying. Also, Sandy Point in the State Park at the southern end of Plum Island offers good surf, beach and rock structure. Crane's Beach in Ipswich and Halibut Point State Park in Rockport are also beautiful spots with good fly-fishing.

I keep a number of different-sized rods rigged on my boat, ready for various situations. A range of from 8- to 11-weight outfits covers all but the truly big-game species. A 9-weight outfit is considered the preferred all-around rod for both boat and wading purposes. For nearly all of my fishing, I prefer to use depth charge or fast-sinking lines. This helps to throw large fly patterns into the wind and gets the fly down deep into the feeding zone in fast-moving water. An intermediate-density line is good for surface-feeding fish and for beach fishing at night. When using sinking lines, I use a short, hard mono butt section looped to a 2- to 5-foot, 20-pound fluorocarbon tippet. For intermediate-density lines, I use a 7- to 9-foot tapered leader with a 12- to 20-pound (depending on water clarity) tippet.

Many creature comforts are available in the nearby cities of Newburyport, Rowley, Ipswich and Essex. Most lodging is of the bed-and-breakfast type. Camping is available in Salisbury State Park, which also includes good trailer accommodations.

Guides (Capt.)	Phone/Fax	Email Address
Fred Christian	978-631-1879	fred@captainfred.com
Barry Clemson	978-948-3750	bclemson@bigfoot.com
Nat Moody	978-525-4477	info@first-light-anglers.com
Rick Southgate	978-768-7471	
Derek Springler	978-525-4477	info@first-light-anglers.com
Bredan Stokes	978-465-5136	

American Angling Supply
23 Main St., Salem, NH 03079
Contact: David
603-893-3333

First Light Anglers
17 Ashland Ave.
Bath, ME 04530
207-442-8239
info@first-light-anglers.com

Orvis - Boston
84 State St.
Boston, MA, 02109
617-742-0288

River Edge Trading
50 Dodge St., Beverly, MA 01915
Contact: David
978-921-8008

Surfland Bait & Tackle
28 Plum Island Blvd.
Newbury, MA 01951
978-462-4202

Capt. Barry J. Clemson has been competently guiding fly-fishers on a full-time basis for over a decade. Barry fishes from a seaworthy 20-foot Action-Craft Flatsmaster boat powered by a 200-horsepower Yamaha outboard. Capt. Clemson's years of experience and dedication to the sport of fly-fishing have given him a broad scope of knowledge to draw upon for both catching and teaching. He has been featured in fly-fisherman magazine and in two fly-fishing videos on the Outdoor Life Network's cable channel. A long-time supporter of the Coastal Conservation Association, he maintains a catch-and-release policy on his boat.

Most Common Prey	Typical Size (inches)	Usual Months of Availability*												Typical Matching Fly Patterns**
		J	F	M	A	M	J	J	A	S	O	N	D	
Crabs	2 - 4				5	5	5	5	5	5	5	5		Del's Crab Fly
Herring	3 - 8				5	5	5	5	4	4	4	3		Wagtail Deceiver
Mackerel	5 - 12					5	5	4	4	5	3	2		Barry's Holy Mackerel
Menhaden	3 - 14					4	5	5	5	5	4	3		Brad Burns' Grocery Fly
Pollack	4 - 12				3	5	5	5	4	4	3	2		Cape Ann Kinky Klouser
Sand Eels	0.5 - 4.0					4	5	5	5	5	4	3		Sparse Chartreuse Clouser
Shrimp	0.5 - 1.5				5	5	5	5	5	5	5	5		Sparse Chartreuse Clouser
Silversides	2 - 5				2	3	4	5	5	3	3	2		Chartreuse Flashtail Clouser

*1=Scarce, 2=Spotty, 3=Available, 4=Readily Available, 5=Widely Available • ** Pattern Recipe in Appendix A.

Chapter 3: Boston Harbor and the South Shore

By Capt. Mike Bartlett

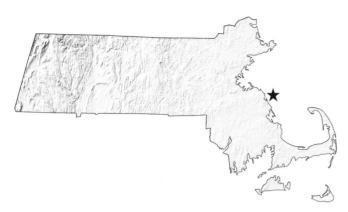

When fly-fishers think about Boston, they usually relate the area to Paul Revere, the Freedom Trail, the Old North Church and the Boston Tea Party. It hasn't been until recently that fly-rodders have turned their attention to the world-class fishing opportunities that now lie within a stone's throw from some of the nation's most historic sites. Boston fishermen haven't always had it so good. Before the late 1980s, Boston had one of the nation's most polluted harbors. Now, it is common to catch striped bass and bluefish just a few yards from Logan Airport, thanks to the joint efforts of former-Governor Bill Weld and a local activist group, Save the Harbor - Save the Bay.

The Boston area is of course a Class-A resort destination because of its historical significance and the many tourist attractions. There are many things to do for the non-fishing visitor, including museums and sports parks. Sleeping accommodations and restaurants are widespread and suitable for a wide range of tastes. Camping facilities are also available on many of the islands which are part of the Harbor Islands National Park. A unique feature of the Harbor's waterfront is that fly-fishing clients can be picked up at Rowe's Wharf in the heart of downtown.

Boston's inner harbor is a thoroughly urban fishery that includes 35 inshore islands that provide enough structure and channels to satisfy the saltwater fly-fisher for a lifetime. The migratory stripers begin to show up near Boston in late April and early May, following schools of alewives and mackerel. The exact timing of their arrival is predicated on water temperature. School-sized stripers precede the larger striped bass, and the first schools can be found in the estuaries and bays where the relatively shallow water and dark-colored peat substrate warms up first. By late May and early June, waves of big stripers patrol the shallows and rocky ledges near the communities of Scituate and Cohasset and the islands of Boston's outer harbor. These large bass, spurred by their increased metabolic activity in the warming waters, aggressively take alewife and mackerel imitator patterns in 3/0 to 5/0 sizes. Some of the most consistent fly-fishing for big stripers can be expected from mid-June through mid-July.

In the Boston area, the most productive fly-fishing is done in a boat. These mobile casting platforms allow fly-fishers to move to the structures which provide edge-effect shelter for the prey species. This acts like a magnet for the predatory stripers. 8- to 10-weight fly rods with 300- to 400-grain fast-sinking, shooting taper lines are the best tools for casting into the wash, tidal surge or current interface. A short 3- to 5-foot length of 20-pound fluorocarbon leader helps in turning over heavily weighted and dressed flies and aids in getting the fly down to the 3- to 5-foot depth strike-zone. The fly reel should be a reliable, corrosion-resistant, disc-drag design, with the capability of spooling at least 200 yards of 30-pound backing line. Striped bass in the 40- to 50-pound range have been caught in the harbor and along the South Shore's rocky coastline.

Boston's inner harbor has a veritable melting pot of prey species. Improved water quality and relatively cold water throughout the summer months yields nutrients and plankton for silversides (sperling), adult herring (alewives) and menhaden (bunker). Every morning from May through October somewhere in the harbor where the current is flowing, stripers push the bait to the surface. This attracts the gulls and terns and, of course, fly-fishers. As the season progresses and the waters warm, juvenile herring, peanut bunker and sand eels add to the feeding frenzy. By August, bluefish begin to frequent the region. Attractor patterns such as the Clouser Deep Minnow in sizes 1/0 to 3/0 mimic these smaller prey. The Clouser Half-and-Half (Flatwing Clouser) in sizes 2/0 to 3/0 are more appropriate for the larger baitfish. In both cases, chartreuse/white color combinations seem to provide the best visibility in Boston Harbor's often-murky water. The majority of stripers caught in the inner harbor are fish between 15 and 30 inches in length. Possibly, this is a result of the relationship

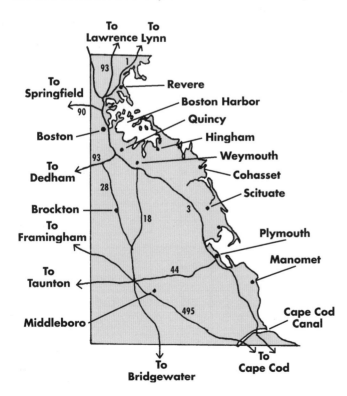

Species	Typical Size - Pounds	J	F	M	A	M	J	J	A	S	O	N	D
Bluefish	1 - 40	1	1	1	1	1	2	3	5	4	2	1	1
Striped Bass	3 - 20	1	1	1	2	4	5	5	5	5	4	2	1

1=Scarce, 2=Spotty, 3=Available, 4=Readily Available, 5=Widely Available

between prey size and predator energy expenditure. At any rate, the sheer biomass that the harbor supports is incredible.

The South Shore of Massachusetts extends from the city of Weymouth to the Cape Cod Canal. The South Shore has long-standing roots in quality fishing, and can be easily reached from Routes 93 and 3. Boston's Water Shuttle is another means of traveling to South Shore destinations while avoiding the congestion of automobile traffic. The fishing on the South Shore is more diverse and scenic than it is in Boston Harbor and the area includes many estuary systems associated with the Back, North and South rivers. There are significant flats in Plymouth and Duxbury, and rock gardens and ledges in Cohasset and Scituate. The fly-fishing season in the estuaries starts early; the mud bottom attracting the sun's rays and warming the water much earlier than in the deeper waters of the area. Accordingly, the first groups of migratory fish can be found here. Fortunately, the deeper water around the rocks and ledges remains cold, attracting both the school fish and the larger fish throughout the heat of July and August.

To properly fish the rocks and ledges you'll probably need an experienced guide to keep away from submerged hazards at all tide levels. However, once you have been introduced to an area and learned its vagaries, you might be able to be successful on your own by exercising considerable caution. Back River in Weymouth, Scituate Harbor, Green Harbor in Marshfield and Plymouth Harbor have state-maintained boat-launching facilities which can be used for a daily fee. Skiffs can also be rented on the North River in Marshfield. For the shorebound angler, the banks of the North and South Rivers coursing the towns of Marshfield, Scituate and Norwell are accessible by foot and can provide excellent early-season fly-fishing; especially during the herring run. The rocky promontories at Third and Fourth cliffs in Scituate and the "Glades" of North Scituate are accessible from shore, as are the wadable barrier beaches, bars and mud flats of Kingston, Duxbury and Plymouth bays.

Fishing in the Boston Harbor and the South Shore is an experience you'll not forget. Where else can the fly-fisher find so much history, good food, comfortable lodging, other activities and world-class fly-fishing within a stone's throw of each other?

Guides (Capt.)	Phone/Fax	Email Address
Mike Bartlett	781-293-6402	Bfast@bigfoot.com
Barry Clemson	978-463-9249	bclemson@valley.net
Wayne Frieden	781-545-6263	reeldream2@mediaone.net
Charlie Lemieux	781-747-2602	charlie@hwoflyfishing.com
Jon Perrette	781-749-9855	
Bill Smith	781-293-7444/ 781-826-8490	dragginfl@aol.com

Concord Outfitters
84 Commonwealth Ave. Concord, MA 01742
Contact: Andy Bonzagni
978-318-0330 /978-318-0880
andy@concordoutfitters.com

Henry Weston Outfitters
15 Columbia Rd. Pembroke, MA 02359
Contact: Jim Mckay
207-442-8239
jim@hwoflyfishing.com

Old Salt Outfitters
Route 3A, Hingham, MA 02043
Contact: Jon Perette
781-749-9855 /781-749-7557
jeffdoyle@emial.msn.com

Orvis - Boston
84 State St., Boston, MA 02109
Contact: Christina Tobias
617-742-9791/617-742-9791

Orvis - Framingham
575 Worcester Rd, Rt 9
Contact: Brad Wolfe
508-872-7711/508-872-5570
darbeflow@aol.com

Stoddard's
50 Temple Place, Boston, MA 02111
Contact: Phil Klug
617-426-4187/617-357-8263
stoddards@worlds.com

Capt. Mike Bartlett grew up in Marshfield on the South Shore and has fished the coastal and offshore waters of Massachusetts for over 35 years. He holds both B.A. and Masters in Biology degrees and has been teaching Marine Biology on the South Shore for the past 27 years. Mike owns and operates B-Fast Sport Fishing Charters, running offshore charters out of Green Harbor in Marshfield and inshore charters out of Cohasset and Boston Harbor. He is the Orvis-endorsed fly-fishing guide for Boston Harbor and the South Shore and is a member of the OMC/HydraSports Fishing Team. Mike is a published author and he regularly presents seminars on saltwater sports fishing throughout the Northeast.

Most Common Prey	Typical Size (inches)	Usual Months of Availability*												Typical Matching Fly Patterns**
		J	F	M	A	M	J	J	A	S	O	N	D	
Alewives	4 - 7	1	1	2	5	5	5	3	3	3	1	1	1	Sar-Mul-Mac, Herring/Alewife
Mackerel	6 - 12	1	1	2	5	5	3	3	2	2	2	1	1	Sar-Mul-Mac, Epoxy-Head Deceiver
Menhaden	2 - 10	1	1	1	2	4	4	5	5	5	4	2	1	Epoxy-Head Deceiver, Afternoon Delight
Sand Eels	3 - 7	1	1	2	2	3	4	4	4	4	3	2	1	Clouser Deep Minnow (A), Epoxy Sand Eel
Silversides	2 - 4	1	1	2	4	5	5	5	5	4	4	2	1	Flat-Wing Clouser, Clouser Deep Minnow (A)

*1=Scarce, 2=Spotty, 3=Available, 4=Readily Available, 5=Widely Available • ** Pattern Recipe in Appendix A.

Chapter 4: The Flats and Backwaters of the Middle Cape

By Capt. Bill Strakele

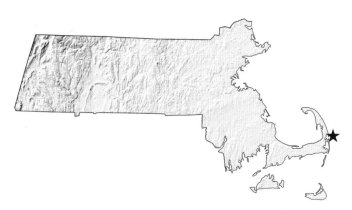

Middle Cape Cod is a typical New England seaside resort area, dotted with a half dozen small towns and the homes of vacationers, retirees and working residents. There are more than enough motels, restaurants, marinas, etc. to satisfy the tastes of the visiting fly-fisher and his family and friends. Nickerson State Park in the town of Brewster has extensive camping facilities on a first-come, first-served basis and also has some excellent fresh-water fishing in several of its lakes. In general, lodging accommodations during the summer should be booked at least 6 to 8 weeks in advance due to the area's popularity as a vacation destination. The middle Cape is particularly pleasant in the spring and fall, before and after the peak vacation season.

Good fly-fishing opportunities are available on both the eastern (Atlantic Ocean) and western (Cape Cod Bay) shores of the middle Cape, with many varied scenarios. The chart below lists the primary gamefish species, as well as their usual times of availability. Nauset Inlet, on the eastern coast and located in the town of Orleans, is a sportsman's paradise and has a legendary reputation for its striped bass fishing. The 20-pound class IGFA record striper of 73 pounds was caught on nearby Nauset Beach.

The Atlantic Ocean beaches north and south of Nauset Inlet are among the most beautiful in the world, and they offer outstanding fly-fishing opportunities.

Nauset Marsh, located just inland and north of Nauset Inlet, is comprised of 750 acres of pristine waterways. The northern half of Nauset Marsh lies within the boundaries of the Cape Cod National Seashore and the southern half lies within the towns of Eastham and Orleans. The Marsh is home to striped bass, bluefish and hickory shad. Ospreys, rosetta terns and piping plovers also make the Marsh and nearby beaches their home.

On the western shore, only a few miles from the eastern shore, is Cape Cod Bay, home to many sport fish including striped bass, bluefish and bluefin tuna. The flats of the Bay extend northward from the town of Dennis, through Brewster and into Eastham. The fly-fishing here is similar to that in Florida; sight-casting to large fish cruising the shallow flats in gin-clear water.

Boat-launching facilities are numerous on both coasts. Most are well maintained and only the facilities at Sesuit Harbor in Dennis charge a fee for use. Local tides must always be considered when selecting launching ramps and fishing areas, since the average tide movement is 9 vertical feet, exceeding 12 feet at times. It is recommended to hire an experienced fly-fishing guide when venturing out in a boat for the first time, to become familiar with local routes and difficult areas. One must be particularly cautious when fishing Nauset Inlet from a boat because of the shallow bars, the aggressive surf, and the 6- to 7-knot current that races through the area. Each year, 6 to 10 boats capsize in the Inlet and some are destroyed on the Inlet's outer bars.

For the wading fly-fisher, the Atlantic Ocean and Cape Cod Bay beaches are readily available. Two of the favorite wading areas on the Bay are Paine's Creek and the Brewster Flats. By selecting the proper tide, one can wade-fish up to a half mile off the beach for both stripers and bluefish. Large areas of this part of Cape Cod Bay are very shallow at low tide and criss-crossed with deeper yet wadable channels. One must take care however to not wait too long to return to shore. The tide can often sweep in behind you, requiring a long swim back to the beach. Both Cape Cod Bay and Nauset Marsh are excellent places to use a canoe or kayak to access good fly-fishing

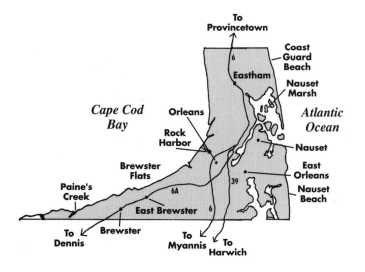

Species	Typical Size - Pounds	J	F	M	A	M	J	J	A	S	O	N	D
Bluefish	5 - 20						2	3	5	5	3	2	
Hickory Shad	1 - 4							2	3	3	4	2	
Striped Bass	5 - 30				2	3	4	5	5	4	3	2	

1=Scarce, 2=Spotty, 3=Available, 4=Readily Available, 5=Widely Available

areas. The marsh has many creeks and coves that hold fish all summer, but be careful to avoid the inlet, especially on strong outgoing tides.

Preferred fly-fishing tackle is a 9-foot, 9- to 10-weight fly rod with either an intermediate-density or fast-sinking line, depending upon the size of the surf. A good-quality reel is required, capable of holding the fly line plus 150-200 yards of 20-pound backing and manufactured from corrosion-resistant materials. Leaders of 7 to 9 feet are quite adequate, with 15- to 20-pound tippets. Below is a chart outlining the prevalent fish prey and their respective fly pattern imitations. One of my favorites is the Clouser Minnow in chartreuse on a 1/0 hook. Poppers also work quite well, producing explosive strikes from aggressive fish. Del's Merkin, also called Del Brown's Permit Fly, is a great fly on the flats when the fish are keying on crabs.

Guides (Capt.)	Phone/Fax	Email Address
Capt. Andrew Cummings	508-349-0819	Bfast@bigfoot.com
Harry Koons*	508-255-4079	ratsass@capecod.net
Capt. Joe Leclair	508-748-3014	
Tony Stetzko*	508-255-2357	
Capt. Bill Strakele	508-255-5223	oca@capecod.net
*shore guides		

Fly Fishing the Cape
Harwich Commons
Harwich, MA 02645
Contact: Peter Alves
508-432-1200

Goose Hummock Shop
Rte. 6A Town Cove, Orleans, MA 02653
Contact: Mike Measkill
508-255-0455
goose@capecod.net

Mac Squids
85 Rte. 6A,
Orleans, MA
508-240-0778

Nauset Angler
2 Beach Rd., E. Orleans, MA
Contact: Harry Koons
508-255-4242
ratsass@capecod.net

Capt. Bill Strakele has been fishing Cape Cod for thirty years and is currently endorsed by Sage, Thomas & Thomas, Tibor, Lund and OMC. A custom fly tier who has developed some very innovative variations on proven patterns, Bill is a frequent guest tier at local fly-fishing events. Capt. Strakele's flies can be found in the finest fly shops on the Cape and nearby islands.

Most Common Prey	Typical Size (inches)	Usual Months of Availability*												Typical Matching Fly Patterns**
		J	F	M	A	M	J	J	A	S	O	N	D	
Bunker	2.5 - 4								3	3				Rat's Arse, Lefty's Deceiver (H)
Crabs	1.25					4	4	4	4	4				Del Brown's Permit Fly
Herring	3.5 - 5.5				3	3			3	3				Roccus Rattle (C), Lefty's Deceiver (C)
Sand Eels	2 - 4.5					4	4	4	4	4				Roccus Rattle (B), Clouser Deep Minnow (B)
Silversides	3 - 4	3	3	3	3	3	3	3	3	3	3	3	3	Roccus Rattle (A), Blonde, Clouser Deep Minnow (A)
General														Roccus Rattle, Bill Strakele's Popper

*1=Scarce, 2=Spotty, 3=Available, 4=Readily Available, 5=Widely Available • ** Pattern Recipe in Appendix A.

Chapter 5: Chatham and Monomoy Island

By Peter Alves

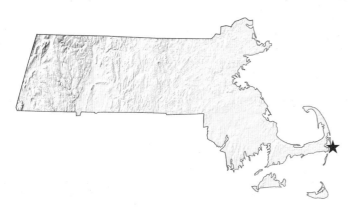

Chatham is a well-known tourist destination on Cape Cod in Massachusetts. This charming town, with its beautiful beaches, attracts visitors by the thousands every summer. Being geared for the tourist season, there are plenty of places right on the main street to get a bite to eat and to find a soft pillow to rest your head. The surrounding towns of Orleans and Harwich also offer numerous restaurants and accommodations. Extensive camping facilities are available in Nickerson State Park, off Route 6A in Orleans.

South of Chatham lies Monomoy, a 2750-acre island managed by the U.S. Fish & Wildlife Service. Monomoy is a flyway refuge to many different species of birds, as well as home to large colonies of gray and harbor seals. Pleasant Bay, north of Chatham, has been the safe harbor for the famous Chatham commercial fishing fleet for many years. The areas around Chatham, especially Monomoy Island and Pleasant Bay, have long been known for their bountiful supply of striped bass, bluefish and other fish species. Boat-launching ramps are located on the Oyster River west of Chatham, in Ryders Cove north of Chatham and at Stage Harbor in Chatham. After June 1, the Stage Harbor ramp can only be used by town residents or permit holders. There are also several marinas in Chatham with launching and docking facilities. Boat rentals are available on the Oyster River and both canoe and kayak rentals can be found in Orleans and Harwich. Navigating the Chatham area can be difficult due to significant tide changes and numerous sand bars, so it is advisable to obtain the services of one of our local guides and to query the local fly shops on fishing conditions.

The best fly-fishing opportunities are available near structure; rocks, edges, points, sand bars, etc. Sight-fishing can be excellent in the crystal-clear waters of Pleasant Bay, since baitfish often follow the incoming tide as the water begins to cover the bars and flats. When the tide turns, the baitfish are flushed to the deeper edge, a perfect place for game fish to ambush their prey. One of the best types of structure to fish off Chatham are the rips around Monomoy, where fast tidal currents pour over steep drop-offs and create turbulent areas. The predator fish know that the baitfish will be swept into these turbulent pockets and they will be waiting there for an easy meal. Boaters need to exercise considerable caution when fishing the rips, especially the larger ones at Bearses Shoals.

Fly fishing from shore can be very productive. Access to fishable water is relatively easy throughout Chatham, but care must be taken to comply with parking restrictions. Striped bass and bluefish are quite active along the beach, especially where there are deep cuts, moving water, visible bait activity and man-made or natural structures. Lighthouse Beach and Hardings Beach in Chatham are well-known striper hotspots because of their proximity to the moving water near the inlets of Pleasant Bay and Stage Harbor. With game fish cruising in the channels and along the beach, both of these beaches offer great wading opportunities for fly-fishers, especially during early morning and evening tides.

A 9-foot, 9-weight fly rod will serve well for catching all of the local game fish except for the bluefin tuna. Wind is a

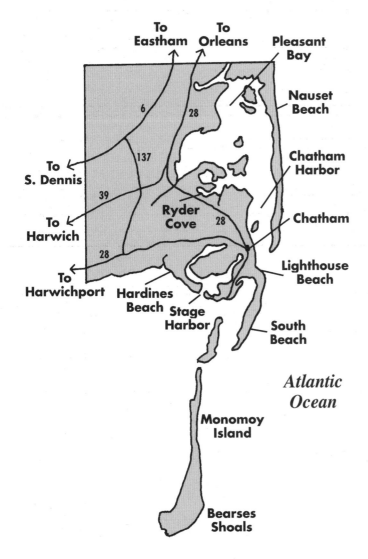

Species	Typical Size - Pounds	J	F	M	A	M	J	J	A	S	O	N	D
Bluefin Tuna	20 - 400							1	3	3	3		
Bluefish	2 - 18				3	4	4	4	4	4	4		
Bonito	4 - 10							1	2	4	2		
False Albacore	4 - 12							1	3	4	3		
Striped Bass	5 - 40				1	5	5	5	5	5	5	1	

1=Scarce, 2=Spotty, 3=Available, 4=Readily Available, 5=Widely Available

constant factor in Chatham, and the 9-weight rod has the extra punch to deal with it and still have sufficient tip flex to have fun landing smaller schoolie bass. The most popular reels are those made from anodized barstock aluminum, with a cork drag system, and able to hold at least 150 yards of 30-pound backing. If I had to pick one fly line with which to fish, it would be an intermediate-density, sinking line. Many anglers also carry a faster-sinking line, with a sink rate of about 5.5 inches per second, to cover fishing depths of 8 feet or more. I would highly recommend carrying such a line on an extra reel spool, remembering to shorten the leader to under 6 feet to promote fast sinking. A 9-foot tapered leader ending in a 12- to 16-pound tippet is usually appropriate for striped bass. Bluefish require an additional 15- to 30-pound wire bite guard, because of their extremely sharp teeth. These feeding machines are really fast and they love to go airborne.

When schools of either bluefish or stripers erupt to chase bait to the surface and the birds join the foray, surface poppers will usually bring quick results. Sand eels are the most abundant baitfish off Chatham and a sparse Clouser or Eric's Sand Eel on a #2 to 1/0 hook will often imitate these prey. When the herring, squid, bunker or silversides are the prey of the moment, a large Deceiver, Pink Squid, Slab Side or Monomoy Flat Wing will usually produce results. Some of the other favorite food of stripers and blues are shrimp, crabs, black eels and mummichogs. Big stripers love to feed on eels, but it is difficult to imitate them effectively. A Hare Eel comes close, with its undulating black body. White Crazy Charlies, Del Brown's Permit Flies and Muddler Minnows are good imitations for shrimp, crabs and mummichogs, respectively. Cinder worm hatches are scarce around Chatham, but when they do occur, Peterson's Cinder Worm works well.

Chatham is near the end of the migratory trail for bonito and false albacore, resulting in a relatively short season; nevertheless the lightning-fast runs of these tackle-busters more than make up for their short residence. In the past several years, these runs of bonito and false albacore have been larger and have been showing up closer to shore. Most fly-fishers use a sink-tip line with a 9-foot leader and 10- to 12-pound tippet for these sometimes-finicky fish. Small flies, imitating juvenile sand eels and silversides, tend to work best. The Johnny's Angel in white or brown/white does quite well imitating the silversides.

The bluefin tuna, the largest game fish available in the Chatham area, requires at least a 12-weight rod and a reel with a smooth drag and a capacity of at least 500-700 yards of 30-pound backing. Intermediate-density lines are fine when the fish are near the surface, but a 500- to 600-grain line may be necessary when the action is deeper. A 9-foot, 20-pound class leader of hard mono is just right for bluefin. Their favorite prey are sand eels and squid and a 6- to 8-inch-long Deceiver with a wide profile works well. These fish are real fighters and all elements of your tackle must be up to the task. Please note that special permits are required to catch these fish and hiring a captain with such a permit may be advantageous.

Chatham has rapidly become one of the premier fly-fishing destinations in the northeast U.S., because of the resurgence of the striped bass fishery, the sight-casting opportunities and the broad spectrum of gamefish species available to fly-fishers at all levels of expertise.

Guides (Capt.)	Phone/Fax	Email Address
Peter Alves*	508-945-1078	pgafish@capecod.net
Capt. Rich Benson	508-432-6264	
Fishing the Cape	508-432-1200	
Guide Service	508-430-1184	
Tony Biski*	508-432-3777	tony@c4.net
Capt. Bill Cooling	508-430-2277	pella@gis.net
Capt. Jim Ellis	508-362-9108	
Capt. Dan Marini	508-945-2006	
Tony Stetzco*	508-255-2357	

*shore guides

Fly fishing the Cape	Goose Hummock Shop
Harwich Commons	Rte. 6A Town Cove, Orleans, MA 02653
Harwich, MA 02645	Contact: Mike Measkill
Contact: Peter Alves	508-255-0455
508-432-1200	goose@capecod.net

Peter Alves has lived and fished the Chatham area of Cape Cod for the past 25 years. As manager of Fishing the Cape, a full-line Orvis dealer in East Harwich, and as an Orvis-endorsed fly-fishing guide, Peter provides a broad spectrum of knowledge for his fly-fishing clients. An avid traveler for bonefish and Atlantic salmon from the Bahamas to New Brunswick, Peter has been featured on both local and national television programs and video productions. In addition to his work and hobbies, he devotes time to various organizations such as the Coastal Conservation Association, Trout Unlimited and the Atlantic Salmon Foundation, and he often shares his knowledge with these local groups with slide and video programs. Peter is indebted to Capt. Will Raye for his considerable help in preparing this chapter.

Most Common Prey	Typical Size (inches)	Usual Months of Availability*												Typical Matching Fly Patterns**
		J	F	M	A	M	J	J	A	S	O	N	D	
Black Eels	6 - 14				3	3	3	3	3	3	3			Hare Eel
Bunker Menhaden	6 - 12					2	3	3	4	4	4			Tabory's Slab Side
Crabs	0.75-1.0				3	3	3	3	3	3	3			Del Brown's Permit Fly
Herring	6 - 12				3	5	3	1						Lefty's Deceiver (D)
Juvenile Herring	2 - 4							2	4	3				Lefty's Deceiver (D)
Mummichogs	0.5 - 4				3	3	3	3	3	3	3			Muddler Minnow (A)
Sand Eels	2 - 10				3	5	5	5	5	5	5			Eric's Sandeel
Shrimp	0.5 - 1.5				3	3	3	3	3	3	3			Crazy Charlie (C)
Silversides	3 - 4					1	2	3	4	5	3			Monomoy Flatwing, Johnny's Angel
Squid	3 - 15					4	5	3	2					Pink Squid (A)
Worms	2 - 3					2	2							Peterson's Cinder Worm
General														Seafoam Popper, Clouser Deep Minnow (B)

*1=Scarce, 2=Spotty, 3=Available, 4=Readily Available, 5=Widely Available
** Pattern Recipe in Appendix A.

Chapter 6: Nantucket Island

By Capt. Tom Mleczko

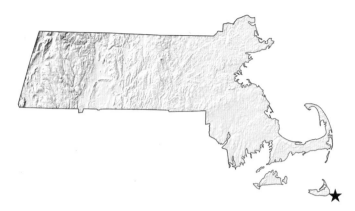

Nantucket is an island located thirty miles off the coast of Cape Cod, Massachusetts. Famous for its history as a whaling port in the 1800s, it has developed into a very busy summer resort community. The year-round population is approximately 9000 and during the summer this population grows to over 40,000 people. The shallow, clear water around the Island makes it a mecca for the saltwater fly-fisher. Striped bass and bluefish start arriving in late April and early May, well before the summer tourist season begins. These game fish remain all summer and do not leave until well into November. The arrival of Atlantic bonito and false albacore follows in late July and August. All of these game fish are terrific fly-rod targets. And, compared to many destinations, Nantucket still receives only light fishing pressure.

The only way to get to the Island is by ferry or plane. Ferries regularly service Nantucket via Martha's Vineyard or Hyannis. A half-dozen airlines service the Nantucket airport from Boston or Hyannis, Massachusetts, New York City and Providence, Rhode Island. There is a wide range of accommodations on the Island, from top-notch hotels to simple boarding houses. Restaurants are also widely available. Prices may be on the high side, but well worth it. Nantucket is well-equipped to support the visiting fly-fisher; the accompanying tables list the local fly shops and the local fly-fishing guides who are well-qualified to answer your questions and help you during your visit. Some of the guides are shore guides who will take you out on the beach, but you can also either bring your own 4x4 or rent one on the Island. Fishing off the beach is a unique and satisfying experience, but it is in the boats where one can fully enjoy the full spectrum of Nantucket's fly-fishing opportunities.

The best overall outfit for fly-fishing Nantucket is with a matched 9-foot, 8- to 9-weight rod, reel and intermediate-density line. Some fly-fishers will lean toward 7-weight

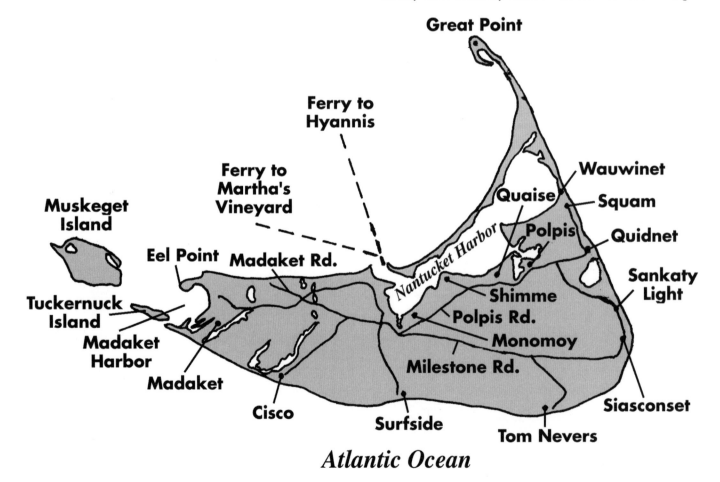

outfits, especially when wading and sight-fishing. Line weights slightly heavier than rod ratings are sometimes recommended for particularly windy conditions. When fishing poppers, a floating line is often preferred, but sinking or sink-tip lines (250+ grains) might be needed when the fish are down deep or in heavy currents or rips. The accompanying chart on gamefish prey lists the more important prey species which we attempt to imitate with our fly patterns, and some representative patterns which have had some local success.

With 55 miles of fishable beaches, crystal-clear water and plenty of fish, Nantucket is a fly-fisher's dream come true. I arrived in 1970 on a weekend invitation from a friend. I always had a passion for fly-fishing and, using an old 6-weight fiberglass fly rod and a size 6 Grey Ghost streamer, I went out and landed my first fly-caught striped bass. Although there's more fishing pressure now, it's still some of the best fly-fishing in the world. To stalk, cast to and hook up with a large striper on the flats is quite a thrill. And, watching your backing disappear when you hook up with a false albacore really gets your heart started. One can fly-fish off the beach, either in the surf on the south shore or by wading the quiet waters of the north shore. Access to a boat gives you the flexibility to cover other areas that are sometimes necessary for success. Many people have told me that fly-fishing takes them to the most beautiful places in the world; living and fishing on Nantucket, I could not agree more.

Guides (Capt.)	Phone/Fax	Email Address
Hal Herrick	508-257-9606	hal@nantucket.net
Jeff Heyers	508-228-4900/ 508-228-4188	crossrip@nantucket.net
Lynn Heyers	508-228-4900/ 508-228-4188	crossrip@nantucket.net
Tom Mleczko	508-228-4225/ 508-228-0598	capttom@nantucket.net
Pete O'Brien	508-228-9127/ 508-228-9109	bass85@hotmail.com
Nat Reeder	508-325-5728/ 508-228-0598	capttom@nantucket.net
Bill Toelstedt	508-228-3181/ 508-228-0598	capttom@nantucket.net

Crossrip Outfitters
Easy Street
Nantucket, MA 02554
Contact: Lynn & Jeff Heyers
508-228-4900/508-228-4188
crossrip@nantucket.net

Bill Fisher Tackle
New Lane
Nantucket, MA 02554
Contact: Bill Pew
508-228-2261
fisherst@nantucket.net

Capt. Tom Mleczko has always had a passion (his wife would say an obsession) for fishing. After starting with sunfish in the ponds around Boston and continuing with the stripers and blues off Long Island's south shore as a teenager, he has spent the last 30 years of his life fishing the water around Nantucket. He has three boats and two experienced captains who work with him. Capt. Tom feels that fly-fishing around Nantucket rates with the best in the world, because of its clean water, light fishing pressure and variety of fishing scenarios.

Species	Typical Size - Pounds	J	F	M	A	M	J	J	A	S	O	N	D
Atlantic Bonito	3 - 8	1	1	1	1	1	1	4	4	2	1	1	1
Bluefin Tuna	10 - 40	1	1	1	1	1	1	1	4	4	1	1	1
Bluefish	2 - 20	1	1	1	1	2	5	5	5	5	5	2	1
False Albacore	4 - 12	1	1	1	1	1	1	3	5	4	3	1	1
Striped Bass	3 - 40	1	1	1	2	4	5	5	4	5	4	3	1

1=Scarce, 2=Spotty, 3=Available, 4=Readily Available, 5=Widely Available

Most Common Prey	Typical Size (inches)	J	F	M	A	M	J	J	A	S	O	N	D	Typical Matching Fly Patterns**
American Eels	4 - 8	3	3	3	4	5	5	5	5	5	5	3	3	Fur Eel, Rat Tail, Sea Serpent
Baby Bunker	1 - 2	1	1	1	1	1	1	2	5	5	3	1	1	Lefty's Deceiver (D), Stir Fry
Butterfish	1 - 3	1	1	1	1	2	4	5	5	4	3	2	1	Lefty's Deceiver (G) - White
Crabs	1 - 3	2	2	3	4	5	5	5	5	5	5	5	1	Del Brown's Permit Fly
Herring (Alewives)	5 - 8	1	1	1	3	5	5	1	1	3	5	4	1	Lefty's Deceiver (D), White/Red/Grizzly Whistler
Sand Eels	2 - 5	1	1	1	2	4	5	5	5	5	5	3	1	Hard Body Shiner, Chartreuse Deep Minnow (N)

*1=Scarce, 2=Spotty, 3=Available, 4=Readily Available, 5=Widely Available • ** Pattern Recipe in Appendix A.

Chapter 7: Martha's Vineyard
By Cooper Gilkes

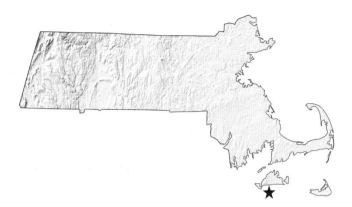

Martha's Vineyard lies along the southern coast of Massachusetts and Cape Cod. The Vineyard is a large island, some 20 miles long as the crow flies from the tip of Cape Poge on the eastern end of Chappaquidick to the cliffs of Gay Head on the western tip, and almost 10 miles wide. The Island is large enough to have distinct regions, the most populated being "down island" where the towns of Vineyard Haven, Oak Bluffs, and Edgartown lie in close proximity. It is here that the majority of the inns, hotels and restaurants are located and offer every type of accommodation to suit all tastes. All three towns are distinctly different and offer completely different experiences; from the stately wealth of Edgartown to the freewheeling nightlife in Oak Bluffs. The Vineyard is accessible by ferry or air. The ferry runs regularly from Woods Hole in Falmouth, Massachusetts for both cars and walk-on passengers. Walking on is easy. Bringing a car across requires advanced reservations.

From the map, it is easy to see why Martha's Vineyard is such a magnificent fishery. The island is riddled with estuarial ponds that feed the sea and serve as great nurseries for baitfish. As the tides move in and out of these ponds in the spring, they bring with them great numbers of young sand eels, herring, silversides and other freshly spawned baitfish. The accompanying chart summarizes the Vineyard's primary prey species, their times of greatest availability, and some productive matching fly patterns. The migrating predators who move up and down this coast during the year are fully aware of the feeding opportunities around the Vineyard and haunt the island's waters. The other factor is the Vineyard's proximity to the estuaries of the mainland and Cape Cod, in particular the Elizabeth Islands that create the southern wall of Buzzard's Bay and the northern wall of Vineyard Sound. These rock-strewn islands and the rocky shores of the Vineyard combine with bountiful bait sources to provide a rich fishery that lasts from late April until well into November.

Perhaps one of the Vineyard's strongest assets is the variety of fishing opportunities that exist. As an island, the Vineyard can offer fishing in almost any weather condition, since there is generally always a protected area on some side of the island. Remarkably, you can be as successful from shore as you can from a boat, since the topography of the island and the estuarial nature of the island create an inshore fishery that is easily accessed by wading anglers. Wading anglers fish very successfully from a number of easily accessible beaches such as Lobsterville Beach in the town of Aquinnah and East Beach out on Chappaquidddick. Rocky shorelines such as the north shore can be reached by hiking from Menemsha. Estuarial flats, canals and ponds like Menemsha, Poge or Tashmoo offer excellent wade and jetty fishing.

Fishing from boats is also excellent since the nature of the island and its waters combine to create rips, currents, tidal flows and heavy structure that provide numerous areas to find fish. Wasque rip off the southeast corner is renowned for its productivity as is Middle Ground on Vineyard Sound and Devil's Bridge off Gay Head. Fly-fishing guides on the Vineyard are all familiar with these areas and the accompanying lists of qualified guides and fly shops can help you with your fly-fishing plans.

If you bring your own boat, there are boat-launching ramps in Vineyard Haven, Katama and Aquinnah. You will have to ferry the boat across on a trailer, which will add significantly to the cost of the ferry ticket.

The fishing season on the Vineyard begins in late April to early May with the arrival of the first small striped bass and bluefish. As May rolls on, the blues and striped bass increase in size and number and by June the traditional bass and blues season is in full swing with fish being taken from all quarters. Billions of sand eels are spewing forth from the estuaries and the fish are on them hard. In late July, the first of

Species	Typical Size - Pounds	J	F	M	A	M	J	J	A	S	O	N	D
Bluefish	4 - 12					4	5	4	3	4	4		
Bonito	5 - 9								3	5	5	4	
False Albacore	4 - 10									4	5	4	
Striped Bass	4 - 35				2	4	5	3	3	4	5		

1=Scarce, 2=Spotty, 3=Available, 4=Readily Available, 5=Widely Available

the bonito show up, soon followed by the false albacore. Fishing then changes from slugging it out with freight trains to hanging on to speed merchants who have the ability to run at 40 miles per hour and to quickly empty your fly reel. Unquestionably, September and early October is the prime time for fishing the Vineyard, with excellent weather and excellent fishing to go with it. The accompanying chart shows the best time of the year for each of these species. It is also during this time of year that the Vineyard puts on its annual fishing derby, a month-long celebration of the island fishing which has been going on now for more than 50 years and is an island institution.

The standard rod for fly-fishing these waters is a 9 foot, 9 weight and it will perform admirably on all four major species; striped bass, bluefish, bonito and false albacore. Some fly-fishers prefer to go lighter, but rarely lighter than an 8 weight. Others may use 10 or even 11 weight outfits, particularly when fishing sinking lines for larger bass in heavy rips and currents. Varying conditions require varying lines and it is a good idea to have a floating or intermediate-density line for beaches and a good sinking line for heavy currents, jetty fishing and boat fishing. A sinking shooting head or the newer sinking heads with attached running lines work well, at weights from 250 to 500 grains, depending on the depth and current. Reels with good drag systems are important when fishing for bonito and false albacore. They can truly stress a reel's drag system. The new large arbor reels are gaining significant popularity because of the speed of their retrieve, which is important if one of these fish turns and runs back toward you. These reels should carry at least 200 yards or more of 30-pound Dacron or 35-pound gel spun backing are recommended. 35 pound gel spun is stronger than Dacron, but significantly thinner and offers much more backing capacity. Both nylon and fluorocarbon leaders are used in the IGFA tippet sizes 12 through 20 pounds. Generally, a 16 pound tippet is standard, but a 20-pound tippet with a 40-60 pound shock leader is recommended for larger bass. Bluefish have very sharp teeth and know how to use them. A wire bite guard between tippet and fly is a must with bluefish.

Guides (Capt.)	Phone/Fax
Capt. Jamie Boyle	508-693-7454
Capt. Bucky Burroughs	508-627-5088
Capt. Mo Flaherty	508-627-5088
Capt. Tim Flaherty	508-627-5088
*Cooper Gilkes	508-627-8202
Capt. Dan Gilkes	508-627-8202
*Lewis Hathaway	508-627-5052
*Chip Leonardi	508-693-6581
Capt. Noah Maxner	508-627-5088
*Rob Morrison	508-627-4422
Capt. Tom Repone	508-627-5786
*Nelson Sigelman	508-696-0476
*Ken Vanderlake	508-696-7551
*shore guides	

Cooper Gilkes has spent his life on Vineyard waters fishing both commercially and recreationally and he now operates Coop's Bait and Tackle in Edgartown, an Orvis-endorsed outfitter. Coop was Orvis Northeast Guide of the Year in 1998, the only wading guide to achieve that distinction, and he is widely regarded as one of the best striped bass anglers in New England. Coop's shop is well-known as the gathering place for anglers on the island and is an excellent source of information for visiting anglers. His guides offer both wade and boat fishing for all four major species.

Coop's Bait & Tackle	Larry's Tackle Shop
RFD, Box 19 Edgartown, MA 02539	15 Columbia Rd. Pembroke, MA 02359
Contact: Coop Gilkes	Contact: Mo Flaherty
508-627-3909 /508-6279551	508-627-5088/508-627-5148
coopsbaitandtackle@yahoo.com	larrys@larrystackle.com

Most Common Prey	Typical Size (inches)	Usual Months of Availability*												Typical Matching Fly Patterns
		J	F	M	A	M	J	J	A	S	O	N	D	
Cinder Worms	1.5					5	2							Cinder Worm
Herring	8 - 12				5	5	4							Herring
Mackerel	4 - 18					5								Mackerel
Sand Eels	2 - 5				1	5	5	5	4	5	5			Sand Eel Fly**
Squid	5 - 12					5	5	2	2	4	4			Squid Fly**

*1=Scarce, 2=Spotty, 3=Available, 4=Readily Available, 5=Widely Available • ** Pattern Recipe in Appendix A.

The Northeast

Chapter 8: East Passage and The Sakonnet River

By Capt. Eric Thomas

The East Passage of Narragansett Bay and the Sakonnet River are the parallel waters surrounding Newport, Rhode Island. The pristine waters of Narragansett Bay are only about one and one-half hours driving time from Boston (and about three hours from New York City). Newport offers a world-class variety of lodging and restaurants. There are probably more bed-and-breakfast establishments per square mile in Newport than anywhere and both extravagant and humble hotels to suit any budget. For the "do-it-yourself" explorer, there are some campgrounds, some of which have travel-trailer facilities. The non-fisher will need a week to fully enjoy the Newport experience. There are the famous summer cottages or mansions, shopping, and the beaches to occupy one's time. The Cliff Walk is a must-see for the fisher and non-fisher alike. This 3.5-mile walk takes you behind the mansions and along the crest of the rock

cliffs which form the shoreline. Some of the best whitewater fishing locations are in the backyards of these "summer cottages."

Newport is also famous as America's first resort town. It is the southern-most town on Aquidneck Island, the largest island in Narragansett Bay. The East Passage lies on the west side of the island and includes Newport harbor. The Sakonnet River lies on the east side of Aquidneck Island. Although Newport is on an island it doesn't have an island feeling. There are three bridges to get on and off the island and the largest, the Claiborne Pell Bridge, connects directly to downtown Newport. All of the waters surrounding the island are easily accessible to shore and boat fishermen alike. Boat-launching facilities are located at Fort Adams, a Rhode Island State Park, and at Weaver Cove, accessible from Burma Road in Portsmouth. Both of these ramps have ample parking with no fee required, and they are also very good fishing holes. Brenton Point State Park in Newport offers one of the easiest access points to the popular cliff fishing of Rhode Island.

Our fishing begins in late April and extends through the fall run of fish in the first part of November. Throughout this time we find striped bass, bluefish, false albacore, bonito, weakfish (squeteague), and on occasion, skipjack tuna and schoolie-size bluefin tuna. These fish show at different times of the season, per the enclosed chart.

The arenas of fishing situations vary widely. You can choose from fishing rocky shores and cliffs, sandy beaches, sunken boulder fields, rips and currents, small flats, and finally, tidal rivers and estuaries. Each of these places is productive at different times during the season. For example, with the tides in June, we see worm "hatches" followed closely by a crab "hatch." The worms range in size from one to four inches. The crabs are in their larval form and they go through a maturation period of approximately two weeks. These crabs, when you can see them, are half as big as your pinky fingernail, and their colors are clear with brown flecks. These are exciting times to be on the water. The striped bass can be seen sipping these crabs off the surface like a trout taking a midge but these fish are five to twenty pounds and are usually in large schools. The enclosed table provides more information on local gamefish prey and some of their imitative fly patterns.

Boating can be treacherous in the best of circumstances. The rocks and covered points are the best places to fish but are difficult to navigate. A half- or full-day guide trip can make the difference between a memorable

Species	Typical Size - Pounds	J	F	M	A	M	J	J	A	S	O	N	D
Bluefin (Schoolies)	12 - 20							2	2	2			
Bluefish	2 - 12				1	3	5	4	4	5	3	2	
Bonito	5 - 7							2	4	3	2		
False Albacore	6 - 13							1	3	4	2		
Skipjack Tuna	8 - 12						1	2	2	2			
Striped Bass	4 - 20	1	1	1	2	5	5	4	4	5	5	2	1
Weakfish	2 - 6						2	3	3	2			

1=Scarce, 2=Spotty, 3=Available, 4=Readily Available, 5=Widely Available

fishing trip or an expensive motor repair. Once you have gathered local knowledge, fishing out of your own boat will be productive and safer. If fishing the rocky cliff is your idea of excitement, you will need some specialized equipment along with some patience. Metal spiked shoes (korkers) are required to grip the very slick rocks and while looking from the rocks to spot fish, you must be aware of the waves and tide. You must examine your fishing place for a while to make sure it is safe so you won't get washed off your perch. It only takes one wave to yank at your knees and sweep you into the water. In spite of the risks, the fish can be literally right at your feet. The stripers feed in the frothy white water and the nastiest-looking water is usually the best place to find them.

A ten-weight outfit and a stripping basket are a must on the rocks. You are always battling wind and currents and the bigger rod will help you accomplish your goal. If you fish the river or the bay, an eight-weight will be perfect. If you can only bring one rod, a nine-weight would be the right choice. The preferred fly line is an intermediate-density clear line matched to the rod. A six- to eight-foot leader with a fifteen-pound tippet is an excellent leader for many situations. A somewhat-longer and lighter-tippet version may be needed if the fish are acting leader shy or if you find yourself in a school of bonito or false albacore. These fish need a longer leader and possibly even lighter tippets. A fluorocarbon leader will also help to increase your odds of hooking one of these speedsters. A good fly selection would include chartreuse Clousers on 1/0 hooks, poppers in white and black, and various Deceivers as standards. There are also some specialized flies that are a must. Those consist of the Rhody Flatwing, Razzle-Dazzle, Ray's Fly, and the White Water Witch. The enclosed list of fly shops can help you with your trip planning.

Guides (Capt.)	Phone/Fax
Chris Aubut	508-636-3267
Steve Cook	401-842-0062
Dave Cornell	508-636-2769
Eric Thomas	401-842-0062
Jim White	401-828-9465

Fin & Feather
95 Frenchtown Rd..
E. Greenwich, RI 02818
Contact: Bryon
401-885-8680

Quaker Lane Bait & Tackle
4019 Quaker Lane
N. Kingstown, RI 02852
Contact: Ed, Justin or Jack
800-249-5400

Robin Hollow Outfitters
4 Brown St., Wickford, RI 02852
Contact: Bill Hatfield
401-267-0102
rho@robinhollow.com

Saltwater Edge
561 Thames St.
Newport, RI 02840
Contact: Tim Sheilds
401-842-0062

Capt. Eric Thomas has been fishing the waters in and around Newport for all of his adult life. He has been guiding clients from shore and boat for the past six years. Eric is the Guide and Educational Director of the Saltwater Edge fly shop in Newport, RI In addition to guiding, Eric's other duties include teaching advanced and introductory saltwater fly-tying, fly-casting and participation in a children's summer fishing camp.

Most Common Prey	Typical Size (inches)	Usual Months of Availability*												Typical Matching Fly Patterns**
		J	F	M	A	M	J	J	A	S	O	N	D	
Anchovies	0.5 - 1.5					2	2	3	4	5	4	2		Bonito Bunny
Bunker (Pogies)	1 - 6					2	3	3	3	4	3			Lefty's Deceiver (M), Rhody Flatwing
Crabs						2	3							Bill's Epoxy Crab
Herring	1 - 6				2	4	4	3	3	2				Blue Black Herring
Mummychogs	0.5 - 2		2	2	3	3	3	3	3	2	2			Quonny Mummy
Sand Eels	0.5 - 2.				2	3	4	4	3	3	2			Rhody Flatwing, Ray's Fly
Silversides	1 - 4				2	3	4	4	4	5	3			Ray's Fly, Rhody Flatwing
Worms	1/16-3/4					3	3							Ken's Clam Worm
General														Razzle Dazzle, Clouser Deep Minnow (L), White Water Witch

*1=Scarce, 2=Spotty, 3=Available, 4=Readily Available, 5=Widely Available • ** Pattern Recipe in Appendix A.

Chapter 9: Rhode Island South Shore and Block Island

By Capt. Mitch Chagnon

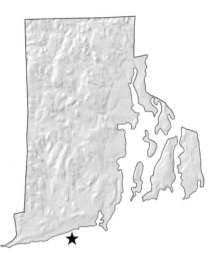

The southern coast of Rhode Island is one of New England's premiere angling destinations. The coastline stretches from Narragansett westward to Watch Hill and contains an interesting mix of barrier beaches, rocky areas and salt ponds; a fly-fisher's paradise. A variety of saltwater game fish can be found along the shoreline, including striped bass, bluefish, seatrout (locally called weakfish or squeteague) and false albacore (little tunny).

The season gets underway during the month of May when the first striped bass find their way into the many salt ponds and inlets. The first arrivals are the two- to five-year-old stripers, ranging in length from 15 to 25 inches. Point Judith, Charleston and Quonochontaug ponds are all good locations for striper fly-fishing during the months of May, June and the early part of July. In quiet coves within the ponds, a 7-weight outfit and a floating line with a sink-tip will allow the best sport for these smaller fish. In more open areas along the barrier beaches where wind is usually an issue, a 9- or 10-weight outfit with a medium-density sinking line is more appropriate.

In the spring, the predominant forage along Rhode Island's south shore are small sea-worms, mummichogs and silversides minnows. During the fall months, small peanut bunker and herring are the main prey for the game fish. The most common of the invertebrate sea worms, known commonly as the cinder worm, stage massive reproductive sessions, or swarms. The timing of the swarms are very temperature-dependent, and are most prolific during the full and new moon phases of May, June and sometimes July. The ideal location for fishing the swarms is where a substrate has been exposed during the hottest part of the daylight hours. If you are fortunate enough to witness this phenomenon, you'll find the action non-stop, starting about an hour before sunset and continuing through the entire night. This event is a regular ritual for local fly-fishers and most fly shops carry a number of flies to simulate the worms. Page Roberts' Worm Fly and Lou Tabory's Snake Fly have long been favorites of mine during this period.

Larger striped bass invade the area by the middle of May, following the herring that travel up the rivers and creeks to spawn each spring. The best areas for fly-fishing can be difficult to locate and access without the help of an experienced guide. Local experts cast large flies with 10- to 12-weight outfits to imitate the small herring, known locally as buckies. By mid-June, the bluefish have moved in to join the striped bass along the beaches and inlets; by mid-August the first bonitos also will be in the area. Although the quality of the fly-fishing is very good from May through August, it is even better from mid-September through mid-October. Large schools of stripers, bluefish and false albacore feed throughout the day as they prepare to make their migration south for the winter. Some days, a significant portion of the southern shoreline is one large mass of feeding fish and diving birds.

If a total getaway is on your agenda, Block Island is definitely the ideal destination. Located 13 miles from the mainland, the "Island" has long been known for outstanding fishing. Over the past 10 years, fly-fishing has taken the island by storm. Block Island now has a full-service fly shop and a number of experienced fly-fishing guides. Around Block Island, the best fly-fishing starts in early July and continues through September. My favorite month is September, when the false albacore and Atlantic bonito are available right off the beach. Off-season rates are available after Labor Day, but advanced reservations are still recommended.

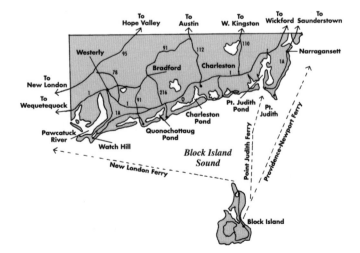

Species	Typical Size - Pounds	J	F	M	A	M	J	J	A	S	O	N	D
Atlantic Bonito	5 - 8							2	4	5	4	1	
Bluefin Tuna	15 - 30							2	3	4	3		
Bluefish	6 - 12					2	4	5	5	5	5	4	1
Blue Sharks	80 - 200					3	4	5	5	5	3		
False Albacore	6 - 14							2	4	4	5	4	2
Hickory Shad	2 - 4				1	4	4	2	2	2	2		
Mako Shark	80 - 120						3	4	3	3			
Oceanic Bonito	5 - 7							2	4	4	3		
Striped Bass	3 - 12				2	3	4	5	5	5	5	4	
Weakfish	4 - 6				1	2	2	2	2	2	2	1	
Yellowfin Tuna	30 - 80							2	3	4	3		

1=Scarce, 2=Spotty, 3=Available, 4=Readily Available, 5=Widely Available

If you enjoy catching big game on a fly, don't overlook the availability of charters for shark and tuna. The shark fishing is best from mid-June through mid-July, whereas September is the best time to fish for yellowfin or bluefin tuna. Twelve- to 15-weight outfits are required for these species, together with an assortment of shooting heads and reels with plenty of extra backing. Stainless-steel bite tippets will also be required for sharks. An assortment of chunk flies, large profile marabou/Krystal Flash streamers tied on long-shank hooks, will round out your artillery for these large game fish. You should definitely plan on bringing your own gear for this big-game fly-fishing, unless you can make advance arrangements with local charter captains.

Public access is quite good along the Rhode Island shore, and of course there are plenty of marinas, tackle shops, restaurants and places to stay. Public launching ramps are numerous and public camping areas remain open through mid-October. Most public beach parking is free after Labor Day weekend and there are many other public access areas. Considerable additional useful information can be obtained from the local Chambers of Commerce and from State and County organizations. Listings of local fly-fishing guides and fly shops are included in this chapter.

Guides (Capt.)	Phone/Fax
Alan Caolo	401-322-8929
Mitch Chagnon	401-789-8801/ 401-783-9015
Pete Farrell	401-466-5232
Johnny Glenn	401-348-8716
Mark Northrup	401-466-5232
Jim White	401-828-9465

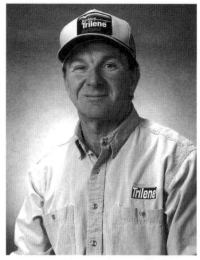

Capt. Mitch Chagnon is a native-born Rhode Islander who has spent his entire life in Narragansett Bay, Block Island and the offshore waters south of Rhode Island. Capt. Mitch holds a Bachelor's degree in Marine Biology, and holds a 100-ton Masters Coast Guard license. He has also attended Johns Hopkins University and the University of Rhode Island for graduate studies in environmental science. Mitch has worked as a Senior Field Scientist and has an extensive background in thermal monitoring, aquatic ecological assessment procedures and energy conservation. For the past 20 years, Capt. Chagnon has guided and operated a charter service in southern Rhode Island and Block Island. He has also worked as a tackle consultant for Berkley Company. His publishing credits include numerous articles in New England Fisherman, Saltwater Sportsman, Sportfishing, Edge Annual Offshore Quarterly, and New England Woods and Waters magazines. He continues to lecture on environmental issues and sport fishing in New England.

Oceans & Ponds
Block Island, RI 02807
Contact: Bruce Johnson
401-466-5131

Quaker Lane Tackle
4019 Quaker Lane, North
Kingston, RI 02852
Contact: Richard Matthews
401-294-3555

Saltwater Edge Fly Fishing Co.
559 Thames St.
Newport, RI 02840
Contact: Eric Thomas
401-842-0062

Most Common Prey	Typical Size (inches)	Usual Months of Availability*												Typical Matching Fly Patterns**
		J	F	M	A	M	J	J	A	S	O	N	D	
Bay Anchovies	2 - 4	1	1	1	1	1	2	2	3	4	5	5	2	Hanson's Glass Minnow
Blueback Herring	2 - 8	1	1	2	3	4	4	4	5	5	5	4	2	Page's Menemsha Minnow
Cinderworms	0.75 - 2.0				1	5	5	4	1					Page's Worm Fly
Grass Shrimp	1 - 2	1	1	1	1	2	2	3	3	2	2	2	1	Ultra Shrimp
Menhaden	2 - 6	1	1	1	1	2	3	4	5	5	5	2	1	Page's Menemsha Minnow
Mummichogs	2 - 3	1	1	3	4	5	5	5	4	4	3	2	1	Clouser Deep Minnow (C)
Sand Lances	2 - 4	3	3	3	4	5	5	5	5	5	4	4	3	Sand Eel
Silversides	2 - 4	2	2	3	3	3	4	4	5	5	4	3	2	Lefty's Deceiver
Offshore - General														Mack Wool

*1=Scarce, 2=Spotty, 3=Available, 4=Readily Available, 5=Widely Available • ** Pattern Recipe in Appendix A.

Chapter 10: The Eastern Connecticut Shore

By Capt. Mike Roback

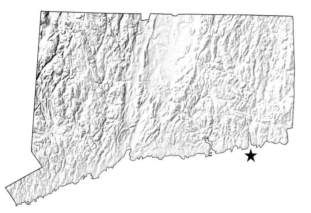

Southeastern Connecticut consists of the old port city of New London plus the towns of Groton, Mystic and Stonington. The waters border those of Fishers Island, N.Y. to the south and Westerly and Watch Hill, R.I. to the east. This tri-state region has some of the most varied structure and inshore fly-fishing in New England. Within a few miles of the geographic intersection of the three states, the angler can fly-fish on flats, jetties, rips, islets, estuaries, beaches, protected bays, breaking reefs, barrier islands, peninsulas and rocky points. If one travels seven miles west along the isolated, boulder-strewn south coast of Fishers Island, you reach the "Race", where twice a day the mouth of Long Island Sound exhales up to 4.2 knots of current of outgoing tide. Five miles to the north and you enter the mouth of the Thames River, southeastern Connecticut's largest river. Heading east back to Rhode Island along the Connecticut coast, one crosses a myriad of more tidal creeks, bays, rocks, reefs and rips.

From the fly-fisher's viewpoint the area is a fantastic nursery for bait, shaped by the glaciers that covered this part of North America 18,000 years ago. Although it is a highly populated area, the discerning angler can enjoy some of the finest and most easily accessible fly-fishing for the striped bass, bluefish, bonito and false albacore that come to feast on the local buffet. By the end of May, the stripers have moved in to the estuaries and are occasionally found pursuing squid and herring on the reefs. By Memorial Day, bluefish can be found prowling the bays, reefs and rips. By the end of June the action should

be in full swing as the fish chase the sand eels in and out of the bays or wait to ambush them as they wash over the reefs. By this time, squid and butterfish are also part of the feast. Through the summer months the fish will often be found in the deeper water and reefs during the day, moving in to feed on sand eels and silversides along the shore during the night.

The first signs of tuna fever begin in mid-August with sporadic sightings and catches of both false albacore (albies) and bonito. Good fishing for bonito can be had some years during the entire second half of August. By the second week of September, the albies are usually in, with the peak fishing usually occurring between September 15 and October 20. The most consistent fishing is during this period, although my personal best days have occurred both before and after these dates. I normally fish hard until November 7 and then catch a few fish and put the boat ashore around Thanksgiving.

The shoreside angler should be well prepared to duplicate the many bait species in this area, including silversides, sand eels, juvenile herring and butterfish. During September and October, bay anchovies will be especially important for those anglers casting to bonito and false albacore. For boat anglers, the addition of squid and menhaden patterns is necessary, especially for those lucky enough to be on the reef when a school of prey is washed over and the larger bass come up in a frenzy. On special occasions, crab and grass shrimp flies can be extremely effective and attractive to fish. One of my most memorable catches last year was an 11-pound blue that took a size-4 grass shrimp dry drifted over Sugar Reef on a mill pond-flat ebbing tide. For those of you a little jaded by a few thousand schoolies, try sight-fishing with a crab pattern the next time you find schoolies on a sand bar.

Normal fly-fishing equipment in our area consists of 8- to 10-weight rods with intermediate lines. In addition, the boat angler should pack a spare spool or rod with a fast sinking shooting head for wind and/or heavy current conditions. You may occasionally use a floating line, but most sliders and poppers can be fished effectively on intermediate lines. I always rig 350- to 450-grain shooting-head lines when fishing from my boat for four reasons; wind, current, depth and big flies. Those reasons are not necessarily listed in order of decreasing importance. It's always preferable to me to catch the fish on intermediate-density lines in the upper fathom of the water column in good weather. However, when that's not possible it's important to be able to get a fly down in a heavy current, or even out fifteen yards in a stiff breeze.

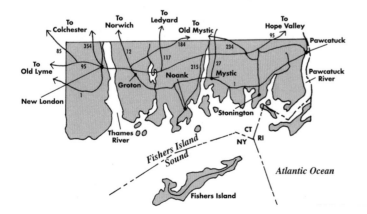

Species	Typical Size - Pounds	J	F	M	A	M	J	J	A	S	O	N	D
Atlantic Bonito	6 - 12						1	3	3	3	1		
Bluefish	1 - 15					3	5	5	5	5	5	2	
False Albacore	4 - 15								2	5	5	1	
Striped Bass	3 - 40					3	5	5	5	5	5	3	

1=Scarce, 2=Spotty, 3=Available, 4=Readily Available, 5=Widely Available

Shore fishermen are generally limited to fishing intermediate lines in rocky areas, and may occasionally use a 225- to 350-grain shooting head when fishing deep over sandy bottoms. We use standard saltwater leaders tied with stiff mono. We use a 15- to 20-pound tippet for bass, but occasionally go down as low as 12 pounds. The addition of a shock tippet consisting of a 6- to 8-inch length of 60- to 80-pound mono connected to the leader with an Albright knot is preferable when fishing for blues under ten pounds. Wire tippets should be considered for bigger blues and are always necessary for fish over 12 pounds. Leaders should be 6 to 9 feet long. When fishing for albies and bonito I use the same leaders with the addition of a 2- to 3-foot, 12-pound soft mono tippet. If I feel that the fish are leader shy in a calm flat day I will add 10-pound or even finer fluorocarbon to this leader system. False albacore and bonito have extremely good eyesight, and proper attention must be paid to tippets and flies, especially in clear conditions. The accompanying chart provides more information on flies for our area.

This is a highly populated area, however, if you are fishing stripers from shore you will have your best fishing at sunset and sunrise and at night during the summer. Boat fishermen will usually find themselves alone as they seek out the same structure that boat traffic avoids; heavy rip lines, boulder piles, reefs, jetties and sand bars. Local knowledge is very important in this area. The strong currents, submerged rocks, reefs, and hazy summer days and nights that can quickly become fog-bound, make it important to do your navigating before you leave the dock, especially for skippers new to the area.

There are plenty of marinas and boat-launching facilities in the area, particularly in Stonington or Mystic.

Guides (Capt.)	Phone/Fax
Jack Balint	860-885-1739
Steve Bellefleur	860-535-4856
Steve Burnett	860-572-9896
Todd Currier	860-691-1382
Johnny Glenn	401-348-8716
Mike Roback	860-561-0232
Dan Woods	860-442-6343

Rivers End Tackle
141 Boston Post Rd.
Saybrook, CT 06475
Contact: Pat Abatte & Mark Lewchik
860-388-3283

The Fish Connection
127 Route 12
Preston, CT 06365
Contact: Jack Balint
860-885-1739

Colonial Sports
431 Fitchville Rd.
Bozrah, CT 06334
Contact: Charlie Connell
860-889-4901

Captain Mike Roback has been guiding saltwater fly-fishers for 8 years out of Stonington Connecticut, on his customized boat, the Double Haul. He has a 100-ton master's license and has logged over 24,000 bluewater miles cruising and racing sailing yachts. Mike has been fly-fishing for thirty years from Labrador to Tierra del Fuego. He spends his winters fishing and guiding in Patagonia with his Argentine wife. His favorite fishing is for the inshore tunas of his own home waters in southeastern Connecticut.

Most Common Prey	Typical Size (inches)	J	F	M	A	M	J	J	A	S	O	N	D	Typical Matching Fly Patterns**
Bay Anchovies	1 - 2.5								2	5	5	2		Generation 7 Epoxy Fly, Page's Slim Jim
Butterfish	1 - 4					2	3	3	3	4	3	2		Lefty's Deceiver (M), Foxy Lady
Herring	3 - 5			3	3	3	3	3	3	3	3	3		Lefty's Deceiver (D)
Sand Eels	1 - 4					3	5	5	5	5	3	2		Page's Sand Eel, Clouser Deep Minnow (H)
Silversides	1 - 4					2	2	4	4	5	4	2		Lefty's Deceiver (M), Foxy Lady
Squid	1 - 6			3	3							3		KZ Squid
General														Estuary Special

*1=Scarce, 2=Spotty, 3=Available, 4=Readily Available, 5=Widely Available • ** Pattern Recipe in Appendix A.

Chapter 11: Western Connecticut Shore

By Capt. Ian Devlin

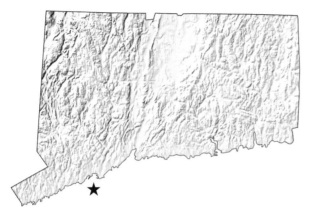

The waters of Long Island Sound from New Haven, Connecticut to the New York State border offer an ideal opportunity for saltwater fly-fishing. Being so close to New York City, this fishery offers the traveling or local fly-fisher an outlet from a busy day's work and provides solid fishing opportunities for the serious angler. Although not primarily a fishing destination like Cape Cod and its outlying islands, the fishing action at times can be very hot. There are many accommodations and good restaurants, plus excellent public transportation for the traveling angler.

The water presents a mixture of fishing opportunities. There is excellent structure in the Norwalk Islands and to the west. This structure will hold fish all season. There are large sections of sand flats, several major reefs and rivers and many tidal outflows. The angler can wade, use a canoe, kayak or a small boat to access this fishery. In years with normal rainfall, the water is off color; accordingly most of the fly-fishing is blind-casting unless the fish are feeding on or near the surface. Because of the poor underwater visibility, soft propellers could save your lower unit. Be sure to carry an extra propeller in case you hit hard. Once you venture out of the main channels and into the fishing areas, there are numerous hidden structures throughout the inner shoreline from Greenwich to New Haven.

Eight-, nine- and ten-weight outfits work well and the intermediate fly line is the most useful. Boat anglers will also find a Depth Charge-type line effective in the deeper rips and a floater or clear tip helpful when using poppers or fishing surface flies.

Shore access is limited during the summer months, but during the fall run many "resident-only" town beaches have access for anglers. Sherwood Island State Park allows fishing all season long on off-peak hours, while "permit-only" Compo Beach in Westport allows fishing in the summer to non-residents late in the evening and early morning. Short Beach in Stratford, which gives access to the mouth of the Housatonic River, has parking all season, although there is a nominal fee during summer. The Bird Sanctuary at the west end of Cedar Beach in Milford has parking for anglers, but a permit is required. There are free state launching ramps in Westport on the east side of the Saugatuck River under Route 95, and in Milford on the east side of the Housatonic River just under Route 95. Also, there is a town ramp at the Veterans Memorial Park on the Norwalk River that charges a daily fee, and a ramp in Stratford that requires a yearly fee.

There are plenty of capable fly-fishing guides who offer both full- and half-day trips. In the peak part of the season, plan to book well in advance because the best guides get booked quickly.

In the spring, early runs of herring and alewives attract the larger stripers into the Housatonic River from the mouth all the way up to the dam in Derby. This action usually starts in early to mid-May. Most of this fishing requires a boat, except for when fishing the water near the dam, which at times can be crowded. Large herring patterns and sinking lines work well here.

During May, in recent years, there has been a good run of weakfish in New Haven Harbor and on the edges of the shallows just west of the harbor called the West Haven sandbar. Small streamers and shrimp flies work well. The best fishing usually occurs during an incoming tide; work the drop-offs with an intermediate line. The sand flats from Frost Point to Compo Beach, in Westport, have a good mix of stripers, bluefish and a few weakfish from mid-May to July. Look for feeding terns just after daybreak, signalling a good run of sandeels. The sandeels are the catalyst that brings the fish into these locations to feed. Sometimes the entire shoreline will have sections of feeding fish when these baitfish are abundant. The lower phases of the tides, both falling and rising, are preferred because they allow easier wading. Boat anglers can find action in the deeper water along the drop-offs. Use 3- to 5-inch long, thin flies or thinly dressed, lightly weighted Clousers.

There are both worm and crab "hatches" that occur from June to August. The worms usually hatch around full and new moons in and around estuaries. Look for crab hatches on foggy, calm mornings in weed lines along the edges of rips. Both hatches require sophisticated techniques; floating lines, small 3-inch-long red or orange worm flies or tiny, dime-size crab flies. In mid to late August there is an influx of juvenile bluefish or "snapper blues." The snappers feed actively on small baitfish and the stripers and larger bluefish feed on them. This can produce catches of really large fish. Many years ago Pete Kriewald

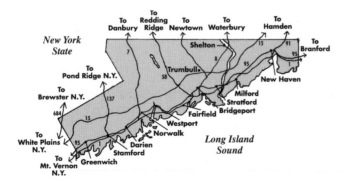

Species	Typical Size - Pounds	J	F	M	A	M	J	J	A	S	O	N	D
Atlantic Bonito	4 - 8								2	3	3		
Bluefish	2 - 14					3	4	4	4	5	5	3	
False Albacore	4 - 8								1	2	3		
Striped Bass	3 - 18			1	3	5	5	4	4	5	5	4	3
Weakfish	2 - 7					2	3	3	2				

1=Scarce, 2=Spotty, 3=Available, 4=Readily Available, 5=Widely Available

took a record 45-pound striper from the Norwalk Islands. The Norwalk Islands between Sprite and Goose Island and the flats at the mouth of the Housatonic River can also offer ideal fishing when the small snappers are around. Poppers work well because the snappers usually feed on the surface. Throughout the Norwalk Islands, inside coves, pockets and even harbors, the 10- to 15-pound bluefish will trap the big bunker available at this time of year. The structure off Darien down to Greenwich offers good night-fishing for stripers in the summer and early fall. There is little shore access so this is all boat fishing. Fish big, dark-colored Snake Flies or Deceivers with an intermediate line and use a slow retrieve.

In September and October, Long Island Sound gets a run of bonito and false albacore. The Housatonic River, outside Southport Harbor, between Sherwood Island and Compo Beach and around the Norwalk Islands is the best place to find them. They feed on spearing, sandeels and bay anchovies. Small epoxy flies 1 1/2 to 4 inches long are the best patterns, using long fluorocarbon leaders. From October to mid-November, schools of small 2- to 4-inch-long bunker provide easy prey for stripers and bluefish. This can be hot fishing because the fish feed intensely and take flies readily. Small herring patterns like Slab Flies, Mark's Baby Bunker or small Deceivers work well.

Poppers are also effective unless the bait concentrations are too thick. If the schools of bait are too thick, use a fast-sinking line and fish the fly below the schools of bait. Expect to find fish in open water, along beaches and against rocky shorelines where the game fish can trap the bait. At times you will find large schools of mixed fish. The late November to mid-December fishing can be great on warm, sunny afternoons. Look for stripers on the reefs and near points on an incoming tide. Large groups of birds sitting on or flying over the water are also a tell-tale sign of fish, but there can be good action even without birds. Outlets are also good late in the season because the water is warm. Small herring patterns fished with intermediate or fast-sinking lines work best.

Guides(Capt.)	Phone/Fax	E-mail
Ian Devlin	203-838-2912	
Glenn Exstrom	203-270-6343	
Bill Herold	914-967-8246	
Scott Locher	203-853-1591	
Jeff Northrup	203-226-1915	Godzilla41@aol.com
Bob Turley	203-378-1160	
Dan Wechsler	203-329-8464	Captaindan@skinniminn.com

Compleat Angler
987 Post Rd.
Darien, CT 06820
Contact: Scott Bennett
203-655-9400

Fairfield Fly Shop
917 Post Rd., Fairfield, CT 06430
Contact: Eric Peterson
203-255-2896
fairfieldflyshop@hotmail.com

Orvis- Darien
432-Boston Post Rd.
Darien, CT 06820
Contact: Mark Kaplan
203-662-0844

Stratford Bait & Tackle
1076-1/2 Stratford Ave.
Stratford, CT 06615
Contact: John Posh
203-377-8091

Capt. Ian Devlin started fishing his local waters as a kid and guided anglers on wading trips when he was still in high school. A full-time guide since 1997, Ian fishes the western Long Island Sound from June to December. From January through May, Capt. Devlin guides out of Englewood Florida. A superb fly-caster and an FFF certified casting instructor, he currently holds an IGFA record for bluefish on 20-pound tippet.

Most Common Prey	Typical Size (inches)	Usual Months of Availability*												Typical Matching Fly Patterns**
		J	F	M	A	M	J	J	A	S	O	N	D	
Alewives	8 - 12				3	3	2							Tabory's Slab Fly, Lefty's Deceiver
Baby Bunker	2 - 4				1	2	3	3	4	5	5	3		Tabory's Slab Fly
Bay Anchovies	1.0 - 2.5								2	3	3			Ian's Anchovy
Bunker	12 - 18				1	2	3	3	4	5	5	3		Lefty's Deceiver
Crabs	1 - 3					3	3	3	3	3	3			Del Brown's Permit Fly
Crab Hatch	0.5						2	2	2					Pop's Bonefish Bitters (Amber)
Herring	8 - 12				3	3	2							Tabory's Slab Fly, Lefty's Deceiver
Sandeels	2 - 5				2	5	5	5	4	3	3			Clouser Deep Minnow (P), Page's Sand Eel
Shrimp	2				3	3	3	3	3	3	3			Ultra Shrimp
Snapper Blues	2 - 8								3	3				Seafoam Popper
Spearing	2 - 5				2	4	3	3	4	5	4	2		Tabory's Snake Fly, Clouser Deep Minnow (P)
Worm Hatch	2 - 3					2	3	3						Tabory's Snake Fly

*1=Scarce, 2=Spotty, 3=Available, 4=Readily Available, 5=Widely Available • ** Pattern Recipe in Appendix A.

Chapter 12: Gardiner's Bay and Montauk
By Capt. Paul Dixon

Extending approximately 100 miles east of New York City, Long Island forms a peninsula at its east end whose waters offer a variety of fly-fishing opportunities. Montauk Highway (Route 27) runs east-west and is the only route which provides good access to both the Atlantic Ocean to the south and a series of large bays to the north. The Atlantic side has miles of sandy beaches, rocky shores and surf. Peconic, Noyack, Gardiner's and Napeague bays to the north are quite different in topography and access. Along Route 27, the towns of Southampton, Watermill, Bridghampton, East Hampton, Amagansett and Montauk are a series of summer vacation villages offering a wide variety of restaurants and places to stay. Advanced reservations are necessary during the vacation season of June through August. Camping is also available at Hither State Park and other parks offer RV and trailer sites.

Eastern Long Island has a cornucopia of fly-fishing opportunities for striped bass, weakfish, bluefish, bonito and false albacore. Understanding the seasonal aspects of the fishing and the topography will greatly enhance your experience and success. For the shore-bound angler, the preferred method of fishing is driving the sand beaches on the Atlantic side. Some beaches on the bay side are also accessible with four-wheel-drive vehicles. All beach vehicles require permits and special equipment. Designated nearby parking areas are available, however, for walking and wading the beach.

Canoe and kayak rentals are quite common along the Montauk Highway, permitting the angler to gain access to both oceanside and bayside areas not available to the walking or wading fly-fisherman. If you have a boat, most of the town halls can provide a launch ramp permit for the town docks. In addition, many of the local marinas have launch ramps available for a small fee.

Without question, using one of our local beach guides or charter captains will greatly enhance your fly-fishing experience. They have the required equipment, and the knowledge of the tides, access points, wind direction, fly selection and fish location to get you to the right place at the right time. In the fall, blitzes of stripers, false albacore and bluefish off Montauk Point provide awesome displays of baitfish carnage. Although these feeding frenzies are often accessible to the wading fly-fisher, boating access is usually more productive.

Fishing at the east end of Long Island tends to be seasonal, with the stripers showing up as early as mid-April, depending on when the fish drop out of their natal rivers (Chesapeake and Hudson systems). By May, the stripers are meandering along the south shore beaches and entering the bays. May also marks the arrival of the bluefish and weakfish, and the variety of baitfish they all prey upon. Some of the stripers become local fish, staying in the area, while others continue north, swimming as far north as Maine. The local stripers plus the bluefish and weakfish provide the fly-rodder with fabulous summer fun. Sand eels, spearing, bay anchovies, menhaden (bunker), shrimp and crabs are the most important prey species on the east end of Long Island. Clouser Minnows tied on size 2/0 to 4/0 hooks in chartreuse/white, tan/white, or olive/white can be deadly. Deceivers on size 2 to 3/0 hooks in most colors also work well. Popovic's Surf Candy in natural colors, sizes 2 to 2/0, mimic the sand eels and spearing perfectly. Weighted flies are important for stripers.

Crab patterns like Merkins, Rattle Crabs and Ragheads can be quite successful in August, when the stripers get a little finicky. Grass shrimp are prolific in the estuaries of the north side, and the stripers will often key in on them, especially at night. The Ultra Shrimp is one of the best patterns to imitate these prey. Poppers and sliders are great flies to work along the beaches and structures and the explosive strikes on flies such as Bob's Banger and the Farnsworth Slider are exciting. A 4-inch trace of wire is useful under these conditions when the bluefish are around.

By August, the baby bunker (menhaden) and bay anchovy (rainbait) begin to show up off Gardiner's Island and Montauk. John Haag's Glimmer Bunker on a 2/0

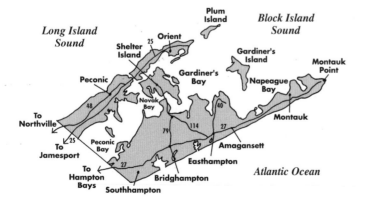

Species	Typical Size - Pounds	J	F	M	A	M	J	J	A	S	O	N	D
Bluefish	1 - 15	1	1	1	1	4	5	5	5	5	5	3	1
Bonito	2 - 10	1	1	1	1	1	1	2	3	4	3	1	1
False Albacore	3 - 15	1	1	1	1	1	1	1	2	5	5	2	1
Striped Bass	3 - 40	1	1	1	2	3	5	5	5	5	5	4	2
Weakfish	1 - 12	1	1	1	1	1	3	4	4	4	4	1	1

1=Scarce, 2=Spotty, 3=Available, 4=Readily Available, 5=Widely Available

hook is my favorite baby bunker imitation. Popovics' 3-D flies and spread flies can also work well in olive/white. The thick schools of bay anchovies are very important to late-summer and fall fly-fishing off Montauk Point. While chasing anchovies, the bonito are breezing through Gardiner's Bay and Montauk in late summer. Epoxy minnows, small poppers and crease flies are good prey imitations. The bonito seem to disappear when the huge schools of false albacore arrive, slashing through pods of bay anchovies in Gardiner's Bay and Block Island Sound in early September. Eventually the bay anchovies drift over to Montauk Point, where migrating striped bass join in the feeding blitzes. Mikkelson's Epoxy Baitfish, Popovics' Surf Candy, Bob Lindquist's Royal Anchovy and the Mystic Bay Hardbody Shiner are all flies that work during this rainbait invasion. Dino Turino's Rattlin Bunny or Popovics' Jiggy will often be preferable when the stripers are thick on the water surface and a light fly tends to simply bounce off their backs.

My choice of tackle for fly-fishing our area consists of several different outfits. Eight- and 9-weight rods with slow-sinking, intermediate-density lines are ideal for shore fishing in the spring. I almost always also carry a 10-weight with a sinking-tip line to fish the rips and the deeper water. A 9-weight rod with a floating line is great fun for casting poppers and for some sight-fishing applications. The 10-weight outfit with an intermediate-density line is a good combination for the fall fishery. One year, we broke over fifteen rods during the fall blitzkrieg.

The east end of Long Island can provide a myriad of fly-fishing opportunities throughout the season. The accompanying list of guides and fly shops can provide you with additional valuable information and gear to make your trip most memorable.

Guides (Capt.)	Phone/Fax	E-mail
David Blinken	212-517-3473	
Paul Dixon	631-324-7979	
Ernie French	631-329-9733	
Scott Gaekle	516-287-3264	
Jim Hull	516-749-1906	
Wally Johnsen	631-725-3548	
James Kang	516-609-9038/	amykang@aol.com
	212-391-6445	
Spot Killen	631-325-1112	brinyfly@worldnet.att.net
Jim Levison	631-907-9004	
Glenn Mikkleson*	631-878-0883	
Ken Rafferty	631-324-8746	
Amanda Switzer	516-324-7979	

*shore guides

Alten Kirch Precision Tackle
Shinnecock Canal
Hampton Bays, NY
631-728-4110

Lure & Feather Company
400 Pantigo Rd.
East Hampton, NY
631-329-5829

The Tackle Shop
470 Pantigo Rd., East Hampton, NY
Contact: Harvey Bennett
631-324-7770

Capt. Paul Dixon has fly-fished for over 25 years. He has worked for the Orvis Company, owned his own fly shop and currently guides full-time. Paul guides half the year in New York's Hamptons and the other half year at the Ocean Resort in Key Largo. Capt. Dixon has been featured on ESPN's "Walkers Cay Chronicles" with Flip Pallot and "The Spanish Fly" with Jose Wejebe. He has also been featured in Outdoor Life, New Yorker, Fast Company and numerous other magazines.

Most Common Prey	Typical Size (inches)	Usual Months of Availability*												Typical Matching Fly Patterns**
		J	F	M	A	M	J	J	A	S	O	N	D	
Bay Anchovies (Rainbait)	0.5 - 2.0	1	1	1	1	1	1	1	2	5	5	4	1	Epoxy Baitfish, Surf Candy, Royal Anchovy, Dino's Rattlin Bunny, Jiggy
Crabs	1 - 3	1	1	1	1	1	3	4	4	2	2	1	1	Del Brown's Permit Fly
Grass Shrimp	0.5 - 2.0	1	1	1	1	3	4	4	3	2	1	1	1	Ultra Shrimp
Menhaden (Bunker)	2 - 8	1	1	1	1	1	2	3	3	4	4	3	1	Haag's Glimmer Bunker
Sand Eels	1 - 3	1	1	1	1	3	4	5	5	4	4	3	1	Surf Candy
Spearing	1 - 3	1	1	1	1	3	4	5	5	5	4	3	1	Surf Candy
General														Bobs Banger, Crease Fly Minnow

*1=Scarce, 2=Spotty, 3=Available, 4=Readily Available, 5=Widely Available • ** Pattern Recipe in Appendix A.

Chapter 13: Moriches and Shinnecock Inlets

By Capt. C. John "Spot" Killen

The south shore of New York's Long Island has approximately 100 miles of ocean-front barrier beaches. This thin strip of sand dunes separates the Atlantic Ocean from numerous shallow-water bays, creeks, canals and small rivers. The south shore has four major inlets, each forming a cut through the barrier beach. This chapter covers the two easternmost inlets, Moriches and Shinnecock, and the area in between. Moriches Inlet is located about 75 miles east of New York City and is on the western edge of a series of high-end resort communities collectively known as the Hamptons.

Route 27A, the Montauk Highway, is the main east-west road through the Hamptons and on, located south of this route are countless hotels, motels, bed & breakfast facilities, marinas, tackle shops, restaurants, boat ramps, boat/canoe rentals, campgrounds, etc. There is a wide range of prices, from the modest to the very expensive. Both Moriches and Shinnecock inlets have county parks on each side, where you pay a daily or longer-term fee for parking. These county parking areas provide immediate access to some great beach and jetty fishing. Usually, the best fly-fishing on the beach is within a mile of the inlet in either direction. The 11 miles of beaches between the two inlets is serviced by Dune Road, which is connected to the mainland via four bridges. The center portion of Dune Road is heavily populated with private homes and offers hardly any public parking. The enclosed charts list the fly-fishing guides and the tackle shops having fly-fishing experience in this area.

Boaters have many choices for launching from the mainland; from marinas that charge a daily fee. There are also several town and county ramps available for use by purchasing a permit. On the water, the shallow bays can be tricky to navigate. If you will be venturing out without a guide, you'll need a local chart and tide table. There are lots of opportunities for exploring the various connecting bays and it is possible to encounter striped bass, bluefish and weakfish just about anywhere between the two inlets on the bay side. From May into November there's a fair amount of surface action to identify the location of schools of fish. Birds in the vicinity will also be an indicator of surface activity.

The inlets are like a magnet for both fish and fishermen and it's recommended that you spend some time at one or both for the best action. Striped bass in particular love moving water, and the inlets are the locations of the faster currents. On a flooding (incoming) tide the fishing around these inlets is safer because the current is pushing you back into the bay. As soon as the tide shifts however to outgoing, the start of the ebb, the inlets will change from millponds to Class 5 rapids, sucking you out into the ocean waves. If you're on a boat in the ocean and it's time to head for the dock during a falling tide, hold outside the breaker line for a while and watch your approach carefully. If you're at Moriches Inlet and it looks too dangerous, run east to Shinnecock Inlet, which is bigger and deeper and a little more boater-friendly.

A 9- to 10-weight fly rod, a reel with a smooth drag and 200-300 yards of 30-pound backing is the outfit of choice for most of your fly-fishing in this area. The fly lines you will need are very dependent upon where you're fishing. When fishing from a boat around the inlets, a 300-to 400-grain (9- to 10-weight) sinking line is my favorite fish producer. There are channels that lead back into the bay which are from 6 to 15 feet deep and that harbor fast currents. Most of the prey and game fish entering or leaving the bays use these channels as a highway and holding area, especially the striped bass. For the beach fly-fisher, a sinking line works well from the rock jetties and for the channels which run close to the beach. Nevertheless, the intermediate-density fly line is used most of the time on the beach. While sight-fishing on the sand flats and in the bays, I'll usually use a floating line, relying on weighted flies like Clousers to reach the correct fishing depth. A floating line is also preferred

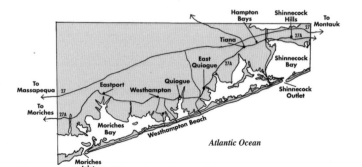

Species	Typical Size – Pounds	J	F	M	A	M	J	J	A	S	O	N	D
Bluefin Tuna	10 - 100						2	3	3	3	2		
Bluefish	2 - 20				2	3	4	5	5	5	5	4	
Bonito	4 - 10						2	3	3	3	3	2	
False Albacore	5 - 15						2	3	4	5	4	3	
Skipjack Tuna	5 - 12							3	4	3	2		
Striped Bass	3 - 30	1	1	1	2	4	5	5	4	5	5	4	2
Summer Flounder	1 - 10					2	3	3	3	3	2		
Weakfish	2 - 12				3	3	3	3	3	3	3	3	

1=Scarce, 2=Spotty, 3=Available, 4=Readily Available, 5=Widely Available

when targeting surface-breaking fish in either the bay or the ocean. A 9-foot leader with a 12- to 20-pound tippet will be quite satisfactory for floating and intermediate-density lines. For sinking lines, a shorter 6-foot leader is preferred. For bluefish, a section of wire bite tippet is also needed.

Oceanside, between the Moriches and Shinnecock inlets, striped bass, bluefish and weakfish can often be encountered between mid-May and November. The fall run along these beaches can be spectacular. From mid-July through mid-October there is sporadic fishing here for bluewater species such as false albacore (little tunny), green bonito, Spanish mackerel, skipjack tuna and schoolie bluefin tuna. These speedsters are usually one to 10 or more miles out in the ocean, but they can occasionally be only a few yards from the beach. Note the species chart for a complete list of available game fish.

Striped bass can be very selective at times, but usually they seem to eat everything and anything. Accordingly, take the fly that you tied and didn't want to show to anybody and give it a try. A striper may think that it's the neatest thing he's ever seen. To be safe, though, bring some Lefty's Deceivers, Clouser Minnows and Glenn Mikkleson's Epoxy Baitfish imitations in size 2 to 3/0 hook sizes. A typical, successful fly can be from 1 1/2 to 7 inches long. The prey chart below lists the more common baitfish as well as crabs, shrimp and squid. Patterns for these other prey are also needed for an all-round arsenal of flies. The permit and bonefish patterns will be good for the flats and squid patterns will be needed for the inlets and ocean.

Guides (Capt.)	Phone/Fax	E-mail
Capt. Joe Blados	631-765-3670	
Capt. Paul Dixon	631-324-7979	
Capt. Scott Gaekle	631-287-3264	sgaeckle@optonline.net
Capt. C. John Killen	631-325-1112	brinyfly@worldnet.att.net
Glenn Mikkleson	631-878-0883	
Capt. Ken Turco	631-728-3797	
Capt. Richie Vitale	631-563-1323	

Altenkirch Precision Tackle
Shinnecock Canal
Hampton Bays, NY
Contact: Hank Altenkirch
631-728-4110

B&B Tackle
320 Montauk Hwy Ctr.
Moriches, NY 11934
Contact: Chet Wilcox
631-329-5829

Cold Spring Harbor Fly Shop
37 Main St.
Cold Spring, NY
Contact: Ken Kuhner
631-673-8937

Fly Fishing Super Store
4105 Sunrise Highway,
Bohemia, NY 11716
Contact: Bill Ballen & Richie Vitale
631-563-1323

Capt. C. John "Spot" Killen has lived on Long Island all of his life and he has been making a living on the water for the past 29 years. This has given him an intimate knowledge of the bays and ocean areas he fishes today. Spot has been fly-fishing exclusively for the past 10 years and has been guiding fly-fishers full-time for the last 4 of those years.

Most Common Prey	Typical Size (inches)	Usual Months of Availability*												Typical Matching Fly Patterns**
		J	F	M	A	M	J	J	A	S	O	N	D	
Bay Anchovies	1 - 4					2	2	2	3	4	5	3		Epoxy Baitfish, Clouser Deep Minnow (H)
Bunker Menhaden	2 - 12			1	2	3	3	3	3	3	3	3		Moriches Mouthful
Butterfish	2 - 6				2	2	2	3	3	3	2	2		Lefty's Deceiver (G)
Grass Shrimp	1 - 2						3	3	3	3				Snapping Shrimp
Herring	4 - 12				3	3	2	2	2	3	3	3		Lefty's Deceiver (D)
Lady & Blue Crabs	1 - 2					3	3	3	3	3	3	3		Acrylic Deer Hair Crab
Sand Eels	2 - 6				1	3	4	4	5	4	3	2		Clouser Deep Minnow (J), Lavendar Eel
Silversides	2 - 4				1	3	4	5	5	5	5	3		Clouser Deep Minnow (I), Epoxy Baitfish(B)
Squid	3 - 12				2	3	3	3	3	3	3	3		AcrylicSquid
Tinker Mackerel	3 - 6				4	5	5	2	2	3	3	2		Lefty's Deceiver, Epoxy Baitfish (A), Clouser Deep Minnow (A)

*1=Scarce, 2=Spotty, 3=Available, 4=Readily Available, 5=Widely Available • ** Pattern Recipe in Appendix A.

Chapter 14: Upper New York Harbor

By Capt. Joe Shastay, Jr.

While in Manhattan, most people don't even realize that they're on an island, not to mention the fact that this island is surrounded by water inhabited by 10- to 30-pound game fish. Manhattan has literally anything that a person could want including, for the past 10 years, quality fly-fishing with convenient Manhattan pickup. The waters around Manhattan consist of three sections of rivers; the Hudson River to the west, the Harlem River to the north, and the East River to the east. The most fascinating aspect of these rivers are the significant current flows, which create estuary-like conditions because of the water dynamics. The Hudson receives fresh water from its headwaters and its tributaries, but it also receives salt water from the bay and from the ocean via tidal influence. The East River is the most dynamic of the three; it is actually a tidal strait whose magnificent range of up to 7-knot currents are separated by slack periods of as little as 8 minutes.

There is no place on the East River that is as spectacular as Hell's Gate, an area that is notorious for shipwrecks and feared by sailors over the years. These rocky, foaming shallows are heaven on earth to game fish because of the concentration of prey on which they feed. Most native New Yorkers still can't believe that such a prolific fishery exists in such close proximity to their jobs or homes. The Harlem River also seems to offer promise of good fly-fishing, although the author has yet to give it adequate attention.

Shorebound anglers are advised to fish the East River side of Manhattan. Here, the water is generally clearer and the fishing is usually better. Another area for wading/walking anglers is where the East River meets its easternmost terminus at Little Neck and Manhasset bays. April is this author's favorite time to fish this area, though the fall also usually provides good fly-fishing. Another shore area worth checking out is Liberty State Park in Jersey City, New Jersey. This one-mile-long waterfront walkway, plus numerous jetties and rip-rap walls, provides many fly-fishing opportunities.

Kayaks can be launched in the Hudson River from Pier 26 on the Manhattan west side. This pier is located 5 blocks north of Chamber Street and 5 blocks south of Canal Street. Fly-fishers can expect to fish in waters whose depth ranges from 6 to 35 feet, with the best fly-fishing occurring in the spring (March-June) and the fall (October-January). Sight-casting is particularly productive at night under lighted piers and docks. Surface feeding by bluefish and striped bass is quite common during

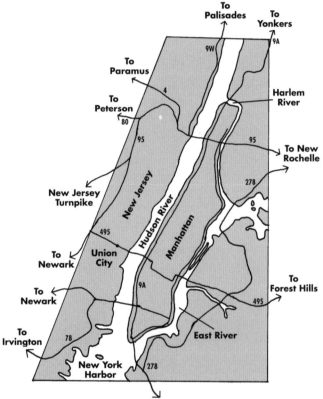

Species	Typical Size - Inches	J	F	M	A	M	J	J	A	S	O	N	D
Bluefish	18 - 35	1	1	1	1	4	5	3	3	5	5	2	1
Striped Bass	18 - 30	4	1	3	5	5	5	3	3	3	5	5	5
Weakfish	14 - 28	1	1	1	1	4	5	3	2	1	1	1	1

1=Scarce, 2=Spotty, 3=Available, 4=Readily Available, 5=Widely Available

May, June, September, October and November, and anglers can participate in the feeding frenzies by following the working birds during the daylight hours. October is probably the best month for this activity. The average size of striped bass landed on the fly is generally from 17 to 21 inches, with occasional brutes in the 28- to 30-inch range being landed. The bluefish will average 22 inches, with quite a few 28- to 34-inch fish also landed. Bluefish are particularly tough on tackle, especially on knots and reel drag systems.

Tackle recommended for bluefish are 8- to 10-weight rods with 250- to 300-grain saltwater sinking lines, although blues are also taken on the surface with poppers and floating lines. Striped bass tackle is more varied. This author recommends 6- to 9-weight rods, with 7- to 8-weights being the best choice for schooling stripers in the 17- to 21-inch range. Floating lines are seldom used and a 250-grain sinking line is best. The author's preferred choices for school bass flies are green/white Clousers, Surf Candies, Glass Minnows and Slab Sides. Most of the fish hooked will be about 10 feet down in a 3-knot current, so one needs to get into the strike zone quickly and then stay there. Polycheate worm flies like the Palolo and Page's Worm Fly are good, but not necessarily optimum during the worm hatches in May and June. Often, spearing, bay anchovy, and shad imitations will work just as well. This author is not a big advocate of matching the hatch. Generally, these fish eat as the opportunity presents itself, though flash and glitter will usually help to get their attention, especially under artificially-lit structures at night. For big bluefish, I like a big moss bunker imitation like the Sedotti Slammer.

Guides(Capt.)	Phone/Fax	E-mail
Joe Shastay	973-239-1988	joejohunt@aol.com
Frank Torino	718-448-1761	

Orvis New York
356 Madison Ave.
New York, NY 10017
Contact: Fishing Dept.
212-697-3133/
212-687-3133

Urban Angler
118 E. 25th St.
New York, NY 10010
Contact: Steve Fisher
212-979-7600/
212-473-4020
urbang@panix.com

Capt. Joe Shastay, 41 years old, has been fishing the local area for about 35 years, 10 years as a licensed charter captain. He enjoys both fly and spin fishing and has the enviable record of 237 consecutive charter trips without failing to have his clients land a fish. Capt. Joe is particularly knowledgeable of the history of the Port of New York. Joe has been featured in articles in both Saltwater Fly Fishing and Sports Illustrated magazines. He enjoys working with children and anglers at all levels of experience.

Most Common Prey	Typical Size (inches)	Usual Months of Availability*												Typical Matching Fly Patterns**
		J	F	M	A	M	J	J	A	S	O	N	D	
American Eels	6 - 10	1	1	1	1	4	4	4	4	4	4	1	1	Black Angus, Catherwood's American Eel
American Shad	2 - 14	3	3	3	2	2	2	1	1	2	3	3	3	Shinabou Shad
Atlantic Herring	6 - 12	3	3	3	1	1	1	1	1	1	1	1	3	Tabory's Slab Side, Hair Head Herring
Bay Anchovies	2	3	3	3	2	2	2	2	2	2	3	3	3	Surf Candy, Green and White Glass Minnow
Killifish	2	3	3	3	3	4	4	4	4	4	3	3	3	Bob's Siliclone Mullet, Whitlock's Matuka Sculpin
Moss Bunker	3 - 14	1	1	1	1	4	4	4	4	4	4	1	1	Sedotti Slammer, & Jelly Fly
Polycheate Worms	1	1	1	1	1	3	3	1	1	1	1	1	1	Palolo Worm, Page's Worm Fly
Spearing	2	3	3	3	3	3	3	3	2	2	2	3	3	Surf Candy (A), Clouser Deep Minnow (I)

*1=Scarce, 2=Spotty, 3=Available, 4=Readily Available, 5=Widely Available • ** Pattern Recipe in Appendix A.

The
Atlantic States

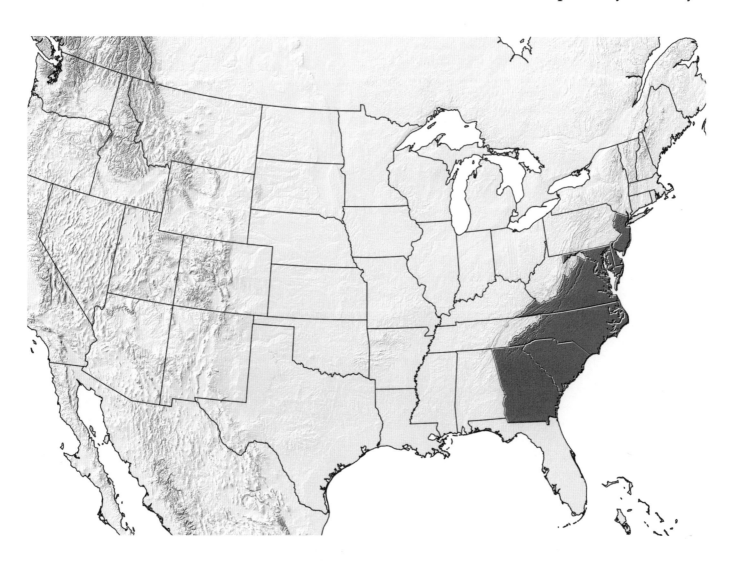

Chapter 15: Sandy Hook and the Raritan Bay Estuary

By Ed Broderick

As shown on the included map, the "Hook" is a six-mile peninsula which acts as a barrier island between the Atlantic Ocean and the bay formed by the confluence of the Raritan, Shrewsbury and Navesink rivers. It sits directly across from the Verrazano Narrows, where the Hudson River spills into the Atlantic Ocean. As fishermen, it's easy to imagine the effect four great rivers can have in creating a spectacular and diverse fishery. The area includes the whole of Raritan Bay stretching west thirteen miles from Sandy Hook, bordered by the first towns of the New Jersey shoreline on the south and Staten Island on the north. In the early season, the western shallows of the bay and the estuary waters of the rivers warm faster than the ocean, acting as an attractant for early runs of striped bass and bluefish.

Sandy Hook is part of the Gateway National Park System and is a primary place for bird watching and general enjoyment of one of the few unspoiled places along the New Jersey shoreline. It is an interesting and ever-changing environment where the sand creeping northward creates a very productive tidal rip at the tip of the peninsula. Although a very dependable area for the

shorebound fly-fisher, it takes a good walk over soft sand, in waders, to reach the most productive stretches. On the bay side there are many good stretches, including Spermacetti and Horseshoe coves, the "Bug" light area around the Coast Guard Station, the rip rap formed from the debris of the old Highlands bridge and in general the entire six-mile bay front. During the fall, large schools of bait move south along the ocean and schools of bluefish, striped bass, false albacore and weakfish pursue them. The enclosed table lists the predominant gamefish species and their availability during the year.

The area considered attractive for shorebound fly-fishing includes all accessible areas of Raritan Bay and the ocean shoreline down to the towns of Deal and Asbury. Jetty fishing is particularly good near these towns. During the high summer months, access to the town beaches and jetties is limited, but the best fishing is near the point of Sandy Hook. The early season in March usually starts with striper action westward along the Raritan Bay beaches of Cliffwood and Union beaches. The arrival of the first schools of silver-sided minnows and large schools of bunker signals the beginning of the fly-fishing season. At the same time, the fishing in the lower reaches of the rivers starts to pick up. The enclosed chart lists the primary prey species and their corresponding productive fly patterns.

When fishing from a boat, one has the choice of structure fishing in areas such as Romer Shoals, Flynn's Knoll and the major and minor rips of Sandy Hook, or locating surface action signaled by feeding birds and oily slicks on the water. Picturesque fly-fishing is found around the Romer Shoals, Old Orchard and West Bank lighthouses of Raritan Bay. Boat fishing is productive from the lower waters of the bay offshore to such areas as the Mud Buoy, 17 Fathoms, and the BA Buoy where there are good opportunities for more exotic species. A favorite trick is to arrive at the offshore areas when the early party boats, who have been chumming all morning, start to leave. From the fish's viewpoint, it's somewhat like taking away your food halfway through dinner.

Our gamefish species include striped bass and blue-fish throughout the spring, with weakfish making a con-

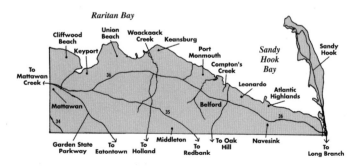

Species	Typical Size - pounds	J	F	M	A	M	J	J	A	S	O	N	D
Bluefish	2 - 20				2	4	5	5	5	5	5	3	
Bonito	2 - 8							3	4	4	4	2	
Dolphin	2 - 20								2	3	3	3	
False Albacore	4 - 15						2	3	4	5	5	3	
Fluke(Summer Flounder)	1 - 10					4	5	5	5	5	5		
Skip Jack	4 - 15								3	4	3		
Spanish Mackerel	2 - 10								1	1	1	1	
Striped Bass (Stripers)	2 - 40			2	3	5	5	5	5	5	5	5	3
Tuna	10-20								2	2	3	2	
Weakfish	1 - 10				2	3	3	4	5	5	4	3	

1=Scarce, 2=Spotty, 3=Available, 4=Readily Available, 5=Widely Available

sistent appearance toward late spring. For those who wish to target them, there is a lot of challenge in the ever-present fluke or summer flounder. Use a Seaducer, tied Clouser-like so that the hook point rides upright. In the summer months, these species are readily available along with occasional appearances of Spanish mackerel. As summer heads toward fall, there are excellent opportunities for false albacore, bonito, skip jack and, in recent years, the occasional small blue and yellowfin tuna. To date, we have not yet landed one on our 9-weight outfits. Though not considered a primary species, there are periodic opportunities to target dolphin on a fly. These fish range from the small chicken dolphin to some nice specimens of around 20 pounds.

When fishing from a boat, you must be prepared to fish deep. The tides can be fast and the fish like to hug the channels; thus there is a need to get the fly down quickly. We use high-density lines that cast well and sink quickly. The technique resembles deep-water nymphing; cast uptide, let the line sink and be very watchful for a strike. Most types of intermediate-density lines perform well for shore fishing. Rods are generally in the 8- to 10-weight range, though one can have a lot of fun using 3- to 6-weight outfits while pursuing the small bluefish almost always found in the waters immediately behind Sandy Hook. Since the blues and stripers can be large, reels with good drag mechanisms are necessary. Good reels are even more important when targeting the little tuna.

Our favorite flies are quite traditional, with size being a primary consideration. We tie our flies oversize and use scissors on the water to cut them back when appropriate. Knowing what bait is in the area is very important. We regard this area as primarily a small-bait fishery, since the bunker are usually hit hard by the commercial netters after the initial spring run. Nevertheless, one must be prepared for a bunker blitz when a school does survive the netting. Clousers and Deceivers in varying sizes and colors cover most situations. Lately, flies imitating small dolphin have been productive due to the dolphin schools that periodically come close to shore and are targeted by larger game fish. When targeting bluefish, we prefer not to use wire leaders, instead using heavy monofilament shock tippets. We usually start fishing with 60-pound tippets, scal-

ing down until we start catching fish. Although 8-pound tippets are common for the little tuna, 12-pound tippets are generally used for stripers and weakfish.

All of Sandy Hook Park is open to fishing before Memorial Day and after Labor Day. Some beaches on the ocean are closed during the summer season, but fortunately the better parts remain open. Accommodations at reasonable rates are readily available in towns such as Leonardo and Highlands. Red Bank and Shrewsbury are upscale and conveniently nearby. Boats can be rented from various marinas in Highlands and Atlantic Highlands, and there are launching ramps at the Leonardo State Marina, at the Municipal Marina in Atlantic Highlands and in the town of Keyport. A good source for additional information are the members of the local Bayshore Flyrodders Club and the guides and fly shops listed in the included tables.

Guides (Capt.)	Phone/Fax	E-mail
Robby Barradale	732-291-1193	captfysh@aol.com
Ed Broderick	908-789-3382	slabfly@aol.com
Frank Tenore	973-763-2876	
Dino Torino	718-356-6436	fly4tuna@cs.com

Fly Hatch
468 Broad St.
Shrewsbury, NJ 07702
Contact: Dave Chouinard
732-530-6784
flyhatch@aol.com

Orvis - Paramus
770 Rte. 17 N.
Paramus, NJ 07652
Contact: John Roetman
201-447-6648/
201-447-5231
flyfishnj.aol.com

Sportsman's Outfitter
1061 Raritan Rd.
Clark, NJ 07066
Contact: Don Madson
732-388-2085/505-213-0741
fishtek@earthlink.net

Ed Broderick started guiding with his son "EJ" in 1990, after a long involvement with both saltwater and freshwater fly-fishing for bass. At the time there were no fly-fishing services available in the Raritan Bay area. We maintain and fish both a 25-foot Steigercraft and a 30-foot Aquasport, to offer comfort and safety even when the wind is strong. These craft offer the option of moving offshore to pursue the small tuna and dolphins which are seasonally available.

Most Common Prey	Typical Size (inches)	J	F	M	A	M	J	J	A	S	O	N	D	Typical Matching Fly Patterns**
Baby Bunker	2 - 4								3	4	5	5	5	Lefty's Deceiver (N), Tabory's Slab Side
Bay Anchovies	2 - 4		1	2	3	4	4	4	4	5	5	5	3	Clear Synthetic Clouser
Bunker	4 - 12			1	3	4	4	4	4	5	5	5		Lefty's Deceiver (N) Tabory's Slab Side
Herring	4 - 8		2	2	1	1	1	1	2	2	2	2	1	Tabory's Slab Side (B)
Killifish	2 - 4		5	5	5	5	5	5	5	5	5	5	2	Clear Synthetic Clouser
Sandeels	3 - 6							1	3	3	3	3	2	Synthetic Clouser
Sea Bass	4 - 6								2	3	3	3	3	Lefty's Deceiver (H)
Snapper Blues	6 - 10							1	3	4	4	2		Lefty's Deceiver (O)
Spearing	2 - 4				1	3	5	5	5	5	5	4	3	Clouser Deep Minnow (A), EJ Sparkle Fly, Surf Candy
Worms	2 - 6				5	5	5	5	5	5	5	5	4	Dixon's Devil Worm

*1=Scarce, 2=Spotty, 3=Available, 4=Readily Available, 5=Widely Available
** Pattern Recipe in Appendix A.

Chapter 16: Barnegat Bay

By Capt. Dick Dennis

Barnegat Bay runs north-south and is approximately 29 miles long and 3.5 miles across at its widest point. Bay depth ranges from one foot on the eastern side to 12 feet on the western side. The bay is mainly nourished by the Manasquan, Metedeconk and Toms rivers, but the Cedar Creek, Forked River and Oyster Creek estuaries also provide bait and warmwater flow. Oyster Creek is particularly important because it is a nuclear power plant discharge location, raising the estuary water temperatures 30 to 40 degrees above the typical wintertime bay temperature of 40 degrees. Accordingly, fish and bait are available at the mouth of this estuary for all 12 months of the year.

The Manasquan and Barnegat inlets each have several square miles of adjacent salt marsh and feeder ditches where bait moves into the bay when bay temperatures reach the mid-50s. The most pristine area is adjacent to Island Beach State Park, a narrow barrier island approximately 10 miles long. The park lies between the Atlantic Ocean and calmer Barnegat Bay. Sand dunes and other habitat, which offer cover to maritime plants and wildlife, extend from the entrance of the park in Seaside Park to the tip of the island at the Barnegat Inlet. The Barnegat Lighthouse is a prominent feature, and can be seen for 10 miles from all directions. Island Beach is one of the few undeveloped area beaches on the New Jersey coast and is home to its largest osprey colony. There are many other species of birds, and today's vegetation is the same as it was hundreds of years ago. The sand dunes are off-limits to ensure the continuing health of the vegetation, but canoeing and kayaking is permitted in the nutrient-rich tidal marsh area. Visitors to Island Beach State Park have access to 3000 acres of clean sandy beaches.

The estuaries of the Manasquan River, the Metedeconk River, the Toms River, Cedar Creek, the Forked River and Oyster Creek provide good fly-fishing in the spring and fall for stripers, weakfish, bluefish, flounder and white perch. Fly fishers can target and catch all of these game fish by fishing structures and drop-offs, and by matching the available bait. Most fishing is done from a boat, but there are limited wading opportunities near Manasquan, Point Pleasant, Bay Head, Mantoloking Point, the Toms River and of course in Island State Park. Restaurants, motels and marinas for launching boats are widely available in Point Pleasant, Toms River, Beachwood, Pine Beach and other locations. The included chart lists the fly-fishing guides who are available in the area; beach guides are also usually available through the many tackle shops in the area. Local fly shops are also listed on a separate chart.

Beach fly-fishing usually targets albacore, bluefish, striped bass and weakfish. The latter are most available on the beach when they leave the bays during the north-south migration. Striped bass, weakfish and bluefish are available in the bay on a regular basis starting in late April. Poppers, sliders and other baitfish imitations "matching the hatch" will usually be productive. When the bluefish come into the bay in late April, they are starting their northerly migration. The weakfish and stripers are also on the move. Bayside fishing is quite good during the warm

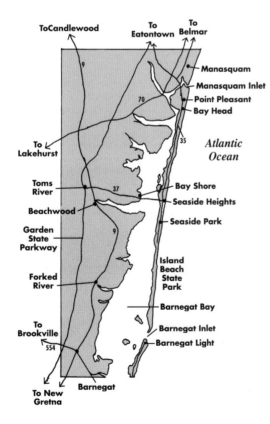

Species	Typical Size – Pounds	J	F	M	A	M	J	J	A	S	O	N	D
Albacore	7 - 10	1	1	1	1	1	1	1	1	4	5	3	2	1
Bluefish	2 - 8	1	1	1	3	4	5	4	3	3	4	4	2
Striped Bass	18-36 Inches	1	1	2	3	4	4	2	2	3	4	5	3
Summer Flounder	2 - 5				3	4	5	5	4	4	2	1	
Weakfish	2 - 7	1	1	1	2	4	5	5	4	4	3	2	1
Winter Flounder	1 - 2	1	3	4	4	2							

1=Scarce, 2=Spotty, 3=Available, 4=Readily Available, 5=Widely Available

weather, particularly near the Barnegat Inlet. The enclosed chart lists the principal game fish available in our area.

Often, the type of fly line used can make the difference between success and failure. I use floating lines for fish who are feeding on the surface, intermediate-density lines for fish feeding below the surface and 250- to 350-grain sinking shooting heads for blind-casting to bottom-feeders. We commonly use 8- to 10-weight fly rods, normally 8 1/2- and 9-footers when fly-fishing from a boat, and 9- to 10-footers when wading or walking the beach. I generally prefer 8-foot leaders for floating lines, 6-foot leaders for intermediate-density lines and 4-foot leaders for sinking lines. Leaders will typically be made from 2 or 3 sections; starting from a 30-pound butt and terminating in a 10- or 15-pound fluorocarbon tippet. We use good-quality fly reels capable of holding 200 yards of 30-pound Dacron backing plus the fly line. We recommend corrosion-resistant reels with good drag systems and a thorough fresh-water washing after each trip.

The accompanying chart lists the main gamefish prey, their times of availability and typical matching fly patterns. In the spring, the baitfish are smaller; in the fall they are larger. The larger bunker, herring and mullet are more ocean-oriented; however they will sometimes frequent the bays and rivers when the ocean conditions are rough. In the spring, we use poppers, sliders, Jiggies or Half-and-Halfs for bluefish, weakfish and stripers. Once the water temperature reaches 55 degrees, the spearing, killifish and shrimp are more active and the pattern choices change. The small crabs and the cinder and clam worms hatch at full-moon phase.

In mid-summer, the bunker and herring leave the bay and head for the sea. After May and until September, the weakfish bottom-feed in the deeper waters since the bay temperatures are approaching 78 to 80 degrees. Under these conditions, we fish deep with flies like the Surf Candy and the Ultra Shrimp. When the baitfish are relatively high-profile like the bunker or herring, the Spread Fly or Dave's Wide Side will often produce good results. The latter is a smaller fly, tied on a circle hook, so it's a bit safer for the fish. Sand eels are a common striper prey in the ocean and they are prevalent in the spring and fall.

Guides (Capt.)	Phone/Fax	E-mail
Dave Chouinard	732-530-6784	flyhatch@flyhatch.com
Dick Dennis	732-530-6784/	hed0075@aol.com
	732-929-0967	
Paul Eidman	732-922-4077	paulyfish@aol.com
Bill Frazier	732-288-0133	wfrazierjr@aol.com
Jim Freda	732-528-1861	jfreda@bytheshore.com
Bill Hoblitzel	732-780-8624	
Brain Pasch	732-350-4528	

Betty & Nick's
8th Avenue.
Seaside Park, NJ 08752
Contact: John Bushell
732-793-2708
cobra76@bettyandnicks.com

The Fly Ranch
468 Broad St.
Shrewsbury, NJ 07702
Contact: Dave Chouinard
732-530-6784
flyhatch@flyhatch.com

Sportsman's Center
Route 130.
Bordertown, NJ 08505
Contact: Bob Atticks
609-298-5300
info@sportsmanscenter.com

Capt. Dick Dennis has lived in Seaside Park and Toms River all of his life. He has been actively fly-fishing since 1975 and fishing in general for 50 years in his native Ocean County. Dick is a charter member of the Atlantic Salt Water Fly Rodders, a group consisting of 240 members. He is a certified FFF Casting Instructor, an accomplished fly tier and a U.S. Coast Guard-certified Captain. Dick has been fishing his native waters as a Charter Captain for Backcast Enterprises and for The Fly Hatch.

Most Common Prey	Typical Size (inches)	Usual Months of Availability*												Typical Matching Fly Patterns**
		J	F	M	A	M	J	J	A	S	O	N	D	
Bay Anchovies	1 - 2	1	1	2	4	4	5	5	5	5	5	4	3	Deep Candy
Bunker	4 - 18	1	1	2	2	3	4	4	4	5	5	5	3	Dave's Wide Side
Cinder Worms	0.75 - 1.0	1	1	1	2	3	3	3	3	2	2	1	1	Dixon's Devil Worm
Crabs	2 - 4	1	1	4	5	5	5	5	5	5	4	4	2	Chernobyl Crab
Grass Shrimp	0.5 - 1.5	1	1	2	3	4	5	5	5	4	3	2	1	Ultra Shrimp (A)
Herring	8 - 12	1	1	2	3	4	4	3	3	4	3	2	1	Lefty's Deceiver (L)
Killifish	1 - 3	1	1	2	3	4	5	5	5	5	4	3	2	Deep Candy
Mullet	3.5 - 4.0	1	1	1	2	2	3	3	4	5	5	4	2	Bob's Siliclone Mullet (A)
Sand Eels	2 - 5	1	1	2	2	3	3	3	3	5	5	4	3	Half-and-Half (D)
Spearing	1.5 - 3.0	1	1	2	3	5	5	5	5	5	3	2	1	Jiggy
General														Bob's Banger (A)

*1=Scarce, 2=Spotty, 3=Available, 4=Readily Available, 5=Widely Available • ** Pattern Recipe in Appendix A.

Chapter 17: Cape May
Chris Goldmark

Southern New Jersey is unique in that very few anglers fly-fish in the area. For years I was under the impression that there were only four fly-fishers in the Cape May area; I've since discovered a few more, most of whom I've never met—and I have lived here a very long time. This gives you an idea of the sheer size of this fishable area. With everybody spread out and all catching fish, none of us would see another fly-fisher for days or even weeks. Nevertheless, there are plenty of sport fishermen and lots of boat traffic, especially during the peak tourist season of June through September. Even so, there are always places to catch fish in complete privacy at any time of the year. Cape May boasts an attractive habitat, easy accessibility and comfortable and affordable accommodations.

The Cape's beaches and inlets are especially accessible and productive for the fly-fisher who is new to the area. Good

spring fishing starts in the middle of May for large weakfish, called trout by locals. These fish won't usually take a fly until the water temperatures reach 56 to 58 degrees F. There are days in March or April when the striped bass fishing can be excellent along the beaches and inlets, but this fishing is highly weather-dependent and it tends to vary from year to year with respect to fish size and availability. In other words, it's kind of hit or miss. The weakfish can be targeted from all the jetties and rock structures from North Cape May, around the Cape May Point and all the way up to Sea Isle and points further north and east. Weakfish prefer the structure and they like tidal flow. Accordingly, this is the scenario for using sinking lines, often called "chuck-and-duck" and "low-and-slow". Clousers, Bendbacks and Jiggys are perennial staples, whereas the best colors seem to change from year to year. Contacting the local fly shops will be of considerable help to you and, of course, our local guides are always very up to date on the most successful fly patterns.

Fall is mullet time. These baitfish usually begin their southerly migration in the middle or end of September. When the mullet school up and come out of the back bays, the beaches and inlets come alive. Stripers, weakfish and bluefish are readily found on all the beaches in knee-deep water. A general rule of thumb in Cape May is that southerly or onshore winds tend to hold the bait tighter against the beach, which makes for some good fly-fishing. On the other hand, northwestern breezes often hold the bait far enough off the beach so as to make the game fish inaccessible to the shore-bound angler. Beach fishing continues to be excellent right up until January, depending on such factors as weather, water temperature and the detailed migration routes of the late-fall forage species like the juvenile bunker and anchovies.

The back bays or meadows can be extremely productive, but the first-timer must use the services of an experienced guide in order to achieve any degree of success. The back bays encompass a very large area and, without local knowledge, you'll spend most of your time getting lost, running aground, swatting greenheads and probably not catching anything. Fall is the best time to fish these waterways, but there is also excellent fly-fishing in the spring for large fluke (summer flounder) and weakfish.

The rips just off Cape May Point are famous all along the Atlantic seaboard. Some of the world's best spring and fall striper fishing occurs on these shoals. Unfortunately, the boat traffic reflects this popularity. This is an area accessible only by boat, and I don't mean a 14-foot skiff. There is a tremendous amount of tidal flow over very shallow water and the slightest amount of offshore wind or swell can make the rips very dangerous. The fish hold tight to the bottom and sinking

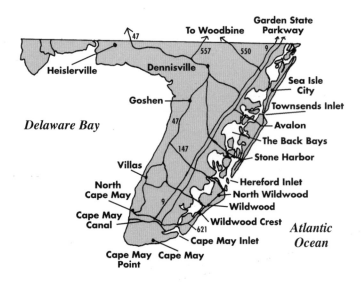

Species	Typical Size - Pounds	J	F	M	A	M	J	J	A	S	O	N	D
Bluefish	1 - 10				3	4	5	5	5	5	5	4	3
False Albacore	5 - 12								2	4	5	4	3
Striped Bass	5 - 25	2		3	4	4	3	3	3	5	5	5	4
Weakfish	2 - 10				3	5	5	5	5	5	5	4	2

1=Scarce, 2=Spotty, 3=Available, 4=Readily Available, 5=Widely Available

lines are necessary. Again, I'd strongly recommend having a guide if this is your first exposure to the rips. Fall is the season for false albacore. This is probably the most unheralded fly-fishery in the mid-Atlantic region. The albacore fishing here in South Jersey can be very intense and very accessible. October is the peak month for action.

For the visiting fly-fisher who wishes to walk and fish on his own, I'd suggest three areas; the sod banks by the free bridge on Great Channel just south of Stone Harbor, the Cape May Point jetties (wear corkers to deal with the slippery rocks), and the Cape May and North Wildwood beaches.

The best all-around fly rod for this area is an 8- to 9-weight. An exception would be when fly-fishing for big stripers in the rips or chasing false albacore. Here, at least a 10-weight rod is needed, plus a reel with plenty of backing capacity. A useful rule for fly lines for this area is to "sink in the spring and float in the fall", but there are many circumstances, especially in the fall in heavy surf where an intermediate-density line will make your fly-fishing a lot easier. Clousers are very popular in South Jersey, but when striper fishing in the fall, Capt. Joe Blados' Crease Fly and Steve Reifsneider's Phantom Mullet are both very productive.

Accommodations in the city of Cape May can be a bit pricey, but are well worth it if you want to be near the beach and in an area just teeming with Victorian heritage. For lower-priced accommodations, the locals recommend going "offshore", which is west of the Garden State Parkway. If you bring your own boat, there are three launching ramps in the immediate area.

Guides (Capt.)	Phone/Fax	E-mail
Gary Gibson	609-263-6540	
Chris Goldmark	609-884-3697	
John Miller*	609-886-1954	mrfish@bellatlantic.net
Lee Schilling	609-729-9269	captainlee@aol.com
*Shore guide		

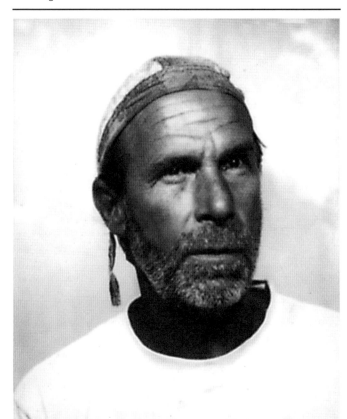

Chris Goldmark is a licensed charter captain and has lived in Cape May for 35 years. For 25 years he made his living as a commercial fishermen, but for the past 10 years he has been guiding sports fishermen on a full-time basis. Chris guides in Cape May during the warmer 6 months and he guides on the island of Culebra in Puerto Rico for the other 6 months, for bonefish, tarpon and permit. His exploits in Puerto Rico have been described and published in several travel magazines and books and in angling publications.

Bob Jackson's
719 Broadway, W
Cape May, NJ 08204
Contact: Bob Jackson
609-898-7950/609-898-7951
mail@fishcapemay.com

Bob's Bait & Tackle
970 Route 109
Cape May, NJ 08204
Contact: Bob Semick
609-884-2248
bob@bobsbaitntackle.com

Gibson's Tackle
42nd & Bay St.
Sea Isle City, NJ 08243
Contact: Gary Gibson
609-263-6540
gibsonstackle@hotmail.com

Jim's Bait & Tackle
970 Route 109
Cape May, NJ 08204
Contact: Chris Poacher
609-884-3900
609-884-3506

Most Common Prey	Typical Size (inches)	\multicolumn{12}{c}{Usual Months of Availability*}	Typical Matching Fly Patterns**
		J	F	M	A	M	J	J	A	S	O	N	D	
Adult Bunker	6 - 12				4	5	5	5	5	5	4	3		Bozo Bunker
Mullet	3 - 5							2	3	5	5	3		Crease Fly, Phantom Mullet
Peanut Bunker	2 - 4							3	4	4	4	5	4	Crease Fly, Bozo Bunker
Sandworms & Bloodworms	6			3	3	3	3	3	3	3	3			Clouser Deep Minnow (O), Deep Candy Bendback
Spearing	3 - 5			3	4	4	4	4	4	4	4	4	4	Clouser Deep Minnow (I), Jiggy

*1=Scarce, 2=Spotty, 3=Available, 4=Readily Available, 5=Widely Available • ** Pattern Recipe in Appendix A.

Chapter 18: Upper Chesapeake Bay
By Capt. Norm Bartlett

Chesapeake Bay is the largest estuary in the United States. The entire length of the Bay, including the portion in Virginia, is about 180 miles long, north to south. The total shoreline is estimated to be 8100 miles, with about half in Maryland and half in Virginia. At its widest point, east to west, the Bay is 30 miles wide. The average water depth is 21 feet. For the purposes of this chapter, the upper Chesapeake begins at the mouth of the Potomac River and extends northward 80 miles to Conowingo Dam on the Susquehanna River. During the spring, the north end of the bay will be almost entirely fresh water, with salinity increasing to about 17 parts per thousand at the mouth of the Potomac River. In the fall, salinity at the north end of the bay rises to only about 3 parts per thousand; accordingly the Bay's upper end and its many con-

tributing rivers contain many freshwater species such as largemouth bass, smallmouth bass and chain pickerel.

The western shore of the Bay is heavily populated and includes the cities of Havre de Grace, Aberbeen, Edgewood, Baltimore, Annapolis, Prince Frederick, Solomon's Island, California, Lexington Park and Wynn, plus many smaller towns. In addition, Washington DC is nearby, at the upper end of the Potomac River. In contrast, the eastern shore of the Bay contains the somewhat smaller communities of North East, Elkton, Rockhall, Stevensville, Easton, Oxford and Cambridge and its major industries are farming and commercial fishing. State parks are located on both sides of the bay; many offer camping as well as bay access for boating and fishing.

While the Upper Chesapeake has thousands of miles of shoreline, there are only a few wading opportunities for the fly-fisher. I recommend the Susquehanna State Park, three miles north of Havre de Grace, especially in the summer when the water is low. Striped bass, largemouth bass and smallmouth bass are often available at this time of the year. When wading, make sure that you wear a life preserver, since water levels can change without warning (the dam generation schedule can be obtained by calling 410/457-4076). I strongly advise that you go with someone who knows the area the first time that you fish here. Fly fishing for hickory shad is also available in Deer Creek, which empties into the Susquehanna River. April is the best month for this fishing. April is also the best time to catch a trophy-size striped bass on a fly, but it must be released. Fish as large as 30 pounds are available during this special catch-and-release season, just below Havre de Grace on the Susquehanna Flats. These trophy fish are in shallow water and are getting ready to spawn. There is also wade-in fly-fishing available at Elk Neck, Sandy Point and Point Lookout state parks. The latter two state parks are best for saltwater species because of the higher salinity levels at the more southern access points. Saltwater fly-fishing is best from April until November. From November through March we concentrate our fly-fishing for chain pickerel in the Severn and Magothy rivers. During the winter, we also fish the hot-water discharges at the Brandon Shores power plant in Baltimore, for both stripers

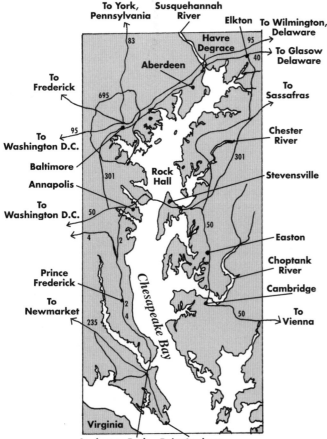

Species	Typical Size	J	F	M	A	M	J	J	A	S	O	N	D
American Shad	2 pounds				1	3	3						
Bluefish	5 - 9 pounds				2	3	3	3	3	3	3	2	
Chain Pickerel	1 - 2 pounds	3	3	3								3	3
Croakers	1 - 3 pounds	1	1	1	3	3	3	3	3	3	3	1	1
Hickory Shad	1 pound				1	3	2						
Largemouth Bass	1 - 3 pounds				2	3	3	3	3	3	3		
Smallmouth Bass	1 - 2 pounds				2	3	3	3	3	3			
Spanish Mackerel	1 - 3 pounds						3	3	3	3	1	1	
Speckled Trout	1 - 2 pounds			3	3	3	3	3	3	3	3		
Striped Bass	2 - 5 pounds	3	3	3	5	5	5	5	5	5	5	5	3
Weakfish	1 - 2 pounds				3	3	3	3	3	3	3		
White Perch	8 - 12 inches	1	1	4	4	4	4	4	4	4	4	1	1

1=Scarce, 2=Spotty, 3=Available, 4=Readily Available, 5=Widely Available

and perch. The enclosed charts list nearby fly shops and fly-fishing guides who regularly fish in the upper Chesapeake Bay.

An 8- or 9-weight fly rod will handle most fishing situations in the upper Chesapeake Bay. A 10-weight outfit might be preferred when conditions are quite windy or when casting large popping bugs for stripers or bluefish. Sinking or sink-tip lines are ideal when fishing streamers in water depths of 4 to 20 feet, and leaders need be no longer than four feet. At greater depths, lead-core lines are required. When fly-fishing with popping bugs, floating lines are preferred with leaders no longer than nine feet. We use braided wire shock tippets for toothy fish such as bluefish and chain pickerel. When fishing for large stripers with large flies or popping bugs, 15-pound-test tippets with 30-pound shock tippets are recommended. A 7-weight outfit can be a lot of fun when fishing for croakers, perch or schoolie stripers or blues.

Guides (Capt.)	Phone/Fax	E-mail
Norm Bartlett	410-679-8790	norman.bartlett2@gte.net
Richard Bornman	410-457-4076	
Brady Bounds	301-862-3166	
Sid Campen	410-226-5647	campen@dmx.com
Michael Critzer	301-253-5605	coastalcmc@aol.com
Steve Culver	410-476-3342	chkurfly@hore.intercom.net
Joe Evans	410-260-2046	hamboat@aol.com
Bruce Foster	410-827-6933	
Richie Gaines	410-827-7210	fishster1@aol.com
Mike Murphy	410-397-3474	mmurphy@dmv.com
Gary Neitzey	410-557-8801	
Bo Toepfer	410-535-6529	captbo@prodigy.net

Angler's Sport Center
1456 Whitehall
Annapolis, MD 21401
Contact: Rob Jebson
410-974-4013
410-257-6940

The Fisherman's Edge
1719 1/2 Edmonson Ave.
Catonsville, MD 21228
Contact: Joe Bruce
410-719-7999/800-338-0053
flies@earl.com

Hudson Trail Outfitters
424 York Road
Towson, MD 21204
410-583-0494

Maclellan's Fly Shop
8592 Leonardtown Rd.
Hughesville, MD 20637
Contact: C.R. Maclellan
301-274-5833

Tocherman's
1919 Eastern Ave., Baltimore MD 21231
Contact: Tony Tocherman
410-327-7744/888-327-7744

Capt. Norm Bartlett has been fishing the Chesapeake Bay for 35 years and has been guiding professionally for eight years. He teaches fly-casting, conservation and performs slide show presentations. Norm's principal hobby is tying flies. He has held six IGFA world fly-rod records and currently holds the IGFA weakfish record, 14 pounds 2 ounces on four-pound-test tippet. Capt. Bartlett currently guides year-round in Maryland and in North Carolina for false albacore during the fall run. Recently, he invented the "Flycasting Trainer" which is used to teach fly-casting. Capt. Bartlett has been on national television twice; once on "Flyfishing America" and once on the "CBS Morning Show." He has also been on local television programs.

Most Common Prey	Typical Size (inches)	Usual Months of Availability*												Typical Matching Fly Patterns**
		J	F	M	A	M	J	J	A	S	O	N	D	
Alewives	2 - 10	3	3	3	3	3	3	3	3	3	3	3	3	Lefty's Deceiver (M), Clouser Deep Minnow (G), Chesapeake Fly
American Eels	4 - 24			3	3	3	3	3	3	3	3	3		Bruce's Suspend Eel
Bay Anchovies	0.5 - 3.0						3	3	3	3	3	3		Crazy Charlie (B)
Blueback Herring	4 - 8			2	5	5	3	3	1	1	1	1	1	Lefty's Deceiver (M), Clouser Deep Minnow (G), Chesapeake Fly
Blue Crabs	0.5						1	2	3	3	3	3		Crystal Crab
Menhaden	2 - 12	3	3	3	3	3	3	3	3	3	3	3	3	Lefty's Deceiver (M), Clouser Deep Minnow (G), Chesapeake Fly
Silversides	2 - 4			3	3	3	3	3	3	3				Lefty's Deceiver (M), Clouser Deep Minnow (G), Chesapeake Fly
White Perch	2 - 12	1	1	3	4	4	4	4	4	4	4	4	4	Lefty's Deceiver (M), Clouser Deep Minnow (G), Chesapeake Fly

*1=Scarce, 2=Spotty, 3=Available, 4=Readily Available, 5=Widely Available • ** Pattern Recipe in Appendix A.

Chapter 19: The Flats of Tangier and Pocomoke Sounds

By Capt. Kevin Josenhans

Tangier and Pocomoke sounds lie at the midpoint of the Chesapeake Bay, equally dissected by the Maryland-Virginia state line. Comprised of a vast area of shallow, grassy flats, this expanse of water stretches from Hooper Straits on the north to the shorelines of Tangier and Watts islands and from the eastern shore of Virginia to the south. Interspersed within this great expanse of water are dozens of uninhabited marshy islands, along with the historic island communities of Smith Island, Maryland and Tangier, Virginia. This low-lying marshy area plays host to a large number of local and migrating waterfowl, including one of the northernmost nesting populations of the brown pelican. The Glenn L. Martin Wildlife Refuge and the island towns on Smith and Tangier are accessible only by boat.

The primary jumping-off spot for shallow-water fishing in this area is Crisfield, Maryland. Located just thirty minutes south of the town of Salisbury, Maryland this working waterman's community has all the amenities needed for a short or extended fishing trip. State-operated Somers Cove Marina has a large deepwater boat ramp. Camping is available at nearby Janes Island State Park, along with boat, canoe and kayak rentals and a concrete launch ramp. The nearest fully equipped fly shop is located in Salisbury.

Although the Crisfield area is perhaps best known for its fantastic bottom fishing, this area is fast being discovered as one of the premier shallow-water fly-fishing destinations on the entire Chesapeake Bay, if not the entire east coast. The area has the appearance of fishing the Carolinas or the Florida backwaters further south. In addition to the underwater grasses, there are many submerged stump fields from long-since-downed cedar trees. Much of what once was land area is now an underwater forest of fish-attracting structure. Care must be used when navigating the shallow flats, since the stumps are not visible from the water's surface. A good guide with local knowledge is a worthwhile investment for the first trip or two. Though treacherous to navigate, it is this underwater minefield that attracts the numerous gamefish species to the shallows.

Striped bass, speckled trout, bluefish and weakfish can be found cruising the shallows from April through November. Seasonally, you may also find redfish (red drum), flounder and croaker. Along the deeper edges of the sound, Spanish mackerel, bluefish and stripers can be seen working the surface from late summer into early fall, with the stripers continuing their feeding binge through November. It is quite possible for an angler to end a day's trip having caught five or more different species on a fly.

An eight-weight rod rigged with matching line is an ideal outfit for these waters, while anything from a six to nine will do. A favorite outfit of mine is an 8-weight rod, rigged with a matched shooting head. For fishing waters averaging two to eight feet deep, I favor a medium-fast sinking line. The bottom contour can change rapidly while drifting the flats and a faster sinking line will allow your fly to work deeper into the water column. When fishing the most shallow flats, or over grass, an intermediate or floater will do fine. A two-piece, 4- to 6-foot leader will suffice, consisting of a 30- to 40-pound butt section followed by a 12- to 20-pound tippet. The heavier tippet is necessary to ward off the barnacle-encrusted stumps, and the fish are generally not leader-shy. I tend to favor the heavier tippet, especially when targeting larger speckled trout, since their violent head shaking will sometimes cut a light leader. Sometimes a bite tippet of 30- to 40-pound. mono is necessary for mackerel and bluefish, or even a trace of wire for the larger blues.

Three basic fly patterns will work for all species. Deceivers, Clouser Deep Minnows and poppers. In fact, it was at Crisfield where Lefty Kreh developed the original Lefty's Deceiver while fishing the flats of nearby Fox Island. A majority of the time I will tie my Deceivers and Clousers quite full with extra flash. The waters can sometimes be slightly off-color and the extra bulk helps push more water, which I feel helps as a fish attractant. Favorite colors are chartreuse/white, gray/white, black and a local favorite, fluorescent yellow with gold flash. Joe Bruce's crab-colored Clouser, a mixture of tan, olive and white bucktail is also popular. Tie these patterns on

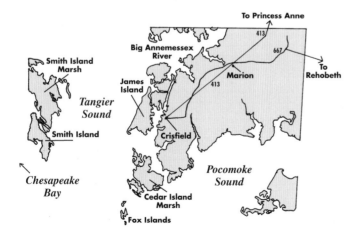

Species	Typical Size - Pounds	J	F	M	A	M	J	J	A	S	O	N	D
Bluefish	1 - 6	1	1	1	2	3	4	5	5	5	4	2	1
Croakers	1 - 2	1	1	1	1	3	4	4	3	2	1	1	1
Redfish (Red Drum)	1 - 40	1	1	1	2	3	3	2	3	3	2	1	1
Spanish Mackerel	1 - 3	1	1	1	1	1	2	3	4	3	2	1	1
Spotted Seatrout	2 - 5	1	1	1	2	5	5	4	4	5	4	2	1
Striped Bass	2 - 10	1	1	2	3	5	5	5	5	5	5	5	4
Weakfish	2 - 6	1	1	1	2	3	4	3	3	4	4	3	1

1=Scarce, 2=Spotty, 3=Available, 4=Readily Available, 5=Widely Available

1/0 or 2/0 stainless hooks in two- to six-inch lengths. This best represents the size of silversides, which are probably the most prevalent baitfish inhabiting the shallows. During the worm swarms of early summer, worm imitation patterns such as Josenhans' Clam Worm will produce great results. Crab patterns, such as Del Brown's Permit Fly (Merkin), will work most anytime of the year. When all else fails, I resort to a pattern that Lefty Kreh introduced to me some years ago called the Cactus Striper. This fly can be tied to resemble the numerous pencil eels that stripers so much enjoy. Tying instructions can be found in the Appendix.

During the fall months of October/November the stripers move up into the creeks of Janes Island near the aforementioned state park. The adventurous angler may rent a canoe or kayak, or launch their own at the park and paddle into the island's interior. Stripers can be caught in many of the island's miles of backwater creeks that are otherwise inaccessible to the boating fisherman. Also, the shorelines of many of Tangier Sound's islands are excellent places to wade this time of the year.

The speckled trout is my bread-and-butter fish, since at times we have fishing that will rival that of any Texas or Louisiana estuary. The specks average two to five pounds and we have caught them, on a fly, as large as nine pounds. The striped bass are the most numerous, averaging two to ten pounds, with fish to fifteen pounds taken on occasion. Though not the trophies found in the deeper sections of the bay, what they lack in size they make up for in sheer numbers. It is quite common for a party of two to catch and release well over one hundred fish on a crisp October day's fishing. May through June, and then again in October and November are the prime times for the stripers. A good run of big weakfish occurs in May and June, with fish to ten pounds possible. Throw in bluefish, red drum and a flounder or two and you have a potpourri of possibilities at your disposal.

Guides (Capt.)	Phone/Fax	E-mail
Dan Harrison	410-986-0219	
Kevin Josenhans	410-968-3579	KJosenhans@aol.com
Mike Murphy	410-968-3286	mmurphy@dmv.com
Matt Tawes	410-968-3286	Capttawes@aol.com

Anglers' Sports Center
1456 Whitehall Rd.
Annapolis, MD 21401
Contact: Rob Jepson
410-974-4013
410-757-6940

The Fisherman's Edge
1719 1/2 Edmonson Ave.
Baltimore, MD 21228
Contact: Joe Bruce
800-338-0053/410-719-799
flies@erols.com

Salisbury Fly Shop
325 Snow Hill Rd.
Salisbury, MD 21804
Contact: Mason Huffman
410-543-8359

Sea Hawk Sports Center
643 Ocean Highway
Pocomoke City, MD 21851
Contact: Jack Redlinger
410-957-0198

Captain Kevin Josenhans has been fishing the waters of Tangier and Pocomoke sounds for twenty years. He has operated a well-respected guide service out of Crisfield, Maryland for the past seven years. Kevin is a member of the G. Loomis Pro Staff and is an accomplished fly tier as well as casting instructor. Kevin is consulted weekly for fishing reports for regional and local periodicals. His guide service has been featured in both national and regional fishing publications, and on national television programs such as ESPN's "Fly Fishing America" and Outdoor Life Network.

Most Common Prey	Typical Size (inches)	Usual Months of Availability*												Typical Matching Fly Patterns**
		J	F	M	A	M	J	J	A	S	O	N	D	
American Eels	4 - 10	1	1	3	4	5	5	5	5	5	5	4	3	Cactus Striper
Atlantic Silversides	2 - 5	1	1	3	5	5	5	5	5	5	5	4	3	Lefty's Deceiver (A), Clouser Deep Minnow (A)
Bay Anchovy	1 - 2	1	1	3	5	5	5	5	5	5	5	5	3	Bruce's Bay Anchovy, Clouser Deep Minnow (A)
Clam Worms	1 - 3	1	1	2	3	5	5	3	3	3	3	3	2	Josenhans' Clam Worm
Crabs	0.75	1	1	2	3	5	5	5	5	5	5	5	3	Del's Crab Fly
Hogchokers	2 - 4	1	1	3	4	5	5	5	5	5	5	4	3	Clouser Deep Minnow (A)
Herring	6 - 12	1	1	4	4	4	3	3	3	3	3	2	1	Big Eye Deceiver
Killifish	1 - 3	2	2	4	5	5	5	5	5	5	5	5	4	Lefty's Deceiver (A) -Blk
Menhaden	2 - 10	1	1	2	3	4	5	5	5	5	5	4	3	Lefty's Deceiver, Clouser Half and Half (A)
Norfolk Spot	3 - 5	1	1	1	1	3	4	5	5	5	4	3	1	Clouser Half and Half (A)
Shrimp	1	2	2	3	4	4	4	4	4	4	4	4	3	Bruce's Crystal Shrimp

*1=Scarce, 2=Spotty, 3=Available, 4=Readily Available, 5=Widely Available • ** Pattern Recipe in Appendix A.

Chapter 20: Northern Outer Banks
By Capts. Sarah Gardner and Brian Horsley

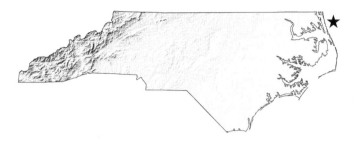

The northern Outer Banks consists of two narrow barrier islands that extend from the Virginia State line to Hatteras Inlet, a distance of nearly 150 miles. The Banks are a very popular vacation destination with plenty of activities for everyone, especially fishermen. Vacation homes, motels, state and national parks and miles of beautiful public beaches make up the landscape. There are a wide variety of rental houses, hotels and restaurants to fit every budget and taste.

Long known for its surf and gulfstream fishing, the Outer Banks is now carving a name for itself in the fly-fishing world. A visiting fly-angler can start by wading the creeks and sloughs of the Pamlico and Roanoke sounds for schoolie stripers, speckled trout and redfish. More adventurous anglers can use small boats to explore grass beds in the

Pamlico Sound, where they will find speckled trout and bluefish. A late-summer trip over the wrecks chasing cobia, albies and amberjack will provide fly-fishing memories for a lifetime. Even gulfstream species such as dolphin, yellowfin tuna or the high-jumping white marlin make excellent fly targets.

The inshore and backcountry fly-fishing is the most popular, probably because it is easily accessible to people without boats. In the spring, the creeks and sloughs around Oregon Inlet begin to warm up and the numerous marsh islands and oyster beds provide excellent structure to fish. With this warm-up, anglers can find schoolie stripers (12 to 24 inches), puppy drum (redfish), bluefish and speckled trout. One of the hottest spots for stripers during the spring is along the coastal bridges. The bridge that connects the mainland to Roanoke Island is the William B. Umstead Bridge. Of all the bridges in the area this is the best for stripers. Along the pilings of the bridge and over the oyster rocks just off the bridge is home to thousands of stripers. Most of the action is subsurface and most of these bridges must be fished from a boat.

Summer in the northern Pamlico Sound is speckled trout season. Large numbers of speckled trout can be found over the grass beds, around Marsh Island and in the sloughs on the north side of Oregon Inlet. The best action is from boats, but wading fly-fishers still take their share of trout. Outside the inlet, cobia make their annual migration to the Chesapeake Bay. This migration gives the fly angler a few shots at a truly great game fish weighing up to 60 pounds. Early summer also brings Spanish mackerel and small bluefish. Mid-summer the nearshore wrecks and artificial reefs are great places to look for amberjack.

Fall is a transition time, but fishing remains excellent. Speckled trout fishing slows, but only just a bit. What we give up in numbers, we make for in size! Both the ocean side and the sounds now have fish. Redfish and speckled trout move into the marshes chasing large schools of finger mullet and shrimp. Along with the cooler water, stripers begin to move in the Croatan Sound and around Oregon Inlet. Late fall is one of the few times we see surface action on stripers in the sounds. The north ends of Roanoke Island and north of the William Umstead Bridge are traditional fall striper hot spots. Stripers are usually chasing baby bunker and glass minnows moving out of the Albemarle Sound system on their way to the ocean. Most of the fish in the fall are from 18 to 25 inches with a few on each side.

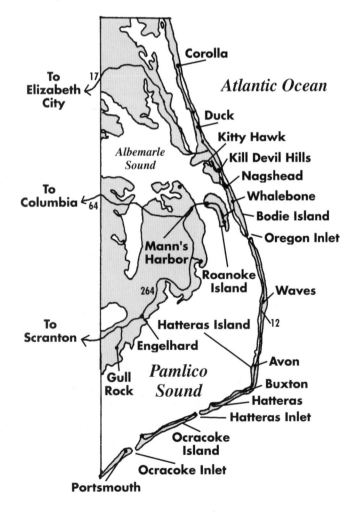

Species	Typical Size - Inches	J	F	M	A	M	J	J	A	S	O	N	D
Bluefish	12 - 24	1	1	1	2	4	4	3	3	3	4	2	2
Cobia	36 - 50	1	1	1	1	3	3	3	2	2	1	1	1
Redfish	14 - 36	1	1	2	3	4	4	2	2	3	3	3	2
Speckled Trout	10 - 26	1	1	1	1	3	5	5	5	5	4	2	1
Stripers (Bay)	14 - 24	2	2	3	4	5	3	2	2	2	3	5	5
Stripers (Ocean)	30 - 50	3	2	2	1	1	1	1	1	1	1	2	5	5

1=Scarce, 2=Spotty, 3=Available, 4=Readily Available, 5=Widely Available

Fall is also the time the false albacore appear in good numbers. The artificial reefs can be alive with albies and there also may be breaking fish along the beaches.

Some of the hottest striper fishing on the east coast can be found on the northern Outer Banks in early winter. Huge schools of migrating menhaden, weakfish and croakers show up and this large amount of bait attracts a significant percentage of the East Coast's wintering stripers. Most of the fly-fishing activity takes place in boats in 15 to 50 feet of water along the beach, but this excellent fishery is not limited to boats. Waders fishing the beaches on both sides of Oregon Inlet have excellent opportunities for taking big bass from the surf. The Green Island Slough on the south side of Oregon Inlet holds many stripers that are easily accessible to shore-bound anglers.

The northern Outer Banks is a huge area and thus far I have only touched briefly on the small area within a dozen miles of Oregon Inlet. The mainland side of Hatteras Island is a vast area offering excellent fly-fishing to both waders and boaters. This area is covered with large areas of shallow water and shoals. This makes it tough and intimidating to the visiting boater; people who trailer boats to the area would be advised to charter a guide for a day. A word of caution; both Oregon and Hatteras inlets are sleeping giants and are likely to wake up at any moment. Wind and tide can quickly turn a placid inlet into your worst nightmare. Seventeen people have lost their lives in Oregon Inlet since 1972.

The Outer Banks does not have any exclusive fly shops, however there are plenty of tackle shops, per the enclosed chart, with employees who know what is happening with fly-fishing and are very generous with helpful information.

A wide range of tackle is required to sucessfully fly-fish all of the many opportunities in the Outer Banks. A fairly standard outfit is a 7- to 8-weight fly rod with a good saltwater reel and an intermediate-density weight-forward fly line. Slow to fast-sinking lines are required when the currents are faster and/or when there is the need to get deeper within minimum delay. Shore-wading fly-fishers will probably prefer 9- to 10-weight outfits when fishing in the winter for the larger fish. Ten-weight outfits are recommended for boating fly-fishers in the winter, and 11-weights are preferred when targeting cobia in the summer. Although longer leaders are best for sight-fishing in shallow water, a four-foot leader is quite satisfactory for use with the sinking lines. As shown on the enclosed prey chart, Clousers and Deceivers are the flies that are most successful locally. Chartreuse/white and black/red are usually good color combinations.

Most Common Prey	Typical Size (inches)	Usual Months of Availability*												Typical Matching Fly Patterns**
		J	F	M	A	M	J	J	A	S	O	N	D	
Blue Crabs	1 - 3	1	1	1	3	4	4	4	4	4	2	2	2	Clouser Deep Minnow (E)
Croakers	1 - 4	1	1	1	1	3	3	4	4	4	3	3	2	Clouser Deep Minnow (E)
Finger Mullet	1 - 5	1	1	1	1	2	2	2	3	4	5	4	2	Lefty's Deceiver (J), Half-and-Half (C)
Glass Minnows	1 - 3	1	1	2	3	3	3	3	3	3	3	3	3	Clouser Deep Minnow (E)
Menhaden	3 - 6	1	1	1	2	3	3	3	3	3	3	3	1	Lefty's Deceiver (J), Half-and-Half (C)
Shrimp	1 - 4	1	1	1	2	3	3	4	4	4	4	4	3	Clouser Deep Minnow (E)
Spots	1 - 4	1	1	1	1	3	3	4	4	4	3	3	2	Clouser Deep Minnow (E)

*1=Scarce, 2=Spotty, 3=Available, 4=Readily Available, 5=Widely Available
** Pattern Recipe in Appendix A.

Guides (Capt.)	Phone/Fax	E-mail
Capt. Zander Brody	252-995-5269	
Capt. Sarah Gardner	252-449-2251	sgardner@beachlink.com
Capt. Brian Horsley	252-449-0562	bhorsley@beachlink.com
Dave Rode	252-480-6416	guides@fish-riomar.com

Capt. Marty's Outer Banks Fishing Co.
PO Box 1078
Nags Head, NC 27959
Contact: Mike Lucas
252-441-3132

Frank & Fran's
Highway 12
Avon, NC 27915
Contact: Frank Folb
252-995-4171
ffff@interpath.com

Frisco Rod & Gun
PO Box 10, Highway 12, Frisco, NC 27936
Contact: Bryan Pery
252-995-5366
frg@interpath.com

TW's Bait & Tackle
815 Ocean Tr., Monteray Plaza
Corolla, NC 27927
252-453-3339

Milepost 4, Highway 158
Kitty Hawk, NC 27949
252-261-7848

Milepost 10.5, Hwy 158
Nags Head, NC 27959
252-441-4807

Capt. Sarah Gardner is a recent transplant to the Outer Banks, from Maryland's eastern shore where she extensively taught fly-casting and fly-fishing. She has been guiding full-time for the past three seasons. Besides guiding, Sarah is also a freelance writer and photographer. She has a weekly column in the Fisherman Magazine *and a monthly column in the* Mid-Atlantic Fishing Journal. *Her articles have appeared in* Fly Fish America, Saltwater Sportsman *and* Fly Fishing in Salt Waters *magazines. Sarah also holds several saltwater fly-fishing world records. On their days off, Brian and Sarah enjoy backcountry and bluewater fly-fishing.*

Capt. Brian Horsley has fly-fished the Outer Banks since the mid-70s and has been guiding there since 1992. Brian is also a freelance writer and photographer, with frequent articles in Fly Fish America, Fly Fishing in Salt Waters *and many regional publications. His photographs have been published in* Sportfishing, *and* Saltwater Sportsman. *Brian and Sarah own and operate Flat Out Fly-Fishing Charters and they specialize in saltwater fly-fishing and instruction. Brian runs a 20-foot Jones Brothers Cape Fisherman and Sarah runs an 18-foot Parker. They are based in the Oregon Inlet Marina.*

Chapter 21: Cape Lookout

By Capt. Joe Shute

The Cape Lookout National Seashore is located midway along the North Carolina coast and is considered to be the southernmost part of the Outer Banks. Included in this area are the cities/towns of Morehead City, Atlantic Beach, Beaufort, Harkers Island and numerous smaller communities. Cape Lookout is probably best known in the fly-fishing world for its fall blitz of false albacore. The fly-fishing for false albacore around Cape Lookout is the best anywhere on the eastern coast, and perhaps the entire U.S. Nevertheless, Cape Lookout has many other fly-rod opportunities. Access to the area is easy, whether you are driving or flying in by commercial or private plane. Overnight accommodations and restaurants are open year-round and suitable for anyone's tastes. Campgrounds and trailer parks are also available, plus marinas and boat-launching areas.

Access to the ocean from all boat ramps is very easy. The Cape Lookout area has two inlets for ocean access; Beaufort Inlet is located just east of the town of Atlantic Beach and Barden Inlet is located inside the hook of Cape Lookout itself. Beaufort Inlet is 45 to 50 feet deep and is a major port for large container and military ships. Bardens Inlet is also a very deep inlet; the channel from Harkers Island to the Cape is marked, but shifting sands and swift currents can make navigation difficult at times for all but the smaller craft.

The back sounds between Morehead City and Harkers Island have many shallow sand bars and oyster rocks. Local knowledge is required in many places. Many areas may appear to have plenty of water in which to run a boat, but those appearances can often be deceiving. It's a good idea to hire a guide for this area, and the local fly shops can also provide useful information on places to

fish and fly patterns to use. The accompanying tables list some of the most qualified fly-fishing guides and the fly shops in the Cape Lookout area.

For fly-fishers that would like to strike out on their own, there are a few businesses that rent power boats in Atlantic Beach and some that rent kayaks and canoes in Atlantic Beach, Beaufort and the Emerald Isle area. Good beach access for fly-fishing can be found at Fort Macon State Park at the east end of Atlantic Beach. One can also take one of the ferries from Beaufort and Harkers Island to Shackleford Banks or to the hook of Cape Lookout. These ferries are quite inexpensive and they can offer convenient access to some excellent beach fishing, especially in the fall.

The species of fish to be caught in the Cape Lookout area will depend on the time of the year that you visit. Generally, there can be good fly-fishing throughout the year, but the season really begins to heat up in April and stays that way through December. Even January and February, though can provide good fly-fishing for redfish. The Spanish mackerel and bluefish usually start off our spring season with a bang; the fall usually ends with our fantastic fly-fishing for false albacore and redfish. We even have some great offshore fly-fishing in the gulf-stream for pelagic species like dolphin and king mackerel. The accompanying chart will give you more detailed information on species availability throughout the year.

The most popular fly rods to use in the area are probably 9-footers for 8-weight and 10-weight lines. The 8-weights are good for redfish, Spanish mackerel, speckled seatrout, and small Atlantic bonito and false albacore. The 10-weights are more appropriate for king mackerel, dolphin, and our larger false albacore in the fall. We usually use 8- to 9-foot tapered leaders with 12- to 20-pound tippets. When fishing for species with sharp teeth, such as the mackerel, you will need to use a heavy monofilament or preferably a wire bite tippet. Mackerel can bite through the monofilament quite easily, guaranteeing the loss of some flies. When fishing for the smaller species, 100 yards of 20-pound line backing is more than sufficient. When tackling the larger species, however, you should have a reel that will hold at least 200 yards of 20-pound backing. For these larger fish like the fall false albacore you should also have a better-quality fly reel with a good and dependable drag system. Many inferior drag systems have met their match and have been destroyed by the blistering runs of the Cape's false albacore and king mackerel. The most popular fly line

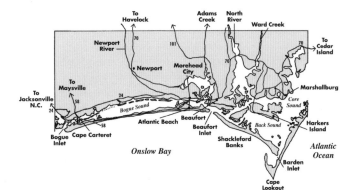

Species	Typical Size - Pounds	J	F	M	A	M	J	J	A	S	O	N	D
Amberjack	20 - 50	1	1	1	2	3	4	4	4	4	4	4	1
Dolphin	5 - 40				2	5	5	5	4	4	3	2	1
False Albacore	8 - 20	2	1	3	2	1	1	1	1	2	4	5	4
King Mackerel	5 - 20	1	1	1	2	4	4	4	4	5	5	5	1
Redfish	18-30 Inches	4	2	2	3	4	4	4	4	5	5	5	4
Spanish Mackerel	1.5 - 5.0				1	4	5	5	5	5	5	1	
Speckled Trout	1.5 - 5.0	1	1	1	2	4	4	4	4	5	5	5	4

1=Scarce, 2=Spotty, 3=Available, 4=Readily Available, 5=Widely Available

is a weight-forward, intermediate-density striper line. This type of line will allow your fly to sink slowly and is easier to cast into the wind. In addition, having a 200-grain full-sinking line for some of the inshore species like the speckled seatrout will help you to get your fly into some of the deeper holes. A 400-grain sinking line is also required when fishing in the ocean for false albacore and king mackerel.

There are a wide variety of baitfish and crustaceans in North Carolina waters. As shown on the accompanying chart, the most abundant species are bay anchovies (glass minnows), menhaden (bunker or shad), finger mullet, threadfin herring (greenies), killifish (mud minnows), crabs, and a variety of different shrimp. Most of the baitfish that we try to imitate are between 3 and 4 inches long, in hook sizes from 2 to 2/0. The most popular flies for the baitfish species are the Clouser Minnows. Using different materials and color combinations, the Clouser will catch any species of smaller fish from seatrout to false albacore. For redfish, a few of the flies that we use don't seem to resemble anything in particular, but they do produce. The Copperhead fly, tied by Capt. Randy Hamilton of Charleston, is a very good pattern to use, as well as the many different variations of spoon flies. A dun-gray Clouser Minnow with a touch of gold Krystal Flash will also produce well for redfish.

By far, the most productive fly for our Spanish mackerel and false albacore is the chartreuse and white Clouser Deep Minnow. Olive and white and brown and white are also good color combinations. For the offshore species such as king mackerel and dolphin, larger flies tied in Half-and-Half or Deceiver patterns also work well. For the king mackerel, different combinations of pink and white, all-pink, green and white, all-green, and brown and white are productive. Dolphin prefer the bright colors of chartreuse, green, and blue and white combinations. Make sure to add plenty of flash material when tying flies for both the kings and for dolphin. When tying the offshore flies I always like to use larger and stronger hooks, even up to 5/0 in size. Some of the above patterns are listed in the prey chart below.

Guides (Capt.)	Phone/Fax	E-mail
George Beckwith	252-249-3101	guide@pamilco-nc.com
Dave Dietzler	252-240-2850	brkwater@bmb.clis.com
Derek Jordan	252-322-5356	
Rob Pasfield	252-728-3907	
Sam Sellars	252-728-3735	jackrabbit@mail.clis.com
Joe Shute	888-856-8554	captjoe@mail.clis.com
	252-240-0276	

Cape Lookout Fly Shop Inc.
601-H Atlantic Beach Causeway
Atlantic Beach, NC 28512
Contact: Joe Shute
888-856-8554/252-240-2744
captjoe@mail.clis.com

Pete's Tackle & Fly Shop
1704 -½ Arendell St.
Morehead City, NC 28557
Contact: Pete Allred
252-726-8644

Capt. Joe Shute of the Cape Lookout Fly Shop and the Fish Finder Light Tackle and Fly Fishing Guide Service was the first full-time inshore guide in the Cape Lookout area. He started his guide service 13 years ago, specializing in light tackle fishing for speckled trout, redfish, king and Spanish mackerel, false albacore, etc. Currently, about half of his charters are for fly-fishing clients. Capt. Joe has taught "how-to" fishing seminars for the last 12 years, has written articles for many outdoor publications, and has appeared on regional TV fishing shows. Capt. Shute helped start the local Inshore Light Tackle Fishing Club and is a board member of the Cape Lookout Fly Fishers Club.

Most Common Prey	Typical Size (inches)	Usual Months of Availability*												Typical Matching Fly Patterns**
		J	F	M	A	M	J	J	A	S	O	N	D	
Bay Anchovies	1 - 4	1	1	3	3	4	4	4	4	5	5	5	3	Deep Candy, Clouser Deep Minnow (F)
Crabs	0.5 - 2.0	1	1	1	2	5	5	5	5	5	5	4	1	Hamilton Copperhead
Finger Mullet	2 - 4	1	1	1	2	3	4	4	4	5	5	4	1	Crystal Chenille Mullet
Killifish	2 - 3	1	1	1	4	5	5	5	5	5	5	4	2	Deep Clouser Minnow (F)
Menhaden	2 - 8	1	1	1	2	3	5	5	5	5	5	5	3	Lefty's Deceiver (K)
Shrimp	0.5 - 4.0	1	1	1	2	3	4	4	4	5	5	4	1	Rattle Shrimp
Threadfin Herring	2 - 5	1	1	1	3	5	5	5	4	4	4	3	1	Lefty's Deceiver (K)

*1=Scarce, 2=Spotty, 3=Available, 4=Readily Available, 5=Widely Available • ** Pattern Recipe in Appendix A.

Chapter 22: Cape Fear

By Capt. Al Edwards

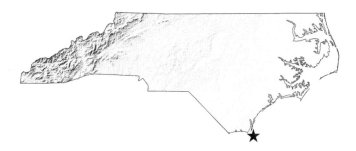

The Cape Fear region of North Carolina covers an area from the city of Southport at the mouth of the Cape Fear River to the resort community of Wrightsville Beach, 25 miles to the north. In between Southport and Wrightsville Beach lie miles of shallow backwater marshes and sloughs that offer fly-fishing for a variety of fish species, as shown on the accompanying chart. Both the wading and the boating fly-fisher will find opportunities to challenge their skills. Launching ramps are readily available in the area, and most of them are state ramps which offer excellent parking and no launching fees. In addition, each local community has one or more marinas and a broad range of restaurants, from gourmet to fast food. Accommodations range from bed-and-breakfast houses to locally-owned and national chain motels.

Fishing the Cape Fear area offers year-round opportunities, but the spring of the year (March through May) really kicks off the start of fishing where even novice anglers should have success with bluefish, Spanish mackerel, spotted seatrout and redfish. Diehard anglers can have good days throughout the colder months of winter on seatrout and redfish, but they must be extra careful wading during this time, since a wrong step could leave you very cold indeed.

The main deep-water channel through this area is the Intracoastal Waterway. It is well-marked and navigation is quite straightforward at all tides. Nevertheless, the creeks and sloughs that branch off from the Waterway have extensive oyster rocks and sandbars, so one must be careful when venturing away from the main channel. When exploring a new area, it is best to enter these waters on a low, rising tide. That way, should you become grounded, waiting a few minutes will result in the rising tide getting your boat afloat, permitting you to continue your trip.

The accompanying chart lists several local fly-fishing guides that are knowledgeable of the area and skilled in the required fly-fishing strategies and techniques. Also included is a list of local fly shops that are fully equipped and stocked with the items required for fly-fishing. Fly shop personnel are an excellent source of information for visiting fly-fishers.

An ideal fly-rod for the area would be a 9-foot for 9-weight. Weight-forward, intermediate-density fly lines are the best choice to cover all fly-fishing scenarios. When fishing in shallow water, using floating or intermediate-density sinking fly lines, a satisfactory, all-purpose leader would consist of 4 feet of 30-pound mono for the butt section, 2 feet of 20-pound mono for the mid-section and about 2 feet of 12- to 17-pound tippet. When fishing the depths around channels and bridges using a full-sinking fly line, you should shorten the length of your leader to 3 feet of 40-pound mono for the butt section, 1 1/2 feet of 20-pound mono for the mid-section, and 1 to 1 1/2 feet of 15- to 17-pound tippet. The shorter leader helps you feel the bites more quickly and allows the fly to remain in the target depth without floating upward 7 or 8 feet from the line. Any fly reel with corrosion-resistant components, a fairly good drag system and a capacity for 150 to 200 yards of 30-pound backing will be satisfactory for our fly-fishing.

As shown on the accompanying chart, our primary prey species will be some form of baitfish. In salt water, like fresh water, the more successful fly-fisher will choose the fly which best "matches the hatch", or in our circumstances closely resembles the local prey species in size, shape and color. Most of the flies should be from 2 1/2 to 4 inches long. I usually tie my flies somewhat

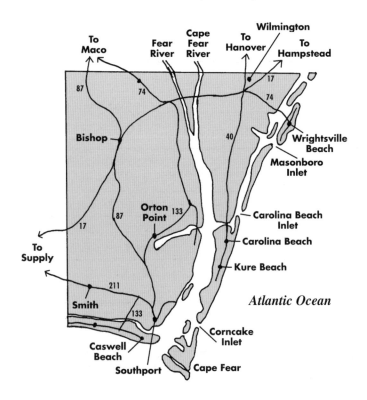

Species	Typical Size - Pounds	J	F	M	A	M	J	J	A	S	O	N	D
Bluefish	1 - 6	1	1	1	2	3	4	4	5	4	4	3	1
Bonito	1	1	1	1	3	5	4	2	2	2	1	1	1
Ladyfish	2 - 4	1	1	1	1	1	3	4	4	3	3	1	1
Pompano	1.5 - 3.0	1	1	1	2	2	3	4	4	4	3	1	1
Redfish	4 - 10	1	1	3	4	4	5	5	5	5	5	3	3
Spanish Mackerel	1.5 - 4.0	1	1	1	1	3	4	5	5	5	4	3	1
Spotted Seatrout	2 - 6	2	2	3	3	3	3	3	2	5	5	5	4

1=Scarce, 2=Spotty, 3=Available, 4=Readily Available, 5=Widely Available

longer, so that I can trim the length of the fly to better imitate the prey available at that moment. Generally, baitfish prey can be successfully imitated by Deceivers and Clousers, provided they are tied with the appropriate materials in the correct sizes. The more blunt-shaped prey like the finger mullet can be successfully imitated by pattern variations of the Woolhead Mullet and the Muddler Minnow. Crabs can often be simulated by patterns like Dell Brown's Permit Fly, also known as the Merkin.

Visiting fly-fishers who would like to do some wade fishing have several choices. Wrightsville Beach, located east of Interstate Route 40 via Highways 74 or 76, offers limited wading on the north and south ends of the island. Kayak rentals are also available here, which will permit access to miles of backwater opportunities. Around Carolina Beach, the fly-fisher will find numerous wading areas along River Road, which turns off Highway 421, the main highway through this town. At the southern end of Highway 421 is the Fort Fisher State Recreation Area, where the fly-fisher will find enough territory for several days of wading and exploring. Southport offers many miles of tidal marsh and river fly-fishing, but most areas are accessible only by boat.

The Cape Fear River upstream of the city of Wilmington is brackish and much further upstream it is strictly fresh water. Excellent fly-fishing can be had here, but the lack of wading access requires the angler to do most fly-fishing from small boats. Here, 5- to 6-weight rods with floating lines and light leaders are the norm with any small popping bugs. These poppers are eagerly received by shellcrackers, bluegill and a host of other pan fish including largemouth bass.

Guides (Capt.)	Phone/Fax	E-mail
Al Edwards	910-313-0702	aedwards@wilmington.net
Lee Parsons	910-350-0890	
Steve Smith	910-457-4655	fins@bcinet.net
Tyler Stone	888-325-4285	tstone@saltwaterfly.com

Digh's Country Sports
1922 Eastwood Rd.
Wilmington, NC 28403
Contact: Bobby Digh
910-256-2060
captaindigh@aol.com

Fins & Feathers
208 N. Howe St.
Southport, NC 28461
Contact: Steve Smith
910-457-4655
fins@bcinet.net

Great Outdoor Provision Co.
3501 Oleander Dr.
Wilmington, NC 28403
Contact: Tim Glover
910-343-1648
scottw@greatoutdoorprovisionco.com

Intracoastal Angler
1900 Eastwood Rd.
Wilmington, NC 28403
Contact: Tyler Stone
910-256-4545
tstone@saltwaterfly.com

Captain Al Edwards has over 15 years of fishing experience in the Cape Fear area. He is a member of the North Carolina Fly Fishing Association and is on the Board of Directors of the U.S. Anglers Association. Al has been a speaker for the Saltwater Sportsman magazine at their seminars and has had articles published in Field & Stream and several other magazines.

| Most Common Prey | Typical Size (inches) | \multicolumn{12}{c}{Usual Months of Availability*} | Typical Matching Fly Patterns** |

Most Common Prey	Typical Size (inches)	J	F	M	A	M	J	J	A	S	O	N	D	Typical Matching Fly Patterns**
Crabs	1.25	1	1	1	2	3	4	5	5	5	4	2	1	Del Brown's Permit Fly
Finger Mullet	2 - 4	1	1	1	2	3	4	5	5	5	4	3	1	Woolhead Mullet, Clouser Deep Minnow (J)
Glass Minnows	2 - 5	1	1	1	2	4	5	5	4	3	2	1	1	Surf Candy, Clouser Deep Minnow (H), Al's Glass Minnow
Mud Minnows	2 - 4	1	1	2	3	4	5	5	5	4	4	3	1	Clouser Deep Minnow (H), Cockroach Deceiver
Pinfish	2 - 3	1	1	1	2	3	5	5	5	5	5	2	1	Lefty's Deceiver (D), Bendback (A)
Shrimp	2 - 4	1	1	1	2	3	4	5	5	5	4	2	1	Ultra Shrimp

*1=Scarce, 2=Spotty, 3=Available, 4=Readily Available, 5=Widely Available • ** Pattern Recipe in Appendix A.

Chapter 23: Cape Romain
By Capt. Randy Hamilton

The intracoastal waterway borders the western edge of the refuge and it is the main route for boat traffic. The other well-maintained watercourse is Five-Fathom Creek. If fishing without a guide, be careful when venturing outside these two areas and have a good tide table in hand. The tide range is up to seven feet, so a creek four feet deep can be bone dry at low tide. It is very important that you hire a local guide to navigate safely and to help you locate fish.

The Santee River dominates the northern end of the refuge. The Santee's influx of brackish water works its way south through the refuge's many creeks; therefore the water can range from slightly off-color to quite muddy. Salinity will vary as well. Knowing that the water clarity can change daily, local guides have adapted various tactics. Top-water poppers, rattling flies and very bright, flashy patterns are a few of the types of patterns you will find in a guide's fly box.

Bull's Bay lies on the southern end of the refuge and is the largest shallow-water bay north of Port Royal Sound. The bay serves as nursery grounds for huge numbers of shrimp and mullet. Depth varies from 40 feet at the tarpon hole near White Banks to inches deep around Bird Island. Again, local knowledge will keep the neophyte out of trouble.

Between Bull's Bay and the Santee River lie hundreds of creeks and small bays. Oyster mounds cover this area and act as a center for fish activity. In the shallow bays, redfish and flounder will target these mounds for ambushing bait. In the deeper creeks, schools of speckled trout, bluefish and ladyfish station themselves along oyster rakes in 3 to 20 feet of water to surprise mullet, menhaden and shrimp. In both habitats, moving water is the key to finding feeding fish.

The eastern coastline has five major inlets to the ocean and outside each inlet are shoal areas that attract large redfish (bulls) during the spring and fall. These big boys can range up to 40 pounds and are almost exclusively caught on surf-fishing gear. Most of these fish are caught in three to six feet of water, so fly-rod opportunities are there. The Cape Romain lighthouse is just north of Key Inlet and is a good landmark for navigation. There is no marked water course to the lighthouse.

Cape Romain has been my home water for several years, and I developed my favorite pattern, the Hamilton Copperhead, to deal with the cloudy water conditions that frequently occur in the refuge. The Copperhead is extremely flashy and can be fished very slowly, allowing redfish, trout and flounder to find it in muddy water.

A good strategy to find fish on your own would be to explore the side creeks of the two main waterways I've

The low country of South Carolina is blessed with expansive estuaries filled with salt marshes, creeks and bays. Covering 20 miles of coastline and over 64,000 acres of marsh and open water, the Cape Romain National Wildlife Refuge is the seasonal home to 337 species of birds including wood storks, bald eagles and the state's only nesting pair of peregrine falcons. The primary targets for fly-fishers are redfish, speckled trout, flounder and ladyfish. Tarpon, bluefish and Spanish mackerel make seasonal appearances but are not reliable.

Virtually all fishing opportunities in Cape Romaine are from a boat. Most areas we fish have a very soft bottom; when wading you can go in up to your knees or up to your chest. There are hard-bottom flats to wade, but you must travel by boat first to reach these areas. There are three public boat ramps that access the refuge. All the ramps are located just off highway 17 and are well marked. The southern-most ramp at Moore's Landing is difficult to use at low tide. The Buck Hall ramp is about six miles south of McClellanville and is adjacent to a nice state campground. The last public ramp is in the fishing town of McClellanville on Pinckney Street.

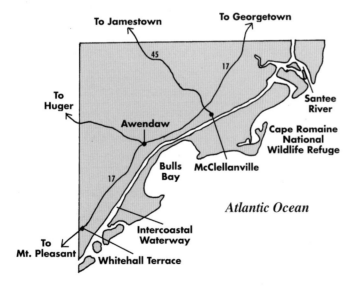

Species	Typical Size - Pounds	J	F	M	A	M	J	J	A	S	O	N	D
Bluefish	1 - 5	1	1	2	2	3	3	2	1	1	1	1	1
Flounder	1 - 7	1	1	2	2	4	5	5	5	5	4	3	2
Ladyfish	0.5 - 4.0					2	3	3	3	2	1	1	1
Redfish	2 - 12	4	4	4	3	5	5	5	5	5	5	5	4
Speckled Trout	0.5 - 5.0	3	3	3	4	4	4	3	3	4	5	4	4
Spanish Mackerel	0.5 - 2.0	1	1	1	1	2	2	1	1	1	1	1	1

1=Scarce, 2=Spotty, 3=Available, 4=Readily Available, 5=Widely Available

mentioned. Once in a side creek, look for even smaller side creeks. Often, these smaller creeks will have a mud or oyster bar at the mouth. While in the small creek, watch your depth finder for the first deep hole. Usually it will be in the first bend. Prospect this hole with a fly that will get to the bottom. Redfish, trout and flounder will hang in these deep holes during falling tides and often stay in the hole through the low tide. The depth in such a hole can vary from 6 feet up to 20 feet. Likewise, if you are in a creek that is 7 feet deep, you should look for holes around 15 feet deep.

Cape Romain also has areas that are ideal for catching redfish in flooded spartina grass. The lighthouse area has several good grass flats for finding tailing fish. The reds will tail for crabs during the moon tides in late spring and throughout the summer. Find a guide who knows the tailing areas. Weedless flies are a must for this fishery. Crab and minnow imitations are very productive but be sure you can accurately present your selected fly.

The village of McClellanville has a few small restaurants and a bed-and-breakfast. Mt. Pleasant and Georgetown, south and north respectively, have a full range of lodging and dining options. The village is just off highway 17. Georgetown is 20 minutes away and Mt. Pleasant is about a 30-minute ride. This area is off the beaten track but the drive is well worth it. Very low boat traffic, few vacation homes and miles of living marsh combine to make a location that is unique in South Carolina.

Barton & Burwell	Buck 'n Bass
47 S. Windimere Blvd.	1040 Anna Knap Blvd.
Charleston, SC 29407	Mt. Pleasant, SC 29464
Contact: Sandy Burton, Ollie Burwell	Contact: Mark Ragsdale
843-766-3220	843-971-9900

Charleston Angler	Hadrells Point
946 Orleans Rd.	885 Ben Sawyer Blvd.
Charleston, SC 29407	Mt. Pleasant, SC 29464
Contact: Rick Hess	Contact: Mike Able

Ludens	Tailwalker Marine
78 Alexander St.	2903 Highmarker St.
Charleston, SC 29403	Georgetown, SC 29440
Contact: Dee Meador	Contact: Stuart Ballard
843-723-7829	843-527-2495

Capt. Randy Hamilton grew up fly-fishing the limestone spring creeks in and around Carlisle, Pennsylvania. For the past 12 years he has fished and guided the Carolina coasts and created fly patterns for our inshore game fish such as redfish, speckled trout and ladyfish.

Guides (Capt.)	Phone/Fax	E-mail
Wally Burbage	843-556-8004	
John Cox	843-727-3901	jhcox@awod.com
Delta Guide Service	843-546-3645	dtp@sccoast.net
Chad Ferris	843-822-3227	cptferris@aol.com
Billy Glenn	843-884-8627	
Randy Hamilton	843-763-6499	copperheadsc@netscape.net
Champ Smith	843-928-3990	
Lee Taylor	843-971-1200	skinnyh2o@aol.com

Most Common Prey	Typical Size (inches)	Usual Months of Availability*												Typical Matching Fly Patterns**
		J	F	M	A	M	J	J	A	S	O	N	D	
Fiddler Crab	1 - 3	1	1	2	3	4	5	5	5	5	4	3	2	Randy's Spoonfly
Finger Mullet	2 - 10	1	1	2	2	4	5	5	5	5	4	3	2	Woolhead Mullet, Clouser Deep Minnow (J)
Glass Minnow	2 - 4	1	1	3	4	4	4	3	3	3	3	3	2	Hanson's Glass Minnow, Clouser Deep Minnow (A)
Grass Shrimp	1 - 3	1	1	2	3	4	4	4	4	4	4	2	2	Crazy Charlie (D)
Menhaden	2 - 8	1	2	2	3	4	5	5	5	5	4	3	2	Lefty's Deceiver (D), Hamilton Copperhead
Mud Minnows	1 - 4	4	4	4	4	4	4	4	4	4	4	4	4	Ridgeway's Food Fly
White Shrimp	3 - 6	1	1	2	2	3	4	4	5	5	5	4	2	Clouser Deep Minnow (H), Hamilton Copperhead, Ridgeway's Food Fly

*1=Scarce, 2=Spotty, 3=Available, 4=Readily Available, 5=Widely Available • ** Pattern Recipe in Appendix A.

Chapter 24: The Lowcountry
By Capt. Richard Stuhr

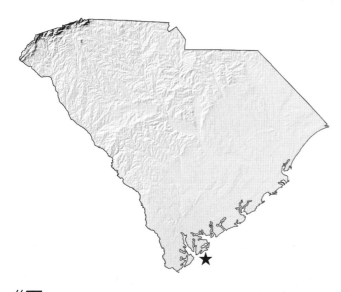

"The Lowcountry" is the name we locals use for the coastal plains area of South Carolina. The area is dominated by barrier islands with fine sandy beaches and vast spartina marshes cut by miles of tide-controlled rivers and creeks. These are ideal nursery grounds for shrimp, crabs, oysters, finfish and a variety of other forms of marine life. This chapter will describe the area around Charleston, Edisto Island and Beaufort/Hilton Head.

Charleston is a historic city and in addition to fishing there is much to see and do for the whole family. Local architecture, museums, plantations, parks and beaches are just samples of the variety of diversions available for the non fly-fisher. Nearby, Mt. Pleasant, Isle of Palms, Sullivan's Island, Folly Beach, Kiawah and Seabrook islands also offer areas of interest. Accommodations and restaurants are abundant and run the full scale of pricing.

For those who want to try fly-fishing on their own, there are many public boat landings around Charleston. Charleston County Parks, Recreation and Tourism (Phone 843-762-2172) can provide further information. Rentals are available for boats, as well as canoes and kayaks. Land-based fly-fishing is best at the inlets between the barrier islands, particularly in May through September for seatrout, flounder, bluefish, Spanish mackerel and ladyfish. Chartreuse Clousers are always good patterns with which to start. A word of caution is necessary for those who are unfamiliar with the area and who will be boating on their own. The coastal region has strong currents which combined with the wind can cause very choppy conditions. It's advisable to check wind forecasts before venturing out too far from the dock. Also, Charleston Harbor hosts heavy shipping traffic, so you must keep an eye out for ships and their wakes.

To the south is Edisto Island. Although somewhat isolated, Edisto still is the essence of the typical lowcountry family vacation beach. Accommodations consist mainly of rental houses or condos, and there is an excellent State campground on the beach. There is a full-service marina on the south end of Edisto Island and restaurants are few, but of good quality. Edisto is a good launch point to explore St. Helena Sound and some of the 350,000-acre ACE Basin National Wildlife Refuge, a pristine example of a typical salt/freshwater ecosystem. Jeremy and Frampton inlets breach the beach and offer good fishing opportunities for the shore-based angler. Further information can be obtained from the Edisto Chamber of Commerce (843-869-3867, website www.edistochamber.com) and Edisto Beach State Park (843-869-2156, website www.southcarolina-parks.com).

Beaufort (pronounced Bewfort) is a quaint little city about one hour south of Charleston, with good accommodations and restaurants to suit any taste. For campers, Hunting Island State Park offers excellent facilities and beach access. One feature unique to the Beaufort/Hilton Head fishery is sight-fishing for cobia in April, May, and June. These large, challenging fish can be found from Port Royal Sound to the Highway 170 bridge.

Though some techniques may vary from place to place, the fly-fishing is quite similar in the lowcountry. During the summer, the ladyfish, Spanish mackerel, bluefish and jack crevalle may be found schooling on the surface nearly anywhere on the lower reaches of the rivers where rips form. In Charleston Harbor, big poppers and streamers are effective for jacks running in the 15- to 30-pound range. In 1999, Ron Silverman, President of the Charleston Longrodders, set a new 20-pound tippet class record for jack crevalle of 39 pounds, 5 ounces. For blues, Spanish mackerel and ladyfish I prefer small poppers, but sometimes one must go sub-surface to entice strikes. Small Clousers and glass minnow patterns work very well, especially those tied with Ultra Hair on 2X-long hooks. Often, smaller is better.

Species	Typical Size	J	F	M	A	M	J	J	A	S	O	N	D
Bluefish	18 - 32 inches	3	2	2	4	5	5	5	5	5	5	5	5
Jack Crevalle	6 - 35 pounds				1	4	5	5	5				
Ladyfish	1 - 3 pounds				2	5	5	5	5	2			
Redfish (Red Drum)	18 - 32 inches	3	2	2	4	5	5	5	5	5	5	5	5
Seatrout	12 - 20 inches	3	1	2	3	5	5	5	5	5	5	5	5
Spanish Mackerel	1 - 4 pounds					4	5	5	5	2			

1=Scarce, 2=Spotty, 3=Available, 4=Readily Available, 5=Widely Available

Around October, the redfish will begin to school on the backwater flats. Shrimp are still around and the reds have a frenzied urgency to get fat while they can. Although mimicking flies work well, I actually prefer bright colors and slow sinkers to catch the attention of redfish. A Cave's Rattler is a very good attractor pattern. We fish the grass edge when the tide drops, when the fish move onto the flats. As the water cools, the bite is more focused around low tide, where the bait will be concentrated. The fishing activity usually slows down in late January through February, depending upon how cold the water becomes during this period. The fish are still there, but their bite cycles slow considerably. In mid-March through May, the redfish are still schooled, but by June bait is so abundant that their preoccupation with the naturals makes hookups difficult. Nevertheless, during the full and new moon tides where the water levels vary by 6 feet or more, the redfish will be eagerly working the flooded marshes for fiddler crabs and other crustaceans. Stalking these tailing fish is the ultimate sport, in my opinion. Crab and other crustacean patterns are productive, as well as the Cave's Rattler.

Fall and winter are excellent seasons for seatrout. When the waters cool, the seatrout will school in the upper estuaries, but are just as available near river mouths and inlets. Really cold weather usually pushes the seatrout to deeper water. In the April/May time period, these trout spawn in the deeper areas nearer the harbors and beaches, particularly around structure. A good time to catch big trout! A floating line with weighted fly and a 9-foot leader with a 6- to 12-pound tippet will usually suffice, but I prefer a sink-tip or 250-grain shooting head in fast currents and/or deeper water. Depending upon water temperature, bait, etc., the seatrout will hold anywhere from the grass edges to the deep holes. The Lowcountry offers a wide range of opportunities for the fly-fisher. The accompanying charts list local fly-fishing guides and fly shops.

Capt. Richard Stuhr is a light-tackle and fly-fishing specialist. A native of Charleston, Capt. Stuhr has lifelong experience fishing and boating the coastal region of the Lowcountry. Richard is an Orvis-endorsed guide and instructor who has fished many regions of the U.S. as well as the Caribbean and Central America. Capt. Stuhr enjoys leading trips to his favorite destinations.

Baystreet Outfitters	Capt. Ed's Fly Shop
815 Bay St.	47 John St.
Beaufort, SC 29902	Charleson, SC 29403
Contact: Tony Royal	Contact: Ed Humphries
843-524-5250/	843-723-0860
843-524-9002	capted@atlanticboating.com

Charleston Angler	Haddrell's Point Tackle & Supply
946 Orleans Rd.	885 Ben Sawyer Blvd.
Charleston, SC 29407	Mt. Pleasant, SC 29464
Contact: Brad Harvey or Rick Hess	Contact: Mike Able
843-571-3899/843-571-4958	843-881-3644/843-849-5480
webmaster@charlestonangler.com	capnmike@haddrellspoint.com

Lowcountry Outfitters	Ludens
1533 Fording Island Rd., Suite 16	78 Alexander St.
Hilton Head Island, SC 29926	Charleston, SC 29403
Contact: Travers Davis	Contact: Dave Crosby
800-935-9666/843-837-6200	843-723-7829/843-723-7433

Guides (Capt.)	Phone/Fax	E-mail
Peter Brown	843-830-0448	
Wally Burbage	843-556-8004	capburbage@aol.com
Chris Chavis	843-795-4707	finstalker@aol.com
Jerry Ciandella	843-971-9111	
John Cox	843-884-1371	jhcox@awod.com
Chad Ferris	843-722-3277	cptferris1@aol.com
George Gallagher	843-884-6410	grgallagher@aol.com
Bill Glenn	843-884-8627	wbglenn@bellsouth.net
Champ Smith	843-928-3990	
Richard Stuhr	843-881-3179/843-849-3970	
Lee Taylor	843-971-1200	skinnyh2o@aol.com
J.R. Waits	843-971-9407	jrwaits@internetx.net

Most Common Prey	Typical Size-Inches	Usual Months of Availability*												Typical Matching Fly Patterns**
		J	F	M	A	M	J	J	A	S	O	N	D	
Blue Crabs	1 - 3	1	1	2	2	3	5	5	5	5	5	3	1	Del Brown's Permit Fly
Fiddler Crabs	1				1	3	5	5	5	5	3	1	1	Chernobyl Crab
Finger Mullet	2 - 4	1	1	2	3	4	5	5	5	5	4	2	1	Lefty's Deceiver (D), Seaducer
Killifish (Mudminnows)	3	1	1	2	2	4	5	5	5	5	5	3	3	Clouser Deep Minnow (K), Half and Half (B)
Menhaden	2 - 6			1	2	4	5	5	5	5	3	1		Lefty's Deceiver
Shrimp	2 - 4				1	2	3	5	5	5	3	1		Bonefish Slider, Scates Shrimp
General														Cave's Rattlin' Minnow

*1=Scarce, 2=Spotty, 3=Available, 4=Readily Available, 5=Widely Available • ** Pattern Recipe in Appendix A.

Chapter 25: The Golden Isles
By Capt. Larry Kennedy

Georgia has approximately 100 miles of shoreline, protected by 15 barrier islands. The area occupies the westernmost portion of the South Atlantic Bight, the curved coastline extending from Cape Hatteras, North Carolina to Cape Canaveral, Florida. This location has considerable protection from wave action and the highest tidal range (up to 9 feet) in the southeastern United States.

Since the area is more affected by tidal action, rather than wave action, the beaches are quite wide and flat with very shallow slopes. The 15 barrier islands known as the Golden Isles lie between the ocean and a band of coastal marshes. The islands are separated by relatively small and deep sounds which are flushed twice daily by the tides. The marshes, up to a mile wide in some places, are mainly filled with spartina grass which at times has a golden hue; thus the label of "The Golden Isles". Some claim the islands were named for the gold booty that Blackbeard the pirate was supposed to have buried here many years ago—a claim not yet proven.

This vast sheltered marsh area is a natural hatchery and nursery for hundreds of species of aquatic creatures ranging from the small grass shrimp and mud minnow to the larger redfish and blacktip shark. For the purposes of this chapter, the overall area will be subdivided into three sections; the North, Middle and South, which are greatly influenced by the Savannah, Altamaha and Satilla rivers, respectively.

The North section excels as a fly-fishing area for seatrout and redfish. At certain times of the year, fishing for striped bass is also an option. Since the local riverine stripers are usually spawning when available, and not as plentiful as their migratory cousins, resource conservation is required and a local guide is suggested to access their locations.

The Middle section offers great sight-fishing for tripletail. This species spawns in the spring off the barrier islands and can often be seen cruising on their sides. The local rationale for this unusual behavior is that the tripletail creates a decoy shelter for smaller prey, and then devours them when the prey draw near. In the summer, this area also provides good sight-fishing for very large tarpon, sharks and jack crevalle.

The South section provides some fantastic surf fishing for seatrout in the spring and early summer, and for bull redfish (red drum) in the fall. The most action occurs primarily off Cumberland Island, the largest of the barrier islands. Behind Cumberland Island there are numerous creeks and flats that would take a lifetime to fully explore. These creeks and flats are excellent locations for cruising and tailing redfish; they congregate here in large numbers before reaching sexual maturity and heading out to the deeper waters of the Atlantic Ocean.

Red drum, or "reds" as they are locally called, are one of the most sought-after species on the Georgia coast. The

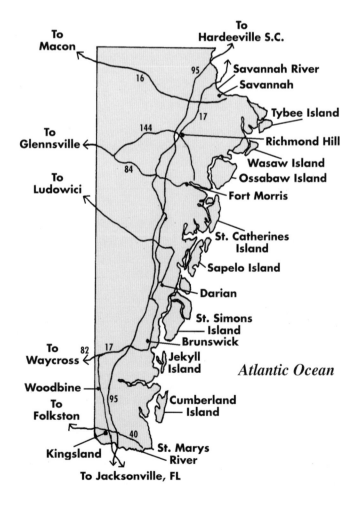

Species	Typical Size - Pounds	J	F	M	A	M	J	J	A	S	O	N	D
Bluefish	1 - 4	1	1	2	3	4	5	5	5	5	4	2	1
Flounder	1 - 8	1	1	3	4	3	3	3	3	5	5	4	2
Jack Crevalle	1 - 30	1	1	1	2	3	4	5	5	5	3	2	1
Ladyfish	2 - 9	1	1	1	1	2	5	5	5	5	4	1	1
Redfish	2 - 50	3	3	3	3	3	3	3	3	5	5	5	3
Spanish Mackerel	1 - 5	1	1	2	3	4	5	5	5	4	3	2	1
Spotted Seatrout	1 - 6	2	2	3	4	3	3	3	3	5	5	5	3
Tarpon	40 - 160	1	1	1	1	2	5	5	5	5	4	1	1
Tripletail	4 - 20	1	1	1	2	5	4	3	3	3	2	1	1

1=Scarce, 2=Spotty, 3=Available, 4=Readily Available, 5=Widely Available

giant reds frequent our shores in the fall to spawn. Their eggs drift inshore, hatch, and the life cycle of the species begins in the creeks and rivers. The reds will spend from three to five years here until they reach sexual maturity, weighing about 6 to 10 pounds at that time. They will then go out to sea, congregate in large schools and then spawn in the fall, starting the process anew. The fishing for reds varies considerably from year to year, depending upon the condition of the main freshwater rivers feeding the area. Spawning reds can sense when the ratio of fresh/salt water is appropriate to permit their eggs to float successfully to a protective inshore sanctuary. They will abort their spawning efforts if the salinity is so low that the eggs will sink rather than float. Accordingly, the annual population of juvenile reds is quite dependent upon the extent of flooding in inland rivers during the fall of the year.

As shown on the included chart, fly-fishing guides are readily available in the Golden Isles. If, however, you plan to explore on your own, rental of a canoe, kayak or jon boat will produce better results than wading. There are flats available, but they are generally quite soft in bottom texture and even so much as to be dangerous in certain places. There are numerous launching sites along the coast and it is highly recommended that those unfamiliar with the area start out at or near low tide, to minimize the likelihood of being aground for a long time period. If one should lose his or her bearings and become lost, remember that following the outgoing tide will always bring you to the open water and civilization.

If one had to choose a single fly-fishing outfit to cover 90% of our local fishing opportunities, it would be an 8-weight with a weight-forward floating fly line. For tarpon or shark, an upgrade to a 12- or 13-weight outfit is essential in order to land these fish within a reasonable period of time. Under those circumstances where it is best to fish deep, and especially where a swift current is involved, a fast-sinking line is required. Taking this approach also permits one to get down to the larger predators when their smaller cousins are in a feeding frenzy at the surface. Proper fly retrieve is critical in this region because of the tremendous amount of natural food available to the game fish. Your fly must behave like it is injured, to suggest an easy prey to the predator. An erratic fly retrieval (strip, strip, pause, strip, etc.) usually produces best.

Interstate 95 runs nearby along the entire coast and hotels, motels, restaurants, marinas, stores and campgrounds are readily available. The local fly shops listed can be very helpful in getting you started in the right direction.

Guides (Capt.)	Phone/Fax	E-mail
Greg Davis	912-355-3271	sltfc@hotmail.com
Kenny Dodd	912-832-6838	
Bob Edwards	912-638-3611	bobedwards@seaisland.com
Mike Kennedy	912-638-3214	charters@saintsimonoutfitters.com
Larry Kennedy	912-638-5454	charters@saintsimonoutfitters.com
Larry Kennedy Jr.	912-638-3214	charters@saintsimonoutfitters.com
Toby Mohrman	912-729-5960	
Greg Smith	912-634-0312	fishingwithducky@technonet.com
Matt Williams	912-355-3271	sltfc@hotmail.com

The Bedford Sportsman South
3405 Frederica Rd.
St. Simons Island, GA 31522
Contact: Ellen Kennedy
912-638-5454/912-638-5493
charters@saintsimonsoutfitters.com

Oak Bluff Outfitters
4501 Habersham St.
Savannah, GA 31405
Contact: Brian Smith
912-691-1115/912-691-1117
oakbluff@worldnet.att.net

Capt. Larry Kennedy has been in the fly-fishing industry for over 30 years, serving as a guide, naturalist, instructor and outfitter. He has fished and toured Georgia's Golden Isles since childhood, and he loves to share what he has learned from his experiences in one of the world's most pristine, majestic and beautiful areas.

Most Common Prey	Typical Size-Inches	Usual Months of Availability*												Typical Matching Fly Patterns**
		J	F	M	A	M	J	J	A	S	O	N	D	
Crabs	2	3	3	3	3	3	3	3	3	3	3	3	3	Crab Pattern
Finger Mullet	3	2	2	3	3	3	3	3	3	3	3	2	2	Lefty's Deceiver (I)
Grass Shrimp	1	3	3	3	3	3	3	3	3	3	3	3	3	Crazy Charlie (A)
Menhaden	6	1	1	1	1	3	3	3	3	3	3	2	1	Leiser's Angus
Mudminnows	2	2	2	3	3	3	3	3	3	3	3	2	2	Clouser Deep Minnow (D)
Mullet	6	2	2	3	3	3	3	3	3	3	3	2	2	Tabory's Slab Side (A)
Shrimp	3	3	3	3	3	3	3	3	3	3	3	3	3	Clouser Deep Minnow (D)
General														Wooly Bugger Express, Bendback (A)

*1=Scarce, 2=Spotty, 3=Available, 4=Readily Available, 5=Widely Available • ** Pattern Recipe in Appendix A.

Florida

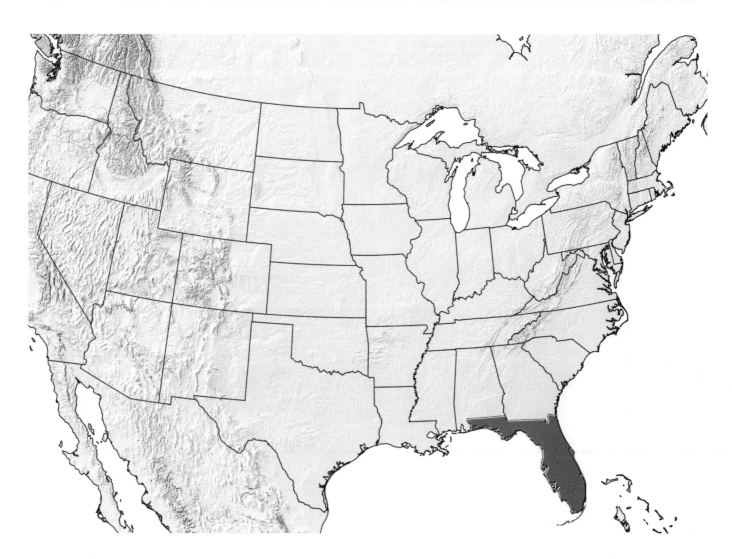

Florida

Chapter 26: Lower Indian River Lagoon and Its Inlets

By Capt. Mike Holliday

The Indian River is not really a river in the true sense of the word. It's actually a 190-mile lagoon stretching from the St. Lucie Inlet in Stuart to Ponce Inlet in New Smyrna Beach. For the most part, the river is anywhere from a half mile to a mile wide, with an average depth of three feet. Littered with grass flats, sandbars, oyster bars and mangrove shorelines, the Indian River is home to over 300 species of fish including snook, tarpon, redfish, and seatrout. The relatively shallow depth of the river allows for some of the best saltwater inshore fishing in the country, be it by wading or from a boat.

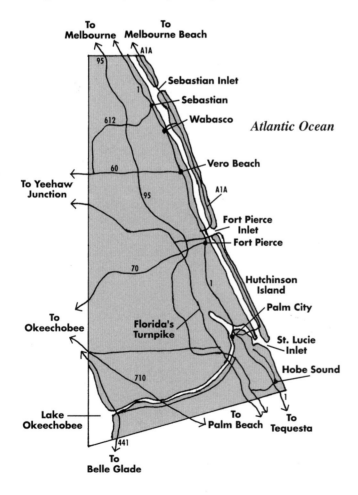

The lower or southern stretch of the river runs from Sebastian Inlet south to the St. Lucie inlet, and is bordered by a handful of barrier islands that separate the river from the Atlantic Ocean. On the mainland side, U.S. Hwy. 1 parallels the Indian River, while A1A runs the length of the barrier islands. Sebastian is the only inlet of the three with a bridge traversing the inlet. Sebastian Inlet sits along a lonely stretch of undeveloped beach, but is home to Sebastian Inlet State Park which has camping, fishing and surfing facilities, boat ramps and a small snack bar. The town of Sebastian on the mainland side of the river is a small Florida fishing village with quaint bed-and-breakfast type hotels.

About 15 miles south is the town of Wabasso, and the Wabasso Causeway which leads to the barrier island just north of Vero Beach. This stretch of the Indian River is dotted with small spoil islands that provide excellent habitat for most inshore game fish. Every one of the causeways that cross the Indian River have boat launch facilities; small parks with boat ramps are also plentiful the length of the mainland and barrier islands. The islands are also a great place to camp and fish at night. Vero Beach is an affluent small town with excellent fishing, dining and overnight options. South of Vero Beach is Fort Pierce, a fairly large town with dining and overnight amenities. At Fort Pierce, the traveler must cross a series of bridges back to U.S. 1, drive a half mile south, and then traverse similar bridges back onto the barrier island.

At Stuart, there is a similar series of bridges on the north side of the inlet, but to access the south side of the inlet requires driving 13 miles south on A1A to Jupiter Island, then north to the Hobe Sound National Wildlife Refuge. There is no public access to the south side of St. Lucie Inlet. The Wildlife Refuge is an 8-mile walk from the inlet. From the Stuart Causeway, MacArthur Boulevard runs a winding course to Bathtub Beach, where it ends at Sailfish Point, a private development. There is no public access to the St. Lucie Inlet, and it's roughly a 1-mile walk from Bathtub Beach to fish the inlet from shore.

Boat rentals are rare on the southern stretch of the Indian River. The shallow configuration of the river allows easy access to wade fishermen who can work the bars and drop-offs, and utilize low tides to wade hundreds of yards out from shore. Shorebound anglers generally target snook, trout

Species	Typical Size - Inches	J	F	M	A	M	J	J	A	S	O	N	D
Jack Crevalle	12 - 30	3	4	4	5	5	3	2	1	2	3	3	3
Ladyfish	15 - 28	5	5	4	3	2	1	1	1	2	3	5	5
Pompano	10 - 20	5	5	5	4	3	1	1	1	1	2	3	4
Permit	20 - 35	3	3	3	2	2	3	3	3	3	2	1	2
Redfish	15 - 30	3	3	4	5	5	5	4	4	4	5	5	4
Snook	20 - 30	1	2	3	3	4	5	5	5	5	5	4	3
Spanish Mackerel	16 - 25	5	5	4	3	2	2	1	1	3	4	5	5
Tarpon	24 - 50	1	1	1	2	3	5	5	5	5	5	4	2
Trout	15 - 25	3	3	3	4	5	5	5	4	3	3	3	3

1=Scarce, 2=Spotty, 3=Available, 4=Readily Available, 5=Widely Available

and redfish in the summer months, however, the mosquito impoundments between Vero Beach and the St. Lucie Power Plant are great areas for fishing juvenile tarpon to 20 pounds.

The fish tend to run larger in the warm months so 8-weight rods, 12-pound class tippets and a good smooth drag reel with at least 250 yards of backing are the standard outfits for that time of year. In the winter, ladyfish, jack crevalle, Spanish mackerel, seatrout, bluefish and pompano are the mainstays. These fish average less than two pounds so it's a good idea to drop down to a 5- or 6-weight outfit with sufficient backing to handle a fish over 15 pounds when they're encountered, which is fairly often. Fluorocarbon bite tippets are commonplace in case snook, bluefish or ladyfish are encountered. Use 30- to 40-pound-test tippets, and in most cases, a floating line will suffice. Sinking lines are better for fishing tarpon in the deeper cuts, and a sink-tip might be nice to have along in the winter months in case a cold front drives the fish to the holes which average four to six feet deep.

Fly patterns should coincide with the baitfish runs that take place throughout the year, starting with shrimp or glass minnows from December through March. Rattling Shrimp patterns tied with some gold in the body and orange eyes are effective on most winter species. As spring approaches, tie them on bendback hooks so they can be fished in the grass and around mangroves. The Borski shrimp patterns are popular options. Clouser Minnows in brown-and-white, red-and-yellow and chartreuse-and-white work well on most gamefish species throughout the cooler months.

April brings the first of the spring run of mullet, most of which are three to five inches in length. By June, pilchards and sardines inhabit the flats close to the inlet. Pinfish and pigfish are abundant on just about every grass flat, and needlefish and ballyhoo can be found around the sandbars and spoil islands. Dahlberg Divers or Mirrolure flies in gray, chartreuse or red-and-white are great for the larger seatrout, snook and redfish feeding on mullet. Any large baitfish pattern that produces a silhouette will fool these fish feeding on pinfish and pigfish over the grass. If tarpon are your targets, the best fishing is by boat in the Sebastian River, Big Mud Creek or the St. Lucie River from June through October, although there is a year-round population of juvenile fish to around 40 pounds. The tarpon will eat standard Cockroach patterns as well as Orange Quindellens and the Black Death. September brings the fall mullet run, and once again mullet patterns are a priority all the way through October. November signals a shift to northeasterly breezes and a change from the larger diet of mullet to shrimp and small baitfish.

Keep in mind that you'll find the best fishing for seatrout around grassbeds that are covered with sandy potholes. The trout like to ambush prey as it moves from the cover of the grass across the open sand. Redfish like dense grass in less than knee-deep water. Fish shallow, and look for tailing fish at dawn and dusk around the edges of sandbars, oyster bars and mangrove roots. Snook can be found at night around any dock with a light, or wherever there is moving water with a drop-off. They're powerful fish with voracious appetites that will crush any offering moving through the entire water column.

The Back Country
2046 Treasure Coast Plaza Unit C,
Vero Beach, FL 32960
Contact: Eric Davis
561-567-6665
Tbackcoun@aol.com

Professional Outfitters
1204 S. U.S. 1
Vero Beach, FL 32962
Contact: Gary Rhinehart
561-569-3666

The Snook Hook
3595 NE Indian River Dr.
Jensen Beach FL 34957
Contact: Henry Caiomonto
561-334-2145

Southern Angler
3585 SE St. Lucie Blvd.
Suart, FL 34997
Contact: Matt Bagley
561-223-1300

Wabasso Bait & Tackle
PO Box 22, 4720 85th St.
Wabasso, FL 32970
Contact: Terry or Steve Parsons
561-589-8518

Guides (Capt.)	Phone/Fax	E-mail
Matt Bagley	561-223-1300	
Lewis Clanton	561-464-2761	
George Geiger	561-388-3183	
Mike Holliday	561-223-7381	mholliday@maverickboats.com
Matt Muer	561-223-1300	
Terry Parsons	561-589-8518	
Tom Pierce	407-259-5911	
Rodney Smith	407-777-2773	camirl@digital.net
Mark Yanno	561-569-7593	
Jack Yanora	561-223-1300	

Capt. Mike Holliday has been fishing Florida waters since the age of six, and has lived on the Treasure Coast for 24 years. Mike has been an outdoor writer since 1986, and has worked as Associate Editor for Florida Sportsman *magazine and as Outdoor Editor for the* Fort Pierce Tribune. *He is also an outdoor writer for the* Miami Herald *and the* Palm Beach Post. *Capt. Holliday is a board member of six fishing clubs and has been a charter captain since 1985. He is a Hewes/Maverick and Penn Fishing Tackle-endorsed guide and appears regularly on regional and national television programs featuring saltwater fishing.*

Most Common Prey	Typical Size (inches)	Usual Months of Availability*												Typical Matching Fly Patterns**
		J	F	M	A	M	J	J	A	S	O	N	D	
Crabs	2 - 3	1	1	1	3	4	5	5	5	3	2	2	1	Kwan Fly
Glass Minnows	2 - 3	5	5	5	4	3	2	2	2	2	3	4	5	DL's Fuzz-Tail Glass Minnow, Clouser Deep Minnow (B)
Mosquitofish	2	2	2	2	2	3	5	5	5	5	4	3	2	Flasher, Almost Nothing Fly
Mullet	2 - 10	3	2	3	4	5	5	5	5	5	5	4	3	Dean's Minnow, Dahlberg Diver
Pilchards	2 - 4	2	2	3	3	4	5	5	5	5	5	4	3	Glades Deceiver
Pinfish	2 - 5	2	2	2	3	4	5	5	5	5	4	3	2	DL's Redbone Fluff
Sardines	4 - 7	1	1	1	2	3	5	5	5	3	2	2	1	Mangrove Minnow, Sar-Mul-Mac
Shrimp	2 - 5	4	5	5	5	5	4	2	2	2	2	3	3	Deer Hair Shrimp
Threadfin Herring	4 - 8	2	2	2	2	3	4	4	4	4	3	2	2	Eat-Em, Abel's Anchovy

*1=Scarce, 2=Spotty, 3=Available, 4=Readily Available, 5=Widely Available
** Pattern Recipe in Appendix A.

Chapter 27: Biscayne National Park and the Upper Florida Keys
By Capt. Barry Hoffman

Off the southeastern coast of Florida lie two national treasures, Biscayne National Park and Florida Bay. Unlike most terrestrial parks, here, sky and water overwhelm the scenery. Both are expansive shallow basins that provide food and habitat for the many species of fish and wildlife that make their home above and below the surface. Collectively, the two parks encompass over one and a half million acres. Biscayne Bay is bordered by the Miami coastline on its west side and a string of low barrier islands to the east. The Upper Florida Keys are an ancient coral reef tract. Bordered by Florida Bay to the west and the Atlantic Ocean eastward, they consist of mainland Key Largo at the north end and the town of Tavernier at the south end.

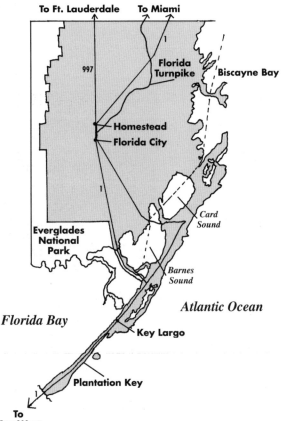

On and around the thousands of miles of shoreline, flats and mangrove islands, there is abundant bird and animal life. The backcountry islands and ocean-side flats provide the fly-fisherman with a unique angling opportunity. The blue-green tinted waters are extraordinarily clear and offer a transparent view of the life below. The primary gamefish targets on the flats are tarpon, permit and bonefish. In the slow-moving waters of the backcountry redfish, snook and seatrout are the most-sought species.

For bonefish, permit and small tarpon, a balanced, nine-weight outfit will cover just about any fly-fishing situation. The ability of these fish to pull several hundred yards of fly line and backing from your fly reel is well known, requiring a relatively large reel with sufficient line backing. Wind is a constant companion on the Keys and using somewhat heavier outfits will improve your casting performance. Redfish, seatrout and snook are more short-range fighters and will require less line backing. An eight-weight rod will cover these backcountry species and a seven-weight would even be more sporting. Giant tarpon will usually destroy anything less than a ten-weight fly rod. The ability to land the fish before exhaustion (for both angler and fish) usually requires stepping up to an eleven- or twelve-weight outfit. These fish can exceed one hundred and fifty pounds and even a small one of eighty pounds will test your tackle to its limits.

The majority of the water fished averages less than two feet in depth and a weight-forward floating line is most commonly used. Occasionally, a sink-tip line can be effectively used to probe the deeper holes and channels of the backcountry islands. Normally, a nine- or ten-foot leader will be suitable for this area. Usually, water clarity and wind strength will determine the length and strength of the tippet. Both of these factors have a significant effect on the ability of the fish to detect the angler. I've often used leaders of twelve feet or more for tailing bonefish under windless conditions. Tippet dimensions are matched to the species. Usually my leaders will terminate in a ten-pound tippet. Redfish, snook and seatrout have abrasive teeth or gills and thus a short length of 20-pound shock tippet is necessary. Large tarpon demand complex leaders constructed with shock tippets testing from 60 to 100 pounds.

Many conventional fly patterns are suitable for this area; I've described a few strategies here to help you with your selection. In clear water, use natural colors such as tans and greens. In turbid water, utilize colors like orange or red and flash to help the fish find your offering. Tie them in varying weights and sizes, to cover various combinations of water clarity, depth and current. Bonefish are not always the finicky eaters of their reputation. While rooting the bot-

Species	Typical Size-Pounds	J	F	M	A	M	J	J	A	S	O	N	D
Bonefish	6 - 12	3	3	5	5	5	4	3	3	4	5	5	4
Permit	3 - 45	2	2	3	3	4	4	4	4	3	3	2	2
Redfish	3 - 12	2	2	3	4	4	4	4	4	5	5	5	3
Seatrout	1 - 3	5	5	4	3	2	2	2	2	3	4	4	5
Snook	5 - 15	3	3	4	4	5	5	5	4	4	4	3	2
Tarpon	10 - 150	1	2	3	4	5	5	4	3	2	1	1	1

1=Scarce, 2=Spotty, 3=Available, 4=Readily Available, 5=Widely Available

tom of a soft flat, they'll eat just about anything. Depending on the time of year, shrimp, crabs, and glass minnows probably make up the majority of their diet, with a few gobies and snails on the side. Gotchas, Clousers and Crazy Charlies imitate these prey nicely. My favorite fly is usually a tricolor Clouser Minnow tied on a number 4 to 2 hook. Permit, without a doubt, love crabs. There are a number of good crab patterns available; Del Brown's Permit Fly and the McCrab seem to work best. The diet of a redfish, snook or seatrout includes shrimp, crabs and various small baitfish. I usually select Deer Hair Sliders, Deceivers and Bendbacks tied on 1/0 or 2/0 hooks. Tarpon fly choices are many, but as a general rule of thumb the cleaner the water and the better the light, the more natural fly colors should be used. In addition, I've downsized most of my tarpon flies lately, using 3x strong hooks up to 3/0 in size. Low light or turbid water require larger, darker flies that the tarpon can see and "feel".

At the end of the Florida Turnpike in Florida City are many small chain hotels for those wishing to explore Biscayne Bay. Since Route 1 is the only main road in the Florida Keys, it's not difficult to find sleeping accommodations ranging from campsites and various mom-and-pop hotels to five-star mini hotels. Most offer access to the water via boat ramps located on their property. Also, there are several islands that offer camping via permit. Restaurants are many and varied, both along Route 1 and in Florida City and Homestead. Although much of the wadeable shoreline is privately owned, there are several points of entry that will enable you to access many shorelines and backcountry islands. For Biscayne Bay, several points of entry are Black Point Park, Homestead Bayfront Park, Alabama Jacks and at the Card Sound Bridge. Along Route 1, there are wadeable flats and canoe entries to Barn Sound between Mile Markers 109 and 111 plus bridge fishing at Jewfish Creek Bridge (MM#108). Also, launching ramp facilities are available at the South Dade Marina (MM#114.5), at John Pennecamp State Park (MM#103) and at the Harry Harris County Park (MM#93). Ramp access to Blackwater and Little Blackwater Sounds is also available at Mile Markers 111 and 113. Several fly shops are conveniently located in the upper Keys.

Due to the very shallow nature of these waters, navigation on and around the flats and backcounty is difficult without local knowledge and a keen understanding of the tidal currents and the wind's influence on the water depth. Careful motoring is very important; sunlight, a good chart and a pair of polarized glasses are a prerequisite for navigation. A wary eye on the water's color provides subtle clues to the depth ahead. It is far better to drive cautiously than to risk injury to one's self, vessel and the living turtle grass bottom. Hiring a guide that has spent years learning the water and habits of the fish can help immeasurably in terms of time and productivity.

Biscayne Bay Outfitters	Bluewater World
8243 S. Dixie Highway,	Mile Marker 100.5,
Miami FL 33143	Key Largo FL 33037
Contact: Franko Zambolie	Contact: Tom Hamilton
305-669-5851	305-451-2511
bonefishfl@aol.com	
Bonefish Bob's Fly Shop	**Charlie Richter's Fly Shop**
81900 Overseas Hwy.,	472 NE 125th St. N,
Islamorada FL 33036	Miami FL 33161
Contact: Bob Berger	Contact: Charlie Richter
305-664-4615	305-893-6663
	crflyshop@aol.com
Florida Keys Outfitters	**World Wide Sportsman**
PO Box 603.,	81576 Overseas Hwy.,
Islamorada FL 33036	Islamorada FL 33036
Contact: Sandy Moret	Contact: Fly Department
305-664-5423	305-664-4615

Guides (Capt.)	Phone/Fax	E-mail
Chris Asaro	305-257-3134	CaptAsaro@aol.com
Duane Baker	305-852-0102	dbaker@keysconnection.com
Rob Fordyce	305-248-6132	
Barry Hoffman	305-852-6918	guide@flatsguide.com
Kiwi Hughes	305-852-8316	
Jack McCoy	305-852-5225	
Rick Murphy	305-242-0099	
Gary Rehm	305-664-2551	rehm@reefnet.com
Bob Rodgers	305-853-0933	brodgers@ddtcom.com
Joe Rodriguez	305-382-4028	

Capt. Barry Hoffman is a native of South Florida, fishing the Southeast coast for nearly 28 years. After moving to the Keys in 1982, Barry began guiding in 1986. A self-taught fly-caster and imaginative fly tier, he has been featured in Saltwater Software's CD-ROM "Saltwater Sportsman" and in Fly Fishing America *magazine. He has published articles on bonefish and tarpon locally (in* Fishing the Florida Keys*), and he currently writes a weekly column for 15 major fishing websites. Barry is an enthusiastic and patient fly-casting instructor/guide.*

Most Common Prey	Typical Size (inches)	Usual Months of Availability*												Typical Matching Fly Patterns**
		J	F	M	A	M	J	J	A	S	O	N	D	
Crabs	.75 - 1.5	3	3	4	4	5	5	5	5	5	4	4	3	Mc Crab
Finger Mullet	2 - 4	3	3	4	4	4	5	5	5	5	4	4	3	Deer Hair Slider
Glass Minnows	1 - 2	5	5	4	3	2	2	1	1	2	2	3	4	Tricolor Clouser
Pilchards	2 - 3	5	5	4	3	2	2	1	1	2	2	3	4	Seaducer (B)
Shrimp	2 - 4	5	5	5	5	5	4	4	4	5	5	5	5	Barry's Dumdrum

*1=Scarce, 2=Spotty, 3=Available, 4=Readily Available, 5=Widely Available • ** Pattern Recipe in Appendix A.

Chapter 28: Islamorada and the Middle Keys Flats

By Capt. David G. Kreshpane

The Middle Keys/Islamorada area is well known for its superb shallow-water angling for bonefish, tarpon, and permit. Fly fishers from around the world travel here each year to challenge trophy game fish on the fly. Islamorada has both large and small fishing resorts, full-service marinas, and a number of first-class fly-fishing outfitters. You don't have to travel very far from Route 1 to find quality fishing.

Southwest on Route 1 into the Middle Keys/Marathon area, fly-fishers can venture onto some productive wadable flats on Lower Matecumbe, Long Key State Park, and Grassy Key. Both kayaking and wading can produce bones, small tarpon, and permit from these areas and they are easily reached from Route 1. There are marinas and camping facilities in Long Key State Park and several small fishing lodges on both Long Key and Grassy Key. Both the Long Key bridge and Channel 5 are tarpon hot spots during the spring and early summer. Although Marathon is not quite as well known as the Islamorada area when it comes to bonefishing, this sleepy town boasts some of the best tarpon and permit fishing found in the Keys.

The first tarpon runs show up by late February, and the flats around Pigeon Key are alive with hungry tarpon in the 25- to 55-pound range. These fish take flies throughout the day and hooking and jumping several fish in a day is not uncommon. May and June are considered prime times for trophy tarpon; the migratory "silver kings" have arrived and the fishing for these 100-plus-pound fish is in its prime. From Islamorada to the Seven-Mile Bridge in Marathon, anxious fly anglers and patient guides are staked-out, waiting for schools of tarpon to cross within casting range. For fly-fishers seeking a lesser challenge, the small 10- to 20-pound "baby" tarpon can be found throughout the Middle Keys' back country and are a blast on lighter 8- and 9-weight fly rods. The smaller fish put on the same aerial show as their larger cousins and are much easier to land.

Permit can be found on the shallow banks and grass flats throughout the backcountry areas from Islamorada down through the Middle Keys. From Nine-Mile Bank in Florida Bay to the Bamboo, Red Bay, and Jacks Banks just north of Marathon, the permit fishing is fantastic. Permit are by far the wariest of the flats species to take a fly; hooking and landing a permit on fly gear is considered a lifetime accomplishment. Fly patterns like Del Brown's Permit Fly (the Merkin), developed over the years to imitate crabs, have proven successful on the wariest of permit.

When it comes to trophy bonefish, it's hard to beat the flats and backcountry banks in Florida Bay. Some of the biggest bonefish in the Keys are found on the flats surrounding the Islamorada area. Although bonefish can be found throughout the Middle Keys, the Islamorada area is considered the hot spot for trophy bones. Of course, when dealing with Mister Bone in the shallows, the angler's fly-fishing skills are put to task. Nothing is more exciting and demanding than poling after tailing bonefish in the shallows, trying to get that pinpoint cast to a fish that once hooked can rip off 90 feet of fly line and 150 yards of backing in the blink of an eye.

There are several hundred guides that work the shallows in the Islamorada-Marathon area, but the list of competent fly-fishing guides narrows considerably. Most of the local fly shops can match you with a guide that specializes in fly-fishing; however it is important that you ask for an experienced fly-fisherman and that all you want to do is fly-fish! Ask as many questions as you can beforehand so both the angler and guide have an idea what to expect. When booking the trip, be honest regarding your casting and flats-fishing ability and experience. Fly casting from a skiff is a completely different

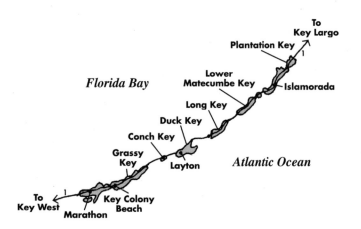

Species	Typical Size - Pounds	J	F	M	A	M	J	J	A	S	O	N	D
Barracuda	5 - 20	3	3	3	4	4	4	4	4	4	4	4	4
Blacktip Sharks	10 - 30	2	2	2	5	5	5	5	5	5	3	3	3
Bonefish	5 - 8	2	4	4	5	5	5	5	5	5	5	5	3
Flats Snapper	1 - 6	5	5	5	3	3	3	3	3	3	3	5	5
Permit	3 - 20	3	3	5	5	5	5	5	3	3	3	3	3
Tarpon	10 - 100	2	3	4	4	4	4	4	3	3	2	2	2

*1=Scarce, 2=Spotty, 3=Available, 4=Readily Available, 5=Widely Available

experience than wading a beach or casting on a trout stream. Some guides are better suited for an instructional day and can offer valuable tips on casting and sight-fishing skills. Other guides will expect you to be prepared and believe that all he has to do is put you on fish.

There are many choices when selecting the correct fly rod, line and reel combinations for fishing the Keys. Try to choose the outfit(s) that can be used under many conditions and fishing situations. A good all-around choice for the bones and permit is a 9-foot rod that throws a 9-weight, weight-forward floating line. A good-quality reel with a smooth drag and the ability to slow down a trophy bonefish or permit is a must. Middle Keys bones average 5 to 7 pounds and the permit on the flats are often in the 15- to 25-pound range. An extra spool pre-rigged with an intermediate-density or sink-tip line will be handy for fishing over bonefish muds in deeper water, or casting to permit on the deep edges of the flats. For the smaller baby tarpon, a 9- or 10-weight outfit will work fine. But when you get into the larger silver kings, an 11- or 12-weight outfit is the wiser choice. There are many great tarpon reels designed solely for handling the large tarpon; investing in one of these quality reels pays off big when you are connected to a trophy fish. Tarpon have an unusual way of mistreating your tackle; if there is a weak link between your fly and your casting arm they will always find it.

Each spring in the waters from Islamorada down through the lower Keys a strange natural phenomenon occurs. Small red worms approximately 1.5 to 3.5 inches in length begin their spawning cycle, setting in motion a feeding frenzy by tarpon, permit, snapper, and other species of fish that feed near the flats bordering the bridges. The worm has been mistakenly identified in the past as palolo worms (*Eunice schemacephala*). Although there are palolos in the Atlantic Ocean, the worms that swarm in the Keys each spring are a species of Nereids (*Nereis riise*). These worms have been positively identified by senior biologists from both the Florida Department of Natural Resources and the Florida Marine Biology Lab.

When the worms are swarming, so are the tarpon; in numbers that stagger the imagination. Fish are rolling by the thousands, with their tails and dorsal fins gliding across the water, gulping worms off the surface like trout feeding during the evening hatch. Watching these 100-pound fish feed only a few feet from the boat can unnerve even an expert tarpon fly-fisher. The swarms last only a few hours and are usually late in the afternoon during an outgoing tide. The worms are normally olive-green in color and only turn red when spawning. Small red flies that "match the hatch" will work during the swarm, but as with all selectively feeding tarpon the presentation must imitate the naturals. Predicting the swarms is like looking into a crystal ball; there are many factors that come into play such as the moon phase, water salinity and wind. If you are lucky enough to be on the water during a swarm, one thing is certain; you will never forget the images of this strange natural phenomenon that few ever get the chance to see!

Bonefish Bob's	Florida Keys Outfitters
Mile Marker 81.6 Bayside	81880 Overseas Highway
Islamorada, FL 33036	Islamorada, FL 33036
Contact: Bob Berger	Contact: Sandy Moret
305-664-9420/305-664-3891	305-664-5423

World Class Angler	World-Wide Sportsman
5050 Overseas H'way.	Mile Marker 81.5 Bayside
Marathon, FL 33050	Islamorada, FL 33036
Contact: Dave Navarro	Contact: Bonnie Beal
305-743-6139	305-664-4615/305-664-3692

Guides (Capt.)	Phone/Fax
Cal Cochran	305-743-6875
Jeff Colmes	305-853-0714
Diego Cordova	305-743-7317
Cy Eastlack	305-743-2589
Steve Huff	305-743-4361
Dave Kreshpane	305-743-9666
Buddy LaPointe	305-743-2871
Albert Ponzoa	305-743-4074
Billy Rabito	305-743-6010
Len Roberts	305-664-5420
Randy Small	305-451-0102
Bruce Stagg	305-853-5818

Capt. David Kreshpane has been guiding and fly-fishing the middle Keys for 9 years. With his wife Ellen and daughter Elizabeth, they run a fishing lodge and fly-fishing schools on the flats in Marathon. David is a former Maine guide and outdoor photographer/writer whose works appear in both national and regional publications. Capt. Dave is an accomplished fly tier and casting instructor who loves challenging trophy bonefish on the Middle Keys flats.

Most Common Prey	Typical Size (inches)	Usual Months of Availability*												Typical Matching Fly Patterns**
		J	F	M	A	M	J	J	A	S	O	N	D	
Blue Crabs	1 - 3	4	4	4	4	4	4	4	4	4	4	4	4	Del Brown's Permit Fly
Grass Shrimp	0.5 - 3.0	5	5	5	5	5	5	5	5	5	5	5	5	Deer Hair Shrimp, Tan Clouser
Hermit Crabs	0.25 - 1.0	3	3	3	3	5	5	5	5	5	5	3	3	Dave's Hermit Crab
Mullet	2 - 6	3	3	4	5	5	5	5	5	5	3	3	3	Wool Head Finger Mullet
Needlefish	3 - 7	5	5	5	5	5	5	5	5	5	5	5	5	Cuda Fly
Pilchards	1 - 4	5	5	5	5	3	3	3	2	2	2	5	5	Blue Back Pilchard
Red Worms	1 - 3	1	1	1	1	1	4	4	4	1	1	1	1	Red-Hot Rat Tail
Shrimp	0.5 - 2.0	5	5	5	5	5	5	5	5	5	5	5	5	Snapping Shrimp

*1=Scarce, 2=Spotty, 3=Available, 4=Readily Available, 5=Widely Available
** Pattern Recipe in Appendix A.

Chapter 29: The Lower Keys and the Marquesas

By Capt. Lenny Moffo

The Lower Keys are considered to be the area from the lower end of the Seven-Mile Bridge (Mile Marker 40) to Key West (Mile Marker 1). Twenty-six miles to the west of Key West lie the Marquesas, a true atoll and donut-shaped group of mangrove-covered islands about three miles in diameter. Within the rim of islands is a lake-like body of water with beautiful flats surrounding the islands inside and out.

The area that lies between Key West and the Marquesas is dotted with myriad flats and mangrove islands. This maze of literally hundreds of flats and mangrove islands continues along the Gulf side of the Keys all the way to the Seven-Mile Bridge. All of the Lower Keys, including the Marquesas, are contained within the Florida Keys National Marine Sanctuary, and this area is home to many fish and bird species.

There are a wide variety of hotels, motels and bed-and-breakfast places throughout the Lower Keys; enough to suit most tastes and budgets. And for those anglers who can't get enough of the outdoors there are campgrounds available for all types of camping. The traveling fly-fisher will also find a varied selection of restaurants and eateries, with the majority located in the Key West area.

For those anglers who would like to try some wading on their own, they will find that there not as many wadable flats as they think there should be in a 40-mile stretch of islands. Much of this is due to private property restrictions and sanctuary closures. One of the places I recommend for wading is Little Duck Key (Mile Marker 40); you can park free at Veteran's Memorial Park (oceanside), with quite a bit of area in which to roam. Also, at Mile Marker 37 there's Bahia Honda State Park, where you will find miles of shoreline, beaches, food concessions, camping and other amenities. The jetty at Fort Zachary Taylor in Key West at the end of Southard Street can provide some fly-fishing opportunities.

Fly fishers who are intent upon striking out on their own will find that there is no shortage of kayak and canoe rental facilities scattered throughout the Lower Keys. This can put the energetic angler in touch with numerous places not readily available by road and open up a whole new world of opportunity. Powerboat rentals are also numerous, but flats skiffs with push poles are generally not available. Most boat rental agencies try to discourage the use of their boats in the backcountry (the Gulf or northern side of Route 1), since navigation can be so difficult and dangerous. In contrast, oceanside in the Lower Keys can also have some great fly-fishing without some of the problems of the backcountry.

For anglers who wish to bring their own boat, there are many boat ramps with good access on most islands throughout the Lower Keys. Most of the ramps are at marinas, and will cost between $5 and $15 per day of use. There are also some County-owned ramps whose use is free to the general public.

My opinion on using guides in the Keys is prejudiced of course, but I think the best way to get the most out of a fly-fishing vacation in the Keys is to hire a guide. When I go on vacation elsewhere I hire guides and some of the things I found valuable in selecting a guide are: 1) Talk to him on the phone to develop rapport and make sure you feel comfortable with him; 2) Ask the hard questions and tell him what your objectives are for the trip. But, don't forget that a lot of what will happen is up to you. "No fly is better than a good cast." Bonefish in the Lower Keys are big and smart. Most fish will range from six to ten pounds, with quite a few larger ones likely to be encountered.

I recommend a 9-foot, 8- or 9-weight fly rod with a reel capacity of at least 180 yards of 20-pound backing and a weight-forward fly line. I prefer an 11- to 12-foot leader with a butt section of 30- to 40-pound test tapering down to a 10-pound-test tippet. The flies that we use in the Keys are tied on bigger hooks than most other bonefish destinations, with size 2 being the average size. Charlie-type flies are productive, as well as some of the new "designer" flies. Sometimes a smaller crab-type fly will work well.

Some of the best permit fishing in the world is found in the Lower Keys; 20- to 40-pound permit are common. For this species, the rod of choice would be a 9-foot 10-weight

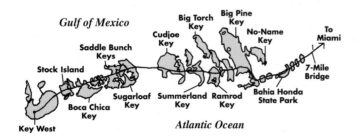

Species	Typical Size - pounds	J	F	M	A	M	J	J	A	S	O	N	D
Baby Tarpon	10 - 40	3	3	3	4	5	5	5	4	4	4	4	3
Barracuda	1 - 50	4	4	4	3	2	2	2	2	2	2	2	3
Big Tarpon	50 - 150	1	1	2	3	5	5	3	2	1	1	1	1
Bonefish	5 - 14	3	3	4	4	4	4	4	4	4	4	3	3
Cobia	10 - 40	3	3	3	2	1	1	1	1	1	1	1	2
Jack Crevalle	1 - 12	3	3	3	3	3	3	3	3	3	3	3	3
Permit	10 - 40	3	3	4	3	3	3	5	4	4	4	3	3
Sharks	10 - 250	3	3	3	4	5	5	5	5	5	5	5	4

1=Scarce, 2=Spotty, 3=Available, 4=Readily Available, 5=Widely Available

rod with a good reel with at least 180 yards of backing with a weight-forward floating fly line or possibly a weight-forward slow-sink-tip line (intermediate density). A 12- to 14-foot leader is preferred, with the butt section of 40- to 50-pound test tapering down to a 12-pound tippet. Crab patterns seem to work best, but shrimp flies are also often successful. I usually use these flies tied on size 2 to 1 or 1/0 hooks, and sometimes fish with flies tied on 2/0 hooks when conditions warrant. All flies should be weighted to sink correctly for the conditions at hand.

I use permit gear on small tarpon, generally weighing between 15 and 40 pounds. These great fish can be found year-around, weather permitting, but you'll have to change your leader to one about 9 1/2 feet long, with a 30- to 40-pound-test shock tippet. Traditional tarpon fly patterns or most streamer-type flies will fill the bill nicely, tied on 1, 1/0 or 2/0 hooks. An 11- to 12-weight rod and line would be the proper tool for large tarpon. These fish generally weigh between 70 and 150 pounds. Your reel should hold at least 200 yards of 30-pound backing and a weight-forward fly line, floating or slow-sink. I personally always carry two 12-weights loaded with one of each type of line density.

Most fly-fishers follow IGFA rules when it comes to tarpon leaders. I like 50- to 60-pound test butt sections, about 5-6 feet long with a loop on the end. There are many different configurations for tarpon leaders but the essence of it is that you must have at least 15 1/2 inches of class tippet (usually 15- or 20-pound test) and no more than 12 inches of shock tippet, which is usually 60-, 80- or 100-pound test. With the necessary maze of mono knots, your leader will end up to about 10 feet long. If you are going to tie your own flies, I would use 2/0 or 3/0 hooks that are quite sharp. Traditional tarpon patterns work well in colors like tan, brown and orange, and you can't go wrong with the standard Cockroach patterns.

Some of this might sound a little overwhelming, but if you fish with a guide he'll provide everything you'll need. If you don't have Keys-type of equipment, you can still have a great time. There are really only two factors that matter in the success of your trip. One factor you can control, and that is how well you can cast the fly. The other factor you can't control and that's the weather. Good luck!

Saltwater Angler
243 Front St.
Key West, FL 33040
Contact: Jeffery Cardenas
800-223-1629
305-294-3248
saltangler@aol.com

Sea Boots Outfitters
29975 Overseas Hwy.
(US Hwy. 1, MM 30)
Big Pine Key, FL 33043
Contact: Christina Sharpe
800-238-1746/305-872-9005
seaboots5@aol.com

Guides (Capt.)	Phone/Fax	E-mail
Vaughn Cochran	305-745-2425	blackflykw@aol.com
Steve Lamp	305-745-2114	drctcher@aol.com
Lenny Moffo	305-872-4683	captlen@earthlink.net
Jeff Segallos	305-744-4422	thinh2o@aol.com
Dave Wiley	305-872-4680	outcast97@aol.com

Capt. Lenny Moffo was raised in New Jersey and has been fly-fishing for 37 years, tying flies for nearly as long. Lenny moved to the Northwest after his school days, in search of the sporting life. He lived and guided in both Montana and Idaho, but wintered in the Florida Keys during vacations. Saltwater fly-fishing and fly tying were just getting noticed by mainstream fly-fishers; Lenny found the possibilities endless and fell in love with saltwater fly tying. Eighteen years later, Lenny is still tying flies and guiding fly-fishers in the Florida Keys. He still goes to the northwestern states in the summer, when on vacation.

Most Common Prey	Typical Size (inches)	Usual Months of Availability*												Typical Matching Fly Patterns**
		J	F	M	A	M	J	J	A	S	O	N	D	
Ballyhoo	5 - 10	4	4	4	4	4	4	4	4	4	4	4	4	Utility Minnow
Crabs	0.5 - 1.5	3	3	3	3	3	3	3	3	3	3	3	3	Lenny's Fleeing Crab, Ribbon Crab
Mullet	4 - 10	3	3	3	3	4	4	3	3	3	3	3	3	Utility Minnow
Needlefish	4 - 8	3	3	3	3	3	3	3	3	3	3	3	3	Utility Minnow
Pilchards	2 - 4	3	3	3	3	3	3	3	3	3	3	3	3	Utility Minnow
Pinfish	2 - 5	5	5	5	5	5	5	5	5	5	5	5	5	Utility Minnow
Shrimp	2 - 4	4	4	4	4	4	4	4	4	4	4	4	4	Lenny's Tarpon Shrimp, Bone Bugger

*1=Scarce, 2=Spotty, 3=Available, 4=Readily Available, 5=Widely Available • ** Pattern Recipe in Appendix A.

Chapter 30: Everglades National Park

By Capt. Chris Asaro

The largest and most diverse of our national parks, Everglades National Park encompasses a large portion of south Florida and all of Florida Bay. This unique environment of mangroves, cypress forests, sawgrass, beaches, flats, creeks, bays and rivers provides a wide range of fly-fishing opportunities over its area. There is first-class freshwater fishing for largemouth bass, guided fishing for 100-plus-pound tarpon and dozens of other venues in-between.

An hour's drive south from the Miami airport brings one past wading woodstorks, dwarf cypress forests, deer grazing habitat, and the oldest mahogany tree in North America. As shown on the enclosed map, Flamingo Outpost and its well-maintained Ranger Station lie at the southern end of Route 9336. Flamingo is the primary southern port of Everglades National Park and one of the two principal boat-launching areas accessing the Gulf of Mexico and the backcountry. The other major point of Gulf/backcountry access is via Everglades City/Chokoloskee Island, at the southern terminus of Route 29, and about one and one-half hours from the airport at Ft. Myers.

Both communities are tourist-friendly and well equipped with restaurants, launching ramps and other accommodations for the visiting fly-fisher. Most of the fly-fishing guides listed on the attached chart use one or both of these communities as the starting point for their excursions to the flats of the Gulf and Florida Bay or the backwaters of the Park. Some guides also access Florida Bay from the mainland of the Upper Keys. Many fully equipped fly shops, as listed on the attached chart, are located in the larger communities of Naples, Miami, Ft. Lauderdale and Boca Raton.

South Florida is the location of the famous "sea of grass," the 50-mile-wide southern flow of water from Lake Okeechobee and central Florida. Along its length, the freshwater flow gradually channels into creeks and rivers and increases its salinity along the way due to tidal influence. This estuarial environment and its transition into the Gulf and Florida Bay creates innumerable, varied fly-fishing scenarios at various times of the year, for the gamefish species listed on the attached chart.

Although the Park offers year-round fishing for various gamefish species, May and June offer the best opportunities for numbers of larger predators. The Backcountry Grand Slam (tarpon, snook and redfish) is always a reasonable target during this period. Tailing redfish and rolling tarpon are very common on the grass flats of Florida Bay and the Gulf, especially during the warmer months. Seatrout, jack crevalle, pompano, Spanish mackerel, ladyfish, tripletail and cobia are also attractive targets. They can be available year-round, but the winter period usually provides the best action.

Guided charters will provide the most reliable access to high-quality fly-fishing, but there are also some reasonable opportunities for the do-it-yourselfer. Wade and bank fishing areas are quite limited, except for the brackish lakes and ponds in the Flamingo area. Flamingo, Everglades City and Chokoloskee all have facilities for renting boats, canoes and kayaks. The nearby flats, oyster bars and creeks are often overlooked, but they can be very productive at times. Of particular importance is the 100-mile, marked trail which connects Everglades City with Flamingo and which has primitive camping sites along the way. Use of this wilderness waterway requires a shallow-draft boat or canoe and a permit from the ranger

Species	Typical Size - Pounds	J	F	M	A	M	J	J	A	S	O	N	D
Black Drum	1 - 40	3	3	4	4	4	3	3	3	3	3	3	3
Cobia	2 - 40	3	3	3	2	1	1	1	1	3	3	4	4
Mackerel (Spanish)	0.5 - 5	4	4	3	2	1	1	1	1	3	4	5	5
Permit	2 - 30	1	1	2	3	3	3	3	3	3	3	3	1
Pompano	0.5 - 4	3	3	3	2	1	1	1	1	2	3	3	3
Redfish (Red Drum)	1 - 15	3	3	3	4	5	5	5	5	5	5	5	3
Snook	1 - 20	3	2	3	4	5	5	5	5	5	5	5	5
Spotted Seatrout	0.5 - 5	5	5	5	5	4	3	3	3	3	4	5	5
Tarpon	5 - 120	2	2	3	4	5	5	3	3	3	2	2	2
Tripletail	1 - 15	3	4	4	4	3	2	2	2	2	3	3	3

1=Scarce, 2=Spotty, 3=Available, 4=Readily Available, 5=Widely Available

station. Care must be taken to prepare for wind, tides and insects.

Fly fishers targeting large tarpon should be prepared with 9-foot, 12-weight outfits and reels with good drag systems and a capacity of at least 300 yards of 30-pound-test backing. Weight-forward floating lines are best, with 9-foot tapered leaders having 15- to 20-pound tippets, plus 80-pound shock tippets. For snook and redfish, 8- or 9-weight outfits are quite satisfactory, with reels having a capacity of about 150 yards of 20-pound backing. Nine-foot tapered leaders with 8- to 12-pound tippets plus a 30- to 40-pound shock tippet are fairly standard. For the smaller game fish such as ladyfish, mackerel, etc. and for unusually calm wind conditions, 5- to 6-weight outfits are quite satisfactory.

Everglades National Park has some significant-sized populations of baitfish; the enclosed table lists the more common species including mullet, menhaden, herring and glass minnows. The most common crustacean prey are crabs and shrimp. From early spring until late fall the baitfish group together in massive schools. In the back-country, these schools often consist of very small min-nows and snook and tarpon may only be fooled by small flies down to size 6. Seaducers and Deceivers are usually quite sucessful for baitfish imitations, with chartreuse being a particularly productive color. Deep Clouser pat-terns also work quite well, especially in the deeper grass flats for seatrout, jack crevalle, ladyfish, pompano and mackerel. Weedguards are highly recommended for fish-ing in the Everglades, especially when fishing in thick turtle grass or tight up against the mangroves.

The most exciting fishing in Everglades National Park is probably sight-fishing for the larger species. Casting skills must be finely tuned and brown or amber polarized sunglasses are a must to permit spotting the fish and getting the fly to him with little delay. One great fly pattern for sight-fishing is Tim Borski's Chernobyl Crab, tied with a weedguard. This is very effective on the mudflats and oyster bars around Chokoloskee and on the grass flats of Flamingo. Clear water makes it easier to see the fish, but it also makes it easier for the fish to see you before you can tempt him with a wisp of fur and feathers. Casting preparation will increase your chances for suc-cess. This wild country can be challenging for even the best, so you should do your homework.

Biscayne Bay Fly Shop
8243 S. Dixie Hwy.
Miami, FL 33143
Contact: Jesus, Franco or Leo
305-669-5851/305-669-5852

Charlie Richter's Fly Shop
472 N.E. 125th St.
N. Miami, FL 33161
Contact: Charlie Richter
305-893-6663/800-866-0763

Everglades Angler
810 12th Ave. South
Naples, FL 34102
Contact: Mark Ward
941-262-8228/941-262-0572
mail@evergladesangler.com

The Fly Shop of Ft. Lauderdale
5130 N. Federal Hwy.
Ft. Lauderdale, FL 33308
Contact: Joe, Gil Martin
954-772-5822
flyshopfl@aol.com

Mangrove Outfitters
4111 E. Tamiami Trail
Naples, FL 34113
Contact: Tom Shadley
941-793-3370
captshadley@mangroveoutfitters.com

Ole Florida Fly Shop
6353 N. Federal Hwy.
Boca Raton, FL 33487
Contact: Kyle
561-995-1929/877-653-3567
oleflorida@aol.com

Guides (Capt.)	Phone/Fax	E-mail
Chris Asaro	305-257-3134	CaptAsaro@aol.com
	941-695-2277	
Andrew Bostick	941-394-3010	wyman1230@aol.com
Robert Collins	941-262-1970	captrscjr@aol.com
Chris Dean	305-666-0908	
John Dickinson	305-669-1721	bonefish@bellsouth.net
Joe Gonzalez	305-642-6727	
Barry Hoffman	305-852-6918	guide@flatsguide.com
Bob LeMay	954-435-5666	lemaymiami@aol.com
Doug Lillard	954-894-9865	captdoug@mindspring.com
Joe McNichol	941-262-4132	
Jim Nickerson	941-262-4132	
Lee Quick	941-695-0032	
Adam Redford	305-255-7618	adam.redford@cwix.com
Tom Tripp	941-775-1917	fishtrpp@aol.com

Capt. Chris Asaro is a native of South Florida and has been fishing the since the age of 4. He lives both in Key Largo and on Chokoloskee Island, and is thus able to conveniently cover all areas of Everglades National Park with both a Hewes Bonefisher and an OMC Roughneck. His past 12 years have been fully dedicated to fly-fishing and exploring the Everglades. An avid fly tier and lecturer, Chris enjoys sharing his secrets to success.

Most Common Prey	Typical Size (inches)	Usual Months of Availability*												Typical Matching Fly Patterns**
		J	F	M	A	M	J	J	A	S	O	N	D	
Crabs	1 - 5	5	5	5	5	5	5	5	5	5	5	5	5	Chernobyl Crab (A)
Glass Minnows	0.25 - 2.	2	2	2	3	5	5	5	5	5	5	5	4	Glades Minnow
Herring	1 - 5	2	2	3	4	5	5	5	5	5	5	5	4	Seaducer (A), Clouser Deep Minnow (B)
Menhaden	1 - 5	2	2	3	4	5	5	5	5	5	5	5	4	Seaducer (A), Lefty's Deceiver (G)
Mullet	1 - 12	4	4	4	5	5	5	5	5	5	5	4	4	Deerhair Bass Bug
Shrimp	0.25 - 4.	5	5	5	5	4	4	4	4	4	4	4	5	Fish Fuzz Clouser
General														Hot Lips

*1=Scarce, 2=Spotty, 3=Available, 4=Readily Available, 5=Widely Available
** Pattern Recipe in Appendix A.

Chapter 31: Marco Island and the 10,000 Islands

By Capt. Matt Hoover

The 10,000 Islands include the city of Marco Island, an up-scale resort community located a dozen miles south of Naples, Florida. East of Marco Island lies the 35,000-acre, 10,000 Islands National Wildlife Refuge, managed by the U.S. Department of Interior's National Fish and Wildlife Service. The Refuge provides protected habitat for a wide range of invertebrates, fishes, amphibians, reptiles, birds and mammals, including several threatened and endangered species. The Refuge's boundaries include Marco Island and Route 92 to the west, the Gulf of Mexico to the south, the Faka Union Canal to the east, and Route 41 (The Tamiami Trail) to the north. Public boat-launching facilities are available on Route 951 just north of Marco Island, at the south end of Marco Island and at Collier-Seminole State Park on Route 41.

Marina launching facilities are also readily available in Marco Island, in the town of Goodland and at the resort community of Port of the Islands. Marco Island, Goodland and Naples have literally hundreds of fine restaurants geared to suit any taste. Overnight accommodations are also readily available at these locations, including campgrounds and trailer parks.

As shown on the map, deep-water access into the interior of the Refuge is provided by several passes and rivers.

Careful navigation is required because of shallow areas, sandbars and oyster bars. It is highly recommended that you hire a competent fly-fishing guide who knows the topography and the tides. It is not very difficult to lose your way or become temporarily stranded in these backwater areas. The accompanying table lists most of the area guides who are skilled with fly-fishing clients and who regularly fish Marco Island and the Refuge. Also included is a table listing the location of nearby fly shops that are fully equipped to support the fly-fisher and able to answer most questions.

Boat, canoe and kayak rentals are available on Marco Island and at the Collier Seminole State Park for those fly-fishers who wish to strike out on their own. Canoes and kayaks are a particularly effective way of getting into the very shallow headwaters of the Refuge where conventional boats or even flats skiffs are unable to access. Shorebound anglers can often find good fly-fishing in the canal adjacent to Route 41. Snook and tarpon are the usual targets, but bass and alligator gar will sometimes bring a welcome surprise. During the late spring and throughout the summer, the beaches adjacent to the Gulf will often produce tarpon, snook, jack crevalle, ladyfish or redfish. This is the time of the year when many fish species are spawning and their need for food is satisfied by the heavy concentrations of baitfish. The snook are particularly accessible at this time, since they will often cruise in small groups extremely close to the shoreline. It was on the beach where I established an IGFA two-pound tippet fly-fishing world record for snook in 1993.

The Refuge tends to be classified into three regions; 1) the "front," consisting of the islands adjacent to the Gulf, 2) the "back," consisting of the back bays, lakes and creeks, and 3) the "middle," which is everything in between. The gamefish species tend to occupy these regions (and the Gulf itself), at various times depending on the tides, water temperature, salinity, food availability, etc. The secret is to learn the effect of these and other variables to locate the species, identify their local prey, and present a reasonable feathered imitation for their approval. The accompanying chart lists the most important gamefish species for our area, together with information on when they are most available.

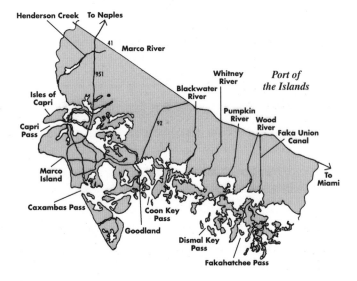

Species	Typical Size	J	F	M	A	M	J	J	A	S	O	N	D
Jack Crevalle	2 - 6 pounds	3	4	4	5	5	5	4	4	4	5	5	4
Ladyfish	0.5 - 4 pounds	5	4	3	2	1	1	1	1	2	3	4	5
Mangrove Snapper	10 - 14 inches	5	5	5	4	4	5	5	4	4	3	3	4
Pompano	2 - 3 pounds	5	5	4	4	4	5	5	4	3	3	4	5
Redfish (Red Drum)	2 - 10 pounds	2	2	3	4	5	5	4	4	5	5	4	3
Snook	2 - 10 pounds	3	3	4	4	5	5	4	4	4	4	3	2
Spanish Mackerel	1 - 3 pounds	5	5	5	4	4	3	3	3	2	3	3	4
Spotted Seatrout	1 - 4 pounds	5	5	4	3	2	2	2	2	3	4	4	5
Tarpon	10 - 150 pounds	1	2	3	4	5	5	4	3	2	1	1	1

1=Scarce, 2=Spotty, 3=Available, 4=Readily Available, 5=Widely Available

The most popular fly rod used in our area is a nine-footer for an eight-weight line. Some fly-fishers use seven- or nine-weights. Ten- to 12-weight rods and lines are suggested for our larger tarpon, whose weight may exceed 100 pounds. We generally use nine-foot tapered leaders with 12- to 20-pound tippets. Since many of our game fish have abrasive mouth interiors, an additional 12- to 18-inch "bite" tippet is recommended adjacent to the fly. We usually use 80- to 100-pound bite tippets for tarpon, though I have on occasion seriously considered going up to 125-pound strengths. Most of our targeted fish that are of legal size have the capability of breaking a 20-pound tippet. Redfish, snook and smaller species will seldom run more than 100 yards after being hooked. Their fight is usually a close-quartered war, so 150 yards of 30-pound Dacron backing on the reel is usually sufficient for the purpose. Tarpon are a different story. I have had tarpon run non-stop for a full 300 yards before being stopped or turned. Two hundred to 300 yards of 30-pound Dacron backing is recommended for this species. Weight-forward floating lines are usually the best choice for all fish species, although a sink-tip line will come in handy on occasion.

As shown on the attached chart, we have many prey species in our area. There are finger mullet, glass minnows, scaled sardines, spanish sardines, threadfin herring, killifish, crabs and shrimp. Most of the prey that we try to imitate are not much longer than four or five inches. I tie most of my snook and redfish flies on number 2 to 1/0 hooks. Finger mullet are a very important source of food for our game fish. There are a variety of flies that will imitate the finger mullet, including the Woolhead Mullet and Pete's Persuader. The scaled sardine or shiner is probably the most-imitated baitfish. Deceiver-style flies and the Matt's 40, on number 1 to 1/0 hooks, are quite effective in lengths from two to five inches. Dahlberg Divers and hair-bug sliders are good imitations for killifish, especially for snook, redfish and jack crevalle. Crustacean patterns like Del's Crab Fly (size 4 hook) are particularly good for tailing redfish in the winter months. "Puff" style flies on size 2 to 1/0 hooks are effective shrimp imitations, especially for winter snook. Small glass minnow imitations like Dave's Glassy are very effective for snook and jack crevalle on the beach and under dock lights at night. We use many differing tarpon flies, but I have found that for our sometimes-stained water, the Black Death pattern developed by the late Harry Kime is very effective. The most effective patterns seem to be in dark colors. Half of the fun in fly-fishing though is in experimenting with different flies. Fly patterns resembling these prey are listed in the table.

Most Common Prey	Typical Size (inches)	Usual Months of Availability*												Typical Matching Fly Patterns**
		J	F	M	A	M	J	J	A	S	O	N	D	
Crabs	0.75	5	5	5	5	5	5	5	5	5	5	5	5	Del's Crab Fly
Finger Mullet	2 - 4	3	3	4	4	4	5	5	5	5	4	4	4	Woolhead Mullet, Pete's Persuader
Glass Minnows	1 - 2	1	1	2	2	3	4	4	5	5	4	4	3	Dave's Glassy, Night Snook Fly
Killifish	3		1	1	3	4	5	5	5	5	4	3	1	Dahlberg Diver
Scaled & Sp. Sardines	2 - 5		1	3	4	5	5	5	5	5	4	3	1	Lefty's Deceiver, Matt's 40
Shrimp	2 - 4	5	5	5	5	5	5	5	5	5	5	5,	5	Puff
Threadfin Herring	2 - 5		1	1	3	4	5	5	5	5	4	3	1	Lefty's Deceiver, Matt's 40
General														Black Death

*1=Scarce, 2=Spotty, 3=Available, 4=Readily Available, 5=Widely Available
** Pattern Recipe in Appendix A.

Guides (Capt.)	Phone/Fax	E-mail
Andrew Bostick	941-394-3010	wyman1230@aol.com
Jeff Brown	941-775-7745	captjbrown@aol.com
Richard D'Onofrio	941-389-5726	
Dave Eimers	941-353-4828	fishflash1@aol.com
Dave Harding	941-643-1261	captdaveh@aol.com
Matt Hoover	941-732-6550/ 941-775-1210	fishhoover@aol.com
Al Keller	941-353-6451/ 941-455-6762	
Bob Marvin	941-455-7548	flyingcaptain@aol.com
Stacy Mullendore	941-261-0618	captstayman@aol.com
Jay Peeler	941-417-3055/ 941-417-1677	capnjaybo@cs.com
Steve Westervelt	941-775-2003	info2@fishing-guru.com
Duane White	941-774-2986/ 941-774-0966	deweycapt@aol.com

Angler's Answer
11387 E. Tamiami Trial
Naples, FL 34113
Contact: Dan Gewant
941-775-7336
mail@anlglersanswer.com

Everglades Angler
810 12th Ave. South
Naples, FL 34102
Contact: Mark Ward
941-262-8228/941-262-0572
mail@evergladesangler.com

Mangrove Outfitters
4111 E. Tamiami Trail
Naples, FL 34113
Contact: Tom Shadley
941-793-3370
captshadley@mangroveoutfitters.com

Marco River Marina
951 Bald Eagle Dr.
Marco Island, FL 34145
Contact: Eric Rodriguez
941-394-2502
marcoriver@mindspring.com

Naples Sporting Goods
779 5th Ave. South
Naples, FL 34102
Contact: Ted Rome
941-262-6752/941-262-7654

Sunshine Ace Hardware
141 9th Street North
Naples, FL 34102
Contact: Tom Reynolds
941-262-2940
sunshine@sunshineace.com

Captain Matt Hoover has been living and fishing in southwest Florida for 23 years. He has been an Orvis-endorsed guide for seven years and a charter member of Naples' Backcountry Fly Fishers, a club now having an active membership of over 100 fly-fishers. Matt is an accomplished fly tier and has developed several patterns that have captured both local and national attention. He is also a skilled fly-casting instructor, a featured fishing columnist for the Marco Island Daily News, and has appeared on several regional television programs featuring fly-fishing.

Chapter 32: Sanibel Island & Pine Island Sound
By Capt. Dave Gibson

Sanibel Island and Pine Island Sound are located on the gulf coast of Florida in Lee County. Approximately 120 miles south of Tampa, this diverse region is comprised of mangrove estuaries, lush grass flats, barrier islands and gulf waters. The area is a birdwatcher's paradise and one of the top three shelling destinations in the world. Nearby population centers include Fort Myers, Sanibel Island, Cape Coral, Pine Island and Fort Myers Beach. Access is easy, with Interstate 75 and the Southwest International Airport located just to the east of Fort Myers.

There is a wide range of accommodations nearby, from the very modest to exclusive island resorts. There are also campgrounds in all parts of the county. Boat, canoe and kayak rentals and charter fishing are readily available. Convenient boat-launching ramps are located at Punta Rassa, Matlacha, Sanibel, and Pine Island, as shown on the enclosed map. Fishing from shore can often be productive; areas that have easy accessibility for land- and canoe-based anglers include Sanibel beaches, Sanibel causeway islands, Sanibel's Ding Darling National Wildlife Refuge, Bunche Beach, Estero Island Beach, Blind Pass, Big Carlos Pass, New Pass and Big Hickory Pass. Don't be surprised to see a variety of species caught in the same area. Spotted seatrout, jack crevalle, ladyfish, pompano, Spanish mackerel, snook, redfish, flounder and even tarpon can be within a cast from shore. Local guides and fly shops are listed on the enclosed tables.

An 8- or 9-weight rod/reel/line outfit is ideal for 75% of the fly-fishing in this area. We use larger equipment when targeting tarpon or when extra pressure is needed to turn fish away from structure after hooking. Ten- and 12-weight outfits are also used offshore for kingfish or other larger quarry such as cobia, monster snook or even grouper. A floating line is quite satisfactory most of the time, however a sink-tip or intermediate-density line may be needed in deeper and fast-moving water. The fly reel must have a good-quality drag system. You never know what you will hook on your next cast. It is a good idea to have at least 200 yards of line backing on your reel to be prepared for long fish runs. Several of our game fish have teeth or a very abrasive mouth and thus a shock tippet of 30-50 pounds is often needed. If I'm targeting pompano or redfish exclusively, I'll simply use a leader tippet of 10-15 pounds strength.

With regard to recommended flies, there are several types which I nearly always carry. The first is a Clouser Minnow, tied in color combinations of chartreuse and white, pink and white, brown and white and all white. Size variations can be covered by hooks ranging from size 1 to 4. Chartreuse and white Deceivers tied on size 1 hooks also work quite well. Yellow and red Seaducers tied on size 1 hooks are also important. With our vast grass flats, we encounter tailing redfish on the lower tides, which presents great opportunities for sight-casting. Lately, I have had quite a bit of success with Muddler-type flies tied on size 1 and 2 hooks. Brown and white, yellow and red, and black and white are good color combinations. A craft fur shrimp pattern tied on size 1, 2 and 4 hook with a double-mono weedguard has also been very effective.

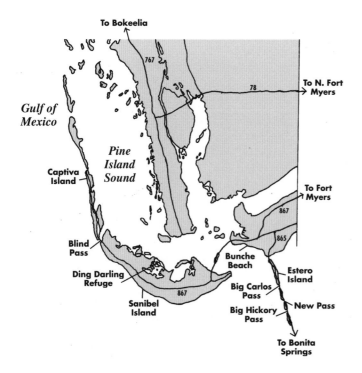

Species	Typical Size	J	F	M	A	M	J	J	A	S	O	N	D
Jack Crevalle	12 - 30 inches	3	3	4	4	4	5	5	5	5	5	4	4
Ladyfish	15 - 24 inches	5	5	4	4	4	3	3	3	5	5	5	5
Pompano	10 - 16 inches	5	5	5	5	4	4	4	3	3	4	4	5
Redfish	16 - 34 inches	4	4	5	5	5	5	5	5	5	5	5	4
Snook	15 - 40 inches	3	3	4	5	5	5	5	5	5	5	4	3
Spanish Mackerel	15 - 25 inches	4	4	5	5	4	4	3	3	4	5	5	4
Spotted Seatrout	12 - 20 inches	5	5	5	5	5	4	3	4	4	5	5	5
Tarpon	25 - 150 pounds	1	1	3	4	4	4	3	3	3	2	1	1

1=Scarce, 2=Spotty, 3=Available, 4=Readily Available, 5=Widely Available

I use weedguards on all my patterns when I'm fishing tailing fish in the grass. A 20-pound mono guard gives me enough protection to slide through the grass without being so stiff as to act as a "fish guard".

The water in the Sound becomes crystal clear as the rains subside in November, which allows for great sight-casting when the water is too deep for spotting tailing fish. Snook, redfish and trout are the main targets along the shorelines and potholes. One can also drift or pole the deeper grass flats and blind cast. The miles of mangrove shoreline and many oyster bars are also great places to cast the edges, since these are also great ambush spots for predatory game fish.

April, May and June means it's tarpon time. The silver kings arrive in great numbers along the gulf beaches and backcountry flats. The average size of these fish is 75 pounds, with fish well over 150 pounds in every school. Eleven- to 12-weight outfits are a must, together with a silky smooth reel drags and line backing up to 300 yards. We literally hunt the fish until located, and then use electric trolling motors to approach them. An 80-pound shock tippet is the minimum used. Successful flies include the Cockroach, crab patterns and other standard patterns. Most of the local guides use 3/0 top-quality hooks for the tarpon flies.

Local game fish feed on three main types of food; shrimp, crabs and baitfish (minnows). Shrimp species include grass shrimp, rock shrimp, and common shrimp. The crabs include blue crabs, mud crabs and stone crabs. Baitfish prey include pinfish, mutton minnows, mullet, pilchards, glass minnows and threadfin herring. I feel that the most important factors in "matching the hatch" are size, shape and color or shade. I'm not concerned about tying an exact replica of the living prey. Silhouette and size are the main keys. The enclosed chart lists the principal prey species and accompanying fly patterns.

Captain Dave Gibson has been a resident of the Sanibel area since 1979 and a full-time fishing guide since 1986. Dave is presently on the pro staff for the Diamondback and Cortland companies and for Harris fly reels. An accomplished fly-casting instructor and fly tier, Dave also has given lectures and seminars from Marco Island, Florida to Chicago, Illinois. His video "Flycasting for Redfish" is quite popular and he has also appeared on local television programs.

Most Common Prey	Typical Size-Inches	Usual Months of Availability*												Typical Matching Fly Patterns**
		J	F	M	A	M	J	J	A	S	O	N	D	
Crabs	2 - 4	5	5	5	5	5	5	5	5	5	5	5	5	Slider
Finger Mullet	1 - 4.	3	3	4	5	5	5	5	5	5	4	3	2	Lefty's Deceiver (B)
Glass Minnow	0.25 - 1.5	2	2	3	4	5	5	5	5	5	5	4	3	Mini Clouser, Mini Deceiver
Pilchard	2 - 5	3	3	5	5	5	5	5	5	5	5	5	5	Lefty's Deceiver (C), Clouser Minnow
Shrimp	2 - 4	5	5	5	5	5	5	5	5	5	5	5	5	Craft Fur Shrimp
Threadfin Herring	3 - 6	2	2	4	5	5	5	5	5	5	4	2	2	Lefty's Deceiver (C), Clouser Minnow

*1=Scarce, 2=Spotty, 3=Available, 4=Readily Available, 5=Widely Available • ** Pattern Recipe in Appendix A.

Chapter 33: Boca Grande & Charlotte Harbor
By Capt. Peter Greenan

Known as the tarpon capital of the world, this pristine estuary presents Florida at its best. Local National Wildlife Refuges covers approximately 85 square miles of mangrove islands and extensive grass flats. Pods of bottle-nosed dolphins, families of manatees and nesting sea turtles are regularly observed. Fly fishers here seek tarpon, snook, redfish, cobia, seatrout and more. The accompanying chart denotes the best season for each species. The many grass flats and oyster bars hold several varieties of shrimp, crabs and bait fish. The area is also home to seven types of herons, four species of egrets, ibis, oyster catchers, osprey and eagles. In addition, winter brings a huge migration of white pelicans from the far north.

Fly fishing is available whether the angler is in a boat or wading. Because of the shallow water and large area a guide is recommended. Several experienced fly-fishing guides are listed for you. Boats can be rented from many places including; Captiva Island, Boca Grande (Gasparilla Island) and Punta Gorda. Kyaking and canoeing are both popular here and both types of craft can be rented at these same locations. Wade fishermen can access the beaches along the Gulf of Mexico at any public beach on all islands. Few locations are appropriate for shore wading in our bays, with the exception of the old railroad trestle at Boca Grande. Here, fly-fishers can get in the water and cover a large area of good flats and potholes. Anglers with boats may launch free at Placida and Punta Gorda public ramps, and at the marina facilities at Boca Grande, Placida, Pineland, St. James City and Captiva Island. Many of these locations also have fine waterside restaurants, hotel accommodations, fuel docks and ship stores.

Additionally, we are blessed with several out-islands that are only accessible by boat. These unique locations include North Captiva Island, Cabbage Key, Useppa Island and Palm Island. All of these islands have accommodations and restaurants. Also, the out-island of Cayo Costa (La Costa) at Boca Grande Pass is primarily a state park and has overnight cabins and hiking opportunities.

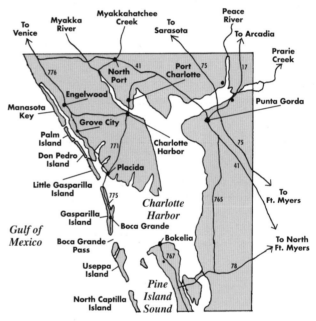

Species	Typical Size - Pounds	J	F	M	A	M	J	J	A	S	O	N	D
Cobia	2 - 15	2	2	3	4	5	5	5	5	4	4	3	2
Jack Crevalle	2 - 12	4	4	4	4	5	5	5	5	5	5	4	4
Ladyfish	2 - 3	5	5	5	5	5	5	5	5	5	5	5	5
Redfish	2 - 5	5	5	5	5	5	4	4	4	5	5	5	5
Seatrout	1 - 2	5	5	5	5	5	5	4	4	5	5	5	5
Snook	2 - 6	2	3	4	5	5	5	5	5	5	5	4	3
Spanish Mackerel	1 - 2	2	2	3	4	4	4	4	4	4	4	3	2
Tarpon	25 - 100	1	1	1	3	5	5	5	5	4	3	2	1

1=Scarce, 2=Spotty, 3=Available, 4=Readily Available, 5=Widely Available

Photo by Capt. Mike Holliday

A "baby" tarpon. Photo by Capt. David Kreshpane

Keys bonefish. Photo by Capt. Lenny Moffo

Big snook. Photo by Capt. Dave Gibson

Skipjack tuna. Photo by Capt. John Killen

Mangrove snapper. Photo by Capt. David Kreshpane

The toothy barracuda. Photo by Capt. Lenny Moffo

A nice weakfish. Photo by Lou Tabory

Bluefish. Photo by Capt. Brian Horsley

Scanning the horizon. Photo by Peter Alves.

Bonito. Photo by Capt. Mike Roback

False albacore. Photo by Capt. Joe Shute

Alabama redfish. Photo by Capt. Rick Haag

The elusive cobia. Photo by Capt. Mike Holliday

Rainbow over Charleston Harbor. Photo by Capt. Jerry Ciandella

Monomoy striped bass. Photo by Peter Alves

The joy of a big red. Photo by Capt. Rick Haag

A calm creek in North Carolina. Photo by Capt. Brian Horsley

World-record jack crevalle. Photo by Stephen Ross

Bluefish blitz at Montauk. Photo by Capt. Paul Dixon

Barracuda. Photo by Capt. Lenny Moffo

NY harbor bluefish. Photo by Capt. Joe Shastay

Holding still at sunrise. Photo by Capt. Larry Kennedy

Feeding birds near a Louisiana tidal drain. Photo by Capt. Kirby Lacour

Guides' favorite flies
Large Favorites of the Northeast

Moriches Mouthful
Capt. John Killen

Grocery Fly (A)
Capt. Doug Jowett

Barry's Holy Mackerel
Capt. Barry Clemson

KZ Squid
Capt. Mike Roback

Northeast Favorites for Stripers and Bluefish

Sar-Mul-Mac
Capt. Mike Bartlett

Haag's Glimmer Bunker
Capt. Paul Dixon

Rhody Flat Wing
Capt. Eric Thomas

Monomoy Flatwing
Peter Alves

Roccus Rattle (B)
Capt. Bill Strakele

Atlantic States Favorites

EJ's Sparkle Fly
Ed Broderick

Dave's Wide Side
Capt. Dick Dennis

Al's Glass Minnow
Capt. Al Edwards

Cave's Rattlin Minnow
Capt. Richard Stuhr

Chesapeake Fly
Capt. Norm Bartlett

Copperhead
Capt. Randy Hamilton

Cactus Striper
Capt. Kevin Josenhans

Woolly Bugger Express
Capt. Larry Kennedy

Phantom Mullet
Chris Goldmark

Florida Favorites

Lenny's Tarpon Shrimp
Capt. Lenny Moffo

Red-Hot Rat-Tail
Capt. Dave Kreshpane

Barry's Dumdrum
Capt. Barry Hoffman

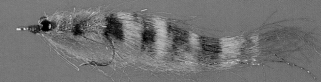

Craft Fur Shrimp
Capt. Dave Gibson

Eat-Em
Capt. Mike Holliday

Chernobyl Crab
Capt. Chris Asaro

Greenan's Shrimp
Capt. Pete Greenan

Matt's 40
Capt. Matt Hoover

Gulf States Favorites

Kirby's Kosmic Killer
Capt. Kirby Lacour

Estaz Borski Shrimp
Capt. Eric Glass

Scates Shrimp
Capt. Sally Moffett

Texas Tout Fly
Capt. Chuck Uzzle

Phillips Header
Capt. Chris Phillips

Middle Bay Eel
Capt. Rick Haag

Favorite Clousers

Clouser Deep Minnow (N)
Capt. Tom Mleczko

Clouser Deep Minnow (I)
Capt. Joe Shastay

Clouser Deep Minnow (C)
Capt. Mitch Chagnon

Clouser Deep Minnow (F)
Capt. Joe Shute

Dave's Seminole Clouser
Dave Settoon

Clouser Deep Minnow (P)
Capt. Ian Devlin

Clouser Deep Minnow (E)
Capts. Sara Gardner & Brian Horsley

Clouser Deep Minnow (M)
Capt. Jeff Poe

Clouser Deep Minnow (G)
Capt. Fred Lynch

Clouser Deep Minnow (B)
Capt. Dan Malzone

The Boca Grande/Charlotte Harbor area is divided into three distinct segments; the backcountry including all the shallow flats behind and between the mangrove islands, the outside, near harbor edges, bars and islands, and the beaches on the numerous barrier islands along the Gulf of Mexico. Water temperature, tides and winds all determine where you should fish on a given day. Certain species are found in each area during different seasons of the year. Here are a few examples. Tarpon are in the backcountry in early spring and are in the gulf and passes during summer. Snook are in the deep backcountry and creeks in winter and off the beaches in the summer. Redfish are in the deep backcountry in winter and on the outside in the summer.

The most common rod in our area is a 9-footer for 8-weight. Some species require special rods. Tarpon are often in the 100-plus-pound range and we use 11- or 12-weight fast-action rods with fighting grips. Sink-tip or intermediate-density sinking lines are preferred for the "silver king." Ladyfish, seatrout and Spanish mackerel can be handled easily on a 5- or 6-weight rod with a floating line. A popular method of snook fishing is night fishing under the lights. A good 8-weight with floating line is appropriate for this type of fly-fishing. In the winter, tailing redfish are on open flats in clear, very shallow water. A delicate presentation with a light rod and long leader is in order under these circumstances. Since the fish can run a long distance without any danger of losing him, a 6-weight rod works well, even on 1- to 12-pound fish.

Here are some hints for catching fish in our neighborhood. Fish for crustacean feeders like redfish, pompano and permit on a rising tide. They are looking for their groceries in the grass and mud of newly covered flats. Baitfish feeders like snook and seatrout have more success finding food when the baitfish bunch up at the bottom of the outgoing tide. When in doubt try a chartreuse fly. For some reason our fish seem to see that color best. A good axiom for redfish is "make it brown and get it down." The enclosed chart contains more information on the species and availability of our local prey, as well as some of the fly patterns that have often proven to be successful. Our local fly shops, list-ed on the accompanying chart, can be quite helpful in answering many of your questions.

Boca Grande Outfitters
P.O. Box 1799
Boca Grande, FL 33921
Contact: Zeke Sieglaff
941-964-2445/941-964-2447
tarpon@ewol/com

Economy Tackle
6018 S. Tamiami Trail
Sarasota, FL 34231
Contact: Mark Goodwin
941-922-9671
hurxthal@netsrq.com

Lehr's Economy
1366 N. Tamiami Trail
Ft. Meyers, FL 33903
Contact: Dave Westra
941-995-2280

Guides(Capt.)	Phone/Fax	E-mail
Denny Blue	941-624-2923	
Pete Greenan	941-923-6095	capt.petegreenan@worldnet.att.net
Ed Hurst	941-349-2086	reelfree@gte.net
Tommy Locke	941-964-0083	tlocke@floridaflyfishing.com
Scott Moore	941-778-3005	scott@floridaflyfishing.com
Brandon Naeve	941-966-4112	brandon@floridaflyfishing.com
Zeke Sieglaff	941-964-2445	tarpon@ewol.com
Roy String	941-379-5083	roy@floridaflyfishing.com

Captain Pete Greenan grew up fly-fishing the streams of New England and New York state for trout. While on vacation in Florida, Pete caught the saltwater fever, decided to become a guide and has been pursuing this dream ever since. Pete has been fly-fishing for 47 years and has been guiding and teaching others for 19 years. He is the owner of the Gypsy Guide  *Service and the Boca Grande Fly Fishing Schools and appears regularly at national fly-fishing shows and international sportsmen's expositions. Capt. Pete has hosted the "Sarasota Saltwater" TV show and was a founding officer for the Mangrove Coast Fly Fishers and the Sarasota chapter of the Coastal Conservation Association. In addition, he has been active in the Connecticut Fly Fisherman's Association, the Federation of Fly Fishers, Trout Unlimited and Ducks Unlimited.*

Most Common Prey	Typical Size (inches)	Usual Months of Availability*												Typical Matching Fly Patterns**
		J	F	M	A	M	J	J	A	S	O	N	D	
Crabs	2 - 4	1	1	2	3	5	5	5	5	4	3	2	1	Phil's Tarpon Crab, Pell Tarpon Fly, Cockroach
Glass Minnows	1 - 4	2	3	4	5	5	5	5	5	5	5	4	4	Gray Blonde, Clouser Deep Minnow (J)
Pilchards	2 - 5	1	1	3	4	5	5	5	5	5	5	4	4	Lefty's Deceiver (Q), Clouser Deep Minnow (J)
Pinfish	2 - 4	3	3	4	5	5	5	5	5	5	5	5	4	Grizzly Bead-Head, Pink/Grizzly Tarpon
Shrimp	2 - 4	5	5	5	5	5	4	3	3	3	4	5	5	Greenan's Shrimp, Greenan's Redfish, Rattlin' Rose
Threadfin Shad	2 - 6	1	1	2	3	4	5	5	5	4	3	2	1	Lefty's Deceiver (Q)

*1=Scarce, 2=Spotty, 3=Available, 4=Readily Available, 5=Widely Available • ** Pattern Recipe in Appendix A.

Chapter 34: Tampa Bay

by Capt. Dan Malzone

Tampa Bay, Florida's largest open-water estuary, stretches to an area of 398 square miles at high tide. Popular for sports and recreation, the bay also supports one of the world's most productive natural ecosystems. Estuaries like Tampa Bay, where salt water from the sea mixes with fresh water from rivers and upland drainage, are nurseries for young fish, shrimp and crabs. More than 70 percent of all finfish, shellfish and crustaceans spend critical stages of their development in these nearshore waters, protected from larger predators that swim in the open sea. Wildlife abounds along the shores of Tampa Bay. As many as 50,000 pairs of birds, from the brown pelican to the colorful roseate spoonbill, nest in Tampa Bay every year. Many other species, like the white pelicans and the sandpipers, are seasonal visitors.

Tampa Bay consists of four distinct areas; the Gulf, the upper, the lower, and the middle regions. In the lower region at the mouth of the bay, Fort DeSoto Park to the north and Terra Ceia Bay to the south are both aquatic preserves with no-motor zones. These are some of the best wading flats in Florida and large schools of redfish, seatrout and jack crevalle are common. Since the adoption of the state inshore net ban, it's also not uncommon to see tailing permit on these flats. All fish coming into Tampa Bay must pass by one of these two flats. Tailing redfish in these areas rate as the supreme fly-rod challenge. The middle region is bounded by Pinellas Point and Weedon Island to the west and the Cockroach Bay Aquatic Preserve to the east. This region of the bay has two of greater Tampa's largest power plants, one on each side of the bay. In the winter, these power plants produce a warmwater outflow which attracts large schools of jack crevalle, tarpon, cobia and ladyfish seeking the comfort of the warmer waters. To some extent, this is somewhat like fishing in a goldfish bowl! During the warmer months, these same fish move out onto the flats, where they make great targets for sight-fishing.

The upper part of the bay is probably the least fished of all four regions. Water clarity can be a problem in the summer because of the influx of silt from the rivers during the frequent rainstorms. Visibility improves during the winter, but wade fishing is difficult because of the soft bay bottom. Nevertheless, there are plenty of fish in this region year-round, for those willing to do lots of blind-casting. This is one of the best areas in Tampa Bay to catch large snook.

The gulf coast region is a mecca for the fly-fisherman seeking multiple species from a boat. Large schools of king mackerel, Spanish mackerel, tuna, bonito, and redfish abound nearshore. Early morning shoreline wading for snook is a popular pastime for the fly-fisherman, during the summer when these superb game fish are in their spawning season. The enclosed table lists the major gamefish species of Tampa Bay and their months of greatest availability.

The land mass surrounding Tampa Bay is a major metropolitan area, with many restaurants and accommodations available to suit a wide range of tastes and pocketbooks. The state of Florida provides a large array of

Species	Typical Size	J	F	M	A	M	J	J	A	S	O	N	D
Cobia	20 - 60 pounds	1	1	2	3	3	4	4	3	2	1	1	1
Jack Crevalle	2 - 15 pounds	2	2	3	4	4	5	5	4	3	2	2	2
Ladyfish	1 - 4 pounds	2	2	3	4	4	5	5	4	3	2	2	2
Permit	12 - 35 inches	1	1	1	2	2	3	4	4	3	2	1	1
Redfish (Red Drum)	18 - 21 inches	2	3	5	5	5	5	4	4	4	3	3	2
Seatrout	12 - 27 inches	4	4	5	5	4	4	2	1	2	3	4	4
Snook	3 - 30 pounds	1	1	2	3	5	5	5	5	4	2	1	1
Tarpon	50 - 150 pounds	1	1	1	1	5	5	5	4	3	2	1	1

1=Scarce, 2=Spotty, 3=Available, 4=Readily Available, 5=Widely Available

publications of interest to the visiting fly-fisherman, including a map of Tampa Bay's boat ramps, sea grass areas, no-motor zones and aquatic preserves. As shown on the enclosed table, several fly shops are available to serve the needs of the fly-fisher. Also, a number of very well-qualified fly-fishing guides are listed below.

The standard fly-fishing outfit for Tampa Bay is a nine-foot for 7- or 8-weight line. Weight-forward, floating lines are usually best, although clear, sink-tip lines can often be useful for deeper runs. Tapered leaders, 8 to 12 feet in length will cover most circumstances, with 10- to 15-pound tippets. If pursuing tarpon, 12- to 13-weight outfits are needed, as well as 60-pound (or more) shock tippets and high-quality reels with considerable backing capacity. The prey species most common in Tampa Bay are shown on the enclosed table, together with some of the imitative fly patterns that have proven to be productive. Most flies are tied on size 2, 1, or 1/0 hooks

Rodbenders
207 11th St.
Tampa, FL 33602
Contact: Dan McKinney
813-223-7754
mail@rodbenders.com

Saltwater Fly Fisherman
623 Cleveland St.
Clearwater, FL 337555
Contact: John Homer
727-443-5000
flyrodz@concentric.net

World Class Outfitters
13911 N. Dale Mabry
Tampa, FL 33618
Contact: Dave Westra
941-995-2280

Guides (Capt.)	Phone/Fax	E-mail
Capt. Buddy	813-253-2878	captbuddy@saltwater-fly-fishing.com
Al Dopirak	727-785-7774	
Dan Malzone	813-831-4052	capt.dan.malzone@worldnet.att.net
Tom Mohler	727-577-7036	tarpon12wt@aol.com
Russ Shirley	727-343-1957	
Neil Siguarsin	727-786-6431	

Capt. Dan Malzone started fly-fishing in the early 1960s in fresh water, and moved to saltwater fly-fishing in the late 1960s. He was one of the early pioneers of fly-fishing for tarpon at Homosassa, where he learned the art under the tutelage of Capt. Gary Maconi and Norman Duncan (of the Duncan LoopKnot fame).

Dan is a three-time winner of the MET Fishing Tournament, Fly Division, for mackerel, seatrout and mutton snapper. He is also a two-time IGFA world-record holder for fly-caught tarpon, and has guided Dr. Clyde Balch of Naples to an IGFA world record for tarpon on a fly. Capt. Malzone also guided his wife at the Hillsborough Tarpon Tournament, where she was cited for the largest tarpon (ladies division), overall tournament champion, most releases and combined weight champion. Dan is a member of the IGFA, the Florida Outdoor Writers Association, the Florida Keys Guides Association, the Miami Rod & Reel Club, and the Coastal Conservation Association of Florida. He is sponsored by Mercury Marine, Maverick Boats and is an Orvis-endorsed guide for the west coast of Florida.

Most Common Prey	Typical Size (inches)	Usual Months of Availability*												Typical Matching Fly Patterns**
---	---	J	F	M	A	M	J	J	A	S	O	N	D	---
Crabs	1 - 3	5	5	5	5	5	5	5	5	5	5	5	5	Del Brown's Permit Fly
Finger Mullet	4 - 6	2	2	3	4	4	5	5	5	5	4	3	2	Woolhead Mullet
Glass Minnows	1 - 2	1	1	3	4	5	5	5	5	5	4	3	1	Epoxy Glass Minnow
Sardines	2 - 5	1	1	3	4	5	5	5	5	5	4	3	1	Lefty's Deceiver (C)
Shrimp	2 - 4	5	5	5	5	5	5	5	5	5	5	5	5	Guide's Bunny, Clouser Deep Minnow (B)

*1=Scarce, 2=Spotty, 3=Available, 4=Readily Available, 5=Widely Available • ** Pattern Recipe in Appendix A.

Chapter 35: Santa Rosa Sound and the Gulf Islands National Seashore
by Dave Settoon

Welcome to the Emerald Coast, a piece of heaven between Destin and Pensacola, Florida. There are approximately 70 miles of white sand beaches, anchored by Choctawhatchee and Pensacola bays. Between the two bays is Santa Rosa Island, a barrier island, and Santa Rosa Sound. Destin, known as the "luckiest fishing village," has one of the largest fleets in Florida and is nestled in the mouth of Choctawhatchee Bay. There are two jetties at the East Pass. The East Jetty is the longest and is known for its great fishing. Along the sandy beaches are miles of wadable water, with opportunities to catch ladyfish, bluefish, cobia, Spanish mackerel, jack crevalle, pompano and redfish. When fishing Choctawhatchee Bay, it is best to hire a guide, because most of the bay is too soft for wading. Destin is a full-service resort community with many restaurants and accommodations ranging from campgrounds and RV parks to high-rise condos. Destin also has facilities available for boat, canoe and kayak rentals.

About a 45-minute drive to the west from Destin lies Santa Rosa Sound and the Gulf Island National Seashore area, my favorite place to fly-fish. The sound side is a great place for the wading fly-fisher; it has miles of grass flats, channels, coves and sandbars. Spotted seatrout, red-fish, ladyfish and jack crevalle are readily available in the sound. Across the road, there are many miles of beaches where ladyfish, pompano, Spanish mackerel, and jack crevalle roam from spring to late fall. Further west is Fort Pickens, at the junction of Pensacola Bay and Santa Rosa Sound. The West Pass is larger than its counterpart at Destin. Fort Pickens has miles of beaches for fishing, but also sand dunes to explore, museums, civil war forts, bicycle paths, picnic facilities, camping areas, etc.

Fishing in the Santa Rosa Sound area is quite seasonal, with the best fishing times between March and late November. A 9-foot, 8-weight fly rod is ideal for the back bays, together with a matched weight-forward floating line and a nine-foot leader. I prefer a 12-pound tippet for seatrout. Nine- and 10-weight outfits will often be needed on the beach to permit casting into the wind, and a weight-forward intermediate-density line is preferred to get below the wave action. Shorter leaders are practical on the beach, but at least a foot of 25- to 30-pound shock tippet is required because of the abrasive mouths of many of our gamefish. A good saltwater fly reel with a capacity for about 200 yards of 30-pound backing is appropriate for most of our game fish off the beach or in the backbay.

There are many different species of prey in this region, with finger mullet, pinfish, menhaden, pilchards, shrimp, crabs and sandfleas being the most important. The two flies that I use most often are the Seminole Clouser and the Ballyhoo Clouser. The Seminole Clouser is most productive for the back bay; the spotted seatrout and redfish can't seem to get enough of the gold flash. The Ballyhoo Clouser is

Species	Typical Size - Pounds	J	F	M	A	M	J	J	A	S	O	N	D
Bluefish	1 - 3	5	5	4	4	4	4	4	4	5	5	5	5
Jack Crevalle	3 - 30	3	3	4	4	5	5	5	5	5	4	4	3
Ladyfish	2 - 3	2	2	3	4	5	5	5	5	5	4	3	2
Pompano	2 - 3	1	2	2	3	5	5	4	4	5	5	4	2
Redfish	2 - 25	3	3	3	4	4	4	4	5	5	5	4	4
Spanish Mackerel	2 - 3	1	2	2	3	4	5	5	4	4	5	4	3
Spotted Seatrout	1.5 - 8.0	3	3	4	5	5	5	5	5	5	4	4	3

1=Scarce, 2=Spotty, 3=Available, 4=Readily Available, 5=Widely Available

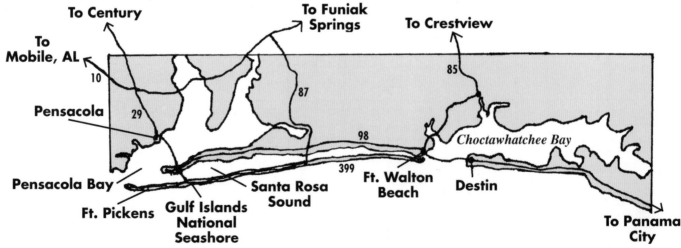

great off the beach for ladyfish, bluefish, Spanish mackerel, bonito and small jack crevalle. Both Clousers are usually tied on a size 2 long-shank hook. Large jack crevalle like a mouthful; thus, Deceivers 4-6 inches long on 1/0 and 2/0 hooks and large poppers and divers are needed for these formidable game fish. These same flies will often work very well during our spring cobia run. In late spring, the pompano run is in full swing and these schooling fish can usually be found in the breaking waves off the beach. Any small bonefish pattern, on a size 4 to 6 hook, should work well. The Absolute Flea pattern is also a good choice for pompano.

Guides (Capt.)	Phone/Fax	E-mail
Paul Darby	850-651-2991	fishnlady@aol.com
Pat Dineen	850-609-0528	Flyliner@aol.com
Joy Dunlap	850-837-8401	papajoyflys@aol.com
Dave Settoon	850-939-4116	
Alan Steele	850-650-6968/	
	877-321-3474	

Blue Bay Outfitters
47 Hwy 98 East
Destin, FL 32541
Contact: Alan & Lousie Steele
850-650-6968/877-321-3474
mail@rodbenders.com

Destin Fly Company
500 E. Hwy 98
Destin, FL 32541
Contact: Joy Dunlap
850-650-1886
papajoyflys@aol.com

Quality Reel Repair
100 Old Ferry Rd.
Shalimar, FL 32579
Contact: Paul & Paula Darby
850-651-2991
fishnlady1@aol.com

Dave Settoon has been living and fishing in northwest Florida for 19 years. He is a store manager for Sockeye's Beach and Sport, with expertise in the full-line Orvis fishing department. Dave has been a fly-fishing guide specializing in wade fishing and teaching fly-fishing for three years. He is a founding member of the Panhandle Fly Fishing Club and provides a weekly fishing report to the Northwest Florida Daily News.

Most Common Prey	Typical Size (inches)	J	F	M	A	M	J	J	A	S	O	N	D	Typical Matching Fly Patterns**
Bay Anchovies	1 - 2	5	5	5	5	5	5	5	5	5	5	5	5	Ballyhoo Clouser
Crabs	1	5	5	5	5	5	5	5	5	5	5	5	5	Del Brown's Permit Fly
Finger Mullet	2 - 4	4	4	4	5	5	5	5	5	4	4	4	4	Woolhead Mullet, Pencil Popper
Glass Minnows	1 - 2	5	5	5	5	5	5	5	5	5	5	5	5	Ballyhoo Clouser
Menhaden	2 - 6	4	4	5	5	5	5	5	5	5	5	4	4	Lefty's Deceiver (P), Pencil Popper
Pilchards	3 - 6	2	2	3	4	5	5	5	5	5	4	3	3	Lefty's Deceiver (E), Hot Butt Bendback
Sand Fleas	1	4	4	5	5	5	5	5	5	5	5	4	4	Absolute Flea
Shrimp	2 - 4	5	5	5	5	5	5	5	5	5	5	5	5	Dave's Seminole Clouser, Cockroach
General														Clouser Deep Minnow (A)

*1=Scarce, 2=Spotty, 3=Available, 4=Readily Available, 5=Widely Available • ** Pattern Recipe in Appendix A.

The Gulf States

Chapter	Destination . . . . .Author/Guide

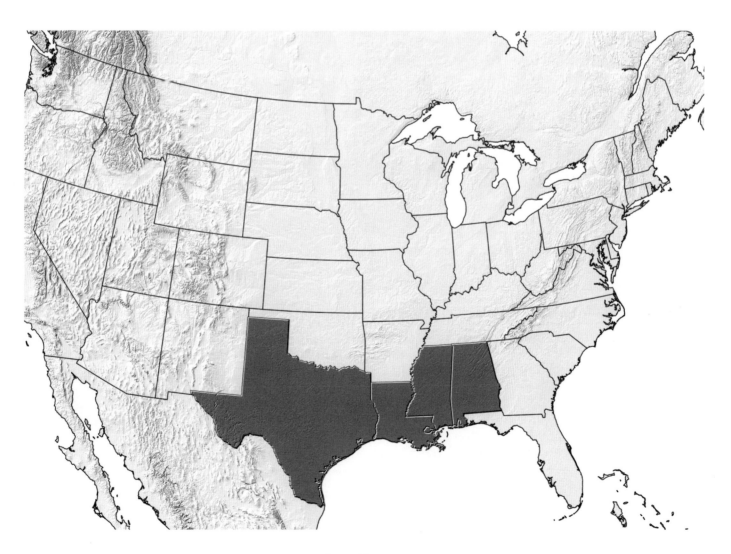

Chapter 36: Orange Beach and the Alabama Gulf Coast

By Capt. Rick Haag

The Alabama Gulf Coast is a geographically short but biologically diverse area. The total coastline is roughly sixty miles long. This small area harbors a broad range of fishing opportunities. The heart of this country is the Mobile Bay Delta and the rivers that feed it. The coastline includes the resort town of Orange Beach, the lightly developed Fort Morgan Peninsula and the City of Mobile. This area's fishery ranges from the migratory Gulf species at or near the numerous offshore oilrigs, to the shallow-water species found in the estuaries, bays, creeks, grass flats and in the fresh waters of the upper Delta system.

There are plenty of places to launch a boat, a kayak or to try your hand at wading. State parks and National Seashore preserves offer some of the most accessible fishing to the fly-fisher on foot. The town of Orange Beach offers many types of accommodations ranging from budget motels to four-star resorts. There is also plenty of shopping, snow-white beaches, and golf for those who would rather not fish. Fly-fishers need only the skills of the sport and a little creativity to open up a world of fishing that many have never seen. Below, I have prepared a calendar-oriented summary of what species are available, when and where the fishing is at its best, and some of the techniques needed to catch fish on the fly. Please refer to the accompanying charts for additional information.

January/February: The upper Gulf is chilly at this time of year, with daytime air and water temperatures in the mid-fifties. Inshore, speckled trout can be found in their winter haunts; namely the deep holes in the area's rivers and creeks. Trout become sluggish in cold water so your presentation must be slow. A 5-weight to 8-weight rod is used, usually with a clear, intermediate-density fly line, and a moderately heavy Clouser minnow with lots of flash. The preferred colors of choice are olive/white and pink/white. One should locate deep pockets, cast across them, and after letting the fly sink at least three-fourths of the way to the bottom, start a slow steady retrieve. Out in the Gulf, bluefish can be found around the nearshore oil platforms; use a flashy Clouser minnow, and strip it in fast. Red and mangrove snapper also can be chummed up to take a fly; I use a white bushy fly and a 10-weight outfit for these brutes. An IGFA fly record for red snapper will soon come from this area.

March/April/May: These months represent a transition period. As the water slowly warms, the trout begin to venture out of the rivers to search for food. Look for them in the lower bays, but not too far from deep water. April brings migrating cobia in world-record sizes. Several fish over 90 pounds are caught each spring. You will need a boat, preferably with a tower, since this is truly sight fishing. You will find them near the surface, swimming from east to west, about a mile and a half or less from shore. Take along a 10- to 12-weight rod, and a reel with a good drag, because these fish are large and strong. Large, flashy flies with a sharp 3/0 hook are the norm; Zonker strip eel patterns can work when all others fail.

In May, the migratory fish start to show, including Spanish, and king mackerel, false albacore, (locally called bonita) and more bluefish. Spanish mackerel and bluefish can be found around schools of bait, and they will pounce on a fast-moving, size 1 minnow pattern when cast into a school of feeding fish. Match the hatch, and stick to natural colors. Do not forget a bite tippet of either 40-pound monofilament or size 2 wire, or you will

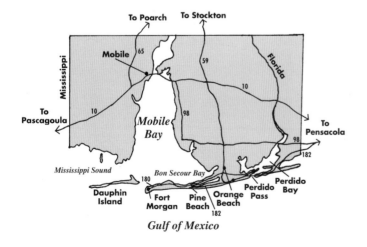

Gulf of Mexico

Species	Typical Size - Pounds	J	F	M	A	M	J	J	A	S	O	N	D
Bluefish	1 - 7	2	2	3	3	4	5	5	5	5	3	2	2
Cobia	10 - 125			2	5	5	4	3	3	3	2	1	
Ladyfish	1 - 4			1	2	3	5	5	5	5	4	1	
Pompano	1 - 5			2	5	5	3	3	3	3	1		
Redfish	2 - 25	3	2	2	2	3	3	3	3	4	5	5	5
Red/Mangrove Snapper	3 - 25	3	3	4	5	5	5	5	4	4	4	4	3
Spanish/King Mackerel	1 - 50			1	2	3	5	5	5	5	4	1	
Speckled Trout	1 - 7	2	2	3	3	4	5	5	5	5	3	2	2
Tarpon	10 - 150						2	3	4	4	1		

1=Scarce, 2=Spotty, 3=Available, 4=Readily Available, 5=Widely Available

lose a lot of flies. Strip your fly fast, and hold on. A 6-weight rod will do the trick for this fishing. False albacore can be really picky. I use no more than a 12-pound fluorocarbon bite tippet and a size 2 or smaller minnow pattern. These fish will hit your fly running, so keep your reel clear, and you will be in the backing before you can blink an eye. In is suggested that you use an 8-weight outfit and a good-quality reel. Pompano can be caught around the passes with small, bright-colored, heavy Clouser Minnows. A sinking fly line is required, and a clear incoming tide is preferable.

June/July/August: Mid-summer is wide open, with all migratory fish available. Trout are thick on the grass flats and around the dock lights at night. Ladyfish will be gorging themselves on anchovies right in the surf. Bluefish are near any structure you can find and acres of false albacore and Spanish mackerel are in the near shore waters of the Gulf, eating anything that gets in their way. August is the time of the year to catch tarpon in Alabama. They can be found cruising the beach less than a half mile offshore. Menhaden flies work well in the more natural colors. Jack crevalle can be found around the near shore shrimp boats; just look for the feeding birds and you will find the fish. Expect a long battle on a 10-weight rod.

September through December: Fall brings giant redfish to the beaches. Follow the birds by boat and use a 10-weight rod with a 400-grain sinking line, working the bait and bird blitzes. Catching ten reds in the morning is not uncommon on days after a cold front. These redfish are generally between 35 and 42 inches long, and weigh in the neighborhood of 20 pounds. This is our most undiscovered fly-fishery and is something to behold, with schools of redfish as large as an acre in area.

Sport fishing has a long history on this stretch of the Gulf Coast, but fly-fishing is relatively new. Currently, there are only a few guides in this vicinity who are adept at guiding fly-fishers. The accompanying charts list these guides and also the fly shops capable of assisting the visiting fly-fisher.

Guides (Capt.)	Phone/Fax	E-mail
Rick Haag	334-981-6012	haagnhaag@gulftel.com
Clifton Jones	334-981-1827	nautico@gulftel.com
Gene Montgomery	334-478-7440	
Mark Pearson	850-470-9626	pearson@networktel.net

McCoy Outdoors
1320 Government St.
Mobile, AL 36608
334-432-3006

Middle Bay Outfitters
231 Fairhope Ave.
Destin, FL 32541
334-432-2231
middlebay@fairhope.com

Pearson & Sons
207 S. Palafox St.
Pensacola, FL 32501
850-470-9626
pearson@networktel.net

Tide Line Outfitters
3702A Dauphin St.
Mobile, AL 36608
334-344-3474
tidelineof@aol.com

Capt. Rick Haag was born and raised on the coast of southwest Florida. In 1988, he moved to the Alabama coast, bringing fly-fishing techniques he had used in Florida with remarkable results. Rick has been a professional fisherman for over 17 years, with experience from billfishing to bonefishing. His fishing travel has taken him throughout the Bahamas, the Virgin Islands and the southeast United States. Capt. Haag is an Orvis-endorsed fly-fishing guide and an original member of the Bay Area Fly Fishers. Rick is an ardent conservationist and is a member of the IGFA, the Coastal Conservation Association and the Billfish Foundation. He is frequently invited to speak to clubs and fly shops throughout the south.

Most Common Prey	Typical Size (inches)	Usual Months of Availability**												Typical Matching Fly Patterns***
		J	F	M	A	M	J	J	A	S	O	N	D	
Anchovies	1	4	3	3	3	3	3	3	4	4	5	5	5	Epoxy Baitfish
Eels	10 - 14			*	*	*	*	*	*	*	*			Middle Bay Eel
Glass Minnows	1	1	1	1	3	4	5	5	5	5	4	2	1	Clouser Deep Minnow (L)
Menhaden	1 - 5	1	1	1	3	4	5	5	5	5	4	2	1	Eric's Baby Bunker
Mullet	2 - 12	3	3	3	4	5	5	5	5	5	5	5	5	Woolhead Mullet
Threadfin Herring	5	2	2	3	4	5	5	5	5	5	4	3	1	Lefty's Deceiver

*1=Scarce, 2=Spotty, 3=Available, 4=Readily Available, 5=Widely Available • ** Pattern Recipe in Appendix A.

Chapter 37: Barataria Estuary System

By Capt. Kirby LaCour

The Barataria Estuary System (BES) is one of the largest brackish estuaries on the Gulf Coast and is probably the greatest natural redfish hatchery in the world. The extent of water salinity depends upon freshwater diversion from the Mississippi River, rain runoff and the strength of tidal flow. It is bordered on the east by the Mississippi River/LA Highway 23 from Belle Chasse to Venice and on the west by Bayou Lafourche/LA Highways 1 and 308 from Lockport to Grand Island. The northern boundary consists of the Intracoastal

Canal from Belle Chasse to Lockport and the southern boundary is the Gulf of Mexico. The freshwater part of this system is actually bordered by the metro area of New Orleans on the north/east and Interstate 310 on the west.

One of the greatest things about the BES is its proximity to a major city such as New Orleans. This provides the non-angler with a host of ventures within the city especially for the food and entertainment. However, for the photographer or wildlife enthusiast the BES is abundant with waterfowl, mammal life, alligators and some of the most fantastic sunrises and sunsets in the world. During fall and winter, the BES is a wintering ground for hundreds of thousands of ducks and other migratory birds. The plant life is unique and is mostly covered with large areas of grass, thus sometimes looking more like a flooded prairie than a marsh. Do not let the proximity of a major city conjure up images of thousands of boats and fishers limiting your area of fishing. It is quite possible to see only a half dozen boats on the water all day, even though you may see many more boats at the marinas. Of course, sleeping accommodations and restaurants are plentiful in New Orleans. In addition, the town of Jean LaFitte, named after the famous buccaneer, has some accommodations and is located on the northern edge of the BES. The eastern side of the BES has motels in Belle Chasse and also in Empire and Venice, the gateway to the offshore fishing. There are a few bed-and-breakfasts establishments also located just outside of Port Sulphur. While restaurants are few on the east side of the BES there are some in Belle Chasse and Jean LaFitte. Many fly-fishers opt for the ride back into New Orleans for an epicurean delight. Most of the fly-fishing guides work out of the Myrtle Grove area, but there are a few in Jean LaFitte.

Navigation within the BES can be difficult due to the fact that most of the average depths are less than three feet and everything looks the same. The marsh is a changing environment and sunken islands can leave a boater stranded in the middle of nowhere. Nevertheless, there are limited but great opportunities for canoe and kayak enthusiasts; checking with the local fly shops can provide you with lots of helpful information. Rental flat boats are available in Jean LaFitte and are rented on a daily basis, but make sure

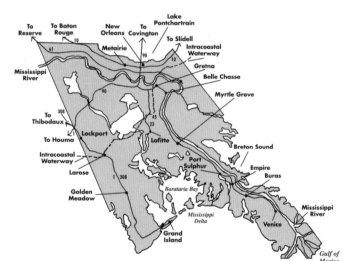

Species	Typical Size – Pounds	J	F	M	A	M	J	J	A	S	O	N	D
Black Drum	1 - 4	2	2	3	4	4	4	3	3	3	2	2	2
Flounder	1 - 3	2	2	3	3	3	3	2	2	2	2	2	2
Redfish	1 - 10	5	5	5	4	4	4	4	4	5	5	5	5
Sheepshead	1 - 3	2	2	3	4	4	4	4	3	3	3	2	2
Speckled Trout	1 - 3	3	3	3	3	4	4	4	4	4	4	4	3

1=Scarce, 2=Spotty, 3=Available, 4=Readily Available, 5=Widely Available

you have reservations for a vessel before driving down there. Some wading is available in the gulf surf along Grand Island. Again, contact local fly shops for details. However, don't even think of wading in the marsh; the bottom is extremely soft and stingrays are plentiful.

Species of gamefish include redfish, speckled sea trout, black drum, flounder, and the most elusive flats fish, the sheepshead. All but the speckled trout are found on the flats in significant numbers and most of your fishing will be done in less than two feet of water for the flats species. The size range for redfish is from one pound to 10 pounds with four-pounders being most common. Black drum and sheepshead average from one to three pounds and speckled trout average from one to three pounds.

Equipment can vary from a 6-weight through 9-weight. An 8-weight outfit is most common for redfish and a 7-weight outfit is best for speckled trout. Weight-forward floating lines are essential and they should have a front taper that is short, to allow for quick accurate casts of up to 50 feet. Too much false casting can spook wary redfish and most casts average 30 to 40 feet in length. A floating line can be used when fishing for speckled trout, but an intermediate-density or sink-tip line is often better. Most fly-casting for speckled trout is blind, in locations where speckled trout usually hang out; once found you often catch many fish. Reels should have a smooth drag and be able to handle 50 to 100 yards of backing. Redfish do not make long runs but their fighting ability is second to none and they do not quit. Leaders can be 7 to 9 feet in length and tip out from 10 to 16 pounds. Shock tippets are not necessary.

Flies used most often are spoon flies, bendbacks, Clousers, crabs and poppers. Sizes and colors vary but they should be tied on size 4 to 1/0 hooks. Guides and local fly shops can provide you with the flies that you need or with useful information on what patterns are working best at the time of your trip.

The BES can be fished 365 days a year. Tropical storms, high winds and frontal activity have a significant impact on fishing. General weather patterns in the summer months are hot and humid with temperatures from 65 to 98 degrees F. The fall and winter are less humid and temperatures ranging from 40 to 80 degrees F. Keep in mind that if the humidity is high, 50 degrees can seem quite cool. Most people enjoy the fall and winter fishing due to the moderate temperatures, but the quality of the fishing during the summer months is hard to beat.

Guides (Capt.)	Phone/Fax	E-mail
Mark Brockhoeft	504-392-7146	cpatmark@bellsouth.net
Barrett Brown	504-908-3474	fish@e-zfly.com
Kirby LaCour	504-464-1697	klacour1@bellsouth.net
Rich Waldner	504-864-1945	

Bayou Specialties
500 River Rd.
Jefferson, LA 70121
Contact: Kenny Cooper
504-835-7221/504-835-1206
coop1@accesscom.net

Lakeside Outfitters
3213 17th St.
Metaire, LA 70002
Contact: Susan Gros
504-834-3473/504-834-3446

Southern Safaris
3792 Vet. Blvd.
Metarie, LA 70002
Contact: John Gesser, Rich Waldner
504-885-3474
flyfishing@southernsafaris.com

Sporting Life
601 Julia St.
New Orleans, LA 70130
504-529-3597

Capt. Kirby LaCour has been guiding fly-fishers full-time for inshore species in the Barataria Estuary System for over 6 years, and he has been fishing the area for over 20 years. He travels throughout the country presenting seminars and casting instruction programs relating to shallow-water sight-fishing. Kirby is also a commercial fly tier and is currently on the Pro Staffs for Scott Fly Rods and Teton Reels.

Most Common Prey	Typical Size (inches)	Usual Months of Availability*												Typical Matching Fly Patterns**
		J	F	M	A	M	J	J	A	S	O	N	D	
Blue Crabs	1 - 2	3	3	4	4	5	5	5	5	5	4	4	3	Del Brown's Permit Fly
Cocahoe Minnows (Anchovy sp.)	2 - 3	5	4	4	3	3	3	3	3	4	4	5	5	Kosmic Killer, Kirby's Cocahoe Clouser Minnow
Glass Minnow	1.5 - 3.0	4	4	4	3	3	2	2	2	3	4	5	5	Bendback (A), Lefty's Deceiver (R)
Shrimp	2 - 3	2	2	3	4	5	5	5	5	5	4	3	2	Seaducer (C), Gold Digger, Kirby's Kosmic Killer

*1=Scarce, 2=Spotty, 3=Available, 4=Readily Available, 5=Widely Available • ** Pattern Recipe in Appendix A.

Chapter 38: Calcasieu Lake

By Capt. Jeff Poe

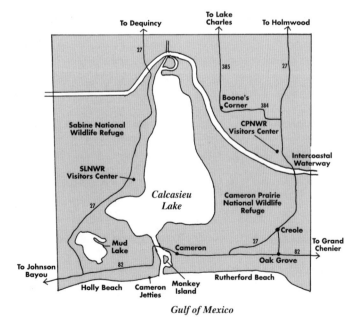

Calcasieu Lake is located south of Lake Charles, Louisiana and about eight miles north of the Gulf of Mexico. The lake is bounded to the south, east and west by two national wildlife refuges, both of which are major nursery areas for many estuarine-dependent marine species. Sabine National Wildlife Refuge lies on the western shore of Calcasieu Lake and extends westward to Sabine Lake and the Texas state line. The Refuge has two public boat ramps that allow easy access to the West Cove area of the "Big Lake," as the Lake is known locally. Speckled trout (spotted seatrout), redfish and flounder may be caught year-round in the canals adjacent to Highway 27.

Although Sabine is the larger of the two refuges, the East Cove Unit of Cameron Prarie National Wildlife Refuge is by far the better area for saltwater fly-fishing. This part of the refuge is accessible only by boat through the Grand Bayou boat bay. The interior of the Refuge contains many bayous, ditches and ponds. The bayous and the borrow ditch adjacent to the Calcasieu Lake shoreline are best fished by blind casting along their banks. Some sight-casting opportunities

will also be available. The ponds in the Refuge range in size from one to several hundred acres and their depth ranges from several inches to about three feet. Shallow draft boats and careful navigation are therefore required when fishing these ponds. The best time to fish the ponds is from mid-July until the first part of November, when the Refuge closes for the duck season. Between July and November is the time when the redfish are schooling and they can be caught on weedless spoonflies, poppers and sliders. Schools of 15 to 30 fish are common and I have seen schools of reds numbering nearly one hundred.

Although many other species are available, redfish and spotted seatrout are the primary targets for visiting anglers. Both the number and the size of the seatrout caught in the Lake are impressive. On a good day, it is possible for a single fly-fisherman to catch and release fifty or more fish. Trophy seatrout of over 28 inches and over 8 pounds are caught regularly, and fish over 30 inches and over ten pounds are caught each year. The state fly-rod record for seatrout of nine pounds, 5 ounces was caught in Calcasieu Lake.

Trout and redfish can also be caught in the Calcasieu Estuary from north of Interstate Highway 10 in Lake Charles to the close-in oil rigs in the Gulf of Mexico south of Cameron. The main factors to consider when determining where to fish are water salinity and clarity. As a general rule, during periods of low salinity the majority of fish and clear water will be found in the southern end of the Estuary. Although spin fishermen will be successful with six inches of water visibility, fly-fishers generally do well with visibility of a foot or more. While fishing the Lake itself, the best areas to fish are over the oyster reefs, found in Turners Bay, The Washout, Nine-Mile Cut, almost all of the West Cove and off of Commissary and Long Points.

An 8-weight fly rod is probably the best choice for inland fishing for seatrout and redfish. Some fly-fishers will select heavier or lighter equipment, depending upon wind conditions. I generally use a 10-foot tapered leader with a 12-pound tippet. I don't find shock tippets necessary, as long as I check for tippet fraying after every three or four caught fish. Weight-forward floating fly lines are usually best, but I always keep a spare rod and reel loaded with sinking line. Although the average water depth of the Lake is only six feet, the depth of the fly and the rate of retrieval are critical. If one chooses to venture into the Gulf to fish

Species	Typical Size	J	F	M	A	M	J	J	A	S	O	N	D
Black Drum	16 - 36 inches	2	3	3	4	5	5	5	4	3	3	3	3
Cobia	15 - 50 pounds	1	1	2	4	4	4	4	4	3	1	1	1
Flounder	12 - 20 inches	2	3	4	4	4	4	4	4	4	5	5	2
Jack Crevalle	20 - 25 pounds	1	1	3	3	4	4	5	5	5	5	2	1
Redfish (Red Drum)	20 - 30 inches	3	3	3	4	4	4	4	5	5	5	5	5
Spotted Seatrout	16 - 23 inches	3	3	4	5	5	5	5	4	5	5	5	4
Tripletail	3 - 15 pounds	1	1	1	2	3	4	4	5	5	3	1	1

1=Scarce, 2=Spotty, 3=Available, 4=Readily Available, 5=Widely Available

around the numerous oilrigs, heavier tackle is in order. The rigs within sight of the beach will hold numerous jack crevalle (20-25 pounds), bull redfish (over 20 pounds) and cobia (15 to 50 or more pounds); accordingly a 10- to 12-weight outfit should be available. Seatrout, bluefish, Spanish mackerel, tripletail and ladyfish are also numerous around the close-in rigs, therefore the lighter outfits are still needed. A fast-sinking line is more appropriate around the close-in rigs, since water depths range from 15 to 40 feet. Great wade fishing is available on the beach between the communities of Holly Beach and Johnson Bayou. The surf holds seatrout, redfish and flounder year-round, with the best fly-fishing available spring through fall. The best water conditions occur with a calm surf and a rising tide.

As shown on the enclosed chart, there are many prey species in the Calcasieu Lake area. The most dominant species are shrimp, menhaden and mullet. Seatrout rely heavy on shrimp while they are juveniles and then consume more fin fish as they age. Accordingly, to target the larger seatrout, use the finfish imitations in larger sizes. I have seen seatrout eat mullet up to a foot long; so, if you can cast it they can eat it. Clouser minnows (shrimp imitations), Deceivers, poppers and sliders make up a rather complete fly box assortment for Calcasieu Lake. The favorite colors for our area are olive, chartreuse and white/red with red, silver or gold flash material. I use a size 1/0 hook for most flies. Larger, heavily dressed flies seem to work best in the brackish water with low visibility.

There are several guides in our area with the knowledge to position you to catch fish. Except for yours truly, none that I know of carry flies or fly-fishing equipment for client use. I can be reached by phone at 337-598-3268, by fax at 337-598-4499 and by email at biglake.guideservice@gateway.net. The nearest fly shops are located in Lafayette, about 70 miles east of Lake Charles.

Capt. Jeff Poe spent his formative years fishing and fly-fishing the lakes, creeks and streams of Alabama. In 1980 Jeff moved to Louisiana to guide for duck hunters and saltwater fishermen on Calcasieu Lake. In 1984 he formally opened his Big Lake Guide Service, located in Sweetlake, on the east shore of Calcasieu Lake. Jeff's specialty is saltwater light tackle and fly-fishing for speckled trout, redfish and flounder. In 1997 Capt. Poe became an Orvis-endorsed guide. He is the current Louisiana state-record holder in the Fly Rod Division for speckled trout at 9.33 pounds. He also holds third place in the speckled trout division. Jeff is a lifetime member of the Coastal Conservation Association and currently operates 6 charter boats and 3 lodges, and arranges regular fall/winter duck hunts.

Lafayette Shooters
3520 Amb. Caffery Pkwy,
Lafayette LA 70503
Contact: Al Bernard
337-988-1191/337-984-5533
Lashoot@bellsouth.com

Lousiana Outfitters Inc.
3809 Amb. Caffery Pkwy,
Lafayette LA 70503
Contact: Justin Mere/Joel Palmer
337-988-9090/337-988-9092

Most Common Prey	Typical Size (inches)	Usual Months of Availability*												Typical Matching Fly Patterns**
		J	F	M	A	M	J	J	A	S	O	N	D	
Menhaden	2 - 10	3	3	4	5	5	5	5	5	5	5	5	4	Clouser Deep Minnow (M)
Mullet	3 - 12	4	4	4	5	5	5	5	5	5	5	5	5	Clouser Deep Minnow (M)
Shrimp	1 - 4	3	3	4	5	5	5	5	5	5	5	5	5	Clouser Deep Minnow (I)
General														Rattling Deceiver

*1=Scarce, 2=Spotty, 3=Available, 4=Readily Available, 5=Widely Available • ** Pattern Recipe in Appendix A.

Chapter 39: The Sabine Lake and River

By Capt. Chuck Uzzle

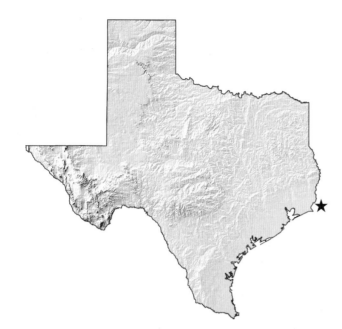

With the hum of the big motor in the background, the two anglers seated at the front of the skiff appear to be disoriented as the slick flats boat settles down in the water and comes to a stop. "Why are we stopping here?" one angler asks. I explain to the fishermen that this is more or less the dividing line between fresh and salt water. From this point in the Intracoastal canal, anglers can run ten minutes either up river or down river and catch over 15 different species of fish. The ability to pursue so many different types of fish is what sets the Sabine system apart

from any other place in Texas. The Sabine system is comprised of the Sabine River and Sabine Lake, these bodies of water comprising the border between Texas and Louisiana. Anglers from all over the world travel here to take part in the adventure that is Sabine fishing. Species such as largemouth bass, Kentucky spotted bass, striped bass, crappie, bream, redfish, speckled trout, flounder, bowfin, sheepshead, black drum, croaker, Spanish mackerel, and alligator gar are some of the species that fly-fishers can target while navigating the Sabine waterways.

The cypress-lined banks of the Sabine River offer up some magnificent scenery as the deep and rich waters of the river flow down toward the Gulf of Mexico. Fly fishers are treated to some spectacular freshwater fishing while quietly casting in the shadows of the ancient cypress and tupelo gum trees. The standard flies for this part of the world are rather basic; mini Clousers in silver, chartreuse, and white are tops on the list. Larger Half and Half (Deceiver-Clouser combinations) flies are successful with some really large stripers as well as redfish along the many drains that empty into the Sabine River. The best colors/patterns for stripers seems to be tan/white, chartreuse/white and occasionally large black Deceivers with strands of silver. Also, let's not forget the top-water poppers; chartreuse and silver are the preferred colors when covering the surface for aggressive largemouth bass and the vicious-striking grinnel.

Saltwater fly-fishers will enjoy some outstanding action on Sabine Lake, since speckled trout and redfish are plentiful in this border lake that sees very little fishing pressure. Blind-casting with shrimp patterns or small crabs is a great way to hook up with some heavyweight trout and reds. Top-water poppers can provide heart-stopping action during the summer and fall as fish begin to school under herds of shrimp in the open water of the lake. Big redfish in the 35-inch class will aggressively cruise the surface of the, inhaling everything that crosses their path. This is a sure-fire way to test your angling skills and your tackle. Along with the reds and specks, fly-fishers also can ply their trade on some of the many flounder that can be found along all the drains on the Louisiana shoreline. Small crab patterns and even spoon flies will produce good numbers of flounder during tidal movements.

The keys to fishing this rich environment are to concentrate on areas that hold bait. Drains and ditches are

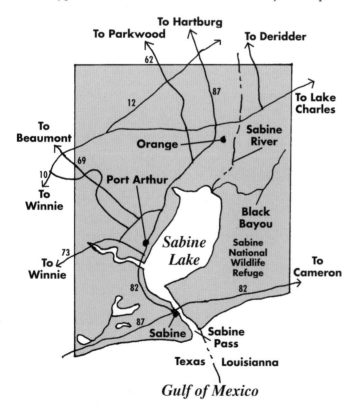

Species	Typical Size - Inches	J	F	M	A	M	J	J	A	S	O	N	D
Bream	4 - 8	2	2	3	4	4	4	4	4	4	4	3	3
Flounder	10 - 18	1	1	2	3	4	3	3	3	4	5	4	3
Largemouth Bass	10 - 18	1	2	3	4	4	4	4	4	5	4	2	2
Redfish	16 - 34	2	2	3	3	3	4	4	5	5	5	5	4
Speckled Trout	14 - 24	3	3	4	4	5	5	5	5	5	5	5	4
Striped Bass	14 - 40	4	4	3	2	1	1	1	1	1	3	4	5	5

1=Scarce, 2=Spotty, 3=Available, 4=Readily Available, 5=Widely Available

prime areas to start looking for fish. In tidal bodies of water it is almost always a rule that some water movement is needed to jump start the fishing. Incoming or outgoing tides are always better than slack water; the tidal movement will concentrate the bait, which in turn draws the fish to these key areas. The tidal movement is extremely important while fishing in the lake. No tide movement usually means no fish. During slack periods it is wise to look for any bait that are schooled up. Shad is the predominant bait during the times of the year when shrimp are scarce. Day in and day out, shad patterns offer up the most consistent bite. Shrimp patterns work great when the lake has a population of either brown or white shrimp during the late summer and fall.

At times, the Sabine River will get muddy due to rainfall, and really make fishing difficult. This muddy water will eventually enter Sabine Lake and settle out after a period of time. Direct rainfall on this area does not appreciably affect water clarity, but upriver runoff from near the Toledo Bend reservoir can be a problem. During muddy water periods, anglers can find better water in the marshes, backwater lakes and sloughs. All along the Sabine River there are horseshoe lakes that can provide some excellent bream and largemouth bass fishing. And the marshes on the lake will harbor many saltwater species along the cane-lined banks. Redfish in the backwaters are perhaps the most common targets in these waters, while flounder and other species like sheepshead rank a close second.

It really doesn't matter which area you fish, freshwater or saltwater, the Sabine system has it all. Hardly a month goes by that an angler cannot be totally engrossed in quality fishing. Generally, the fishing is seasonal for several species; therefore when it is a slack time for one species it is a hot time for another. During a typical calendar year there are times in late summer and throughout the fall into early winter when an angler can catch anywhere from 5 to 10 different species in one day. That period would probably be considered the prime times to be on the Sabine. Late winter and early spring are without a doubt the most unpredictable times for fishermen; on the other hand these are also the best times to catch trophy fish like huge stripers and Texas-sized speckled trout. The Sabine sytem has something for every fly-fisher.

The accompanying chart lists the experienced fly-fishing guides for our area. We have no local fly shops,

but the visiting fly-fisher would be advised to contact the Orvis shop in Houston (Danno Wise, 713-783-2111) for help in advanced trip planning. The local communities of Port Arthur and Orange are very convenient for fishing the Sabine River or Lake and they have all the necessary amenities for supporting a fly-fishing trip.

Standard equipment for fishing the Sabine River and Lake are an 8-weight rod with a weight-forward, floating line and an extra spool of slow to moderate sinking line. The floating line will take care of 90% of all the situations you may encounter. The sinking line is preferred for fishing the stripers in the river when they suspend at deeper depths or for open-water fishing for saltwater species in the lake. The floating line covers all the basics, whereas the sinking line is used for only special situations. Tippet size varies from 8 to 20 pounds. Species like largemouth bass, speckled trout, flounder etc. will require no more than a 10- or 12-pound tippet, while big redfish and stripers may need as much as a 20-pound tippet. A variety of sizes will permit proper presentations for any water conditions. If you had to choose only one size, probably a 12- to 14-pound tippet will do the best all around job.

Guides (Capt.)	Phone/Fax	E-mail
Dickie Colburn	409-883-0723	
Johnny Comier	409-886-7873	
Chuck Uzzle	409-886-5222	cuzzle@pnx.com

Capt. Chuck Uzzle has fished the waters of the Sabine system for nearly 20 years. Capt. Chuck is the only guide who specializes in fly-fishing the Sabine area, and he is a member of the Orvis pro staff and is also sponsored by Hewes, Yamaha, Shimano, Dawson Marine and others.

Growing up near the water has given Chuck a great feel for the waterways and all the creatures that inhabit its surroundings. Chuck was taught to fly-fish by his grandfather at an early age and has developed a love for the sport that has now grown into a passion he enjoys sharing with other anglers at all skill levels. Chuck is an extremely personable and skillful guide who gives all his clients an enjoyable time on the water.

Most Common Prey	Typical Size (inches)	Usual Months of Availability*												Typical Matching Fly Patterns**
		J	F	M	A	M	J	J	A	S	O	N	D	
Brown Shrimp	1 - 3	1	1	2	3	5	5	4	3	3	3	2	1	Kraft Fur Shrimp, Petrie Shrimp, Texas Tout Fly
Crabs	1 - 5	3	3	4	5	5	5	5	5	5	5	4	4	Del Brown's Permit Fly
Mullet	2 - 8	3	3	4	4	5	5	5	5	5	5	4	3	Half and Half (E), Lefty's Deceiver (S)
Shad	0.75 - 5.0	2	2	3	4	5	5	5	5	4	3	3		Clouser Deep Minnow (G)
White Shrimp	1 - 4	1	1	2	3	3	3	3	4	5	5	5	4	Petrie Shrimp, Texas Tout Fly

*1=Scarce, 2=Spotty, 3=Available, 4=Readily Available, 5=Widely Available
** Pattern Recipe in Appendix A.

Chapter 40: Galveston Bay
By Capt. Chris Phillips

Galveston Bay is the largest bay system on the Texas Gulf coast, covering over 600 square miles. Comprising Galveston, Trinity, East, West and Christmas bays, it offers almost every type of fishing situation a saltwater fly-fisher could imagine. And, with Galveston and Texas City nearby, there is no shortage of sleeping accommodations, restaurants, marinas, launch ramps, etc. For surf-fishing enthusiasts, there are many miles on Galveston Island where one can park on the beach and have immediate access. For fly-fishers who don't mind walking on rocks, the Galveston Jetties extend four miles into the Gulf of Mexico and afford many fly-fishing opportunities. Also, there are smaller erosion-preventing jetties or rock groins which extend nearly 100 yards off the beach, located along the Galveston seawall.

The Bays offer sand and grass flats, oyster reefs, tidal lakes, bayous and flooded marshes; all of which hold different types of prey and opportunities for fly-fishing. Generally, access to Galveston and Trinity bays requires a boat, canoe or kayak. There is however reasonable park-and-walk-in access to Dollar Flats and the Texas City Dike. For most of East Bay, a boat is needed to cross the Intracoastal Canal and gain access to the better fishing areas. Nevertheless, the eastern end often has roaming schools of redfish and trophy speckled seatrout which are available to the fly-fisher with wheels, by way of the Anahuac National Wildlife Refuge.

West Bay provides the most ready access for the visiting fly-fisher. There are numerous places where one can park and walk to the bay side of Galveston Island. Probably the best access is from Galveston Island State Park, whose entrance can be reached by traveling west on Farm Road 3005. There, the fly-fisher will find over 1.5 miles of public access to coves, sand flats, grass flats and marsh lakes. Further west on Farm Road 3005 is San Luis Pass, which marks the west end of Galveston Island. Oceanside or bayside, fishing near the pass from spring through fall is one of the premier fishing areas on the upper Texas coast. The fly-fisher may encounter speckled seatrout, redfish, Spanish mackerel, huge jack crevalle and monster tarpon. Further west beyond the San Luis Pass bridge, Farm Road 3005 heads toward Freeport. To the north is Christmas Bay, whose pristine waters offer grass flats, sand potholes, oyster reefs and some of the best sight casting opportunities on the upper Texas coast.

The sheer size of the Galveston Bay system may intimidate the fly-fisher, but a day with a competent guide will give you a great head start on learning the better places, access points and techniques. Currently, I am the only experienced fly-fishing guide who regularly works the Galveston Bay system on a full time basis, and I would be pleased to help you get started (Phone 409-935-0208).

Most fly-fishers in this area use 9-foot fly rods matched to 6- to 8-weight lines. The 8-weight is required when dealing with the wind (the constant bane of the coastal fly-fisher) or when casting larger flies. Since speckled seatrout are usually found in waist-deep water, an intermediate-density fly line is usually the best choice for the wading fly-fisher. Usually, 40-foot casts are required when sight-casting. Casting accuracy is most important; on relatively calm days, experienced casters often scale down to 6-weight outfits for a quieter presentation. In the surf, an 8-weight outfit is the best choice, with both intermediate-density and slow-sinking lines used quite often.

Species	Typical Size – Inches	J	F	M	A	M	J	J	A	S	O	N	D
Black Drum	12 - 30	1	1	2	3	4	5	5	5	5	4	4	4
Flounder	12 - 26	2	2	3	4	5	5	5	5	5	5	4	3
Jack Crevalle	26 - 40	1	1	1	2	2	3	4	5	5	4	2	1
Redfish	18 - 30	3	3	4	5	5	5	5	5	5	5	4	3
Sheepshead	12 - 24	3	3	3	4	5	5	5	5	5	5	5	4
Spanish Mackerel	14 - 26	1	1	1	2	3	4	5	5	4	3	2	1
Speckled Seatrout	15 - 28	2	3	3	4	5	5	5	5	5	5	4	3

1=Scarce, 2=Spotty, 3=Available, 4=Readily Available, 5=Widely Available

Around the jetties or when drift fishing deeper areas from a boat, high-density, fast-sinking lines are preferred.

For most situations, 9-foot leaders tapered to a 12- to 15-pound tippet work best. I also sometimes use a straight 9- to 10-foot length of hard Mason monofilament instead of a tapered leader. The Mason material is quite hard and stiff, it turns over well and seldom is the cause for breakoffs. If the fish seem particularly spooky, a 10- to 12-foot leader can provide an advantage to the angler. When fishing sinking lines, leaders can simply be 4- to 5-foot lengths of 12- to 16-pound hard Mason mono. In the surf, addition of a shock tippet of 20- to 40-pound mono is recommended to withstand the encounters with Spanish mackerel, jack crevalle or even bluefish.

For most flats fishing in the bays, 100 yards of 20-pound line backing is adequate. However, 200 yards of 20-pound backing is considered a minimum for beach and surf fishing, because the fish are usually large and you are not in a position to chase them to deeper water. A 25- to 40-pound jack crevalle will easily strip out 200 yards of backing on their initial run.

The included chart depicts the prey species which are available in the Galveston Bay area, and when they are most prevalent. Mullet are present year-round and shrimp, menhaden, glass minnows, crabs and killifish are here in all months except for the middle of winter. Fly patterns that imitate mullet include 3- to 5-inch Deceivers in white, red/white, chartreuse, and chartreuse/white on size 2 to 2/0 hooks. My favorite mullet replica is the Phillips Header, tied in the same colors and hook sizes and also in red/yellow. The most effective shrimp flies are Patrick's Shrimp (a rattler) and Walter's Shrimp tied on size 2 and 4 hooks in shades of white, brown and olive. Good glass minnow imitations include the Myglass Minnow and Walter's Minnow. These are especially effective at night under the lights and in the surf (for mackerel).

On the flats, both sheepshead and black drum (the Texas permit) can be very difficult to hook. Small Clouser-type patterns in black will work at times for the black drum and small olive or tan Clousers can be effective for sheepshead. To imitate killifish and menhaden, I use Cary's Minnow and small Double Bunnys in olive/white and black/white. When redfish are feeding on small crabs, I suggest using the Flex Crab, Capt. Scott's Matagorda Crab or Del's Merkin (Del Brown's Permit Fly) in brown or olive.

Fly patterns tied with rattle chambers can be tied to imitate most baitfish and crustaceans and they are very effective in off-color water. Redfish and flounder seem unable to resist them when they are tied in gold.

Capt. Chris Phillips has been fly-fishing for 42 years and has been fly-fishing in salt waters for 26 years. Chris has been guiding now for 15 years and is an active participant in some of the better-known Florida fly-fishing tournaments. He has participated in the Gold Cup Tarpon Tournament in Islamorada, Florida for the past 5 years and he won Fishing International's Florida Keys Tarpon Classic in 1984. Chris has been a member of the Texas Fly Fishers since 1976 and served as its president in 1981. Capt. Phillips is also a member of Mercury's Saltwater Team.

Most Common Prey	Typical Size (inches)	Usual Months of Availability*												Typical Matching Fly Patterns**
		J	F	M	A	M	J	J	A	S	O	N	D	
Crabs	0.5 - 2.0	1	2	3	4	5	5	5	5	5	5	4	3	Flex Crab, Del Brown's Permit Fly, Capt. Scott's Matagorda Crab
Finger Mullet	2 - 6	3	3	4	5	5	5	5	5	5	5	4	4	Lefty's Deceivers (C,M&P), Phillips' Header, Rosario's Minnow
Glass Minnow	1 - 3	2	2	3	4	5	5	5	5	5	5	4	4	Myglass Minnow, Walter's Minnow
Killifish	0.5 - 2.0	2	2	3	4	5	5	5	5	5	5	4	4	Cary's Minnow, Rattle Rouser
Menhaden	1 - 4	1	2	2	3	4	5	5	5	5	4	3	2	Double Bunny, Rattle Rouser
Shrimp	2 - 3	1	2	3	4	5	5	5	5	5	4	3	2	Patrick's Shrimp, Walter's Shrimp

*1=Scarce, 2=Spotty, 3=Available, 4=Readily Available, 5=Widely Available • ** Pattern Recipe in Appendix A.

Chapter 41: The Back Bays and Lakes of the Coastal Bend

By Capt. Sally Moffet

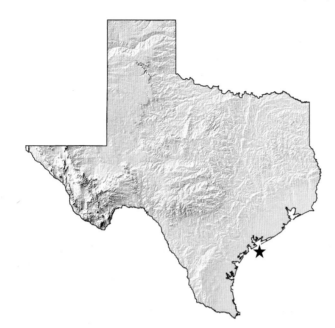

At the heart of the Texas Coastal Bend lies the historic and friendly communities of Rockport and Fulton, and the location of some the most fertile estuaries, lakes and bays on the Texas coast. The Aransas National Wildlife Refuge borders the area to the north, while the quiet islands and flats of Redfish Bay lie to the south. In between are rich tidal zones, estuaries, bird sanctuaries and untouched back lakes that host everything from shrimp nurseries to the endangered whooping crane.

Along Texas Highway 35, small and fishing-friendly towns from Austwell to Ingleside provide ample facilities to launch a boat, purchase gear, tackle, food and drinks, and pick up fishing tips from the local fishermen and women. There are also many walk-in areas that are available for wade fishermen without boats, and many kayak launching

areas in close proximity to these prime fishing areas. There are several places to rent suitable boats and kayaks as well. Since this entire area caters to all types of fishing, you will find a good variety of accommodations in all price ranges and locations, good food, good ramps, experienced fly fishing guides and helpful fly shop personnel

The northern bays of San Antonio, Mesquite, Carlos and St. Charles are filled with oyster reefs and grassy shorelines. Each bay also supports many back lakes that, during certain tidal conditions, hold redfish, trout and black drum. During most wind conditions you can find protected areas to pole a boat, kayak or wade fish. Trout lurk around the shell reefs year-round and these reefs can be waded for miles. San Antonio Bay is quite large and can be tricky to navigate. Hiring a professional guide that is familiar with this bay will make your trip more productive. Mesquite, Carlos and St. Charles bays are smaller and each can be explored in a day. These smaller bays also support many reef systems, tidal flow lakes and grassy/sandy shorelines. St. Charles Bay is surrounded by the Aransas National Wildlife Refuge. You will have many opportunities to view interesting wildlife and birds while exploring this area, making it a real outdoor adventure, especially in the winter months when the refuge is inhabited by the protected and endangered whooping crane. Mesquite Bay is also the gateway to Cedar Bayou, a Gulf of Mexico fish pass accessible only by boat. Depending on the time of year and the surf conditions, redfish, trout, tarpon, ladyfish, and flounder all feed along the beachfront sand guts, at the mouth and just inside of the pass, making for some interesting fly-fishing. At the entrance of the pass, Cedar Flats is a well known and wind protected area that is a favorite of fly-fishermen in the area, along with the cove and lakes on the southeast shore.

In the central area, Aransas is a large primary bay. On its east side is the expansive shoreline of San Jose Island, which holds many guts, sand pockets, grassy islands and lakes. It offers the possibility for fly-fishing in almost any condition of wind, weather and tide. Areas of particular interest include Mud Island and its back shoreline and lakes, Allyns Bight, Allyns Lake, the North Pass and the Middle Pass. Intermittent oyster reefs, sandy pockets and good water flow from the deeper Lydia Ann Channel makes this area rich with bait almost all year round. On the west side of Aransas Bay is Traylor Island whose shoreline is easy to pole, kayak or wade fish.

Of special interest for kayakers is an area located behind the lighthouse on the south end of the Lydia Ann Channel. There are miles of lakes, cuts and marshes to explore, which will soon be marked for ease of navigation. All of these areas hold redfish, trout and flounder. On the

Species	Typical Size - Inches	J	F	M	A	M	J	J	A	S	O	N	D
Ladyfish	10 - 26	1	1	1	1	3	4	5	5	5	3	2	1
Redfish	18 - 36	3	3	2	3	5	5	5	5	5	5	4	3
Speckled Trout	14 - 32	2	2	3	4	5	5	4	3	3	3	2	1
Tarpon	36 - 60	1	1	1	1	2	3	4	5	5	5	3	1

1=Scarce, 2=Spotty, 3=Available, 4=Readily Available, 5=Widely Available

west end of this very large tidal flow area is South Bay which is another expanse of very shallow flats and islands. Copano Bay is a secondary bay that is famous for its long deep reefs and its trout fishing. Fly fishers have a large selection of smaller lakes and bays within this system.

In the southern area, Redfish Bay can be reached from Aransas Pass or Ingleside. There are lots of island shorelines to pole, kayak or wade and there is good access to the Ransom Island and Dagger Island shorelines and cuts, that provide many options for sight casting in clear water. Across Redfish Bay to the northeast are favorite fly-fishing spots; the East Shore and the Brown and Root Flats. Both of these areas provide pristine wading, kayaking and poling around islands and grassy areas. Most conventional bay boats cannot enter this super skinny water. This area is easy to access and easy to fish with generally good wading bottom and usually lots of targets, especially in the early morning.

Walk-in, wading fly-fishers have good access to St. Charles Bay in Lamar, to Copano Bay from West Park Rd. 13 and to the Rockport shoreline along the intracoastal canal by way of several side roads along Highway 35 South. In Aransas Pass there is good wading and kayak access south of Hampton's Landing along the intracoastal canal.

The hard-fighting redfish and the sleek speckled trout are the most commonly targeted fish species in the Coastal Bend back bays, however, other species like tarpon, lady-fish, Spanish mackerel, jack crevelle and bonita are also available in the surf and jetty areas.

Our most popular fly rod is a 9-foot for 8-weight. Depending on personal preference and wind conditions, some fly-fishers elect to use either a 7-weight or a 9-weight rod. Reds rarely run more than 200 feet, so a reel that can hold an 8-weight, weight-forward floating line and 150 yards of 20-pound backing is sufficient. Because you will most often be casting in very shallow water, floating lines work well. You may want to use a stiffer line with shorter front tapers to help when shooting line in our warm climate. We have had good results using a stiff 9-foot tapered leader with an 8- to 12-pound tippet. It can be easily fabricated by starting with a 4-foot butt section of 30-pound mono, adding a 3-foot mid section of 20-pound mono and then a 2-foot tippet.

With redfish and trout, you can present a wide variety of fly patterns and get their attention. Patterns like Scates' Shrimp, Seaducers, Deceivers, crab patterns, Clousers,

Bendbacks and small deer-hairs or poppers on size 4 through 1/0 hooks are irresistible to redfish on the flats. The Coastal Bend area is a rich and fertile estuary system that supports many forage species; hence the large and hungry population of game fish. The following chart portrays the types of prey available and the extent to which they are available.

The Coastal Bend of Texas has been a fishing destination since the 1930s with private fishing and hunting clubs in continuous operation since then. Fly-fishers will find many unspoiled places to explore. The locals are tourist-friendly and most needed services can be easily found. The Coastal Bend is still relatively "undiscovered" as a tourist destination.

Guides (Capt.)	Phone/Fax	E-mail
Paul Brown	361-729-0095	
Brian Holden	361-729-0764	
Sally Moffett	361-729-9095	sally@trip.net
Chuck Naiser	361-729-9314	
Chuck Scates	361-727-1200	cscates@interconnect.net
Bill Smith	361-749-6638	frequentfly-er@centurytel.net
Ethan Wells	361-729-7221	

Gruene Outfitters	J&J Tackle Town
1233A Airline Rd.	3010 Hwy 35 N
Corpus Cristi, TX 78412	Rockport, TX 78382
Contact: Barry Box	361-729-1841
361-994-8361/361-994-8364	361-729-7942
bbox5433@uorld.att.net	

Capt. Sally Moffett has been living and fishing in the Rockport area since 1984. She has been a professional guide for one year, but in that time has gained wide recognition as one of the few female fishing guides and the only female fly-fishing guide on the Texas coast. Sally is a member of the G. Loomis Pro Staff, the Federation of Fly Fishers, the Coastal Bend Fly Fishers, the Aransas Bay Chapter of the Coastal Conservation Association and the Coastal Bend Guides Association.

She conducts a weekly radio segment in Houston that is broadcast throughout the coastal area, has been featured in many magazine and newspaper articles and is a regular contributor to the "Guide Lines" column in the Corpus Christi Caller-Times.

Most Common Prey	Typical Size (inches)	Usual Months of Availability*												Typical Matching Fly Patterns**
		J	F	M	A	M	J	J	A	S	O	N	D	
Crabs	2 - 4	2	3	4	5	5	4	3	3	3	3	3	3	Nix's Crab, Del Brown's Permit Fly
Croakers	2 - 4	1	1	2	3	5	5	5	4	3	1	1	1	Lefty's Deceiver (M)
Mudminnows	2 - 4	3	3	3	4	4	5	5	5	4	3	3	3	Hot Butt Bendback
Mullet	2 - 5	1	1	1	2	3	5	5	5	5	4	3	2	Red Nose Mudminnow
Piggie Perch	2 - 3	1	1	2	2	3	4	5	5	5	4	3	1	Lefty's Deceiver (M)
Shrimp	1 - 2	3	3	3	4	4	5	5	5	5	4	4	4	Scates' Shrimp

*1=Scarce, 2=Spotty, 3=Available, 4=Readily Available, 5=Widely Available • ** Pattern Recipe in Appendix A.

Chapter 42: Upper Laguna Madre

By Capt. Fred Lynch

The Upper Laguna Madre is most easily accessed through Corpus Christi. Air connections are mostly from the Dallas-Fort Worth or the Houston airports. Alternately, one could drive the 140 miles from San Antonio via Route 37, the 200 miles from Houston via Route 59, or the 150 miles from the Rio Grande Valley via Route 77. Hotel accommodations and restaurants are readily available in Corpus Christi and numerous tourist attractions make this a good year-round family destination. For assistance with further information, fly-fishers are encouraged to call Gruene Outfitters Fly Shop at 361-994-8361 or one of the guides listed on the accompanying chart.

A 9-foot, 8-weight fly rod outfit is a good all-around choice for the Laguna Madre area. Many fly-fishers will fish with as light as 5-weight outfits or as heavy as 9-weight outfits. A weight-forward floating fly line is recommended for most of our fishing conditions. Laguna Madre frequently has light to moderate wind conditions and some anglers might wish to use a slightly heavier fly line when these conditions are encountered. A good-quality fly reel with a basic drag and about 90 yards of 20-pound backing will be quite adequate for our area, since the shallow-water redfish rarely run much further than a few yards into the backing. What they may lack in distance running, however, they make up for in bulldog persistence. Tapered 9-foot leaders

The Laguna Madre (Mother Lagoon) is truly a world-class fly-fishery offering a variety of challenges in a variety of fishing environments. Protected from the prevailing southerly winds by Padre Island (Father Island), one of the world's longest natural barrier islands, the Laguna Madre offers exceptional shallow water fly-fishing for redfish and speckled trout. During the summer, there are also fly-fishing opportunities somewhat offshore for kingfish, ling and bonito. A long-kept secret among anglers, Laguna Madre is starting to attract the attention of fly-fishers from all over the world.

For the purposes of this chapter, the Upper Laguna Madre is defined as the area adjacent to and south of Corpus Christi, starting at Dead Man's Hole just north of the JFK Causeway Bridge and extending approximately 50 miles south to Baffin Bay and the Land Cut. It includes such colorfully-named areas as Night Hawk Bay, Nine Mile Hole, the Graveyard, Yarborough Pass and the Badlands. Baffin Bay is world-renowned for some of the largest speckled trout ever caught and it is consistently the location for Texas state trout records.

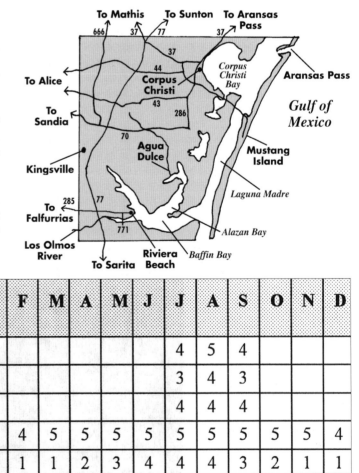

Species	Typical Size - Pounds	J	F	M	A	M	J	J	A	S	O	N	D
Bonito	5 - 6							4	5	4			
Kingfish	15 -35							3	4	3			
Ling	15 - 40							4	4	4			
Redfish	4 - 12	4	4	5	5	5	5	5	5	5	5	5	4
Speckled Trout	2 - 12	1	1	1	2	3	4	4	4	3	2	1	1

1=Scarce, 2=Spotty, 3=Available, 4=Readily Available, 5=Widely Available

in the 8- to 12-pound tippet class are just about ideal all year. Additional lighter tippets are also sometimes recommended. A quality pair of sunglasses with amber or vermillion-colored polarized lenses are a necessity for sight-casting on the flats. Other colors may protect the eyes, but do not enable the novice to easily spot the redfish.

Sun protection is a must all year long in south Texas. Sunscreen, a broad-brimmed hat, a ventilated long-sleeved shirt with a roll-up collar and long pants are the standard attire of the prepared fly-fisher. Clothing of Supplex or other light and quick-dry material works best. Also, bring along some type of aloe-based sunburn lotion and a pair of sun checker-type gloves. Wading on the flats is quite common and, therefore, a hard-sole wading shoe or bootie is essential. There are many miles of oyster shell reefs that can easily cut through a low- to mid-quality wading shoe. Also, make sure that the soles of your shoes are light colored or are otherwise protected so that your guide's boat is not marked up during your fishing day. A camera and a small pair of binoculars are recommended, because of the many sights and bird-watching opportunities that will occur during your fishing day. For your non-fishing time, plan to dress south Texas casual. Our climate is warm from April through October and moderate from November through March.

Laguna Madre fly-fishers have a choice for pursuing their quarry. Many anglers fish on the bow of a flats-equipped boat with a poling platform. However, this setup is not absolutely necessary since an abundance of locations are available for the angler who only has a car and a good pair of wading shoes. For the first-timer to the area, the hiring of a professional fly-fishing guide is a good investment to prepare for further ventures on your own. Most guides don't mind sharing some of this knowledge, especially if you discuss this with him or her in advance. A good map of the area is also a good idea. Local shops and marinas are willing to help you orient yourself and target some good areas.

When wading, it is important to position the sun and wind in favorable positions when possible. Most of the time you will need to spot the fish before you cast the fly; therefore having the sun at your back and having suitable polarized sunglasses gives you a distinct advantage with regard to underwater visibility. Wading slowly and being observant of all that is going on around you is of vital importance. Be on the lookout for baitfish such as mullet working in an area. Study the water for any deviations in surface pattern such as nervous water or wakes that might be created by redfish cruising the flats seeking some lunch.

A variety of saltwater fly patterns are effective on the Laguna Madre flats, depending upon the season and water conditions. Please refer to the accompanying charts for basic information on the gamefish of the area and the prey that they seek. Most prey imitations are tied on size size 8 to 4 hooks and various color combinations of chartreuse, white, pink, red, tan, green, silver, brown, blue, copper, gold black and olive will work at one time or another. In addition to the patterns listed on the accompanying chart, bonefish flies like the Nasty Charlie, Banana Peel, Mini-Puffs, etc. will often work quite well in chartreuse, pink and natural colors.

Guides (Capt.)	Phone/Fax	E-mail
Randy Charba	361-993-5944	
Don Clotiaux, Jr.	361-949-9708	
John Fails	361-949-0133	
Fred Lynch	361-992-4863	
Joe Mendez	361-937-5961	sightcast1@aol.com
Billy Sandifer*	361-937-8446	Billysandifer@aol.com
Bill Smith	361-749-6638	frequentfly-er@centurytel.net

Capt. Fred Lynch has been fishing the Texas coastal region for the last 22 years. For the past 6 years, Fred has been guiding fly-fishing-only on an exclusive basis. Capt. Fred is an active member of the local chapter of the Coastal Conservation Association and the Texas Fly Fishers Association.

Most Common Prey	Typical Size (inches)	Usual Months of Availability*												Typical Matching Fly Patterns**
		J	F	M	A	M	J	J	A	S	O	N	D	
Crabs	0.5 - 2.0			4	5	5	5	5	5	5	5	4	4	Del Brown's Permit Fly
Mud Minnows	0.5 - 4.0	3	3	3	3	3	3	3	3	3	3	3	3	Bonefish Slider
Mullet	1 - 15	5	5	5	5	5	5	5	5	5	5	5	5	Clouser Deep Minnow (G), Seaducer (A)
Shrimp	2 - 4			4	5	5	5	5	5	5	5	5	4	Deer Hair Shrimp, Bendback (B)

*1=Scarce, 2=Spotty, 3=Available, 4=Readily Available, 5=Widely Available • ** Pattern Recipe in Appendix A.

Chapter 43: Lower Laguna Madre and Padre Island

By Capt. Eric Glass

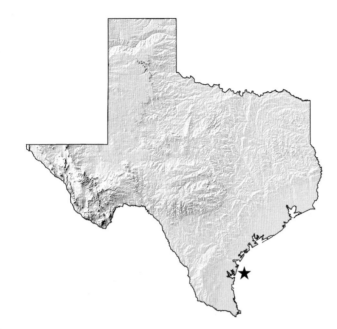

The Laguna Madre of south Texas is the largest hypersaline lagoon system in the United States. The lower basin is approximately 50 miles in length, with an average width of four miles. Laguna Madre is bounded on the east by 115-mile-long Padre Island. Much of the western margin of the lagoon is part of the 50,000-acre Laguna Atascosa National Wildlife Refuge, which provides important habitat for the endangered ocelot and several hundred species of birds. Several of these bird species, including aplomado falcon, plain chachalaca, green jay and great kiskadee, are unique to south Texas.

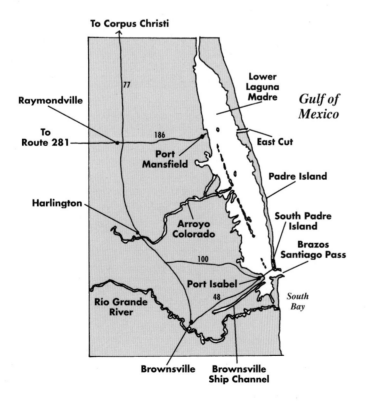

In an average year, the south Texas coast receives less than 30 inches of rainfall; the upland plant community is dominated by hardy species well adapted to the arid climate. Elevated areas are typically covered with a dense growth of mesquite, huisache, yucca, prickly pear, retama, cenizo and other species. Red mangroves are absent in south Texas because hard winter freezes cause complete mortality. Nevertheless, a narrow belt of black mangroves exists along many of the shorelines, especially near Brazos Santiago Pass at the extreme southern end of the lagoon. Because freshwater flow into the lagoon in the recent past has been only slight and because much of the lagoon floor is occupied by seagrass meadows, Laguna Madre is one of the clearest bay systems on the Texas coast. Flats on the western side of the lagoon support luxuriant beds of turtle, shoal and manatee grass. In contrast, the flats along the eastern margin are covered by wind and storm-deposited sands and resemble misplaced bonefish habitat.

A variety of game fish may be encountered on the clear sand and grass flats of the lagoon, but redfish (red drum) and seatrout are the undisputed main attractions. Anglers search for "tailing" fish in grassy areas and "backing" fish along the shorelines. These two "showy" forms of behavior are most common early and late in the day, and during overcast periods. Large seatrout are often encountered in extremely shallow water in spring and summer, especially during the early morning; three IGFA record seatrout have been landed here.

As the prey chart illustrates, a wide assortment of forage species occur here. Most local fly-fishers favor fairly small shrimp and crab imitations (size 4- 6 hooks), and the concensus is that larger baitfish imitations (size 2-1/0 hooks) are often more productive for the larger (25 inches plus) seatrout. For school seatrout in 4- to 5-foot deep basins and along channel edges, small Clousers (size 4-2) fished on sink-tip lines are hard to beat.

Three species of snook occur in the lagoon and are most commonly encountered at the southern end of the basin. The Brownsville Ship Channel, Arroyo Colorado and the Rio Grande River appear to be the principal wintering areas for resident south Texas snook, with dispersal in the spring toward Brazos Santiago Pass, the Padre Island surf and the lower end of the main lagoon. Carry an assortment of finger mullet, sardine and bay anchovy imitations and let the fish pick their favorites. Snook are regarded as relatively

Species	Typical Size	J	F	M	A	M	J	J	A	S	O	N	D
Black Drum	18 - 28 inches	3	3	3	3	2	2	2	2	3	4	4	4
Cobia	12 - 30 pounds	1	1	1	2	3	3	3	3	3	3	2	1
Dorado	3 - 12 pounds	1	1	1	2	4	4	4	4	4	3	2	1
False Albacore	6 - 12 pounds	1	1	1	2	4	3	5	5	5	5	2	1
Jack Crevalle	15 - 20 pounds	2	2	2	3	5	2	2	2	3	5	3	2
King Mackerel	10 - 20 pounds	1	1	1	2	3	4	4	4	4	3	2	1
Ladyfish	18 - 24 inches	2	2	2	3	3	4	5	5	5	4	3	2
Redfish	18 - 26 inches	2	3	3	4	5	5	5	5	3	5	5	4
Snook	18 - 30 inches	2	2	3	3	3	3	3	3	4	4	4	3
Spotted Seatrout	14 - 23 inches	3	3	3	5	5	5	4	4	4	4	4	3
Tarpon	15 - 40 pounds	1	1	1	1	2	3	3	3	4	4	2	1
Tripletail	15 - 24 inches	1	1	1	1	2	3	3	3	3	4	4	2

1=Scarce, 2=Spotty, 3=Available, 4=Readily Available, 5=Widely Available

rare jewels in Texas, and the Lower Laguna Madre Fly Fishing Association is working by example to promote a catch-and-release-only fishery for them.

The communities of Port Mansfield, Port Isabel, Arroyo City and South Padre Island are the principal access points for anglers fishing Laguna Madre. All of them have a range of available lodging, good restaurants, public boat-launching facilities and marinas. Guides familiar with the technical aspects of fly-fishing are available in each of these communities. A partial list of these guides is provided on the enclosed chart. Visiting anglers wishing to explore on their own can find shallow draft rental boats in each of the coastal towns. With the notable exception of South Bay, extensive oyster reefs are absent within the lagoon, but vast expanses of very shallow water are present. Consult the charts, navigate cautiously and monitor depth closely.

A productive venue for shorebound anglers is the Padre Island surf. A 4-wheel-drive vehicle will allow you to patrol the 28 miles of beach between the southern tip of Padre Island and the East Cut, a manmade channel that bisects the island to the north and provides Gulf of Mexico access from Port Mansfield. During late summer and fall, the surf can be calm and clear, with a variety of gamefish present. Spanish mackerel, ladyfish, seatrout and redfish are fairly common, with jack crevalle and tarpon showing up from time to time, particularly in the vicinity of large schools of scaled sardines, bay anchovies, gulf menhaden and Atlantic thread herring. The granite jetties at Brazos Santiago Pass and the East Cut are good places to try and jump a tarpon. Local tarpon anglers fish 3- to 4-inch sardine imitations (1/0 to 3/0 hooks) at dawn and dusk, keeping an eye out for the rolling pods of tarpon. Migratory groups of large jack crevalle are usually present along the beach and around the jetties during May and October. When the light is good, look for their silhouettes in the nearshore swells.

Local fly-fishers favor 7- or 8-weight outfits for the mid-size game fish such as redfish, seatrout, black drum and snook. During calm conditions, we occasionally scale back to 5- or 6-weight outfits for these same species. For tarpon, king mackerel, cobia and large jack crevalle, a 10- or 11-weight is more appropriate. Most tarpon fly-caught locally are not especially large, but they can be difficult to lift up from deep water; a bigger gun will allow you to release them in good condition. Reels for these inshore species should be capable of holding a floating line plus 125 to 150 yards of 20-pound backing. For sight-fishing to redfish and seatrout on very shallow flats, I prefer 12-foot leaders with 10- to 12-pound tippets. Shock leaders are required for tarpon and snook; 60- and 30-pound, respectively, work well. The only full-service fly shop in the area is The Fly Shop (Larry Haines), 318 Queen Isabella Blvd., Port Isabel TX 78578, Phone 956-943-1785.

Guides (Capt.)	Phone/Fax	Port Location
Steve Ellis	956-943-4525	South Padre Island
Cliff Fleming	956-943-3311	South Padre Island
Dale Fridy	956-943-7666	Port Isabel
Eric Glass	956-761-2878	South Padre Island
Bill Hagen	956-761-8876	South Padre Island
Terry Neale	956-944-2629	Port Mansfield
Skipper Ray	956-761-4565	South Padre Island
Randy Rogers	956-761-1663	South Padre Island
Scott Sparrow	956-748-4350	Arroyo City
H.E. Steussy	956-944-2339	Port Mansfield
Jim Stewart	956-943-7395	South Padre Island
Jeff Waugh	956-944-2868	Port Mansfield

An avid fly-fisher since age 12, Capt. Eric Glass has fished the lower Laguna Madre for 16 years; working as a full-time fly-fishing guide for the past six years. His credentials include a degree in aquatic biology. Eric has made numerous instructional appearances for regional angling expositions, fly-fishing clubs and fly shops, plus an appearance on ESPN's "Orvis Sporting Life" with Rick Ruoff. Eric has been a Scott Fly Rod Pro Staff member for the past three years.

Most Common Prey	Typical Size (inches)	Usual Months of Availability*												Typical Matching Fly Patterns**
		J	F	M	A	M	J	J	A	S	O	N	D	
Ballyhoo	4 - 8	1	1	1	3	4	4	4	4	4	3	2	1	Haines Ballyhoo
Bay Anchovies	1.0 - 1.5	3	3	3	3	4	4	4	4	4	4	3	3	Tan/White Clouser
Blue Crab	1 - 2	3	3	3	4	4	4	4	4	4	4	4	3	Furry Foam Crab
Brown Shrimp	2 - 3	3	3	3	4	4	3	3	3	3	3	3	3	Estaz Borski Shrimp
Gulf Menhaden	3 - 12	3	3	3	3	3	3	3	3	4	4	4	3	Epoxy Head Bunker
Lug Worm	3 - 4	3	3	3	4	4	4	3	3	4	4	3	3	Chocolate Eel
Mud Crab	0.5 - 0.75	3	3	3	3	3	3	3	3	3	3	3	3	Tan Turneffe Crab
Needlefish	2 - 6	3	3	3	3	3	3	3	3	4	4	4	3	Needlefish Zonker
Pinfish	2 - 4	3	3	4	4	4	4	4	4	4	4	4	3	Epoxy Head Pinfish
Scaled Sardines	1 - 3	1	1	1	2	3	3	4	4	4	4	3	2	Epoxy Head Sardine
Sheepshead Minnow	0.5 - 0.75	3	3	3	3	3	3	3	3	3	4	3	3	Variegated Clouser
Striped Mullet	2 - 4	3	3	3	3	3	3	3	3	3	4	4	3	Jimmy Nix Mullet
White Shrimp	2 - 3	3	3	3	3	3	3	3	3	3	4	4	3	Estaz Borski Shrimp

*1=Scarce, 2=Spotty, 3=Available, 4=Readily Available, 5=Widely Available
** Pattern Recipe in Appendix A.

Appendix: Fly Pattern Recipes

Following are the recipes for the many fly patterns that our guides have found to be productive in their destination area. Some are classical patterns that have been in use for decades, some are modifications to these classical patterns and others are unique to the local areas and probably new to the literature of fly-fishing. The materials lists for these recipes were provided by the guides or, in some cases, by fly tiers who work closely with the guides. The tying sequences and instructions were written by your editor, based upon the raw material provided by the guides.

While preparation for this book was in full swing, each guide was asked to identify his "favorite fly" and to send one to your editor for photography purposes. Each of these favorite fly patterns are identified by an asterisk (*) following the fly pattern's name in this Appendix. In addition, a full-color photo showing all favorite flies are included in the color section of this book, photographed by one of the best, Jim Schollmeyer.

There was no practical way for your editor to trace the unequivocal source for each of the hundreds of fly pattern recipes included in this Appendix. The distinction between one pattern and another can of course be quite subtle, and even invisible, to the casual eye. Each guide identified the originator of the pattern, if he or she knew it. In some instances, your editor identified the originator, based upon his knowledge. In addition, all the participants in this project referenced literature sources for the recipes when the fly pattern was the same or quite similar to that printed in the literature. The literature sources referenced in this Appendix are as follows:

Reference Number	Title	Publisher	Author	Edition
1	Salt Water Fly Patterns	MARAL, Inc.	Lefty Kreh	First
2	Flies for Saltwater	Mountain Pond	Dick Stewart, Farrow Allen	First
3	Saltwater Flies: Over 700 of the Best	Frank Amato Publications	Deke Meyer	1995
4	Innovative Saltwater Flies	Stackpole Books	Bob Veverka	First
5	A Fly Fisher's Guide to Saltwater Naturals and Their Imitations	Ragged Mountain Press	George V. Roberts Jr.	1994
6	Lou Tabory's Guide to Saltwater Baits & Their Imitations	Lyons & Burford	Lou Tabory	1995
7	Stripers On A Fly	Lyons Press	Lou Tabory	1999

Photo by Randy Hamilton

Absolute Flea

Originator: Capt. Rick Ruoff
Hook: #6 to 4 Mustad 34007
Thread: Tan
Tail: Pair of grizzly hackles
Body: White chenille, badger hackle and tan yarn
Eyes: Lead or plastic dumbbells, depending on desired sink rate

Tie on the dumbbell eyes about 1/8 inch in back of the hook eye. Tie on a short butt of white chenille well past the hook bend. Tie on the grizzly hackles at the hook bend, splayed outward, tie on one end of a piece of tan yarn, and tie on the butt of a badger hackle. Cement the windings at this point. Wind the hackle forward to the hook eye, with most of the hackle fibers located at the hook bend. Tie off the hackle tip and wind the yarn body through the palmered hackle. Tie off at the hook eye, whip finish and cement. Trim the palmered hackle fibers flat on top.

Acrylic Deer Hair Crab

Originator: Glen Mikkleson
Hook: #4 to 2/0 Mustad 34007
Thread: White size A
Body: Natural deer body hair plus thinned acrylic glue and lead tape
Claws: Webby hackle
Legs: Neck hackles
Eyes: Heavy monofilament stems with melted ends
Antennae: 10-pound monofilament

Cover the hook shank with thread and then spin and tie on the deer hair up to the hook eye. Tie off and cement. Trim the body to a crab shape, with a flat side opposite the hook point and slightly tapered (down toward the hook eye) with rounded edges on the opposite side. Soak the deer hair body with thinned acrylic glue and allow to set. Glue on lead tape to obtain appropriate sink rate (none, for a floating crab) and then glue on the eyes, legs and claws. Glue in two pieces of the 10-pound mono between the eyes. Add speckling with a permanent pen marker and add clear epoxy as needed to add weight, strengthen bonds and smooth contours. This recipe is the same as on page 124 of Reference 4.

Acrylic Squid

Originator: Glen Mikkleson
Hook: 1/0 to 5/0 Mustad 34011
Thread: White size A
Tail: 2 long and 8 short saddle hackles (red, gray, white, orange or pink) plus a mixture of different colors of Krystal Flash
Body: Poly yarn, same color as hackles, plus clear acrylic caulking
Eyes: #4-1/2 Witchcraft Stick-ons, silver with black pupils
Fins: Sections of webby saddle or neck hackles

Tie in first the long hackles at the sides of the hook shank at the hook bend. Then tie in first the Krystal Flash and then the short hackles around the hook shank, at the same place. Build up a body of poly yarn, tapered down from back to front, ending at the hook eye. Whip finish and cement. Cover body with clear acrylic coating and allow to dry for 24-48 hours. After drying, coat the entire body with a clear epoxy and mark body and tail hackles with marking pen to give a speckled appearance. Glue fins to the body. This recipe is the same as on page 126 of Reference 4.

Afternoon Delight

Originator: Winslow
Hook: 3/0 Mustad 34011 or equivalent
Thread: 3/0 prewaxed mono
Tag: White chenille

Tail: 5 or 6 extra-long white saddles and a few strands of pearl Krystal Flash
Underbody: White chenille
Body: EdgeWater foam slider cone, color of choice
Eyes: Optional

Tie on a white chenille tag at the hook bend and then tie on the Krystal Flash on top. Tie on the saddle hackles on top of the hook shank and cement thoroughly. Tie on more white chenille, wrap and saturate with crazy glue. Allow to dry. Recoat the chenille underbody with Crazy Glue or epoxy and, before the glue sets, slide on the slider cone from the front, over the hook eye.

Al's Glass Minnow*

Originator: Capt. Al Edwards
Hook: #2 - 1/0
Thread: Clear mono cord
Eyes: Black medium lead dumbbells
Throat: Light olive Ultra Hair
Wing: White Ultra Hair plus pearl Flashabou

Tie on the dumbbell eyes on top of the hook shank, midway between the hook eye and hook bend. Tie on a small clump of light olive Ultra Hair, on top of the hook shank, before and after the dumbbell eyes. Invert the hook in the vise and tie on the white Ultra Hair and pearl Flashabou on top of the hook shank, in front of the dumbbell eyes. Wrap the tying thread back to just behind the dumbbell eyes and then wrap forward, tying off at the hook eye. Whip finish and cement.

*Favorite Fly of Capt. Al Edwards

Almost Nothing Fly

Originator: Tony Route
Hook: Straight eye, standard length
Body: Pearlescent Mylar tinsel
Wing: 6 - 8 strands of pearl Krystal Flash

Wrap the hook shank from bend to hook eye with the Mylar tinsel. Tie off at the hook eye and tie on the Krystal Flash under the hook shank, building thread under the rear so that the fibers extend upward toward the hook bend. Whip finish and cement. This is the same recipe shown on page 22 of Reference 2.

And Jelly Fly

Originator: David E. Azar
Hook: 1/0 to 2/0 Mustad 34007
Thread: White flat waxed nylon
Underwing: White bucktail
Overwing: Olive bucktail and pearl Krystal Flash
Eyes: Large black bead chain

Use a hair stacker to make a small pile of white bucktail fibers whose tips all line up. Select a matchstick-size clump of white bucktail and tie it onto the underside of the hook shank, just before the hook bend. The butt ends should be lined up square, about 1/4 inch in front of the tie-down point. Repeat for a similar bunch of white bucktail on top of the hook shank. Cement both bunches before proceeding. Advance the thread to just in front of the butt ends and tie in another similar-sized clump of white bucktail under the hook shank, keeping the thread in front of the rear bunches. Tie in another similar-sized clump of white bucktail under the hook shank, in front of the last clump. Again, cement each clump as you proceed. Tie in the Krystal Flash on top of the hook shank, at the hook eye, so that it will extend the full length of the fly. Tie on a small clump (half-matchstick size) of olive bucktail on top of the hook shank, so that its fibers extend the same length as the white bucktail fibers. Then tie in the bead chain eyes under the hook shank. Tie in 2 more clumps of white bucktail under the hook shank and one more small clump of olive bucktail on top of

the hook shank. Cement each clump after tying on. Wrap a small tapered head, whip finish and cement.

Ballyhoo Clouser

Originator: Robert Boyle and Dave Whitlock
Hook: Straight eye, long or standard length
Thread: White
Tail: White and olive Ultra Hair and silver Flashabou
Eyes: Lead dumbbells
Nose: White thread

Tie on the dumbbell eyes on the top of the hook shank, just forward of the hook bend. Tie on the white Ultra Hair on top of the hook shank, in front of and behind the dumbbell eyes. Invert the hook in the vise and tie on the olive Ultra Hair just behind the dumbbell eyes, spacing the fibers equally on each side of the hook bend. Fan out the tail end and, while holding it in the fanned position, wrap the fibers with thread and tie off. Saturate the tail end with epoxy and cut a V-notch in it after dry. Build up thread around the dumbbell eyes and wrap a tapered nose with thread, down to the hook eye. Whip finish, paint the top of the nose section with an olive marking pen and paint the nose tip with fluorescent red paint. Coat the entire nose with epoxy. This recipe is similar to that shown on page 38 of Reference 2.

Barry's Dumdrum*

Originator: Capt. Barry Hoffman
Hook: #4 Mustad 34007
Tying Thread: Danville flat waxed brown
Tail: Red and gold Krystal Flash and tan or brown foxtail
Body: Soft webby hackle, hot orange or brown
Head and Body: Copper tinsel chenille
Weedguard: 16-pound Mason (optional) monofilament
Eyes: Brass bead chain

Wrap hook shank with thread. Tie in bead-chain eyes 1/4 inch behind hook eye. Starting at the bend of the hook, tie in 6 strands of red Krystal Flash and 6 strands of gold Krystal Flash. Trim flash so that it extends beyond hook about 1 inch. For a tail, tie in two hot orange hackles, utilizing the soft, webby part of the feather. The length of the tail should be about 3/4 inches, or extending just beyond the hook bend. Starting at the eyes, wrap the body of the fly with copper tinsel chenille back over the orange hackle and again forward over the eyes. Forward of the eyes on the bottom of the hook shank, tie in a length of tan or brown foxtail, so that it extends over and past the hook point. Whip finish and cement the head.

*Favorite Fly of Capt. Barry Hoffman

Barry's Holy Mackerel*

Originator: Capt. Barry Clemson
Hook: 4/0 to 6/0 Mustad 7766
Thread: White Flymaster Plus
Underbody: 0.030 lead wire
Anti-fouling Loop: 30-pound Mason monofilament
Skirt: White bucktail
Wing: 4 medium blue and 4 green grizzly saddle hackles, 15 strands of peacock herl, 10 strands of pearl and 5 strands of blue Flashabou, plus 10 strands of pearl Krystal Flash
Head & Body: Acrylic fiber
Eyes: Prizmatic Stick-ons

Wrap about 10 turns of lead wire onto the hook shank, up to about 1/4 inch from the hook eye. Tie in the horizontal anti-fouling loop and then a skirt of white bucktail, just in front of the hook point. At the same place, on top of the hook, tie on first the blue saddles, then the green grizzly saddles, the flash material and finally the peacock herl. Starting over the wing butts, spin and pack clumps of acrylic fiber forward to the hook eye. Whip finish and cement. Trim the acrylic fiber to shape and attach the eyes with a drop of Goop.

*Favorite Fly of Capt. Barry Clemson

Bendback (A)
Originator: Chico Fernandez
Hook: 1/0 Mustad 34007, debarbed and with bent shaft
Thread: Prewaxed 6/0 red
Body: White chenille or yarn
Wing: Royal or sky blue over white bucktail
Place hook in vise, inverted so that point rides up. Tie on chenille at the hook bend and wrap the thread forward to the hook eye. Wrap the chenille forward to the hook eye and tie off. Tie on the two clumps of bucktail so that they extend over the hook point and well beyond the end of the hook. Tie off, build up thread head, whip finish and cement. This pattern is a variation of the pattern shown on page 7 of Reference 1.

Bendback (B)
Originator: Chico Fernandez
Hook: 1/0 Mustad 34007, with bent shaft
Thread: Prewaxed 6/0 red
Body: White chenille or yarn
Wing: Pink over white bucktail
Place hook in vise, inverted so that point rides up. Tie on chenille at the hook bend and wrap the thread forward to the hook eye. Wrap the chenille forward to the hook eye and tie off. Tie on the two clumps of bucktail so that they extend over the hook point and well beyond the end of the hook. Tie off, build up thread head, whip finish and cement. This recipe is a variation of the pattern shown on page 7 of Reference 1.

Big Eye Deceiver
Originator: Lefty Kreh
Hook: Straight eye, standard length
Wing: 6 to 10 white saddle hackles
Body: Tying thread
Collar: White bucktail
Throat: Red hair or fur
Topping: Peacock herl
Cheeks: 2 mallard breast feathers
Eyes: Painted yellow with black pupils
Head: Red thread
Tie on saddle hackles at the hook bend so that they curve inward together. Wind tying thread forward about 2/3 of the way to the hook eye. Tie on two bunches of bucktail for the collar, one bunch on each side and extending beyond the hook point. Tie on the throat and topping materials just forward of the collar. Tie on the two cheek feathers, after treating with flexible cement and trimming to shape. Build up head with tying thread and whip finish. Add cement to head and paint yellow eyes and black pupils on the cheek feathers.

Bill's Epoxy Crab
Originator: Bill Peabody
Hook: #2 Eagle Claw 254SS
Thread: Clear mono
Body: Tan business card, cut to shape of crab shell
Claws: 2 badger hackle tips
Legs: Strands of peacock herl
Epoxy the business card to the top of the hook shank. Color the top with olive, tan, green and brown markers and cover with a thick coat of clear epoxy. Invert the hook in the vise and epoxy the other side of the card, adding herl legs and hackle-tip claws as the epoxy sets.

Bill Strakele's Popper
Originator: Capt. Bill Strakele
Hook: 3/0 stainless
Tail: 6 chartreuse saddle hackles (3 to 4-1/2 inches long) and 8-10 strands of pearl Krystal Flash or Flashabou
Body: Chartreuse Estaz
Head: White closed-cell foam cylinder, 3/4 inch diameter and 7/8-inch long
Eyes: 3/8 epoxy stick-ons
Tie on the saddle hackles on the side of the hook shank, at the hook bend. Also tie in 4-5 strands of the Krystal Flash or Flashabou in the same place. Glue the wraps to lock them in place. Wrap 6 or 7 turns of the Estaz over the hackle butts and tie off in place. Cut off one end of the foam cylinder at about a 60-degree angle, so that the cylinder's upper length is about 7/8 inches long and its lower length is about 5/8 inches long. Pierce a hole in the lower section of the foam cylinder, so that the hole is about 1/8 inch from and parallel to the lower edge of the cylinder. Add a small amount of epoxy to the hook shank and then push the cylinder onto the hook, from the front end of the hook, turning the cylinder back and forth to distribute the epoxy. The rear of the cylinder should butt against the Estaz body, and the hook eye should protrude just beyond the angled face. Heat the end of a 3/8-inch diameter metal rod and press eye sockets into the foam cylinder. Press the eyes into the eye sockets.

Black Angus
Originators: Eric Leiser and Angus Cameron
Hook: #1 to 2/0
Wing: 4 black saddle hackles
Body: Black marabou plumes
Head: Black dyed deer body hair
Tie on the saddle hackles on the sides of the hook shank, at the hook bend. Cement the butts. Tie in a series of black marabou plumes, winding them forward until about 3/8 inch from the hook eye. Then spin and pack the black deer hair up to the hook eye, tie off, whip finish and cement. Trim the front portion of the head to a pointed shape. This recipe is very similar to that shown on page 60 of Reference 1.

Black Death
Originator: Harry Kime
Hook: Straight eye, standard or 2x short length
Thread: Fluorescent red
Wing: 2 bright red and 4 - 6 black saddle hackles
Collar: Bright red hackle
Head: Fluorescent red
Tie on 1 red and then 2 - 3 black saddles on each side of the hook shank, at the hook bend. Tie on a red hackle stem and wrap so that it fully covers the saddle butts. Tie off the red hackle and build up a thread body, slightly tapering to the hook eye. Tie off, whip finish and epoxy the entire body.

Blonde
Originator: Joe Brooks
Hook: #4 to 6/0
Tail: Bucktail
Body: Bodi Braid
Wing: Bucktail
Eyes: Stick-ons
Head: Thread
Tie on the bucktail tail, first wrapping at the hook bend. Fiber butts should extend up to the hook eye. Tie on the Bodi Braid and wrap forward, over the bucktail underbody. Tie off at the hook eye. Tie on a bucktail wing, on top of the Bodi Braid, just behind the hook eye. Build up a thread head, whip finish and tie off. Attach stick-on eyes and coat the head with

clear 5-minute epoxy. Material colors are at the option of the tier. This recipe is very similar to the ones shown on page 11 of Reference 1.

Blue Back Herring
Originator: Bill Peabody
Hook: 1/0 Eagle Claw 254SS
Thread: Mono
Tail: White bucktail, 1 each white, gray, olive and light blue saddles plus 2 strands each of pearl, pearl blue and pearl olive Flashabou
Skirt: White bucktail
Body: Pearl Bill's Bodi Braid
Collar: White bucktail
Wing: Light gray, medium dark blue and gray Flashabou, 8 strands each
Eyes: Prizmatic stick-ons, silver with black pupils
At the hook bend, tie on the bucktail tail and the 6 strands of Flashabou. On top, tie in the white, gray, olive and light blue saddles flatwing style. Add a white bucktail skirt around the hook shank. Wrap the Bodi Braid up to the hook eye and tie on the white bucktail collar under the hook shank. Tie on the Flashabou wing, build up a large thread head, whip finish and cement. Attach the Prizmatic eyes and coat with epoxy.

Blue Back Pilchard
Originator: Unknown
Hook: #1 - 2/0 Mustad 34011
Thread: Black flat waxed nylon
Tail: Black blood marabou
Body: Pearl Crystal Chenille or Estaz
Underwing: Green and silver Krystal Flash
Overwing: White bucktail and peacock herl
Head: Thread
Eyes: Doll's eyes or stick-on holographic eyes
Tie on a clump of the blood marabou at the hook bend so that it extends about 1 inch beyond the hook bend. Wrap the hook shank from the hook bend to about 1/8 inch behind the hook with the Crystal Chenille. At the hook eye, tie on an underwing of green and silver Krystal Flash, trimming at the marabou. At the same point, on top of the hook shank, tie on a clump of white bucktail and then several strands of peacock herl. Build up a thread head, whip finish and cement. Attach the eyes and coat entire head with either Softex or clear epoxy.

Bob's Banger
Originator: Bob Popovics
Hook: 2/0 Tiemco 911S
Thread: Size A rod-wrapping thread
Tail: White bucktail
Skirt: Large pearl Crystal Chenille or Estaz
Body: Live Body cylinder, covered with silver Banger tape
Eyes: #8 Stick-ons
Tie on the bucktail tail at the hook bend, about twice the length of the hook. Tie in the Crystal Chenille and wrap forward to where the rear end of the body will rest. Prepare the body material by making a hole through its center with a hot bodkin. Wrap the outer surface with Banger tape. Push body onto hook from the front and affix eyes. Epoxy eyes onto cylinder. Either leave body as-is, for future replacement, or epoxy in place. This recipe is the same as shown on page 33 of Reference 2.

Bob's Banger (A)
Originator: Bob Popovics
Hook: 2/0 Tiemco 911S
Thread: Size A rod-wrapping thread
Tail: White bucktail

Skirt: Large chartreuse Crystal Chenille or Estaz
Body: Live Body cylinder, covered with green Banger tape
Eyes: #8 Stick-ons

Tie on the bucktail tail at the hook bend, about twice the length of the hook. Tie in the Crystal Chenille and wrap forward to where the rear end of the body will rest. Prepare the body material by making a hole through its center with a hot bodkin. Wrap the outer surface with Banger tape. Push body onto hook from the front and affix eyes. Epoxy eyes onto cylinder. Either leave body as-is, for future replacement, or epoxy in place. This recipe is very similar to that shown on page 33 of Reference 2.

Bob's Silicone Mullet
Originator: Bob Popovics
Hook: Straight eye, standard length
Wing: Yellow bucktail, 8 to 10 yellow saddle hackles, and pearl Krystal Flash
Collar: Yellow lamb's wool
Head: Yellow lamb's wool and clear silicone rubber with glitter flakes
Eyes: Stick-on Prizmatic eyes

Near the hook bend, tie on first some Krystal Flash and then a bunch of yellow bucktail around the hook shank. Then, tie in 6 to 8 long saddles on the sides of the hook shank, splayed inward. Tie on the other 2 saddles on top, splayed downward. Tie on bunches of long and then short sections of lamb's wool on top, to give a high profile. Tease the wool fibers into position, trim to size and then coat the entire head with a thin layer of clear silicone rubber. Sprinkle glitter flakes onto the silicone rubber and allow to set. After the silicone has set, attach the stick-on eyes and add a final rubber coat to the head. This recipe is the same pattern as shown on page 40 of Reference 2.

Bob's Silicone Mullet (A)
Originator: Bob Popovics
Hook: Straight eye, standard length
Wing: White bucktail, 8 to 10 white saddle hackles, and pearl Krystal Flash
Collar: White lamb's wool
Head: White lamb's wool and clear silicone rubber
Eyes: Stick-on Prizmatic eyes

Near the hook bend, tie on first some Krystal Flash and then a bunch of white bucktail around the hook shank. Then, tie in 6 to 8 long saddles on the sides of the hook shank, splayed inward. Tie on the other 2 saddles on top, splayed downward. Tie on bunches of long and then short sections of lamb's wool on top, to give a high profile. Tease the wool fibers into position, trim to size and then coat the entire head with a thin layer of clear silicone rubber. After the silicone has set, attach the stick-on eyes and add a final rubber coat to the head. This recipe is similar to the pattern as shown on page 40 of Reference 2.

Bone Bugger
Originator: Capt. Lenny Moffo
Hook: #4 to 1/0 Mustad 34007
Tail: Brown or tan schlappen, tan mallard flank fibers, 3 or 4 gold Sili-legs and tan marabou
Eyes: Lead dumbbell type
Body: Tan chenille and 2 to 4 badger hackles
Back: Tan Ultra Hair

Tie in the lead dumbbell eyes about 3/4 of the distance from the hook eye to the hook bend. Just to the rear of the dumbbell eyes, tie in first the schlappen and then the mallard flank fibers, the Sili-legs, more mallard flank fibers and the marabou, in that order. Then, tie in a large group of Ultra Hair fibers, leaving

about 1 3/4 inches extended to the rear. Tie on the badger hackle stems and cement the entire area thoroughly. Palmer the badger hackles forward, through the dumbbell eyes and up to the hook eye. Wind the thread back to the dumbbell eyes, bring the Ultra Hair forward, tie it down and wind the thread forward, repeating to obtain a segmented look for the back. Tie off at the hook eye, leaving about 1/4 inch of the Ultra Hair extending forward. Tease and trim the badger hackle as necessary.

Bonefish Slider
Originator: Tim Borski
Hook: Straight eye, standard length
Wing: Clear craft fur and pearlescent Krystal Flash
Hackle: Long, soft grizzly hackle
Eyes: Lead dumbbells, painted yellow with black pupils
Collar: Dark deer body hair
Head: Natural dark and light deer body hair

Tie on the dumbbell eyes on top of the hook, about 1/4 inch from the hook eye. Invert the hook in the vise. Tie on a large clump of the craft fur around the hook shank at the hook bend. Bar the fur with an olive waterproof marking pen. Tie on the grizzly saddle hackle and palmer forward over the rear half of the hook. Trim the bottom of the grizzly hackle fibers and tease the remainder rearward. Spin and pack the dark deer-hair body. Then spin and pack the dark and light deer-hair head, achieving a mottled effect. Trim the bottom of the head and body flush and the rest round and tapered to the front. Add marker pen color as desired. Tie off, whip finish and cement. This recipe is the same as on page 22 of Reference 2.

Bonito Bunny
Originator: Unknown
Hook: #1 Ower Fly Liner
Thread: Clear mono
Tail: White bunny strip and gold or root beer Krystal Flash
Body: White crosscut bunny strip
Eyes: Small stick-ons

Tie on the Krystal Flash and the bunny strip at the hook bend. Tie on and palmer forward the crosscut bunny strip all the way to the hook eye. Place a small blob of epoxy on each side of the head, and attach the eyes when dry. Cover the eyes with more epoxy for durability.

Bozo Bunker
Originator: Steve Reifsneider
Hook: 1/0 to 4/0 Tiemco 911S
Thread: White 3/0
Body: White, pink and blue Bozo Hair plus silver Krystal Flash
Topping: Black Bozo Hair
Eyes: 3 mm doll eyes

Start thread about 1/4 inch behind the hook eye. Tie in a clump of white Bozo Hair on top of the hook shank, so that an equal amount of hair extends fore and aft of the thread wraps. Tie down securely and then fold the front section of hair over the rear section and again tie down securely. Then tie in, successively in the same way, the Krystal Flash, the pink Bozo Hair, more Krystal Flash, the blue Bozo Hair and the black Bozo Hair. Each clump of material should be butted against the previous clump tightly, to force the fibers to extend in an increasingly upward direction, to increase the fly's lateral profile. Tie off the thread at the hook eye and cement. To maintain the fiber positions, add Zap-a-Gap at the base area of the windings. Glue on the doll eyes and allow to set.

Brad Burns' Grocery Fly
Originator: Brad Burns
Hook: 4/0 Mustad 7766
Thread: White flat waxed nylon
Underbody: 0.030 lead wire
Tail: 8 white schlappen feathers and 10 strands of pink Flashabou
Collar: White bucktail
Wing: Pink, yellow and gray bucktail plus peacock herl and rainbow Flashabou

Tie on the schlappen feathers on top of the hook shank, at the hook bend. Add the pink Flashabou on the sides of the feathers. Tie on clumps of white bucktail on the bottom and sides of the hook shank, about 1/4 inch from the hook eye. Then hi-tie additional clumps of white bucktail for the upper collar. Mix some pink and yellow bucktail and tie a clump of this mixture over the hi-tied collar. Over this, tie on the rainbow Flashabou, the peacock herl and the gray bucktail, in that order. Build up a large head with the white thread, whip finish and cement. Attach the eyes with Goop behind the head on the upper section of the fly.

Bruce's Bay Anchovy
Originator: Joe Bruce
Hook: #2 Mustad 34011
Thread: Fine, clear monofilament
Body: Kreinik 1/8-inch pearl flat ribbon. Wide holo graphic tinsel or Mylar tubing can be substituted
Abdomen: Silver Krystal Flash
Overbody: Polar Bear Ultra Hair
Lateral Line: Wide silver tinsel
Back: Smoke Ultra Hair
Iridescence: Silver Krystal Flash
Top: Gray Ultra Hair
Head: Silver Krystal Flash
Eyes: 3mm silver/black pupil paste-on eyes

Tie in mono thread behind the hook eye and wind to hook bend. Tie in 4 1/2 inches of Kreinik ribbon at this point. Advance thread almost to hook eye and wind ribbon up to thread and tie off. Invert hook in vise so that point and bend are on top. Take about 15-20 strands of Krystal Flash and tie in where the ribbon ends. Wind the Krystal Flash back about 1/8 inch and tie off, trimming the fibers to about 1/4 inch in length. This serves as the abdomen. Invert the hook to its normal position and tie in 10-15 strands of Polar Hair Ultra Hair behind the hook eye. This overbody should extend beyond the hook bend by about 1/2 inches. Tie in the wide silver tinsel on each side of the hook shank, trimming to extend only to the hook bend. Tie a small bundle of smoke Ultra Hair on top of the Polar Bear Ultra Hair, with the butts just to the rear of the Polar Bear butts. Trim to the same length as the Polar Bear hair. Tie about 8-10 strands of silver Krystal Flash on top of the smoke Ultra Hair, trimming to extend about 1/4 inch beyond the Ultra Hair. Get about the same amount of dark gray bucktail and tie down on top of the hook shank, a little further back than the smoke Ultra Hair. Advance the thread to the middle of the head, tying in about 8-10 strands of silver Krystal Flash. Advance the thread to just behind the hook eye and wind the Krystal Flash over the head to cover completely. Wind the mono thread back over the head to cover completely; then cut off the tag ends and whip finish. Apply paste-on eyes to each side of the head and coat the head and eyes with epoxy.

Bruce's Crystal Shrimp
Originator: Joe Bruce
Hook: #4 and 1/0 Mustad 34007
Thread: Fire-Orange flat waxed nylon

Eyes: 1/50 oz. dumbells for #4 hooks (1/36 oz. for 1/0 hooks). Plain lead eyes for light-colored chenille and chrome-plated for the darker bodies.

Antenna: 4 strands each of pearl Flashabou and copper Krystal Flash for #4 hooks, 6 strands each for 1/0 hooks.

Body: Tan, pearl, white, root beer, or pink flash chenille (Estaz)

Tail: Natural deer body hair

Tie on thread behind the hook eye and wind back to a position between the point and barb. Attach lead eyes at this point with figure-8 wraps. Lash tightly by wrapping the thread under the lead eyes and over the hook shank several times. Wind the thread back halfway between the lead eyes and the hook bend and tie in the Flash Chenille at this point. Tie in the Flashabou and the Krystal Flash at this point and then advance the thread back to the hook eye. Invert the hook in the vise, straighten a small bunch of natural deer body hair and tie in with the tips extending about 1/4 inch beyond the hook eye. Advance the thread back to the lead eyes, binding down the deer-hair and keeping it on top of the hook. Trim off excess deer hair butts and finish binding them down. Advance the thread up to the hook eye, invert the hook again and wind the chenille up to and around the lead eyes, passing twice over each side. Then wind the chenille up to the hook eye, tie off, whip finish and apply cement.

Bruce's Suspend Eel
Originator: Bruce Foster
Hook: #1 to 2/0 long shank
Thread: Olive
Tail/Wing: 7 to 9 inches of olive-dyed rabbit fur, 1/8 inch wide
Underbody: Wrapping of 0.010 lead wire to get proper sink rate
Body: Combed olive-dyed wool plus clear silicone
Eyes: Small lead dumbbell eyes

Tie in the dumbbell eyes about 1/4 inch from the hook eye. Wrap the lead wire from the dumbbell eyes to the hook bend. Paint the eyes yellow or gold with black pupils. Tie on the rabbit fur over the length of the hook shank. Tie on the olive wool along the body, whip finish and cement near the hook eye, and trim to the shape of an eel. When the shape is correct, coat the body with clear silicone and allow to dry.

Cactus Striper*
Originator: Lefty Kreh
Hook: 1/0 to 2/0 Mustad 34007 or 34011
Thread: Danville fluorescent red, flat waxed nylon
Tail: Long, slender chartreuse or white saddle hackles with white Krystal Flash or Flashabou
Body: Chartreuse or Pearl Cactus Chenille (Estaz)
Head: Nickel-plated lead eyes, 1/24 or 1/16 oz., with dots of black epoxy for eyes. May substitute Spirit River/Prizmatic tape eyes.

Tie on 4 to 8 saddles at the hook bend. Optionally, also tie on several strands of Krystal Flash or Flashabou. Wrap thread forward and tie on eyes with figure-eight wraps, just to the rear of the hook eye. Wrap thread back to the hook bend and tie on Cactus Chenille. Wrap the chenille forward to the hook eye, with a series of figure-eight wraps over the lead eyes. All thread should be covered at this point. Tie off the chenille just forward of the lead eyes and whip finish.
*Favorite Fly of Capt. Kevin Josenhans

Cape Ann Kinky Klouser
Originator: Capt. Barry Clemson
Hook: 2/0 Mustad 34007
Thread: Medium brown flat waxed nylon

Eyes: Medium lead dumbbells, painted black
Throat: Medium brown Kinky Fiber
Wing: Medium brown and black Kinky Fiber and 25 strands of gold Flashabou

Tie on the dumbbell eyes on top of the hook shank, about 1/4 inch behind the hook eye. Tie on a throat of medium brown Kinky Fiber, tied fore and aft of the dumbbell eyes. Invert the hook in the vise and tie in the gold Flashabou in front of the dumbbell eyes, so that it extends about 1/2 inch longer than the throat fiber. Then, in the same place, tie on first a clump of medium brown Kinky Fiber and then a clump of Black Kinky Fiber. Wrap a large thread head, whip finish and cement. Paint on black eyes with a marking pen.

Capt. Scott's Matagorda Crab
Originator: Capt. Scott Sommerlatte
Hook: #4 Mustad 34011
Thread: Tan Flymaster Plus
Tail: 4 to 6 dark olive saddle hackles, blue Krystal Flash and olive Fly Fur
Body: Cream & olive deer body hair
Legs: Blue Sili-Legs
Eyes: Medium non-toxic dumbbells, painted red or yellow with black pupils

Tie on the saddle hackles on the sides of the hook shank at the hook bend. Tie on the Krystal Flash on top of the hook shank and use tying thread to splay the saddles and Flash so that the tail is V-shaped. Tie on a small clump of olive Fly Fur at the same place. Tie on the dumbbell eyes on top of the hook shank and then tie on 3 pieces of Sili-Legs material onto the hook shank, one in front and the other 2 in back of the dumbbell eyes. Spin and pack the deer hair around the hook shank, keeping the cream hair on top and the olive hair on the bottom, all the way to the hook eye and tie off. The hair near the bend of the hook should flare back over the v-shaped tail. Whip finish and cement near the hook eye. Mark the head and body as desired with permanent marking pens.

Cary's Minnow
Originator: Cary Marcus
Hook: Straight eye, long shank
Thread: Olive
Underbody: White chenille
Throat: Red marabou
Eyes: Solid plastic
Body & Tail: Pearl, peacock and black Krystal Flash
Weedguard: Monofilament loop

Tie on one end of the monofilament weedguard onto the top of the hook shank, wrapping from hook eye to hook bend. Tie on the white chenille at the hook bend and wrap forward to about 1/4 inch from the hook eye. Tie on the plastic eyes, the red marabou throat and then tie on the other end of the monofilament weedguard loop just to the rear of the look eye. Tie on the pearl Krystal Flash evenly on the sides and bottom of the hook shank, just behind the hook eye. Then tie on the peacock Krystal Flash evenly over the top of the hook shank in the same place. Also, tie on a few strands of black Krystal Flash over the peacock Krystal Flash. Move the fibers evenly around the plastic eyes , grasp all of the Krystal Flash fibers at the end and push slightly forward to bow out the middle into the shape of a minnow. While holding the end in place, saturate the front end of the fly with 5-minute epoxy or quick-setting superglue. After the glue has set, wind over all of the Krystal Flash fibers near the tail end, tie off and cement. Trim the tail to shape. This recipe is the same as on page 41 of Reference 2.

Catherwood's American Eel
Originator: Bill Catherwood
Hook: Mustad 34007/3407, Daiichi 2546 or Tiemco 811S
Belly: Olive marabou
Wing: Black, blue-grizzly and drab olive hackle
Head: Black or dark brown deer body hair
Eyes: Glass or plastic, amber with black pupils

At the hook bend, tie on the marabou belly. On the sides, tie on the black hackle. On top, tie on the blue-grizzly and then the drab olive hackle. Tie on the eyes about 1/8 inch behind the hook eye. Spin and pack the deer hair from the hook bend up to the hook eye, through and over the eyes. Tie off at the hook eye, whip finish and cement. Trim the deer hair so that the head has a bullet-nose shape, with the rear fibers tilted back without trimming. This pattern is the same as shown on page 46 of Reference 3.

Cave's Rattlin' Minnow*
Originator: Jon Cave
Hook: Straight eye, standard length, bend-back style
Thread: Orange
Underbody: Glass, plastic or metal rattle chamber, flat twist-on lead
Body: Gold Mylar tubing
Tail: Ends of Mylar tubing strands
Wing: Brown bucktail, pearl Flashabou and copper Krystal Flash
Cheeks: Short, Red Krystal Flash
Head: Orange thread, painted yellow with black pupils

Tie the rattle chamber onto the top of the hook shank with tying thread. Tie lead strip onto the top of the rattle chamber, if you want the hook to ride point up. Slip the Mylar tubing over the rattle chamber and lead strip and secure to the hook bend, leaving some loose Mylar strips as the tail. Tie off with half hitches and cement the tail area. Reattach the tying thread to the front of the fly near the hook eye. Tie down the front end of the Mylar tubing and trim loose ends. Invert the hook in the vise. Tie on a large clump of brown bucktail on top of the hook shank at the hook eye, plus a few strands of Flashabou and a dozen strands of the Krystal Flash. Build up the head with tying thread and paint on eyes and pupils. This recipe is very similar to the one on page 41 of Reference 2.
*Favorite Fly of Capt. Richard Stuhr

Chartreuse Flashtail Clouser
Originator: Bob Clouser
Hook: 2/0 Mustad 34007 or Eagle Claw 413
Thread: Chartreuse flat waxed nylon
Eyes: Medium lead dumbbell eyes
Throat: Chartreuse bucktail
Wing: Chartreuse bucktail and 25 strands of gold Flashabou

Tie on the dumbbell eyes on top of the hook shank, about 1/4 inch behind the hook eye. Tie on a throat of bucktail fore and aft of the beadchain eyes. Invert the hook in the vise and tie on the Flashabou (about 1/2 inch longer than the bucktail) in front of the bead chain eyes, on top of the hook shank. In the same place, tie on a clump of chartreuse bucktail, whip finish and cement.

Chernobyl Crab
Originator: Tim Borski
Hook: Straight eye, standard length
Tail (Claws): White calf tail, orange Krystal Flash and 2 dark furnace hackles
Body: Natural brown deer body hair
Legs: Long, soft brown hackle

Eyes: Lead dumbbells, painted yellow with black pupils

Tie dumbbell eyes on top of hook shank, near hook eye. Wrap thread back to hook bend and tie on 2 clumps of calf tail, one to each side of hook. Tie on Krystal Flash and then the furnace hackles, splayed outward, also on the side. Tie on the brown saddle hackle at the same point. Then spin and pack the deer hair all the way up to the eyes. Trim the deer hair to the shape of a crab. Palmer the brown saddle hackle through the body, tying off at the eyes and trimming off the bottom. Whip finish at the hook eye and cement. This recipe is the same as on page 8 of Reference 2.

Chernobyl Crab (A)*
Originator: Tim Borski
Hook: #2 - #1
Thread: Brown 2/0 nylon
Tail: Brown calf tail, 8 strands of pearl Krystal Flash and 2 grizzly neck hackles
Body: Natural deer body hair, brown saddle hackle
Eyes: Very small to small lead dumbbells, painted yellow with black pupils
Weedguard: Loop of 15-pound Mason hard mono

Tie on dumbbell eyes, on top of hook shank and close to hook eye. At hook bend, tie on one end of mono weedguard, brown calf tail and 8 strands of pearl Krystal Flash. Also, tie in grizzly hackles on the side, splayed outward. Tie on brown saddle hackle and then spin and pack deer hair up to dumbbell eyes. Trim deer hair to shape and then palmer brown saddle through the deer hair, tying off at dumbbell eyes. Tie off other end of mono loop weedguard just to the rear of the hook eye, build up head with thread, whip finish and cement. Paint optional yellow eyes with black pupils on dumbbells. This recipe is a variation of the pattern shown on page 8 of Reference 2.
*Favorite Fly of Capt. Chris Asaro

Chesapeake Fly*
Originator: Capt. Norm Bartlett
Hook: 2/0 Wright McGill 635 jig hook
Thread: White
Body: Iridescent white pipe stem chenille
Wing: White bucktail
Eyes: Silver bead chain

Tie on the bead-chain eyes on top of the hook shank, between the jig bend and the hook eye. Wrap the thread back to the hook bend and tie on the chenille. Wrap the chenille forward, over and through the bead chain eyes, and tie off at the hook eye. Invert the hook in the vise and tie in a large clump of bucktail just to the rear and under the bead-chain eyes. Bucktail should extend about an inch beyond the end of the hook. Wrap the thread forward to the hook eye, tie off and cement.
*Favorite Fly of Capt. Norm Bartlett

Chocolate Eel
Originator: Capt. Eric Glass
Hook: #6 Tiemco 811S
Thread: Black Danville
Tail: Light brown bucktail, 8-10 strands of gray/brown ostrich herl and 6-8 strands of mixed orange and copper Krystal Flash
Body: Medium variegated black/tan chenille
Eyes: Medium bead chain, copper or black
Head: Black tying thread
Weedguard: V-style, 20- to 30-pound fluorocarbon

Tie in a sparse bunch of the bucktail, about 1 to 1.5 inches long, on the top of the middle of the hook shank. Tie in the ostrich herl strands over the bucktail and then tie in 1 or 2 strands of both the orange and the copper Krystal Flash on each side. Tie in one end of the variegated chenille, carry the thread forward and tie on the bead-chain eyes and the weedguard. Then, wind the chenille forward, through and around the eyes, and tie off at the hook eye. Position the weedguard legs, whip finish and cement.

Clear Synthetic Clouser
Originator: Bob Clouser
Hook: Straight eye, standard length
Eyes: Lead dumbbells, painted red with black pupils
Throat: Pearl Flashabou
Wing: Pearl Krystal Flash, silver Flashabou, and pearl Flashabou

Tie the dumbbell eyes on top of the hook, about 1/4 inch behind the hook eye. Tie on a bunch of pearl Flashabou, fore and aft of the eyes, so that the length extends about 2-3 hook lengths beyond the end of the hook. Invert the hook in the vise. Tie on first the Krystal Flash and the silver Flashabou, then a clump of pearl Flashabou, in front of the dumbbell eyes. Tie off, whip finish and cement the head. This recipe is similar to the pattern on page 52 of Reference 2.

Clouser Deep Minnow
Originator: Bob Clouser
Hook: Straight eye, standard length
Eyes: Lead dumbbells, painted red with black pupils
Throat: White bucktail
Wing: Silver Krystal Flash, silver Flashabou, gray bucktail and red bucktail

Tie the dumbbell eyes on top of the hook, about 1/4 inch behind the hook eye. Tie on the white bucktail, fore and aft of the eyes, so that the length extends about 2-3 hook lengths beyond the end of the hook. Invert the hook in the vise. Tie on first the Krystal Flash and the Flashabou, then the gray bucktail and then the red bucktail, in front of the dumbbell eyes. The flash material and the gray bucktail should be as long as the white bucktail throat, but the red bucktail should extend to just beyond the end of the hook. Tie off, whip finish and cement the head. This recipe is the same as on page 52 of Reference 2.

Clouser Deep Minnow (A)
Originator: Bob Clouser
Hook: #1 - 3/0 Mustad 34007
Thread: Danville flat waxed chartreuse nylon
Throat/Wing: Bucktail or Kinky Fiber (olive/white, fluorescent yellow or black), plus silver Krystal Flash, Flashabou and/or Holographic Flashabou
Eyes: Nickel-plated dumbell (1/36 to 3/16 oz.) with holographic stick-on eyes

Tie on dumbell eyes about 1/4 inch behind hook eye, on the top of the shank, opposite hook bend. Then turn the fly over and tie on a small amount of bucktail on top, between the dumbell eyes and the hook eye. Tie on Flashabou to extend 1/2 to 1 inch beyond the bucktail. Then, tie on the Krystal Flash the same length as the bucktail. Tie on the darker shade of bucktail on top (if applicable) and whip finish. This recipe is a variant of the Clouser Deep Minnow pattern on page 42 of Reference 2.

Clouser Deep Minnow (B)*
Originator: Bob Clouser
Hook: #2 - 2/0 Mustad 34007
Body: Pearl Krystal Flash
Thread: 2/0 nylon in white, chartreuse or brown
Eyes: Very small to medium lead dumbbells
Throat: White bucktail
Wing: Silver Krystal Flash and Flashabou, plus chartreuse and white bucktail
Weedguard: 15-pound hard mono loop

Tie dumbbell eyes on top of the hook, about 1/8 inch from hook eye. Tie on the white bucktail throat in back of the dumbbells. Wrap the body with pearl Krystal Flash. Invert the hook in the vise and tie on a clump of white bucktail wing and the Krystal Flash and Flashabou on top of the hook shank. Then tie on a clump of chartreuse bucktail on top of the hook shank. Use brown bucktail here to imitate a young glass minnow. All wing fibers should extend about 2 to 3 hook lengths beyond the hook end. This recipe is similar to the pattern on page 42 of Reference 2.
*Favorite Fly of Capt. Dan Malzone

Clouser Deep Minnow (C)*
Originator: Bob Clouser
Hook: #2 - 2/0 Mustad 34007
Thread: 2/0 nylon in white, chartreuse or clear
Eyes: Medium lead dumbbells
Wing: Few strands of pearl Flashabou, plus chartreuse and white bucktail
Weedguard: 15-pound hard mono loop

Tie dumbbell eyes on top of the hook, about 1/8 inch from hook eye. Invert the hook in the vise and tie on a sparse clump of white bucktail wing and the Flashabou on top of the hook shank. Then tie on a sparse clump of chartreuse bucktail on top of the hook shank. All wing fibers should extend about 2 hook lengths beyond the hook end. This recipe is similar to the pattern on page 42 of Reference 2 and is sometimes tied with a short pearl Flashabou body.
*Favorite Fly of Capt. Mitch Chagnon

Clouser Deep Minnow (D)
Originator: Bob Clouser
Hook: #2 or 1/0 Mustad 34007 debarbed
Thread: Prewaxed 6/0 white and red
Eyes: Lead dumbbells, red with black pupils
Wing: Bucktail, tan/orange, chartreuse/white or all black

Tie on the dumbbell eyes on top of the hook with white thread, near the hook eye. Invert the hook in the vise. Tie on the bucktail wing materials and then tie off the white thread with red thread. Build up the head with thread, tie off, whip finish and cement. This pattern is a variant of the pattern shown on page 42 of Reference 2.

Clouser Deep Minnow (E)*
Originator: Bob Clouser
Hook: 1/0
Thread: Black Danville flat waxed nylon
Eyes: Medium lead dumbbells
Throat: Black bucktail
Wing: Red bucktail plus a few dozen strands of copper Flashabou

Tie on the dumbbell eyes on top of the hook, about 1/4 inch behind the hook eye. Tie on the copper Flashabou on top of the hook, just behind the dumbbell eyes, and then tie on the red bucktail wing over the Flashabou in front of and behind the dumbbell eyes. The Flashabou and red bucktail should extend about two to three hook lengths beyond the end of the hook. Invert the hook in the vise and tie on a clump of black bucktail on top of the hook, just in front of the dumbbell eyes. The black bucktail should extend about one to two hook lengths beyond the end of the hook. Build up a small head with thread in front of the dumbbell eyes, whip finish and cement. Paint the dumbbell eyes your choice of colors. This pattern is a variation of the pattern on page 42 of Reference 2.
*Favorite Fly of Capts. Sarah Gardner and Brian Horsley

Clouser Deep Minnow (F)*

Originator: Bob Clouser

Hook: #2 - 2/0 Mustad 34007

Thread: 3/0 chartreuse nylon flat waxed

Head/Eyes: 3/16 oz. nickel dumbbell eyes

Wing/Throat: Chartreuse and white bucktail, plus silver Krystal Flash

Tie on the dumbbell eyes on the top of the hook shank about 1/4 inch back from the hook eye. Tie on the white bucktail and tie it down, both in front of and behind the dumbbell eyes. Invert the hook in the vise and tie on the Krystal Flash fibers just behind the hook eye. Then, tie on the chartreuse bucktail in the same place. Whip finish and cement the head and eyes. This recipe is very similar to the pattern on page 42 of Reference 2.

*Favorite Fly of Capt. Joe Shute

Clouser Deep Minnow (G)*

Originator: Bob Clouser

Thread: Chartreuse or gray

Head/Eyes: Lead dumbbell eyes, painted yellow with black pupils

Wing/Throat: 2 grizzly dyed chartreuse saddle hackles, chartreuse and white bucktail or Super Hair, plus pearl Krystal Flash or Flashabou

Tie on the dumbbell eyes on the top of the hook shank about 1/4 inch back from the hook eye. Invert the hook in the vise and tie on the grizzly saddles and some white bucktail just behind the hook eye. Then, tie on the Krystal Flash fibers and then the chartreuse bucktail in the same place. Whip finish and cement the head and eyes. This recipe is very similar to the pattern on page 42 of Reference 2.

*Favorite Fly of Capt. Fred Lynch

Clouser Deep Minnow (H)

Originator: Bob Clouser

Hook: Straight eye, standard length

Eyes: Lead dumbbells, pointed red with black pupils

Throat: White bucktail

Wing: Silver or pearl Krystal Flash, silver Flashabou, tan bucktail and white bucktail

Tie the dumbbell eyes on top of the hook, about 1/4 inch behind the hook eye. Tie on the white bucktail, fore and aft of the eyes, so that the length extends about 2-3 hook lengths beyond the end of the hook. Invert the hook in the vise. Tie on first the Krystal Flash and the Flashabou, then the white bucktail and then the tan bucktail, in front of the dumbbell eyes. The flash material and the white bucktail should be as long as the white bucktail throat, but the tan bucktail should extend to just beyond the end of the hook. Tie off, whip finish and cement the head. This recipe is very similar to the pattern shown on page 52 of Reference 2.

Clouser Deep Minnow (I)*

Originator: Bob Clouser

Hook: Straight eye, standard length

Eyes: Lead dumbbells, painted red with black pupils or white with black pupils

Throat: White bucktail

Wing: Silver Krystal Flash, silver Flashabou, and white bucktail

Tie the dumbbell eyes on top of the hook, about 1/4 inch behind the hook eye. Tie on the white bucktail, fore and aft of the eyes, so that the length extends about 2-3 hook lengths beyond the end of the hook. Invert the hook in the vise. Tie on first the Krystal Flash and the Flashabou, then the white bucktail, in front of the dumbbell eyes. The flash material should be as long as the white bucktail throat, but the white bucktail wing should extend to just beyond the end of the hook. Tie off, whip finish and cement the head. This recipe is very similar to the pattern shown on page 52 of Reference 2.

*Favorite Fly of Capt. Joe Shastay

Clouser Deep Minnow (J)

Originator: Bob Clouser

Hook: Straight eye, standard length

Eyes: Lead dumbbells, painted red with black pupils

Throat: White bucktail

Wing: Silver or chartreuse Krystal Flash, silver Flashabou, and gray/white bucktail

Tie the dumbbell eyes on top of the hook, about 1/4 inch behind the hook eye. Tie on the white bucktail, fore and aft of the eyes, so that the length extends about 2-3 hook lengths beyond the end of the hook. Invert the hook in the vise. Tie on first the Krystal Flash and the Flashabou, then the white bucktail and the gray bucktail, in front of the dumbbell eyes. The flash material and the gray bucktail should be as long as the white bucktail throat, but the white bucktail wing should extend to just beyond the end of the hook. Tie off, whip finish and cement the head. This recipe is very similar to the pattern shown on page 52 of Reference 2.

Clouser Deep Minnow (K)

Originator: Bob Clouser

Hook: Straight eye, standard length

Eyes: Lead dumbbells, pointed red with black pupils

Throat: White bucktail

Wing: Silver Krystal Flash, silver Flashabou, green bucktail and white bucktail

Tie the dumbbell eyes on top of the hook, about 1/4 inch behind the hook eye. Tie on the white bucktail, fore and aft of the eyes, so that the length extends about 2-3 hook lengths beyond the end of the hook. Invert the hook in the vise. Tie on first the Krystal Flash and the Flashabou, then the white bucktail and then the green bucktail, in front of the dumbbell eyes. The flash material and the white bucktail should be as long as the white bucktail throat, but the green bucktail should extend to just beyond the end of the hook. Tie off, whip finish and cement the head. This recipe is very similar to the pattern shown on page 52 of Reference 2.

Clouser Deep Minnow (L)

Originator: Bob Clouser

Hook: #2 - 2/0 Mustad 34007

Thread: 2/0 nylon in white, olive or clear

Eyes: Medium lead dumbbells

Wing: Few strands of pearl Flashabou, plus olive and white bucktail

Weedguard: 15-pound hard mono loop

Tie dumbbell eyes on top of the hook, about 1/8 inch from hook eye. Invert the hook in the vise and tie on a sparse clump of white bucktail wing and the Flashabou on top of the hook shank. Then tie on a sparse clump of olive bucktail on top of the hook shank. All wing fibers should extend about 2 hook lengths beyond the hook end. This recipe is similar to the pattern on Page 42 of Reference 2.

Clouser Deep Minnow (M)*

Originator: Bob Clouser

Hook: Straight eye, standard length

Eyes: Lead dumbbells, painted red with black pupils

Throat: White bucktail

Beard: Red Krystal Flash

Wing: Pearl and red Krystal Flash, chartreuse and olive bucktail, and peacock herl

Tie the dumbbell eyes on top of the hook, about 1/4 inch behind the hook eye. Tie on the white bucktail, fore and aft of the eyes, so that the length extends about 2-3 hook lengths beyond the end of the hook. Tie on a short beard with red Krystal Flash, in front of the dumbbell eyes and on top of the hook shank. Invert the hook in the vise. Near the hook eye, on top of the hook shank tie on first the pearl Krystal Flash, then chartreuse bucktail, then the olive bucktail, and then the red Krystal Flash and the peacock herl. Tie off, whip finish and cement the head. This recipe is similar to the pattern on page 52 of Reference 2.

*Favorite Fly of Capt. Jeff Poe

Clouser Deep Minnow (N)*

Originator: Bob Clouser

Thread: Chartreuse

Head/Eyes: Brass-plated dumbbell eyes with black/white stick-ons

Wing/Throat: Chartreuse and white bucktail, plus gold Flashabou

Tie on the dumbbell eyes on the top of the hook shank about 1/4 inch back from the hook eye. Tie on a generous amount of gold Flashabou on top of the hook shank, behind the dumbbell eyes. Then, tie on the white bucktail, both in front of and behind the dumbbell eyes. Invert the hook in the vise and tie on the chartreuse bucktail just behind the hook eye. Whip finish and cement the head and eyes. This recipe is very similar to the pattern on page 42 of Reference 2.

*Favorite Fly of Capt. Tom Mleczko

Clouser Deep Minnow (O)

Originator: Bob Clouser

Hook: #1 to 2/0 Tiemco 811S

Thread: White 3/0

Eyes: Lead dumbbells

Throat: White bucktail

Wing: 8-12 strands of pearl Krystal Flash and pink bucktail

Tie the dumbbell eyes on top of the hook, about 1/8 inch behind the hook eye. Tie on a clump of white bucktail, fore and aft of the eyes, so that the length extends well beyond the end of the hook. Invert the hook in the vise. Tie on first the Krystal Flash and then the pink bucktail, in front of the dumbbell eyes. The flash material should be as long as the white bucktail throat, but the pink bucktail wing should extend to just beyond the end of the hook. Tie off, whip finish and cement the head. This recipe is very similar to the pattern on page 52 of Reference 2.

Clouser Deep Minnow (P)*

Originator: Bob Clouser

Hook: #2 - 2/0 Mustad 34007

Thread: 2/0 nylon in white, olive or clear

Eyes: 7/32 oz. Spirit River nickel dumbbells with Real Eyes stick-ons

Body: Pearl EZ Bodi Braid

Wing: Few strands of pearl Flashabou and silver Krystal Flash plus olive, red and white bucktail

Tie dumbbell eyes on top of the hook, about 1/8 inch from hook eye. Wrap the Bodi Braid from the hook bend to and through the dumbbell eyes and tie off. Invert the hook in the vise and tie on a clump of white bucktail wing and the Krystal Flash and Flashabou on top of the hook shank just behind the hook eye. Then tie on a very sparse clump of red bucktail at the same place. Finally, tie on a clump of olive bucktail in the same place. All wing fibers should extend about 2 hook lengths beyond the hook end. This recipe is similar to the pattern on page 42 of Reference 2.

*Favorite Fly of Capt. Ian Devlin

Clouser Minnow

Originator: Bob Clouser

Hook: #2 - 4
Thread: Chartreuse
Wing: White and chartreuse bucktail, plus pearl
    Krystal Flash
Eyes: Small silver bead chain
Weedguard: 20-pound double mono
Invert hook in vise (hook and bend up) and tie in bead-chain eyes about 1/8 inch from hook eye, using a figure-8 wrap. Tie on one end of the mono weedguard loops near the hook bend. Tie in first the white bucktail and then 4 strands of Krystal Flash on the side of the bucktail. Then, tie in the chartreuse bucktail on top of the white bucktail. Bucktail should be about twice the length of the hook. Finally, tie on the two ends of the mono weedguard loops, whip finish the head and cement. This recipe is an adaptation of the Clouser Deep Minnow pattern described on page 42 of Reference 2.

Cockroach

Originator: John Emery
Hook: Straight eye, standard length
Thread: Black
Wing: 4 to 8 grizzly hackles
Collar: Natural brown bucktail, gray or
    red squirrel tail
Head: Black thread
Tie in the grizzly hackles on the sides of the hook shank, at the hook bend. Cement the hackle butts and then wrap the tying thread forward to the hook eye. Tie on the bucktail or squirrel tail evenly around the hook shank so that the fibers extend about an inch beyond the rear of the hook. Build up a thread head, whip finish and cement. This recipe is the same as shown on page 3 of Reference 2.

Cockroach Deceiver

Originator: John Emery, Lefty Kreh
Thread: Black or brown
Tail: 8 to 15 grizzly hackles plus and 6-8 strands of
    gold Flashabou or Krystal Flash
Collar: Natural brown bucktail
Head: Thread
Tie in the grizzly hackles on the sides of the hook shank at the hook bend. Tie in the Flashabou on top of the hook shank. Wrap the thread forward and tie on large clumps of brown bucktail around the hook shank, adjacent to the hook eye. Build up a thread head, whip finish and cement. This recipe is the same as shown on page 17 of Reference 1.

Craft Fur Shrimp*

Originator: George Close
Hook: #2 or #4 Mustad 34007
Thread: 6/0 red nylon
Eyes: Silver bead chain
Tail: Tan craft fur and 4 strands of pearl Krystal Flash
Body: Blend of tan craft fur dubbing and hare's ear
    Lite Brite
Wing: Red-brown craft fur
Weedguard: 20-pound hard Mason mono
Debarb and sharpen the hook. Tie a pair of eyes on top of the hook, about 1/4 inch behind the eye. Add super glue to keep the eyes from turning. Blacken the eyes with a permanent marker and coat with Hard As Nails clear fingernail polish or Loon's Hard Head fly finish. Tie in the Krystal Flash behind the eyes, to extend 2 and 1/2 inches beyond the hook and trim the ends so that they are uneven in length. Cut off a small clump of tan craft fur close to the backing. Clean out and save the underfur. Tie in the 3-inch-long clump behind the eyes and bind down to the hook bend. Chop the Lite Brite into 3/4 inch lengths and blend with the saved tan craft underfur to make

a sparkling dubbing. Spin to form a chenille about 4 inches long. Wrap the chenille from the hook bend to the eyes, figure-eight around the eyes and tie off in front of the eyes. Cut and clean out a small clump of red brown craft fur and tie in on the bottom side of the hook in front of the eyes. Flatten about 1/8 inch of a short piece of the mono. Treat the flattened section with super glue and tie in just behind the hook eye. Tie off, cement wraps and trim the weedguard to the proper length. Finish off the fly with permanent markers, black and red, to create a segmented-body appearance.
*Favorite Fly of Capt. Dave Gibson.

Crazy Charlie (A)

Originator: Bob Nauheim
Hook: #6 Mustad 34007, debarbed
Thread: Prewaxed 6/0 red
Body: Gold or silver Mylar tinsel
Wing: Black/yellow or white calf tail or squirrel tail
Eyes: Silver bead chain
Tie on the tinsel at the hook bend and wind the thread forward to the hook eye. Wrap the tinsel forward to the hook eye and tie off. Tie on the bead-chain eyes on top of the hook, near the hook eye. Invert the hook in the vise and tie on the wing material so that it covers the hook point and extends well beyond the end of the hook. Tie off, whip finish and cement the head area. This is a variant of the pattern shown on Page 25 of Reference 2.

Crazy Charlie (B)

Originator: Bob Nauheim
Hook: Mustad 34007 or 3407
Thread: White
Tail: Pearl Flashabou
Body: Pearl Flashabou and clear mono
Eyes: Silver bead chain
Wing: 2-4 cream hackle tips
Tie on the bead-chain eyes on top of the hook shank near the hook eye. Tie on a few strands of pearl Flashabou so that they extend beyond the hook bend about 1/2 inch. Then tie on the clear mono. Wrap the Flashabou forward, tying it off at the bead-chain eyes. Then wrap the mono up to the hook eye and tie off. Invert the hook in the vise. Tie on the hackle tips just behind the bead-chain eyes. Wrap the tying thread around the bead-chain eyes and up to the hook eye, forming a small head. Whip finish and cement. This pattern is very similar to the original Crazy Charlie pattern on page 18 of Reference 3.

Crazy Charlie (C)

Originator: Bob Nauheim
Hook: #6 - 2, Mustad 34007 or 3407
Thread: White
Tail: Pearl Flashabou
Body: Pearl Flashabou and 15- to 20-pound clear
    mono
Eyes: Silver bead chain
Wing: White calf tail and 2 grizzly hackle tips
Tie on the bead-chain eyes on top of the hook shank near the hook eye. Wrap the tying thread back to the hook bend and tie on the Flashabou tail. Then tie on the clear mono and a few strands of pearl Flashabou. Wrap the Flashabou forward, tying it off at the bead-chain eyes. Then wrap the mono up to the hook eye and tie off. Invert the hook in the vise. Tie on the calf tail and grizzly hackle tips just behind the bead chain eyes, building some thread behind the wraps so that the hackles and calf-tail fibers point toward the hook point. Wrap the tying thread around the bead-chain eyes and up to the hook eye, forming a small head. Whip finish and cement. This pattern is very similar

to the original Crazy Charlie pattern on page 18 of Reference 3.

Crazy Charlie (D)

Originator: Bob Nauheim
Hook: #6 - 2, Mustad 34007 or 3407
Thread: White
Tail: Pearl Krystal Flash
Body: Pearl Krystal Flash and 15- to 20-pound clear
    mono
Eyes: Silver bead chain
Wing: White bucktail
Tie on the bead-chain eyes on top of the hook shank near the hook eye. Wrap the tying thread back to the hook bend and tie on the Krystal Flash tail. Then tie on the clear mono and the pearl Krystal Flash. Wrap the Krystal Flash forward, tying it off at the bead-chain eyes. Then wrap the mono up to the hook eye and tie off. Invert the hook in the vise. Tie on the bucktail just behind the bead-chain eyes, building some thread behind the wraps so that the fibers point toward the hook point. Wrap the tying thread around the bead-chain eyes and up to the hook eye, forming a small head. Whip finish and cement. This pattern is very similar to the original Crazy Charlie pattern on page 18 of Reference 3.

Crease Fly

Originator: Capt. Joe Blados
Hook: 1/0 to 4/0 Mustad 34011SS
Thread: White K-Thread
Tail: Bucktail, bunny strip, feathers, etc and Krystal
    Flash to match the Fun Foam body
Body: Fun Foam, color of your choice
Eyes: Witchcraft stick-ons
Weedguard: Optional
First tie in the tail, at the hook bend, and then cover the hook shank with tying thread. Take a piece of rectangular Fun Foam about the size of the hook, fold it in half, and trim it so that it simulates a baitfish profile. Cut the head end of the foam flat (blunt), to prevent the fly from spinning when retrieved. Place the foam over the hook shank (folded edge up) so that most of the body is above the hook shank and the hook eye is just inside the mouth. Glue the lower edges of the body together with thick cyano-acrylate glue, using an accelerator spray to ensure instant bonding. Push down on the head of the fly to promote a cupped face. Squeeze the body's tail section down onto the tail material and run some more glue down the hook shank to the tail, from the mouth section. Spray with accelerant to seal the rear of the body. Use permanent marking pens to create a colorful and realistic fly. Draw in a gill opening and add the stick-on eyes. Cover the entire fly with 5-minute epoxy, lightly sprinkle on some fine glitter flakes and allow to cure.

Crease Fly Minnow

Originator: Joe Blados
Hook: Straight eye, long shank
Tail: Blue-gray bucktail, olive-brown bucktail, pearl
and peacock Krystal Flash
Body: Live Body foam sheet
Eyes: Prismatic stick-ons
At the hook bend, tie on some pearl Krystal Flash, then blue-gray bucktail, sparse olive-brown bucktail and peacock Krystal Flash, in turn. Crease a piece of Live-Body foam and trim so that is has a minnow profile. Coat the inside with super glue and attach over and around hook shank. Squeeze the halves together and adjust to an appropriate position before the glue sets. Color the body surface as desired with permanent marking pens and add the stick-on eyes. Coat the entire body with clear epoxy.

Crystal Chenille Mullet

Originator: Unknown
Hook: 2/0 Mustad 90233S
Thread: White 3/0 flat waxed or fine clear mono
Tail: Brown or green saddle hackle with pearl
  Flashabou
Body: Large Crystal Chenille
Eyes: 3-D stick-ons
Tie on several saddle hackles and the Flashabou at the hook bend. Tie in the chenille over the butt wraps and wrap forward to the eye of the hook. Tie off, whip finish and cement. Trim body to desired shape. Stick on eyes and cover with epoxy or Softex. Use permanent marker to darken the top of the fly.

Crystal Crab

Originator: Joe Bruce
Hook: #1 to 2/0
Thread: Red
Claws: Clumps of natural deer hair
Eyes: 2 lengths of silver bead chain, 3 beads each
Legs: Rubber-band strips or live-rubber kegs
Body: Root beer Krystal Flash
Tie on the 2 bead-chain links on the top of the hook, at mid shank, so that the links lay side by side with 2 beads each extending off to one side and one bead each extending off to the other side. Paint the outer 2 beads black. Tie on a thick clump of deer hair at mid-shank, so that the fibers extend about 1/3 of an inch beyond the hook bend. Repeat at the other end of the hook, so that the fibers extend about 1/4 inch beyond the hook eye. The butt ends of the 2 clumps should meet each other at mid-shank. When the thread tension is correct to obtain the proper position of both clumps, saturate the clump butts with cement. Then tie on a large number of Krystal Flash fibers at the hook bend and wrap forward over the deer hair and tie off and cement.

Cuda Fly

Originator: Unknown
Hook: 1/0 to 2/0 Mustad 34007
Thread: Black flat waxed nylon
Body/Tail: Pearl Flashabou, plus white, fluorescent
  green and brown FisHair
Tag: Fluorescent orange thread
Head: Thread
At the hook bend, first tie in several strands of pearl Flashabou. Then, add a layer of white, then fluorescent green and then brown FisHair on top. Build up a thread head, behind which is a few wraps of orange thread. Then wrap a tapered needle or beak down to the hook eye. Coat the thread wraps with epoxy. Eyes are optional.

Dahlberg Diver:

Originator: Larry Dahlberg
Hook: Straight eye, standard length
Tail: Several light ginger variant hackles, plus cream
  and tan marabou and gold Flashabou
Collar: Golden-tan deer body hair
Head and Diving Collar: Golden-tan deer body hair
At the hook bend, tie on some gold Flashabou and then the ginger hackles and a short bunch of tan and cream marabou. Wrap and spin the body hair, tightly packing it all the way to the hook eye. Tie off, whip finish and cement at the hook eye. Trim all deer hair so that the fly's bottom is flat and nearly flush with the hook shank. Also, trim and taper the head top and sides back to a steep flair at the collar. Finally, trim the collar fibers so that they are even in length. This pattern is the same as shown on page 43 of Reference 2.

Dave's Glassy

Originator: Capt. Dave Harding
Hook: #4 stainless steel, laser-sharpened
Thread: White Danville, flat waxed nylon
Tail: White rabbit fur
Body: 20-pound monofilament plus 2 strands silver
  tinsel
Wing: White and chartreuse bucktail
Topping: 6 strands clear or rainbow light Krystal Flash
Eyes: (2) - 3/16 hologram-type
Tie a small tuft of rabbit fur at hook bend for tail. Tie monofilament on top of hook, starting at hook eye and extending over hook bend. Wrap over with tying thread 3 or 4 times to secure mono to hook and build up body. Tie in 2 strands of silver tinsel at hook eye and wind down to hook bend, back again to eye and tie off. Wrap monofilament tightly over silver tinsel, with no gaps. Trim off excess mono. Tie sparse white bucktail wing on both sides, near hook eye. Leave hook shank bottom exposed. Tie 6 strands of Krystal Flash on top of hook near eye, extending to length of wings. Tie a sparse wing of chartreuse bucktail on top of hook, over the Krystal Flash. Build up head with tying thread and tie off. Cement eyes to each side of head and seal head with head cement.

Dave's Hermit Crab

Originator: Capt. David Kreshpane
Hook: #4 - 6 Mustad 34007
Thread: White 3/0 monocord
Tag: Pink Krystal Flash
Legs (Claws): 3 tan grizzly hackle tips
Body: White chenille
Shell Back: EZ Shape Sparkle Body
Head: Thread
Weedguard: Stiff mono piece
Tie on a short bunch of the Krystal Flash at the hook bend. Then tie in the hackle tips near the middle of the hook shank, making sure that they stick out perpendicular to the hook shank about 1/4 inches. Wrap the chenille body from the hook bend to the hook eye, through and around the hackle tips. Tie off the chenille at the hook eye, add a mono weedguard, whip finish and cement. Coat the top of the fly, just over the hackle tips, with the Sparkle Body, being careful not to coat the hackles.

Dave's Seminole Clouser*

Originator: Bob Clouser
Hook: #2 Mustad 34011
Thread: Size G, fluorescent orange
Eyes: 3/16 small gold Super Eyes
Throat: Orange bucktail
Wing: Gold Holographic Tinsel and gold Krystal Flash,
  over burnt orange bucktail, topped with dark red
  bucktail and red Krystal Flash
This fly is tied in standard Clouser Minnow style, with the eyes tied near the hook eye, opposite the direction of the hook bend. The orange bucktail is tied on fore and aft of the Super Eyes shank, and on the same side of the hook shank. On the opposite side of the hook shank, tie on first the gold Holographic Tinsel, then the burnt orange bucktail, and then the gold Krystal Flash. Finish by tying on the red bucktail and then the red Krystal Flash. Form a small head with the orange tying thread and then tie off and saturate the head with cement.
*Favorite Fly of Dave Settoon

Dave's Wide Side*

Originator: Capt. Dave Chouinard
Hook: 3/0 to 5/0 Eagle Claw L2222 Circle Hook
Thread: 3/0 white
Wing: Yellow bucktail or Kinky Fiber, green and gold

Flashabou, polar flash and pink and olive FisHair
Eyes: Small Mylar or epoxy eyes
Place hook in vise with gap up. Starting near the hook bend, tie on 10-15 strands of yellow bucktail, angling the fibers so that they extend approximately parallel to an imaginary line between the hook eye and the hook point. Repeat with 5 to 7 strands of Polar Flash, alternating these two materials until just before you reach the hook eye. Mix a bunch of olive FisHair with several strands each of gold and green Flashabou and pink FisHair, and tie onto the top of the hook, adjacent to the hook eye. Form a thread head, whip finish and cement. Epoxy the eyes to the hook shank and FisHair, allow to set and then recoat the eyes with epoxy.
*Favorite Fly of Capt. Dick Dennis

Dean's Minnow

Originator: Chris Dean
Hook: #6 to 2
Thread: 6/0 white monocord
Wing: Blonde or white Craft Fur or Fly Fur, plus green
  and black Krystal Flash
Body: 40-pound monofilament and silver Mylar tinsel
Eyes: Painted yellow with black pupils
Wind a thread base from the hook eye to the hook bend and back. Tie on a piece of 40-pound monofilament on top of the hook shank, leaving the remainder hanging for now. Tie in the Mylar tinsel just behind the hook eye. Wind back to the hook bend, back to the hook eye and then tie off. Wrap the mono forward over the Mylar and tie down just behind the hook eye. Tie on a one-inch-long, small clump of Craft Fur just behind the hook eye, on both the top and the bottom of the hook shank. Tie on a sparse topping of both green and black Krystal Flash on top of the hook shank. Build a thread head, whip finish and cement. Paint on the eyes. This recipe is the same as shown on pages 136-137 of the February 1998 issue of *Florida Sportsman* magazine.

Deep Candy

Originator: Bob Popovics
Hook: #1 Tiemco TMC 811S
Thread: 3/0 white
Tail: White Super Hair plus pearl and silver Flashabou
Head: Silver saltwater bead
Body: 5-minute epoxy
Eyes: Black/silver stick-on eyes
Position and tie on the silver bead on the hook shank, to the rear of the hook eye. Tie on the white Super Hair, followed by first the pearl and then the silver Flashabou. Whip finish and cement. Build up the body with the 5-minute epoxy and allow to set. Affix the stick-on eyes and add a thin coat of epoxy to secure the eyes.

Deep Candy Bendback

Originator: Bob Popovics
Hook: #4 to 1/0 Tiemco 911S, bendback-shaped
Thread: Clear Danville mono
Head: Lead Conehead
Tail: Pink and white Super Hair
Lateral Line: 2 strips of holographic silver Witchcraft
Body: Pearl Flashabou
Eyes: Silver Prism Witchcraft
Slide the conehead onto the hook and position it behind the hook eye with winding thread. Tie in the white Super Hair behind the conehead, on top of the hook shank. Next, tie in the pink Super Hair on top, in the same place. Tie on the lateral line strips on the sides of the hook shank. Tie on a sparse clump of pearl Flashabou under the hook shank. Coat the head and the hook shank area immediately behind the

conehead with 5-minute clear epoxy After drying, apply the eyes to the conehead and cover the eyes with more clear epoxy.

Deer Hair Bass Bug

Originator: Unknown
Hook: 2/0
Thread: 2/0 nylon, either brown or black
Tail: White or black calf tail, plus 6 white or black saddle hackles and strands of Krystal Flash or Flashabou
Body: Spun and packed deer hair, either white or black
Weedguard: 20-pound hard mono loop

Tie on one end of the mono weedguard, from hook eye to hook bend. Tie on the calf tail on the top of the hook shank at the hook bend. Also tie on the Krystal Flash on the top of the hook. Then tie on the saddle feathers at the hook bend, on each side of the hook shank. Spin and pack the deer hair from hook bend to hook eye, followed by whip-finishing and cementing. Trim the deer hair to the desired shape.

Deer Hair Shrimp

Originator: Tim Borski
Hook: #1 Tiemco 811S
Tail: Tan craft fur
Legs: Long tan hackles
Body: Natural deer body hair
Eyes: Burnt Monofilament

Tie on the tan hackles on the side of the hook shank, at about the mid-point. At the same point, tie on a clump of tan craft fur. Take a short piece of monofilament and light each end briefly, to form dark balls of melted mono. Just to the rear of the hook eye, tie on the mono eyes, so that the monofilament is perpendicular with the hook shank. Spin and pack the deer body hair on the hook shank, starting over the tail butt wraps. Pull the rearmost fibers so that they flare to the rear. Spin and pack tightly and tie off just to the rear of the mono eyes. Trim the body bottom fairly flat and the top and sides into a tapered half-round shape, much like a slider. Give the body a barred appearance by marking with an olive marking pen. This recipe is identical to the one shown on page 28 of Reference 4.

Deer-Hair Slider

Originator: Larry Dahlberg
Hook: #1 - 3/0, 3-4XL
Tail: Tan marabou or feathers, often with Flashabou or Krystal Flash added to each side
Body: None
Head: Natural deer body hair
Weedguard: Mono loop

Tie in thread at hook bend and tie in marabou and Krystal Flash at that same point. Attach one end of mono weedguard and advance forward 2/3 of the hook shank. Pack or spin deer hair all the way to hook eye, attach other end of mono weedguard, tie off and add cement. Trim deer hair so that the head has a flaring collar and a pointed nose. This pattern is based on the Dahlberg Diver, page 9 of Reference 1.

Del Brown's Permit Fly

Originator: Del Brown
Hook: Straight eye, standard length
Thread: Fluorescent green
Tail (Claws): 4-6 ginger variant hackle tips plus sparse pearl Flashabou
Legs: White rubber with red tips
Body: Tan and brown yarn
Eyes: Chrome lead dumbbells

Tie dumbbell eyes onto top of hook shank, close to hook eye. Wrap thread back to hook bend and tie on

hackle tips, splayed outward. Also tie on Flashabou. Tie on strands of yarn on top of the hook, perpendicular to the hook shank. Alternate tan and brown strands. Trim yarn profile to shape of crab carapace. Tie on 3 sets of rubber legs among yarn strips, using an overhand knot. Tie off, whip finish and cement eye area. Also, thoroughly cement knotted legs and yarn ties. This recipe was prepared from the pattern on page 8 of Reference 2.

Del Brown's Permit Fly (A)

Originator: Del Brown
Hook: 1/0 Mustad 34007, debarbed
Thread: Plain Kevlar
Body: Aunt Lydia's Craft & Rug Yarn, brown or yellow
Eyes: Red dumbbell
Legs: Rubber

Tie on yarn strips tightly along the hook shank up to the hook eye. Comb the yarn and trim to the shape of a crab carapace. Tie on the dumbbell eyes at the hook eye. Tie on 3 rubber legs. Tie off in front of the eyes, whip finish and cement. This pattern is a variant of the pattern shown on page 8 of Reference 2.

Del's Crab Fly

Originator: Del Brown
Hook: #6 to #4, Mustad 34007
Thread: Brown Danville, flat waxed nylon
Tail: 4 small brown neck hackles
Body: Brown Antron or Aunt Lydia's Rug Yarn
Legs: Round rubber
Eyes: Small lead dumbbell or bead chain

Tie in the small neck hackles splayed out just ahead of the bend of the hook. Take a one-inch piece of the yarn and tie it next to the hackle butts, oriented perpendicular to the hook shank. Tie in additional pieces of yarn by wrapping a figure-eight thread over each strand, until you have reached a point about 2/3 of the way up the shank toward the eye. Tie the eyes on between the yarn and the hook eye and whip finish the head. Tie in 4 sets of rubber legs by using a figure-eight wrap on the strands of rubber. Cut the yarn and the legs to shape and tease out the yarn with a bodkin. The completed fly shouldn't be larger than your thumbnail. This recipe is largely based upon Del Brown's Permit Fly or Merkin, described on page 8 of Reference 2.

Dino's Rattlin Bunny

Originator: Dino Torino
Hook: 1/0 Mustad 34007, or equivalent
Thread: White
Rattle: Small, 3 mm
Tail Guard: 20-pound mono loop
Tail: White Zonker strip
Body: Small pearl Crystal Chenille
Wing: Olive, chartreuse, tan, white or yellow Fly Fur or Polar Fibre
Eyes: Size 2.5 yellow Witchcraft stick-ons

Tie on a small loop of mono at the hook bend (to prevent tail wrapping of rabbit strip). Loop ends should be under the hook shank and the plane of the loop should be horizontal. Tie on the rattle on top of the hook shank at about its midpoint. Use plenty of thread, and saturate with clear epoxy. Tie on the Zonker-strip tail and build up a small thread ramp to transition from the rabbit strip to the rattle. Tie on the Crystal Chenille plus a small piece of white tying thread and wrap the chenille forward to the hook eye. Then overwrap the chenille with the tying thread, in an even spiral pattern, tying off at the hook eye. Tie a clump of the Fly Fur on top of the hook, at the hook eye, whip finish and cement. Coat the front half-inch of the fly with clear epoxy or equivalent, being care-

ful to keep the Fly Fur on top of the fly. After the epoxy is dry, add the stick-on eyes, draw in gill markings with red paint, and add another coat of clear epoxy.

Dixon's Devil Worm

Originator: Capt. Paul Dixon
Hook: #2 Mustad 34007
Thread: Black
Tail: Clump of blood-red marabou
Body: Pink and black-green Lite Brite

Tie on a large clump of the marabou somewhat past the hook bend. Wrap the rear 3/4 of the hook shank with the pink Lite Brite and the front 1/4 with the black-green Lite Brite. Tie off at the hook eye, whip finish and cement. This recipe is the same as shown on page 54 of Reference 3.

DL's Fuzz-Tail Glass Minnow

Originator: D.L. Goddard
Hook: #6 to 1/0 Mustad 34011
Thread: Fine, clear monofilament
Body and Tail: Fine, pearl Mylar tubing and Prizmatic ultra-fine glitter
Eyes: 2.5 mm black/silver stick-ons

Cut a 4 1/2-inch piece of the pearl Mylar tubing, poke a hole through the center of this tubing, and slip it over the eye of the hook. Tie it in place right behind the hook eye, so that the two ends point up and down, aligned with the hook bend. Wind the mono thread back to the hook bend, pull the upper section of tubing back tightly and bind it down at the hook bend, on top of the hook shank. Repeat with the bottom section of tubing, tying it down under the hook shank. Cut the tag ends of the tubing off, leaving 1/4-to 1/2-inch unraveled sections for the tail. Color the frayed Mylar tail with a yellow marker, if desired. Color the top length of tubing black, olive or green to simulate the minnow's back. The hook shank serves as the minnow's lateral line. Use a bodkin to stretch the upper and lower tubing sections, achieving a minnow-like lateral shape. Apply the stick-on eyes to the front of the hook shank. Mix a small amount of clear 5-minute epoxy, with a small amount of glitter added. While rotating the hook in the vise, add very small amounts of the epoxy/glitter to the Mylar tubing frame pieces, being careful to maintain the tubing and the hook shank in a flat plane. Continue rotating the hook until the epoxy has set enough to prevent sagging and distortion. This recipe is the same as shown on pages 158 to 161 of the May 2000 Issue of *Florida Sportsman* magazine.

DL's Redbone Fluff

Originator: D.L. Goddard
Hook: #4 to 3/0 Mustad 34007 or Tiemco 811S
Thread: Clear, fine monofilament
Body: Tan, cream, golden variant, olive variant or crawfish orange crosscut rabbit strip
Antennae: Stiff peccary hair or moose mane
Eyes: Large gold bead chain or 1/30 to 1/36 ounce lead dumbbell eyes
Weedguard: 3 1/2-inch piece of 25-pound hard Mason monofilament

Fold over the monofilament material at its midpoint, and while squeezing the bent end with serrated pliers, bend the two legs downward. Burn the ends of the mono lightly with a butane lighter, to form a pair of clear eyeballs. Tie in the dumbbell eyes on top of the hook shank, quite close to the hook eye. Wind the thread down to the start of the hook bend and tie in two peccary hairs on top of the hook shank, parallel to each other. Adjust the hairs so that they angle slightly downward, and cement. Tie in the rabbit strip over the peccary hair base and apply some head cement. Wind the thread forward and then palmer the rabbit strip forward to the dumbbell eyes. Tie the strip down, but do not cut off. Invert the hook in the vise and tie on the weedguard base on top of the hook shank, over the dumbbell eyes. Tie in the weedguard securely, so that the mono legs extend well beyond the hook point. Wrap the rabbit strip one more turn, to hide the weedguard base and tie off at the hook eye. Whip finish the head and cement. This recipe is the same as shown on pages 88-89 of the October 1999 Issue of *Florida Sportsman* magazine.

Double Bunny

Originator: Scott Sanchez
Hook: #2 to 3/0 Dai-Riki 930
Thread: 3/0 nylon
Underbody: .035 inch lead wire
Body/Wing: Dark and light rabbit strips and several strands of pearl Flashabou
Eyes: 5/16 inch stick-ons
Weedguard: Hard mono loop (optional)
With the hook out of the vise, wrap the lead wire over the front half of the hook shank, leaving only a small area open behind the hook eye. Impale the light belly strip leather with the hook point. Place the hook in the vise, secure the lead wraps, and tie down the belly strip just in back of the hook eye. Use a bodkin to put contact cement on the leather portions of the darker rabbit strip and the lighter rabbit strip and on the top and bottom of the thread-covered lead wrapping. Holding the tail end of the two strips together with the left hand, use the right hand to pinch the leather sides of the strips together and against the lead wrappings. Then, add a few strands of the Flashabou on each side of the hook, tying them off at the head. Finish the head, whip finish and cement. Lightly coat the area with contact cement where the eyes will be and allow to dry. Attach the eyes and coat with epoxy. This recipe is the same as on page 141 of Reference 4.

Eat n' Em

Originator: John Sweeney
Hook: 2/0 to 3/0 Tiemco 800S
Thread: 6/0 Danville flat waxed nylon
Wing: White, emerald green and black Super Hair plus 8 to 12 strands of Krystal Flash
Eyes: Medium red Spirit River stick-on epoxy eyes
Wrap a short thread base behind the hook eye and tie down a very large clump of white Super Hair at the rear end of this thread base. This clump should be about 9 inches long, with only about 3 inches extending toward the rear. Pull the forward portion of this hair back over the rear portion and tie it down. Trim the top portion so that it's about 1 inch longer than the underlying portion. Now repeat these steps with the remaining white Super Hair, tying it down in front of the previous clump. While tying it down, prop it up by winding the thread behind and under the wing 2 or 3 times, pulling forward. Then, tie in a clump of the green Super Hair in front of the white clumps, repeating the same steps and trimming so that it is longer than the white. Tie in a much sparser clump of black Super Hair in front of the green clumps in the same manner, trimming so that it's a little longer than the green clumps. Divide the Krystal Flash in half and tie each half on the side of the hook shank, to the rear of the hook eye. Trim the overall wing so that the fibers are progressively longer from white to black. Attach the eyes on the side with hot glue and then add clear epoxy to the eyes and thread windings, to lock in place.

EJ's Sparkle Fly*

Originator: Capt. E.J. Broderick
Hook: 2/0 Mustad 34007 or 34011

Thread: Black
Underbody: 10 wraps of 0.030 lead wire
Wing: White Super Hair, white marabou, pearlescent Krystal Flash and chartreuse Flashabou tinsel
Eyes: Stick-on eyes
Wrap the hook shank with a layer of black thread, from the hook eye to the hook bend. Wrap the lead wire, starting about 1/4 inch from the hook eye. Tie on a sparse amount of super hair in front of the lead wire. Add a drop of fast-drying super glue. Tie on some white marabou hair, sparingly, in the same place, around the hook shaft. Tie in 10-15 strands of Krystal Flash on each side of the hook and then about 40-50 strands of Flashabou, distributed evenly around the upper 75% of the hook. All of this material is tied in between the front edge of the lead wire and the hook eye. Build up a small thread head, whip finish and cement. Add the eyes and coat with a few coats of clear epoxy.
*Favorite Fly of Ed Broderick

Epoxy Baitfish

Originator: Glen Mikkleson
Hook: #8 to 1/0 Mustad 34007
Thread: Size A, tan
Tail: Tan bucktail plus red and black Krystal Flash
Body: Rust or copper Mylar braided yarn
Wing: Rust and tan bucktail plus one strand of red Flashabou
Head: Tan thread
Eyes: #2 Witchcraft Stick-ons, silver with black pupils
Tie on the bucktail tail at the hook bend. Also tie on the Krystal Flash. Tie on the Mylar braid and wind forward to just short of the hook eye. At the hook eye, tie on first a clump of the tan and then a clump of the rust bucktail, also including the red Flashabou in between the two clumps. Build up the head with thread and then coat with red nail polish. After drying, add the stick-on eyes and then several coats of clear epoxy on the head. This recipe is very similar to that shown on page 126 of Reference 4.

Epoxy Baitfish (A)

Originator: Glen Mikkleson
Hook: #8 to 1/0 Mustad 34007
Thread: Size A, tan
Tail: White bucktail plus pearl and olive Krystal Flash
Body: Olive Mylar braided yarn
Wing: Olive and white bucktail plus one strand of red Flashabou
Head: White thread
Eyes: #2 Witchcraft Stick-ons, silver with black pupils
Tie on the bucktail tail at the hook bend. Also tie on the Krystal Flash. Tie on the Mylar braid and wind forward to just short of the hook eye. At the hook eye, tie on first a clump of the white and then a clump of the olive bucktail, also including the red Flashabou in between the two clumps. Build up the head with thread and then coat with red nail polish. After drying, add the stick-on eyes and then several coats of clear epoxy on the head. This recipe is very similar to that shown on page 126 of Reference 4.

Epoxy Baitfish (B)

Originator: Glen Mikkleson
Hook: #8 to 1/0 Mustad 34007
Thread: Size A, white
Tail: White bucktail plus pearl and olive Krystal Flash
Body: Silver Mylar braided yarn
Wing: White bucktail plus one strand of red Flashabou
Head: White thread
Eyes: #2 Witchcraft Stick-ons, silver with black pupils
Tie on the bucktail tail at the hook bend. Also tie on the Krystal Flash. Tie on the Mylar braid and wind for-

ward to just short of the hook eye. At the hook eye, tie on a large clump of the white bucktail, also including the red Flashabou. Build up the head with thread and then coat with red nail polish. After drying, add the stick-on eyes and then several coats of clear epoxy on the head. This recipe is very similar to that shown on page 126 of Reference 4.

Epoxy Glass Minnow

Originator: Unknown
Hook: #4 - 2/0, straight eye, standard length
Thread: White flat waxed nylon
Tail: 6 to 8 white saddle hackles plus 6 strands of pearl Krystal Flash
Body: 2 Silver Mylar strips, plus clear 5-minute epoxy
Eyes: Stick-ons, silver with black pupils
Tie on the saddles at the sides of the hook shank at the bend of the hook, curved inward. Also tie in the Krystal Flash at the top of the hook shank. Wrap the thread forward to the hook eye, whip finish and cement. Trim 2 identical pieces of silver Mylar to a fish profile and glue together, with the hook shank in between. Add clear epoxy from the hook eye to and around the hackle butts, shaping it until it has a narrow, oval cross-section. After drying, color the body as desired with marking pens and add the stick-on eyes. Cover with an additional coat of clear epoxy.

Epoxy Head Bunker

Originator: Unknown
Hook: 1/0 to 3/0
Tail: 6 to 8 white saddles plus pearlescent Flashabou
Body: Pearlescent Flashabou
Wing: Mixed black and chocolate brown bucktail, white bucktail, and pearlescent Flashabou
Eyes: Prizmatic stick-ons
Tie on the white saddles on the sides of the hook shank at the hook bend, Tie on several strands of the Flashabou on top. Wrap a Flashabou body up to the hook eye. Tie on the white bucktail on the sides and bottom of the hook shank, just behind the hook eye. Tie on more white bucktail on top of the hook shank, followed by a few strands of Flashabou, and the black and chocolate bucktail. The bucktail on top should be hi-tied; i.e. groups of fibers braced by thread wraps to the rear so that the fibers angle sharply upward to give the fly a broader side profile. Saturate the front portion of the fly with epoxy so that the high profile is retained. After setting, apply the stick-on eyes and add another coat of epoxy.

Epoxy-Head Deceiver

Originator: Lefty Kreh
Hook: 1/0 to 3/0 Mustad 34007 or 34011
Thread: Danville flat waxed nylon
Wing (Tail): 4 to 8 white saddle hackles plus Krystal Flash, Flashabou and/or holographic Flashabou
Shoulder (Collar): Blue and white bucktail, optional peacock herl on top
Beard: Red Krystal Flash
Head: 5-minute epoxy
Eyes: Prizmatic stick-ons
Tie on hackle, Krystal Flash, and Flashabou on at the bend of the hook. Flashabou should extend about 1/2 inch beyond the hackle ends. Tie in bucktail approximately 1/4 to 1/2 inch behind hook eye, blue over white. Tie in optional topping of peacock herl. Turn fly over and tie on 1/2 inch beard of red Krystal Flash. Wrap generous amount of thread behind hook eye and whip finish. Form built-up head with 5-minute epoxy and allow to set. Apply stick-on eyes on head and cover with 5-minute epoxy. This recipe is an adaptation of Kreh's recipe on page 15 of Reference 1.

Epoxy Head Pinfish

Originator: Unknown

Hook: #2 to #1

Tail: 6 to 8 white saddles plus pearlescent Flashabou

Body: Pearlescent Flashabou

Wing: Light green or aqua bucktail, white bucktail, and pearlescent Flashabou

Topping: Peacock herl

Eyes: Prizmatic stick-ons

Tie on the white saddles on the sides of the hook shank at the hook bend, Tie on several strands of the Flashabou on top. Wrap a Flashabou body up to the hook eye. Tie on the white bucktail on the sides and bottom of the hook shank, just behind the hook eye. Tie on more white bucktail on top of the hook shank, followed by a few strands of Flashabou, light green bucktail and several strands of peacock herl. The bucktail on top should be hi-tied; i.e. groups of fibers braced by thread wraps to the rear so that the fibers angle sharply upward to give the fly a broader side profile. Add vertical barring with a permanent marker. Saturate the front portion of the fly with epoxy so that the high profile is retained. After setting, apply the stick-on eyes and add another coat of epoxy.

Epoxy Head Sardine

Originator: Lefty Kreh's Deceiver with several modifications

Hook: 1/0 to 3/0 Tiemco 800S or #1 - 3/0 Daiichi 2546

Thread: Clear nylon sewing thread

Tail/Shoulder: 3 to 4 pairs of white saddle hackles

Wing: Pale olive/white bucktail plus pearl Krystal Flash, silver Flashabou and olive Flashabou

Head: Clear thread and 5-minute epoxy

Eyes: Red/black Prizmatic stick-ons

Tie on the saddle hackles on each side of the hook shank at the hook bend, Save the butt sections cut from the saddles. Tie on a clump of white bucktail just behind the hook eye. Tie a mixture of the pearl Krystal Flash and the silver Flashabou on top of the white bucktail and then tie on a clump of the olive bucktail on top, followed by a topping of olive Flashabou. Add 2 or 3 of the saddle butts to each side, just behind the hook eye. Build up a large thread head, whip finish, cement and then glue the eyes behind the head. Liberally coat the head, eyes and first 1/4 inch of the wing section with clear epoxy and allow to set.

Epoxy Minnow

Originator: Unknown

Hook: #1

Wing: 20 strands of white and 10 strands of olive FisHair, Fly Fur or Craft Fur, plus 6 strands of Holographic Tinsel

Eyes: Silver with black pupils, stick-ons

Tie on the white FisHair on top of the hook shank, behind the hook eye. Tie on the olive FisHair on top and then tie on the tinsel on each side. Total fly length should be about 3 inches. While holding the wing parts in place, coat the entire fly with 5-minute epoxy and allow to dry. Draw in the gill plates with black marking pen. Apply the stick-on eyes and add a coat of Hard-As-Nails finish.

Epoxy Sand Eel

Originator: Unknown

Hook: #1 or #2 Mustad 7766

Thread: Danville clear, fine monocord

Wing: Chartreuse and white bucktail plus pearl or lime Krystal Flash

Body: Fine Mylar tinsel for slender-bodied patterns, Mylar braid over built-up thread for bigger bodies

Head: 5-minute epoxy

Eyes: Small stick-ons

Tie on Krystal Flash and then white bucktail and chartreuse bucktail near hook bend. Install Mylar body up to hook eye. Form epoxy head with 5-minute epoxy and allow to set. Stick-on the eyes and coat with epoxy.

Eric's Sand Eel

Originator: Eric Peterson

Hook: #4 - 2, long shank

Thread: White

Tail and Underbody: White, yellow, lavender and tan craft fur

Eyes: Stick-on Prizmatic eyes

Overbody: 12- to 15-pound mono

Tie on the white craft fur tail, at the hook bend and around the hook shank. On top, successively add the yellow, lavender and tan craft fur. Tie on one end of the piece of mono and wrap the tying thread forward to just behind the hook eye. Bring about half of the tail forward and tie off just behind the hook eye, keeping the various color fibers in the same position as in the tail. Attach the stick-on eyes about 1/8 inch behind the hook eye. Wrap the mono forward, over the underbody and eyes, and tie off at the head. Tie off, whip finish and cement. Coat the entire body with clear epoxy. This recipe is nearly identical to the pattern shown on page 45 of Reference 2.

Estaz Borski Shrimp*

Originator: Tim Borski

Hook: #4 - 6 Tiemco 811S

Thread: Danville, chartreuse for darker fly (or Gotcha Pink for pale fly)

Tail: Tan or rust brown Craft Fur (or cream) plus 6-8 strands of Krystal Flash (orange with tan tail, copper for rust tail or pearl for cream tail)

Legs: Webby cree hackle (light cree for cream tail, dark cree for tan or rust tail)

Body: Tan, peach or brown Estaz or Ice Chenille

Head: Thread (pink for pale fly, chartreuse for dark fly)

Weedguard: V-style, 20- to 30-pound fluorocarbon

Eyes: Extra-small, yellow with black pupils

Tie in the fur tail with 3-4 strands of Krystal Flash on each side. Tie in the cree hackle and the Estaz. Wind the thread forward and tie in the eyes and the weedguard near the hook eye. Wind the Estaz to the hook eye, through and over the eyes, and tie off. Palmer the cree hackle over the body and eyes and tie off at hook eye, taking care to work around weedguard filaments. Build up a thread head, whip finish and cement. Add abdominal bands with a permanent marker (cool gray for pale flies and black for dark flies). This fly is a bulky version of Tim Borski's Swimming Shrimp.

*Favorite Fly of Capt. Eric Glass

Estuary Special

Originator: Jim Tierney

Hook: #2 Mustad 34-7

Thread: Chartreuse 6/0

Tail: 5 green and 5 chartreuse saddle hackles, green Krystal Flash, silver Flashabou, gold Craft Fur and peacock herl

Eyes: Small red lead dumbbell

Body: Chartreuse saddle hackle

Tie in the green and chartreuse saddle hackles on the sides of the hook shank, at the hook bend. At the same place, on top of the hook shank, tie in first the Krystal Flash, the Flashabou, the Craft Fur, and then the peacock herl. Tie on the dumbbell eyes under the hook shank, about 1/4 inch behind the hook eye. Tie on a chartreuse saddle hackle over the tail wraps and palmer it forward to the dumbbell eyes. Build up a moderate-sized head with tying thread, wind forward

to the hook eye, whip finish and cement. Coat the head with 2 coats of clear epoxy.

Fish Fuzz Clouser

Originator: Bob Clouser

Hook: #2 - 2/0

Thread: 2/0 Nylon, either white, brown or chartreuse

Tail: Tan Fish Fuzz

Body: Clear V-Ribbing

Beard: Tan Fish Fuzz

Eyes: Very small to medium lead dumbbells

Tie on the dumbbell eyes to the top of the hook, about 1/8 inch in front of the hook eye. Tie on one end of the mono loop weedguard, from the dumbbell eyes to the hook bend. Tie on a generous tuft of Fish Fuzz at the hook bend, surrounding the hook shank. Tie on the Fish Fuzz beard, before and after the dumbbell eyes. Tie on a generous clump of Fish Fuzz before and after the dumbbell eyes, whip finish and cement. This recipe is based upon the pattern on page 42 of Reference 2.

Flasher

Originator: Unknown

Hook: #2 to 3/0 Mustad 34001 long shank

Tail: Size 00 to size 0 Colorado-style spinner blade and a short piece of 80-pound monofilament

Body: 1/8-inch Mylar braid and optional lead strip

Wing: Dark bucktail plus a lighter-colored underwing of lighter Craft Fur, FisHair or Super Hair (blue/white, red/white, chartreuse/white, red/yellow, or brown/orange work well)

Bend the front half inch of the hook downward, so that it will ride upside down (hook point up) with buoyant material on the hook point side. Tie on a strip of lead wire, if desired, on top of the hook shank. Remove the lacquer on the spinner blade by polishing, to get down to the shiny base material. Tie on one leg of the 80-pound mono on top of the hook shank, slip the spinner blade over the mono and also tie down the other length onto the hook shank. Make sure the spinner blade is free to flutter. Tie on the Mylar braid behind the hook eye and bind it in top of the hook shank while wrapping with thread. Wind the thread back to the hook eye and then wind the braid forward, tying it off at the hook eye. Invert the hook in the vise and tie on the underwing at the hook eye. Then tie on the bucktail overwing, making sure that it extends upward, so that it will not interfere with the spinner blade motion. Build a small thread head, whip finish and cement. Apply the stick-on eyes and add more cement or epoxy to lock in the eyes. This recipe is the same as shown on pages 180-183 of the March 2000 Issue of Florida Sportsman magazine.

Flat-Wing Clouser

Originator: Unknown

Hook: #2 to 3/0 Eagle Claw 254 SS, or equivalent

Thread: 3/0 prewaxed mono

Tail: 2 extra-long white saddle hackles

Wing: Chartreuse/white, olive/white, blue/white or all-black bucktail, with pearl Krystal Flash or Glimmer

Eyes: 5/32 or smaller lead dumbbells

Tie in the white saddles on top of the hook, flatwing-style. Install the lead eyes on top of the hook, about 1/4 inch from the hook eye. Tie on a clump of white bucktail, binding it down in front of and behind the lead eyes. Invert the hook in the vise and tie on the Krystal Flash and the chartreuse bucktail just behind the hook eye. Build up a thread mound under the chartreuse bucktail so that it angles upward to cover the hook point. Form a small thread head, whip finish and cement. This recipe is very similar to the pattern on page 42 of Reference 2.

Flex Crab

Originator: Unknown
Hook: #6 Tiemco 800 S
Thread: Tan 3/0 monocord
Body: Small 1/8 inch tan Flexi Cord
Underbody: White Dipit
Weight: X-Small lead dumbbells
Legs: Brown Sili-Legs
Eyes: Small mono and black beads
Pincers: Pheasant body feathers

Cut off a small piece of Flexi Cord and slide it on the hook. Tie down one end just past the hook bend. Expand and flatten the Flexi Cord profile to a carapace shape and then tie down the other end near the hook eye. Tie on the dumbbell eyes on top of the hook shank, near the hook eye. Knot 4 short pieces of Sili-Legs, coat the ends with a generous drop of super glue gel and insert on one edge of the flattened Flexi Cord. Coat the ends of 2 short pieces of mono with super glue gel and insert into opposite edge. After setting, trim the mono ends, slip 2 small black beads over the ends and superglue the ends. Super glue the ends of 2 small, short clumps of pheasant body feather fibers, and insert into the edge of the Flexi Cord, on both side of the mono/bead eyes. Dab the top side of the Flexi Cord with white Dipit or similar material. Coat the Flexi Cord lightly with thinned epoxy to help it keep its flattened shape.

Foxy Lady

Originator: Jim Tierney
Hook: #2 Mustad 3407
Thread: White 6/0
Tail: 8 white saddle hackles and small silver and pearl Flashabou
Body: White arctic fox fur strip
Wing: Blue artcic fox fibers and small silver, blue and pearl Flashabou Krystal Flash
Eyes: Small lead dumbbells with black/silver stick-ons

Tie on the white saddle hackles and the Flashabou on the top of the hook shank, at the hook bend. Tie on the white fur strip and palmer forward to just behind the hook eye. Tie on the blue fibers and the Krystal Flash on top of the hook shank, just behind the hook eye. Tie on the dumbbell eyes under the hook shank, just behind the hook eye. Build up a moderate thread head over the dumbbell eyes, whip finish and cement. Add the stick-on eyes on the dumbbell eyes and add a generous coat of clear epoxy to the head and eyes.

Fur Eel

Originators: Salty Fly Rodders
Hook: 1/0 to 3/0, either one or two
Underbody: Length of 20-pound monofilament
Body: Strip of mink fur

For flies longer than 5 inches, cut off a length of mono and tie a hook onto one end. Attach the other end of the mono to a second hook by wrapping it with thread on top of the hook shank. Cut a piece of mink fur about 2 to 3 inches longer than the 2-hook fly and about 1/2 inch wide. Taper the front end of the mink strip to facilitate tying it to the front hook bend. Then, fold the mink strip over the top of the hooks and mono and stitch together the full length of the body, taking care to lock in the hook bends of the two hooks. Tie off the front of the mink strip onto the front hook, just behind the hook eye, whip finish and cement. For flies shorter than 5 inches, eliminate the front hook and tie the mono directly to the leader tippet. This recipe is the same as shown on page 54 of Reference 1.

Furry Foam Crab

Originator: Jerry Loring
Hook: #4 - 2 Tiemco 811S
Thread: White Danville
Mouth Parts: Fluffy fibers from cree hackle plus 4 or 5 strands of pearl Krystal Flash
Underbody: 10-12 wraps of 0.030 fuze wire over hook shank
Body: Tan and cream Furry Foam
Claws: Cree or furnace hackle tips
Eyes: Melted heavy monofilament, painted black
Legs: Salt/pepper Sili-Legs
Weedguard: V-style, 20- to 30-pound fluorocarbon

Tie in the fluffy cree fibers and the Krystal Flash at the hook bend. Wrap the fuze wire near the center of the hook shank. Wrap the thread forward and tie in the weedguard under the hook shank. Cut the furry foam pieces to the shape of a crab carapace; glue the cream Furry Foam piece to the underside of the hook shank. Add dabs of super glue gel to the upper part of the hook shank and to the inside of the cream underbody. Build a sandwich consisting of the underbody, 2 pairs of Sili-Leg strands, mono eyes, the hackle-tip claws and the overbody piece of Furry Foam. Press together until the glue sets. Position the weedguard projections in place, whip finish and cement.

Generation 7 Epoxy Fly

Originator: Jim Tierney
Hook: #4 Mustad 3407
Thread: Larva Lace mono
Tail: Polar white Craft Fur
Body: Small lead keel and pearl Krystal Flash
Wing: Olive green and polar white Craft Fur, silver Krystal Flash and pearl Flashabou
Eyes: Small black/silver stick-ons

Tie the lead keel under the hook shank and cement. Wrap the body entirely with the pearl Krystal Flash. Tie on the Craft Fur (olive/white), the silver Krystal Flash and the pearl Flashabou on top of the hook shank, just behind the hook eye. Whip finish and cement. Coat the entire body with clear 5-minute epoxy and rotate until dry. Attach the stick-on eyes, draw in some gills with a red marking pen. Add an additional smooth coat of clear epoxy over the body and rotate until dry.

Glades Deceiver

Originator: Flip Pallot
Hook: #2 or 1, standard length
Thread: 3/0 black monocord
Tail: 2 matched pairs of grizzly saddle hackles
Collar: White and brown bucktail and copper or silver Krystal Flash
Topping: 6 to 8 strands of peacock herl
Eyes: Painted yellow with black pupils

Tie in the grizzly saddles at the sides of the hook, at the hook bend. The feathers should curve inward. Also, tie in 3 or 4 strands of Krystal Flash to each side, and cement the windings. Invert the fly in the vise and tie on a clump of white bucktail (about twice the length of the hook shank) on top of the hook shank to form part of the collar, just to the rear of the hook eye. Invert the fly again, add a smaller clump of white bucktail and then a very sparse clump of brown bucktail to complete the collar. Be sure to distribute the white bucktail around the hook shank before tying down tightly. Add the peacock herl topping on top of the collar, so that the herl strands are slightly longer than the bucktail strands. Wind a thread head, whip finish and cement. Paint on the eyes. This recipe is the same as shown on page 101 in the January 2000 issue of *Florida Sportsman* magazine.

Glades Minnow

Originator: Unknown
Hook: #4 - #1
Thread: 2/0 Olive nylon
Wing/Body: White, tan and olive Ultra Hair, plus strands of white and pearl Flashabou
Topping: Dark olive Fish Fuzz
Beard: White Fish Fuzz
Eyes: Stick-ons, red with black pupils
Weedguard: 15-pound hard mono loop

Tie on one end of the mono weedguard, on top of the hook shank at the hook bend. Tie on the Flashabou at the hook bend. Tie on a clump of white Ultra Hair on top of the hook shank, about 1/8 inch behind the hook eye. Then, tie in clumps of first the tan and then the olive Ultra Hair on top of the hook, each slightly to the rear of the preceding, to create a tapered hair base. Tie in a clump of dark olive Fish Fuzz topping just behind the hook eye and trim so it blends in with the profile of the Ultra Hair. Tie on the other end of the mono loop weedguard under the hook shank, to the rear of the hook eye. Tie on the white Fish Fuzz beard under the hook shank, so that the fibers extend to the hook point. Build up a tapered head with thread, whip finish and cement the head. Spread all fibers so that they splay away from the hook shank, trim to desired shape and saturate the forward third of the fly with clear epoxy so that a high profile is maintained. Add the stick-on eyes and add some more epoxy over the head and eyes for durability.

Gold Digger

Originator: Kirby LaCour
Hook: #4 - 1 Mustad 3407
Thread: Red flat waxed nylon
Tail: Mixture of gold and copper Flashabou plus gold/red Sparkle Flash by Tie-Well
Body: 2 chartreuse or orange saddle hackles
Eyes: Painted
Weedguard: 40# single-post mono or 20# mono loop

Tie on one end of mono loop weedguard, along the top of the hook shank, between the hook eye and the hook bend, if using the loop-type weedguard. Then tie on the Flashabou and Sparkle Flash mixture as a tail on top of the hook shank, at the hook bend. Tightly palmer the saddle hackles at the hook bend, tie off and cement. Build up a thread head just forward of the hackle windings and then wind the thread forward to the hook eye, tapering to a small diameter at the hook eye. Tie on the other end of the mono loop weedguard, whip finish and cement. Paint on white eyes with black pupils at the head and apply clear epoxy from the head to the hook eye. This fly is very similar to a standard Keys-style tarpon fly.

Greenan's Redfish

Originator: Capt. Pete Greenan
Hook: #2, long shank
Thread: Dark red monocord
Body: Olive chenille plus optional 0.030 dia. lead wire
Shoulder: Pheasant body feathers (window pane)
Wing: Dark hair from olive-dyed bucktail plus gold Krystal Flash
Head: Olive chenille
Eyes: Black Bright Eyes (by Phil Camera)

At a point about 1/4 inch from the hook eye, bend the hook eye so that the hook point is approximately even with the hook shank. Place the hook in the vise point-down and then tie on the eyes on top of the hook shank, about 1/8 inch back from the hook eye. Add 4 wraps of lead wire on the hook shank behind the eyes, if desired. Wrap a double layer of chenille for the body, from the hook bend up to the eyes. Tie on the wing fibers on top of the hook shank, just to the rear of the hook eyes. Then tie on a few strands of Krystal Flash at the same place, on each of the sides of the hook shank. Tie on a pheasant body feather over the Krystal Flash, wrap the head with olive chenille, whip finish and cement.

Greenan's Shrimp*
Originator: Capt. Pete Greenan
Hook: #1
Thread: Chartreuse or red monocord
Tail: 4 - 6 grizzly hackle tips plus pearl Krystal Flash
Body: Two long, narrow palmered grizzly hackles and thin gold wire
Eyes: White plastic
Weedguard (Optional): 25-pound hard mono
Tie in the eyes, about 1/4 inch back from hook eye. Tie in hackle tails and Krystal Flash, on the side of the hook shank, at the hook bend. Hackles should be splayed out to the side. Palmer the body up to the hook eye with the grizzly hackle, and reinforce with the wire overwrap. Tie in the weed guard at the hook eye, to leave a single protruding stem for shielding the point. Whip finish and cement.
*Favorite Fly of Capt. Pete Greenan

Gray Blonde
Originator: Joe Brooks and Carl Hanson
Hook: #6 to 2/0
Thread: Black
Tail: White bucktail
Body: Silver Mylar and 10-pound clear or yellow mono
Wing: Gray bucktail
Throat: White bucktail
Head: Thread
Tie on a small clump of white bucktail on top of the hook shank at the hook bend. Taper the end of a short piece of 10-pound mono and tie on at the hook bend. At the same place, tie on the silver Mylar, wrap forward to the hook eye and tie off. Tie on the gray bucktail wing on top of the hook shank next to the hook eye. Pull the wing backward and down, holding it parallel over the top of the Mylar body, while wrapping the mono over the wing and body. Tie down the mono behind the hook eye. Tie on a short white bucktail throat under the hook shank at the hook eye. Build a small thread head, whip finish and cement.

Green and White Glass Minnow
Originator: Carl Hanson
Hook: Up to 1/0 Mustad 34007
Body: Silver Mylar and clear 12- to 20-pound monofilament
Wing: Green and white bucktail plus 2 strands of 1/8-inch silver Mylar
Head: Thread, painted green
Eyes: Painted white with a black pupil
Tie on the Mylar and the monofilament at the hook bend, and wrap the tying thread up to the hook eye. Wrap the hook shank with the Mylar and tie off at the hook eye. Overwrap the Mylar with the monofilament and tie off at the hook eye. Tie on the white bucktail at the hook eye, on top. Repeat with the green bucktail, on top of the white bucktail. Both clumps of bucktail should not extend more than one shank's length past the bend. Flank the bucktail with the 2 strips of Mylar, build a small thread head, whip finish and cement. Paint the head green. When dry, paint on the eyes. When dry, coat with a few drops of cement or epoxy. This recipe is the same as shown on page 105 of Reference 5.

Grizzly Bead Head
Originator: Unknown
Hook: #1

Thread: Black
Tail: Gray squirrel and pearl Krystal Flash
Wings: 6 grizzly saddle hackles
Body: 2 grizzly or red grizzly saddle hackles
Head: One, single bead-chain element
Tie in the squirrel tail short and thick, at and around the hook shank at the hook bend. Tie in the Krystal Flash at the same place. Then, tie in the wing hackles on the sides of the hook shank, at the hook bend, splayed outward. Palmer the remaining two grizzly saddles from the hook bend to within 1/8 inch from the hook eye. Whip finish and cement the windings. With pliers, open a single large bead chain element and crimp it over the thread windings on top of the hook shank, just behind the hook eye. Epoxy the bead-chain eye in place and paint the bead red. Paint white eyes on the red bead and also paint on black eye pupils.

Grocery Fly (A)
Originator: Brock Apfel
Hook: Mustad 7766 or equivalent, up to 5/0 or 6/0
Thread: 3/0 Danville Flymaster Plus or equivalent
Tail: 8 long, white saddle hackles plus clumps of white bucktail and 4 strands of pearl saltwater Flashabou
Wing/Body: Clumps of long bucktail, white, pink and chartreuse, plus 6-8 strands of pearl or rainbow Flashabou. Precede with a full-length base of Big Fly Fiber, to add lightweight bulk for larger flies
Belly: Clump of long white bucktail
Topping: 8-12 strands of peacock herl
Gills: 12 strands of red Krystal Flash
Head: Heavy white thread, overwound with 6/0 white thread
Eyes: Stick-on Mylar or taxidermy eyes
Apply thread the full length of the shank and tie on the 8 white saddles at the hook bend, surrounding the shank. Next, add the 4 strands of saltwater Flashabou to the top, bottom and both sides. Flashabou should extend well beyond the hackle tips. Just forward of the hackle butts, tie in an 1/8-inch clump of white bucktail on top, wrapping in front and back to achieve a standing angle of 45 degrees (hi-tie). Tie on a sparser clump of white bucktail on each side, adhjacent to the hi-tied clump. Glue all wraps. Tie in another hi-tied 3/16-inch clump of white bucktail on top of the hook, just in front of the first one. Then, tie in another 3/16-inch clump underneath the hook, not hi-tied. Tie in small clumps of first pink and then chartreuse bucktail just in front of the last hi-tied white clump. Tie in the strands of peacock herl over these last clumps. Glue all new wraps and, after the glue has dried, add a few more small clumps of white bucktail to the sides of the fly. Spread the red Krystal Flash around the bottom of the fly's head and tie on to form the gills, and then spread the 6-8 strands of Flashabou on each side of the fly, trimming just beyond the bend of the hook. Finally, add a very sparse clump of white bucktail on top of the herl to lock in the herl fibers. Finish the head by forming with heavy thread, overwrapping with the fine thread and adding the eyes. Generously glue all wraps and hang to dry, hook eye up to allow seepage into the wraps. This recipe was adapted from an article, "Delivering the Groceries," by Brad E. Burns, in Fly Fishing in Saltwaters, Sept/Oct 1997.

Grocery Fly (B)
Originator: Brock Apfel
Hook: Mustad 7766 or equivalent, up to 5/0 or 6/0
Thread: 3/0 Danville Flymaster Plus or equivalent
Tail: 8 long, white saddle hackles plus clumps of white bucktail and 4 strands of pearl saltwater Flashabou

Wing/Body: Clumps of long bucktail, white, pink and brown, plus 6-8 strands of pearl or rainbow Flashabou. Precede with a full-length base of Big Fly Fiber, to add lightweight bulk for larger flies
Belly: Clump of long white bucktail
Topping: 8-12 strands of peacock herl
Gills: 12 strands of red Krystal Flash
Head: Heavy white thread, overwound with 6/0 white thread
Eyes: Stick-on Mylar or taxidermy eyes
Apply thread the full length of the shank and tie on the 8 white saddles at the hook bend, surrounding the shank. Next, add the 4 strands of saltwater Flashabou to the top, bottom and both sides. Flashabou should extend well beyond the hackle tips. Just forward of the hackle butts, tie in an 1/8-inch clump of white bucktail on top, wrapping in front and back to achieve a standing angle of 45 degrees (hi-tie). Tie on a sparser clump of white bucktail on each side, adhjacent to the hi-tied clump. Glue all wraps. Tie in another hi-tied 3/16-inch clump of white bucktail on top of the hook, just in front of the first one. Then, tie in another 3/16-inch clump underneath the hook, not hi-tied. Tie in small clumps of first pink and then brown bucktail just in front of the last hi-tied white clump. Tie in the strands of peacock herl over these last clumps. Glue all new wraps and, after the glue has dried, add a few more small clumps of white bucktail to the sides of the fly. Spread the red Krystal Flash around the bottom of the fly's head and tie on to form the gills, and then spread the 6-8 strands of Flashabou on each side of the fly, trimming just beyond the bend of the hook. Finally, add a very sparse clump of white bucktail on top of the herl to lock in the herl fibers. Finish the head by forming with heavy thread, overwrapping with the fine thread and adding the eyes. Generously glue all wraps and hang to dry, hook eye up to allow seepage into the wraps. This recipe was adapted from an article, "Delivering the Groceries," by Brad E. Burns, in Fly Fishing in Saltwaters, Sept/Oct 1997.

Guide's Bunny
Originator: Unknown
Hook: Straight eye, standard shank
Thread: Tan flat waxed nylon
Tail: White polar bear hair or equivalent, plus a few strands of pearl Krystal Flash
Body: Fawn or tan rabbit fur strips
Head: Thread
Tie on a short clump of polar bear hair at the hook bend around the shank. Also tie in Krystal Flash at that point. Tie in a rabbit fur strip and palmer forward to the hook eye. Tie off, build a small thread head, whip finish and cement. Eyes may be painted on.

Haag's Glimmer Bunker*
Originator: John C. Haag
Hook: 2/0 to 3/0 Mustad 34007 or Gamakatsu SL11-3H
Thread: White flat waxed nylon
Tail: 8 - 10 strands of silver Glimmer
Body: 35 to 50 strands of pearl Glimmer
Sides: 15 - 20 strands of Live-Glow Comes Alive
Throat: Light gray Bozo Hair
Wing: Light blue and dark blue Bozo Hair
Eyes: 4-1/2 mm molded eyes, silver with black pupils
Fold the strands of silver Glimmer around the tying thread and tie them onto the hook shank at the hook bend over the hook point. Fold about one third of the pearl Glimmer around the tying thread and tie onto the hook shank in the hi-low style, directly in front of the tail wrappings. Repeat this step two more times, working toward the hook eye so that the third group of pearl Glimmer strands is tied off just behind the

hook eye. Each group of pearl Glimmer strands should rest against the bump of the previous group of strands, causing the strands to flare up and down for a wide fly profile. Tie in 8 to 10 strands of the Comes Alive on each side of the hook shank, just behind the hook eye. Tie in a light gray Bozo Hair throat under the hook shank, just behind the hook eye. Tie in first the light blue Bozo Hair and then the dark blue Bozo Hair as a wing, on top of the hook shank just behind the hook eye. Both the throat and wing should flare up and down. Wrap thread around the head, keeping the sides relatively flat for placement of the eyes. Attach each of the eyes with a drop of Goop. Stipple the fly with Softex from the hook eye to the hook bend, to maintain its high profile, and add dots along the wing sides for false eyes.
*Favorite Fly of Capt. Paul Dixon

Haines Ballyhoo
Originator: Larry Haines
Hook: #1 Tiemco 811S
Thread: White
Tail: White and pale olive Neer Hair or Ultra Hair plus pearl and silver Flashabou
Body: Thread
Eyes: Stick-ons, silver with black pupils
Tie in the tail materials at the hook bend, the white hair on the sides and then the Flashabou and olive hair on top. As in a tarpon fly, build up a thread head at the hook bend and gradually taper it to a small blunt end at the hook eye. Tie in and wrap a few turns of pink thread just to the rear of the hook eye and whip finish. Color the top of the fly from the hook eye back to the thread head with an olive permanent marker. Apply the stick-on eyes to the head and add a few coats of epoxy to the fly's front end.

Hair Head Herring
Originator: Bill Catherwood
Hook: 7/0 Mustad 94151
Underwing: White, light pink and light blue marabou feathers with rigid stems
Wing: 2 light blue and 2 pearl gray hackles
Sides: Pink, light blue and dark blue Krystal Flash
Head: White and light blue deer body hair
Eyes: Solid glass
Tie on the marabou stems at the hook bend, with the white feathers located on the bottom and the top of the hook shank. The pink feathers should be tied on the lower sides of the hook shank and the light blue feathers tied in on the upper sides of the hook shank. At the same place, on the sides, tie in first the light blue hackles and then the pearl gray hackles, so that the base fluff is showing. Tie in the Krystal Flash on the sides and then tie on the glass eyes. Starting over the feather butts, spin, and pack the deer hair up to the hook eye, over and through the glass eyes. Mix the colors to obtain a mottled look. Trim the front to a bullet shape and allow the rear deer hair fibers to flare back over the feather base. This recipe is the same as shown on page 44 of Reference 4.

Half and Half (A)
Originator: Bob Clouser
Hook: 2/0 Mustad 34007 or 34011
Thread: White Danville flat waxed nylon
Tail/Wing: 4 to 8 white saddle hackles plus one grizzly saddle hackle.
Body: White bucktail or Kinky Fiber, plus peacock herl and rainbow Krystal Flash
Eyes: Nickel-plated dumbell eyes, 1/24 to 1/16 oz., plus large Prizmatic tape eyes
Tie on dumbell eyes on top of hook, about 1/2 inch behind hook eye. Tie on white and grizzly saddle

hackles on the top of the hook, midway between the hook eye and hook bend. Tie on Krystal Flash at the same location. Turn the fly over and tie on the bucktail on top, just forward of the dumbell eyes. Tie bucktail again just to the read of the dumbell eyes. Tie on more Krystal Flash to the rear of the dumbell eyes. At the same place, tie on more white bucktail and some peacock herl. Whip finish at the head of the fly and glue the large prizmatic eyes onto the body, just behind the dumbell eyes. The fly should be bulky in appearance. This recipe is a variant of the Clouser Half and Half on page 42 of Reference 2.

Half and Half (B)
Originator: Bob Clouser
Hook: Straight eye, standard length
Thread: Brown
Eyes: Lead dumbbells
Rear Wing: 6-10 olive-dyed grizzly saddle hackles
Front Wing: Yellow bucktail, 10-15 strands of copper Krystal Flash and brown bucktail
Tie on the lead dumbbell eyes, about 1/4 inch back of and on top of the hook eye. Invert the hook in the vise. Wind the thread rearward and tie on the rear wing saddles at the hook bend, on the sides of the hook. Move thread halfway forward on the hook shank and tie on the yellow bucktail. On top of that tie on first the copper Krystal Flash and then the Brown bucktail. Build up the head with thread, whip finish and cement. This recipe is a variant of the recipe on page 42 of Reference 2.

Half and Half (C)
Originator: Bob Clouser
Hook: 1/0 to 3/0 Gamakatsu SC-15
Thread: White Danville flat waxed nylon
Tail: Three or four pairs of chartreuse saddle hackles or grizzly neck hackles, plus holographic gold flash
Eyes: Lead dumbbell eyes, medium for 1/0 hooks and large for 2/0 and larger
Body: Thread base plus holographic gold flash
Wing: White bucktail
Throat: Chartreuse bucktail plus pearl Krystal Flash
Tie on the dumbbell eyes on top of the hook shank, about 1/4 inch behind the hook eye. Tie on the saddle or neck hackles and the holographic gold flash on the sides of the hook, at the hook bend. Hackles and gold flash should extend about 2 hook lengths beyond the end of the hook. Build up a thread base between the hook bend and the dumbbell eyes; then tie on more Holographic gold flash at the tail and wind forward to the dumbbell eyes. Tie off the gold flash and then tie on the white bucktail wing on top of the hook, both in front of and behind the dumbbell eyes. The white bucktail should be slightly shorter than the tail hackles. Invert the hook in the vise and tie on first the Krystal Flash and then the chartreuse bucktail collar on top of the hook, just behind the hook eye. The chartreuse bucktail and Flashabou should extend about the same length as the white bucktail wing. Build up the head with thread, whip finish and cement. This pattern is a variation of the pattern on page 42 of Reference 2.

Half and Half (D)
Originator: Bob Clouser
Hook: #2 to 3/0 Mustad 34007
Thread: 3/0 flat waxed nylon or fine, clear mono
Tail: 2 pairs of white saddle hackles (gray, chartreuse/white, pink, blue or yellow is also productive), plus green Flashabou
Eyes: Gold-plated lead dumbbell eyes, medium for 1/0 hooks and large for 2/0 and larger
Body: Thread base plus Bill's Bodi Braid or pearl

Krystal Flash
Wing: White bucktail
Throat: Gray bucktail plus pearl Krystal Flash
Tie on the dumbbell eyes on top of the hook shank, about 1/4 inch behind the hook eye. Tie on the saddle or neck hackles on the sides of the hook at the hook bend. Hackles should extend about 2 hook lengths beyond the end of the hook. Tie on the Flashabou on top. Build up a thread base between the hook bend and the dumbbell eyes; then tie on the braid and wind forward to the dumbbell eyes. Tie off the braid and invert the hook in the vise. Then tie on the white bucktail wing on top of the hook, behind the dumbbell eyes. The white bucktail should be slightly shorter than the tail hackles. Tie on first the Krystal Flash and then the gray bucktail collar on top of the hook, just behind the hook eye. The Krystal Flash should extend about the same length as the white hackle wing. Build up the head with thread, whip finish and cement. This pattern is a variation of the pattern on page 42 of Reference 2.

Half and Half (E)
Originator: Bob Clouser
Hook: 2/0 Mustad 34007 or 34011
Thread: White Danville flat waxed nylon
Tail/Wing: 4 to 8 white saddle hackles plus one grizzly saddle hackle.
Body: White and black bucktail or Kinky Fiber, plus peacock herl and rainbow Krystal Flash
Eyes: Nickel-plated dumbell eyes, 1/24 to 1/16 oz., plus large Prizmatic tape eyes
Tie on dumbell eyes on top of hook, about 1/2 inch behind hook eye. Tie on white and grizzly saddle hackles on the top of the hook, midway between the hook eye and hook bend. Tie on Krystal Flash at the same location. Turn the fly over and tie on the white bucktail on top, just forward of the dumbbell eyes. Tie down the bucktail again, just to the rear of the dumbbell eyes. Tie on more Krystal Flash to the rear of the dumbbell eyes. At the same place, tie on black bucktail and some peacock herl. Whip finish at the head of the fly and glue the large prizmatic eyes onto the body, just behind the dumbbell eyes. The fly should be bulky in appearance. This recipe is a variant of the Clouser Half and Half on page 42 of Reference 2.

Hamilton Copperhead*
Originator: Capt. Randy Hamilton
Hook: 1/0 or 2/0 Gamakatsu SC15 or SS15
Thread: 6/0 tan or brown UNI-Thread
Wing: Copper Flashabou
Underwing: Copper Krystal Flash
Body: Copper Crystal Chenille
Tail: Copper Flashabou
Eyes: Medium (1/24 oz.) chrome dumbbell
Tie on the dumbbell eyes on top of the hook shank, about 1/8 inch from the hook eye. Cement the dumbbell eyes in place. Wrap the thread back to the hook bend and tie about 8 to 10 one-inch strands of the Flashabou onto the hook shank. Cement in place. Tie on a 3-inch strand of Crystal Chenille and wrap first the thread and then the chenille back to the dumbbell eyes. Tie off the chenille, but leave the remaining segment hanging for now. Invert the hook in the vise and tie in about 8 to 15 strands, 2.5 to 3 inches long, of Krystal Flash on top of the hook shank, just behind the dumbbell eyes. Cut 10 to 20, 2.5 to 3 inch strands of the Flashabou and tie in over the Krystal Flash. Wrap the remaining segment of Crystal Chenille around and through the dumbbell eyes and tie in just behind the hook eye. Whip finish and cement.
*Favorite Fly of Capt. Randy Hamilton

Hanson's Glass Minnow

Originator: Carl Hanson
Hook: 1/0 straight eye
Thread: Red 2/0 nylon
Wing: White and blue bucktail
Body: Continuation of wing materials, plus silver
    Mylar and 12-pound mono
Head: Thread

Tie on a clump of white bucktail behind the hook eye, on top of the hook shank. Then tie on an equal clump of blue bucktail on top. Work the thread back to the hook bend and tie on a strip of silver Mylar and a length of mono. Wrap the tying thread back to the hook eye. Position the wing materials over the top of the hook shank, keeping the blue over the white) and wrap the Mylar forward, tying it off at the hook eye. Then wrap the mono forward over the Mylar, also tying it off at the hook eye. Build a small thread head, whip finish and cement. Coat the head and body with clear 5-minute epoxy. This recipe is identical to that shown on page 46 of Reference 2.

Hardbody Shiner

Originator: Unknown
Hook: Mustad 34007/3407, Daiichi 2546 or
    Tiemco 811S
Thread: White
Tail: Olive and white Craft Fur, black Krystal Flash
    and silver Flashabou
Body: Lead wire and pearl Krystal Flash
Eyes: Painted black over white
Gills: Red marking pen

Wrap lead wire over the hook shank, from the hook bend to within 1/8 inch from the hook eye. Lock in with tying thread and cement. Overwrap the lead with pearl Krystal Flash. Tie on the tail materials just behind the hook eye, positioning the materials to simulate a shiner's profile and coloration. Coat the entire body with clear 5-minute epoxy, keeping the tail materials in their correct positions. After setting, paint on the eyes and the gills and add another coat of clear epoxy. This recipe is the same as shown on page 64 of Reference 3.

Hare Eel

Originator: Unknown
Hook: #1 to 2/0 Mustad 3407
Thread: Black
Tail: Black rabbit fur
Body: Black rabbit fur
Eyes: Plastic black on yellow
Weedguard: Mono loop

Tie on the plastic eyes on top of the hook shank, about 3/16 inch behind the hook eye. Tie on a piece of mono on the bottom of the hook shank, and let it extend past the hook bend for now. Tie on a long strip of rabbit fur, on top of the hook shank and past the hook bend. Then tie on a length of cross-cut rabbit fur strip and palmer up to and around the plastic eyes, up to the hook eye. Tie off, tie on the other end of the mono loop just to the rear of the hook eye, under the hook shank. Whip finish at the hook eye and cement. This recipe is the same as shown on page 64 of Reference 3.

Herring/Alewife

Originator: Unknown
Hook: 3/0 or 4/0 Mustad 7766, Tiemco 800S or
    equivalent
Thread: 3/0 white monocore
Tail: 4 extra-long white saddle hackles
Wing: Blue/white bucktail (brown/white for
    menhaden) or equivalent Angel Hair or FisHair,
    plus pearl Glimmer or Krystal Flash

Eyes: Prizmatic stick-ons, 3-D or flat
Head: 5-Minute epoxy

Tie on the saddle hackles on top of the hook shank, about midway between the hook eye and the hook bend. At the same point, tie on the white bucktail on the sides and bottom and Krystal Flash and the blue bucktail on the top. Form an epoxy head and, after setting, stick on the eyes and recoat the head with epoxy.

Hot Butt Bendback

Originator: Capt. Chuck Scates
Hook: Straight eye, standard length, bend-back style
Thread: White
Butt: Fluorescent pink chenille
Body: Fluorescent white chenille
Wing: 2 to 4 white hackles, white bucktail, pearl
    Krystal Flash and peacock herl

Invert the hook in the vise, with the hook point riding above the hook shank. Tie on and wrap a small amount of pink chenille on the hook shank, well past the hook bend. Wrap the white chenille all the way to the hook eye and tie off. Tie in first the hackles, then the Krystal Flash, a sparse clump of bucktail and a dozen strands of peacock herl, all on top of the hook. The natural curve of the hackles should point downward and the material should generally cover the hook point to assist its weedless character. Build up a small thread head, whip finish and cement. This recipe is the same as on page 38 of Reference 2.

Hot Lips

Originator: Steve Huff
Hook: 2/0
Thread: Yellow or red 2/0 nylon
Tail: 2-4 olive-dyed grizzly saddle hackles, plus strands
    of Flashabou and Krystal Flash
Body: White foam strip, cut oval-shaped with small
    tab at rear and rounded front, plus yellow saddle
    hackle
Beard: Red Fish Fuzz or Krystal Flash
Weedguard: 20-pound hard mono loop

Tie in one end of the mono loop, the saddle hackles, the Flashabou and the Krystal Flash at the hook bend. Tie on the large yellow saddle hackle and the foam strip tab at the hook bend, with the foam strip extending back past the hook bend. Wrap the tying thread forward and tie on the red beard under the hook shank. Palmer the large yellow saddle forward and tie off at the hook eye. Then tie the other end of the mono loop at the hook eye. Tease all upper yellow saddle fibers flat, bring foam strip forward over the back and tie it off at the hook eye, leaving a short, rounded flared section covering the hook eye. Tie off and cement the head under the foam strip flap. This recipe is very similar to the Gurgler pattern on page 33 of Reference 2.

Ian's Anchovy

Originator: Capt. Ian Devlin
Hook: #2 - 6 Mustad 34007/3407
Body: Pearl flat braid
Wing: Tan or olive and white Craft Fur plus pearl
    Krystal Flash
Eyes: Small black over yellow stick-ons

Wrap the braid material onto the hook shank, from the hook bend to just short of the hook eye. Coat with clear epoxy and allow to dry. Tie on the white Craft Fur just behind the hook eye, on top of the hook shank. In the same place, tie on the Krystal Flash and the darker Craft Fur. Make a small thread head, whip finish and cement. Add clear epoxy to the front portion of the fly and allow to dry. Apply the stick-on eyes and add another coat of clear epoxy. This recipe is

very similar to the Hog Fry Minnow shown on page 94 of Reference 3.

Jiggy

Originator: Bob Popovics
Hook: #2 - 1/0 Mustad 34011
Thread: Clear, fine mono
Body: Silver Flashabou
Wing: Gray and white bucktail, plus Krystal Flash
Head: Medium-sized Jiggy head
Eyes: Stick-ons

Slide Jiggy head up to eye of hook and lock in place with thread and cement. Twist on 4 turns of medium-gauge wire and push into Jiggy head recess. Wrap front half of hook shank with silver Flashabou. Tie on white bucktail to the rear of the head, on the sides and bottom of the shank, followed by 6 strands of Krystal Flash, followed by gray bucktail. Tie off and cement tail and head. Add 5-minute epoxy to taper body from head to tail, and allow to set. Set stick-on eyes into recessed eye socket of Jiggy and cover with epoxy.

Jimmy Nix Mullet

Originator: Lefty Kreh, Jimmy Nix
Hook: #2 to 2/0
Thread: Tan
Tail: 8 to 10 wide, light gray saddle or neckhackles
Collar: Light gray marabou and 2-inch strands of
    pearl Krystal Flash
Beard: Small tuft of red marabou
Head: Natural deer body hair
Eyes: 2 glass doll eyes
Weedguard: Loop of 15-pound mono

Tie in one end of the mono weedguard loop along the top of the hook. Tie in the gray saddles equally on both sides of the hook shank, at the hook bend. At the mid-shank, tie in the marabou and the strands of pearl Krystal Flash around the hook. Tie in a red marabou beard on the bottom of the hook, about 1/4 inch from the hook eye. Spin and pack a deer-hair head, trimming it to an oval fish shape. Tie in the other end of the mono loop on the bottom of the hook shank next to the hook eye. Whip finish next to the hook eye and cement. Glue the doll eyes on the deer-hair head. This recipe is the same as shown on page 62 of Reference 1.

Johnny's Angel

Originator: Unknown
Hook: #2 - 1/0
Thread: White
Body/Tail: White Ultra Hair, brown FisHair, pearl
    Flashabou and silicone
Eyes: Stick-on Prizmatics

Tie on the Ultra Hair at the hook bend, surrounding the hook shank. Similarly, tie on some pearl Flashabou and the FisHair, over the Ultra Hair. Wind the tying thread forward and repeat the process, tying the hair and Flashabou just behind the hook eye. Add 2 short strips of wide pearl Flashabou along the sides. Tie off, whip finish and cement. Add clear silicone rubber to the front half of the fly, stroking the fibers into an appropriate shape. Allow to set and apply the stick-on eyes. Add another thin coat of clear silicone.

Josenhans Clam Worm

Originator: Capt. Kevin Josenhans
Hook: #2 Mustad 34007
Thread: Black waxed Nylon
Tail: Red and brown marabou
Body: Root beer Cactus Chenille (Estaz)

Tie in red marabou at the bend of the hook, to approximately one inch beyond the bend. Tie in a small amount of the brown marabou over the red marabou (the red should be the dominant color). Tie in the root beer Cactus Chenille at the hook bend and wrap forward to the hook eye. Build up a small head (just enough to be visible) with the black thread just behind the hook eye and whip finish.

Keel Eel
Originator: Bob Popovics
Hook: Straight eye, long shank, in bend-back style
Underwrap: Flat gold Mylar
Wing: Polar Bear Ultra Hair and dark brown Ultra Hair
Head: Epoxy
Eyes: Stick-on Prizmatic yellow eyes with black pupils
Gills and Mouth: Painted on with a red marking pen
Wrap straight section of hook shank (before the bend) with flat gold Mylar. Tie on small bunch of Polar Bear Ultra Hair at the head, extending somewhat over twice the length of the hook. Then tie on an additional small bunch of the dark brown Ultra Hair on top of the Polar Bear Ultra Hair, extending an additional hook length beyond the Polar Bear Ultra Hair. Saturate the head over the gold Mylar with epoxy to establish shape. Stick-on the Prizmatic eyes and paint on the gills and mouth. Apply an additional light coat of epoxy over the head. This recipe is from page 48 of Reference 2.

Ken's Clam Worm
Originator: Ken Abrames
Hook: #4, short-shanked egg-type hook
Tail: Chartreuse Glo Bug yarn
Wing: Steelhead orange Glo Bug yarn
Invert the hook in the vise so that the point rides above the hook eye. Tie on a very tiny wisp of the chartreuse yarn, about 3/4 inch long, on the hook bend. Tie on a very sparse clump of the orange yarn, about 1 inch long with the fibers facing the hook eye and pulled back to veil the hook point. Whip finish and cement. This recipe is the same as shown on page 34 of Reference 5.

Kirby's Cocahoe Clouser Minnow
Originators: Bob Clouser, Kirby LaCour
Hook: #4 - 2 Mustad 3407
Eyes: Lead dumbbells, painted yellow with black pupils
Belly: White bucktail
Wing: Purple bucktail, 4 - 7 strands each of gold and copper Krystal Flash
Tie the dumbbell eyes on top of the hook, about 1/4 inch behind the hook eye. Tie on the white bucktail, fore and aft of the eyes, so that the length extends about 2 hook lengths beyond the end of the hook. Invert the hook in the vise. Tie on the purple bucktail and then the Krystal Flash, in front of the dumbbell eyes. Tie off, whip finish and cement the head. This recipe is similar to the pattern shown on page 52 of Reference 2.

Kirby's Kosmic Killer*
Originator: Kirby LaCour
Hook: #1 to 4 Mustad 34011 bent to a keel hook, or #4 to 6 keel hook
Thread: 3/0 orange
Tail: Gold Flashabou
Underbody: 6-8 turns of 0.030 lead wire, or equivalent
Body: Root beer or orange Crystal Chenille
Wing: Chartreuse or olive bucktail
Overwing: Gold/pink Reflections by Tie-well
Head: Built-up thread
Eyes: Painted
Tie on the gold Flashabou at the bend of the hook and then tie on the Crystal Chenille. Wrap the hook shank

with a lead wire underbody and tie the wire to the hook shank with tying thread. Wrap the Crystal Chenille forward and tie off at the hook eye. Tie on the bucktail wing on top of the hook shank at the hook eye, followed by the overwing strands. Build up a thread head, coat with cement, and paint on black eyes with a white pupil.
*Favorite Fly of Capt. Kirby LaCour

Kosmic Killer
Originator: Kirby LaCour
Hook: #1 to 4 Mustad 34011 bent to a keel hook, or #4 to 6 keel hook
Thread: 3/0 black
Underbody: 6-8 turns of 0.030 lead wire, or equivalent
Body: White Crystal Chenille
Wing: Purple bucktail
Overwing: Gold/pink Reflections by Tie-well
Head: Built-up thread
Eyes: Painted
Tie on one end of the Crystal Chenille at the bend of the hook. Wrap the hook shank with a lead wire underbody and tie the wire to the hook shank with tying thread. Wrap the Crystal Chenille forward and tie off at the hook eye. Tie on the bucktail wing on top of the hook shank at the hook eye, followed by the overwing strands. Build up a thread head, coat with cement, and paint on white eyes with a black pupil.

Kraft Fur Shrimp
Originator: Tim Borski
Hook: #4 to 1/0 Mustad 34007 or Tiemco 811S
Thread: White
Tail: #1872 Tan Craft Fur with hot orange Crystal Flash
Body: Thread
Hackle: Wide grizzly or badger
Eyes: Lead dumbbells, painted black on yellow
Weedguard: Single or double 15- to 20-pound Mason mono
Tie on the tan Craft Fur at the hook bend and give it a barred look, by marking with a #1457-M Pantone marker. Add some Krystal Flash on the sides. Wrap the hook shank with thread. Tie on the hackle and palmer forward to within about 1/4 inch from the hook eye. Clip off the top hackle fibers. Invert the hook in the vise and tie on the lead eyes. Tie on the weedguard and build up the thread over the dumbbell eyes and the weedguard base. Whip finish and cement. Paint the eyes and pupils. This recipe is the same as shown on page 31 of Reference 4.

Kwan Fly
Originator: Pat Dorsy
Hook: #4 to #1, standard length
Thread: Chartreuse or tan, 6/0 to 3/0
Tail: Craft Fur and a few strands of Krystal Flash
Collar: One cree saddle hackle
Eyes: Bead chain, plastic or small to medium lead dumbbells
Body: Tan, brown/tan or olive/tan strands of Sparkle Yarn
Weedguard: 15- to 20-pound Mason mono, 2-pronged
Wind a thread base from the hook eye to just beyond the start of the hook bend. Tie in the dumbbell or bead-chain eyes on top of the hook shank, about 1/8 inch behind the hook eye. Then tie in the Craft Fur and Krystal Flash at the hook bend, on top of the hook shank, building up thread wraps behind the tail so that it is canted upward. Tie in the saddle hackle stem. Cement the eye wraps and the tail wraps. Wind on the saddle hackle to form a collar. Tie in one-inch strands of the yarn on top of and perpendicular to the hook shank, from the collar to

the dumbbell eyes. Alternate yarn color where appropriate. Trim yarn body to an elongated oval shape. Tie on the 2-pronged mono "mustache" weedguard in front of the dumbbell eyes, whip finish and cement. This recipe is the same as described on pages 124-127 of the June 2000 Issue of *Florida Sportsman* magazine.

KZ Squid*
Originator: Jim Tierney
Hook: 4/0 Mustad 34007
Thread: Pink 6/0
Tail: 15 pink and peach saddle hackles, plus pearl and pink Krystal Flash
Mouth: Red Crystal Chenille
Eyes: Large aluminum dumbbells with epoxy inserts
Skirt: Pink and peach marabou
Body Extension: 300-pound mono
Body: Pink and peach Crystal Chenille
Front Hackle: Pink and peach marabou
Cut off a 5-inch piece of 300-pound mono and make a small loop at one end. Whip finish the loop tightly and cement. Attach the mono to the hook shank by wrapping it with thread, allowing it to extend about 3 inches beyond the front of the hook eye, and glue to secure. Tie the Krystal Flash on top of the hook shank, at the hook bend. Tie on the saddle hackles all around the hook shank, at the same place. Tie on the marabou skirt over the saddle butt wraps and tie on the dumbbell eyes just in front of the skirt. Wrap the entire body with Crystal Chenille, up to the mono loop. Wrap the front hackle just to the rear of the mono loop, whip finish and cement.
*Favorite Fly of Capt. Mike Roback

Lavender Eel
Originator: Glen Mikkleson
Hook: #8 to 1/0 Mustad 34007
Thread: White size A
Tail: Sparse white bucktail and mixed silver and light purple Krystal Flash
Underbody: Silver Mylar braided yarn
Overbody: 4 strands of pearl-dyed lavender (#6968) Flashabou
Wing: Lavender bucktail, pearl-dyed lavender Flashabou and olive dun bucktail
Head: Painted with lavender, pearl and olive dun nail polish
Eyes: #2 Witchcraft Stick-ons, silver Mylar with black pupils
Gills: Tiny bits of red (#6911) Flashabou
Tie in the tail of white bucktail at the hook bend, adding in the Krystal Flash. Wrap the underbody with the silver Mylar braided yarn and overwrap with the pearl-dyed lavender Flashabou. Both wraps are to just short of the hook eye. Tie on the lavender bucktail, followed by first the lavender Flashabou and then the olive dun bucktail. Build up a thread head and coat with the pearl, lavender and olive dun nail polish. After drying, give the fly a coat of clear two-ton epoxy and attach the stick-on eyes and the gill bits. Add another 2 coats of two-ton epoxy, even beyond the hook bend, to keep the wing from wrapping around the tail. This recipe is the same as on page 124 of Reference 4.

Lefty's Deceiver
Originator: Lefty Kreh
Hook: Straight eye, standard length, up to 4/0
Thread: Green thread
Wing: 6 to 10 matched white saddles, 2 grizzly saddles dyed olive and a few strands of pearl or olive Krystal Flash or Flashabou

Body: Tying thread
Collar: White bucktail
Throat: Red Krystal Flash
Topping: Peacock herl
Head: Green Krystal Flash, painted eyes optional

Tie on the white saddles on the sides of the hook, at the hook bend. Then add the grizzly saddles and the Flashabou on each side. Wrap the thread back close to the hook eye. Tie on one clump of bucktail on each side of the hook, extending well past the hook point. Tie on the herl topping, the red Krystal Flash throat and build up the head with thread. Cover the head with the green Krystal Flash, whip finish and add epoxy to the head.

This recipe is the same as on page 49 of Reference 2.

Lefty's Deceiver (A)

Originator: Lefty Kreh
Hook: 1/0 to 3/0 Mustad 34007 or 34011
Thread: Danville flat waxed nylon
Wing (Tail): 4 to 8 saddle hackles (white, black or
    chartreuse), plus Krystal Flash, Flashabou and/or
    Holographic Flashabou
Shoulder (Collar): Bucktail (chartreuse/white,
    gray/white or black). Optional peacock herl on top.
Beard: Red Krystal Flash
Head: Large holographic eyes placed on thread

Tie on hackle, Krystal Flash, and Flashabou on at the bend of the hook. Flashabou should extend about 1/2 inch beyond the hackle ends. Tie in bucktail approximately 1/4 to 1/2 inch behind hook eye, darker color over the lighter shade. Tie in optional topping of peacock herl. Turn fly over and tie on 1/2-inch beard of red Krystal Flash. Wrap generous amount of thread behind hook eye and whip finish. Apply holographic eyes on head and cover with 5-minute epoxy. This recipe is an adaptation of Kreh's recipe on page 15 of Reference 1.

Lefty's Deceiver (B)

Originator: Lefty Kreh
Hook: 1/0
Thread: Tan
Wing: 6 to 12 tan saddle hackles
Gill: 4 strands red Krystal Flash
Collar: Tan and olive bucktail, plus 12 strands of pearl
    Krystal Flash
Head: Olive thread with painted white eye and black
    pupil

Tie in the saddle hackles at the hook bend. Tie in gill material under hook shank, near hook eye. Tie in tan bucktail on bottom and sides and olive bucktail on top for collar. Add pearl Krystal Flash on sides, build up olive head and whip finish. This recipe is an adaptation of the Deceiver pattern shown on page 15 of Reference 1.

Lefty's Deceiver (C)

Originator: Lefty Kreh
Hook: 1/0
Thread: Chartreuse
Wing: 6 to 12 white saddle hackles
Gill: 4 strands red Krystal Flash
Collar: White and chartreuse bucktail, plus 12 strands
    of pearl Krystal Flash
Head: Chartreuse thread with painted white eye and
    black pupil

Tie in the saddle hackles at the hook bend. Tie in gill material under hook shank, near hook eye. Tie in white bucktail on bottom and sides and chartreuse bucktail on top for collar. Add pearl Krystal Flash on sides, build up thread head and whip finish. This recipe is an adaptation of the Deceiver pattern shown on page 15 of Reference 1.

Lefty's Deceiver (D)

Originator: Lefty Kreh
Hook: #1 to 4/0
Thread: White
Wing: 6 to 12 white saddle hackles and 2 grizzly
    saddle hackles
Gill: 4 strands red Krystal Flash
Collar: White and blue bucktail, plus a few strands of
    pearl Krystal Flash or Flashabou
Topping: Several strands of peacock herl
Head: White thread, eyes optional

Tie in the saddle hackles at the hook bend, grizzly on the outside. Tie in gill material under hook shank, near hook eye. Tie in white bucktail on bottom and sides and blue bucktail on top for collar. Add herl topping, pearl Krystal Flash on sides, build up thread head and whip finish. This recipe is an adaptation of the Deceiver pattern shown on page 49 of Reference 2.

Lefty's Deceiver (E)

Originator: Lefty Kreh
Hook: 1/0
Thread: White
Wing: 6 to 12 white saddle hackles and 2 grizzly
    saddle hackles
Gill: 4 strands red Krystal Flash
Collar: White and green bucktail, plus a few strands of
    pearl Krystal Flash
Topping: Several strands of peacock herl
Head: White thread, eyes optional

Tie in the saddle hackles at the hook bend, grizzly on the outside. Tie in gill material under hook shank, near hook eye. Tie in white bucktail on bottom and sides and green bucktail on top for collar. Add herl topping, pearl Krystal Flash on sides, build up thread head and whip finish. This recipe is an adaptation of the Deceiver pattern shown on page 49 of Reference 2.

Lefty's Deceiver (F)

Originator: Lefty Kreh
Hook: 1/0
Thread: White
Wing: 6 to 12 white saddle hackles and 2 grizzly
    saddle hackles
Gill: 4 strands red Krystal Flash
Collar: White, blue and purple bucktail, plus a few
    strands of pearl Krystal Flash
Topping: Several strands of peacock herl
Head: White thread, eyes optional

Tie in the saddle hackles at the hook bend, grizzly on the outside. Tie in gill material under hook shank, near hook eye. Tie in white bucktail on bottom and sides and first blue and then purple bucktail on top for collar. Add herl topping, pearl Krystal Flash on sides, build up thread head and whip finish. This recipe is an adaptation of the Deceiver pattern shown on page 49 of Reference 2.

Lefty's Deceiver (G)

Originator: Lefty Kreh
Hook: Straight eye, standard length
Wing: 6-10 matched black or white saddle hackles,
    plus 2 grizzly saddle hackles and several strands of
    pearl Krystal Flash or Flashabou
Body: Black or white tying thread
Collar: White or black bucktail
Throat: Red Krystal Flash
Topping: 6-8 strands of peacock herl
Head: Green Krystal Flash

Tie on the Krystal Flash at the hook bend, extending 2 hook lengths beyond the hook end. Tie in an equal number of saddle hackles on each side of the hook, extending the same length. Then tie on a grizzly saddle of the same length on each side. Wind thread

forward to approximately 1/4 inch from the hook eye. Tie in the red throat on the bottom of the hook shank. Tie on 2 bunches of bucktail collar, one bunch on each side of the hook. The collar should extend about a hook's length beyond the end of the hook. Tie on the herl topping, whip finish the head and cement. This pattern is usually tied in either all white or all black. The recipe is based upon the pattern on page 49 of Reference 2.

Lefty's Deceiver (H)

Originator: Lefty Kreh
Hook: Straight eye, standard length
Tail: 4 long, matched white saddle hackles, including
    the webby portions, plus several strands of pearl
    Flashabou
Body: Built up with white tying thread and covered
    with pearl Flashabou
Collar: White bucktail on the sides and bottom and
    olive bucktail on the top
Throat: Red Krystal Flash
Head: Built up with white thread
Eyes: White stick-ons, with black pupils

Tie on the Flashabou at the hook bend, extending several hook lengths beyond the hook end. Tie in an equal number of saddle hackles on each side of the hook, extending to the same length. Wind thread forward and backward to build up body. Tie on the Flashabou and wind forward to hook eye. Tie on white and olive bucktail clumps and then tie on the red throat on the bottom of the hook. The collar should extend about a hook's length beyond the end of the hook. Build up the head shape with thread, whip finish the head and cement. Add stick-on eyes to the head and add additional cement. This recipe is based upon the pattern on page 49 of Reference 2.

Lefty's Deceiver (I)

Originator: Lefty Kreh
Hook: #2 Mustad 34007, debarbed
Thread: Prewaxed 6/0 red
Tail: White saddle hackles
Body: Red thread
Collar: White bucktail on the bottom, green bucktail
    on the top
Beard: Red Krystal Flash

Tie on the saddle hackles at the hook bend. Wind the thread forward, close to the hook eye. Tie on a clump of green bucktail on top of the hook and a clump of white bucktail on the hook underside. Tie on a red Krystal Flash beard, build up head with red thread, whip finish, and cement. This pattern is a variant of the pattern shown on page 16 of Reference 2.

Lefty's Deceiver (J)

Originator: Lefty Kreh
Hook: #1 to 3/0 Gamakatsu SC-15
Thread: Danville flat waxed nylon, color of your
    choice
Tail: Three or four pairs of white saddle hackles or
    grizzly neck hackles plus holographic gold flash
Body: Diamond Braid or chenille
Collar: White bucktail
Wing: Green, gray or olive bucktail plus pearl Krystal
    Flash
Topping: Peacock herl

Tie on the holographic gold flash on the sides of the hook, at the hook bend. Then tie on the saddle or neck hackles in the same place. Tie on the body material to within 1/4 inch of the hook eye. Tie on the black bucktail on the bottom and sides of the hook near the hook eye. Then tie on the Krystal Flash, the olive bucktail and then the herl topping at the hook eye, on top of the hook. Wind on a head with the thread, whip finish and cement with Dave's Flexament. After drying, paint on eyes or apply Prizmatic eyes and epoxy the head. This pattern is quite similar to the pattern on page 15 of Reference 1.

Lefty's Deceiver (K)
Originator: Lefty Kreh
Hook: Mustad 34007, size dependent upon prey being imitated
Tail: 4 to 6 saddle white hackles plus a few strands of flash material
Wing/Collar: Bucktail, white, blue, olive or other color to match prey
Topping: Peacock herl
Throat: Red flash material
Eyes: Stick-on type
Tie on the saddle hackles at the hook bend, on each side of the hook shank. When tied, the saddles should be curved inward. Also tie on the flash material on each side. Wrap the thread to within 1/4 inch of the hook eye. Tie in a clump of bucktail on each side of the hook shank. Tie on several strands of peacock herl on the top of the hook shank for the topping. Then, tie in several strands of red flash on the bottom of the hook shank. Build up a head from the tying thread, whip finish and cement. Color the head to suit. Add the stick-on eyes and cover with a coat of clear epoxy for durability. This recipe is similar to the original pattern shown on page 15 of Reference 1.

Lefty's Deceiver (L)
Originator: Lefty Kreh
Hook: #2 - 3/0 Mustad 3407
Thread: Clear, fine mono
Wing: 6 yellow saddle hackles, including the webby portions
Body: Bill's Bodi Braid (gold or silver) or pearl Krystal Flash
Gill: 6 strands red Krystal Flash
Collar: Yellow bucktail
Topping: Several strands of peacock herl
Head: Thread
Eyes: Stick-ons, red/black
Tie in the saddle hackles at the hook bend. Wrap body material to the front of the hook. Tie in yellow bucktail on bottom, top and sides for collar. Tie in gill material under hook shank, near hook eye. Add herl topping, build up thread head and whip finish. Add stick-on eyes to the thread head and epoxy in place. This recipe is an adaptation of the Deceiver pattern shown on page 49 of Reference 2.

Lefty's Deceiver (M)
Originator: Lefty Kreh
Wing (Tail): 6 to 12 white saddle hackles plus a dozen strands of silver Krystal Flash or Flashabou
Shoulder (Collar): White bucktail
Head: White thread
Tie on hackle and Krystal Flash or Flashabou on at the bend of the hook. Krystal Flash or Flashabou should extend about 1/2 inch beyond the hackle ends. Tie in bucktail approximately 1/4 to 1/2 inch behind hook eye. Wrap generous amount of thread behind hook eye and whip finish. Cover head with 5-minute epoxy. This recipe is an adaptation of the recipe shown on page 15 of Reference 1.

Lefty's Deceiver (N)
Originator: Lefty Kreh
Hook: #1 to 4/0
Thread: White
Wing: 6 to 12 white saddle hackles and 2 grizzly saddle hackles
Gill: 4 strands red Krystal Flash
Collar: White, olive and blue bucktail, plus a few strands of pearl Krystal Flash
Topping: Several strands of peacock herl
Head: White thread, eyes optional
Tie in the saddle hackles at the hook bend, grizzly on the outside. Tie in gill material under hook shank, near hook eye. Tie in white bucktail on bottom and sides and then the olive and blue bucktail on top for collar. Add herl topping, pearl Krystal Flash on sides, build up thread head and whip finish. This recipe is an adaptation of the Deceiver pattern shown on page 49 of Reference 2.

Lefty's Deceiver (O)
Originator: Lefty Kreh
Hook: #1 to 4/0 Mustad 34007
Tail: 4 to 6 saddle white hackles plus a few strands of flash material
Wing/Collar: White, brown and black bucktail
Throat: Red flash material
Eyes: Stick-on type
Tie on the saddle hackles at the hook bend, on each side of the hook shank. When tied, the saddles should be curved inward. Also tie on the flash material on each side. Wrap the thread to within 1/4 inch of the hook eye. Tie in a clump of white bucktail on each side and under the hook shank. Tie on first a clump of brown and then a clump of black bucktail on the top of the hook shank for the topping. Then, tie in several strands of red flash on the bottom of the hook shank. Build up a head from the tying thread, whip finish and cement. Color the head to suit. Add the stick-on eyes and cover with a coat of clear epoxy for durability. This recipe is similar to the original pattern shown on page 15 of Reference 1.

Lefty's Deceiver (P)
Originator: Lefty Kreh
Hook: 1/0
Thread: White
Wing: 6 to 12 white saddle hackles and 2 grizzly saddle hackles
Gill: 4 strands red Krystal Flash
Collar: White and red bucktail, plus a few strands of pearl Krystal Flash
Topping: Several strands of peacock herl
Head: White thread, eyes optional
Tie in the saddle hackles at the hook bend, grizzly on the outside. Tie in gill material under hook shank, near hook eye. Tie in white bucktail on bottom and sides and the red bucktail on top for collar. Add herl topping, pearl Krystal Flash on sides, build up thread head and whip finish. This recipe is an adaptation of the Deceiver pattern shown on page 49 of Reference 2.

Lefty's Deceiver (Q)
Originator: Lefty Kreh
Hook: 1/0
Thread: White
Wing: 6 to 12 white saddle hackles and 2 grizzly saddle hackles
Gill: 4 strands red Krystal Flash
Cheek: 2 light mallard breast feathers
Collar: White and green bucktail, plus a few strands of pearl Krystal Flash
Topping: Several strands of peacock herl
Head: White thread, eyes optional
Tie in the saddle hackles at the hook bend, grizzly on the outside. Tie in gill material under hook shank, near hook eye. Tie in white bucktail on bottom and sides and green bucktail on top for collar. Add herl topping, pearl Krystal Flash on sides, and mallard feather cheeks. Build up thread head and whip finish.

This recipe is an adaptation of the Deceiver pattern shown on page 49 of Reference 2.

Lefty's Deceiver (R)
Originator: Lefty Kreh
Hook: #4 - 2
Wing: 6-10 matched white saddle hackles plus pearl Krystal Flash
Body: White tying thread
Collar: White bucktail
Throat: Red Krystal Flash
Topping: Purple bucktail
Head: Pearl Krystal Flash
Tie on the Krystal Flash at the hook bend, extending 2 hook lengths beyond the hook end. Tie in an equal number of saddle hackles on each side of the hook, extending the same length. Wind thread forward to approximately 1/4 inch from the hook eye. Tie in the red throat on the bottom of the hook shank. Tie on 2 bunches of bucktail collar, one bunch on each side of the hook. The collar should extend about a hook's length beyond the end of the hook. Tie on the bucktail topping, whip finish the head and cement. The recipe is based upon the pattern on page 49 of Reference 2.

Lefty's Deceiver (S)
Originator: Lefty Kreh
Hook: #1 to 4/0
Thread: White
Wing: 6 to 12 white saddle hackles and 2 grizzly saddle hackles
Gill: 4 strands red Krystal Flash
Collar: White and brown bucktail, plus a few strands of pearl Krystal Flash or Flashabou
Head: White thread, eyes optional
Tie in the saddle hackles at the hook bend, grizzly on the outside. Tie in gill material under hook shank, near hook eye. Tie in white bucktail on bottom and sides and brown bucktail on top for collar. Add pearl Krystal Flash on the sides, build up a thread head and whip finish. This recipe is an adaptation of the Deceiver pattern shown on page 49 of Reference 2.

Leiser's Angus
Originator: Eric Leiser and Angus Cameron
Hook: 4/0 Mustad 34007 debarbed
Tail: Green saddle hackle
Body: Green marabou
Head: Green deer body hair
Tie on saddle hackle tails. Tie on clumps of green marabou, winding forward to about half the hook shank length. Spin and tightly pack the deer hair up to the hook eye. Tie off, whip finish and cement. Trim the deer hair to a pointed head. This pattern is a variation of the pattern shown on page 60 of Reference 1.

Lenny's Fleeing Crab
Originator: Capt. Lenny Moffo
Hook: #1 to #6 Mustad 34007
Thread: 3/0 pink or brown flat waxed
Tail: 7 to 12 rubber legs or Sili-legs, white with brown markings
Eyes: Lead dumbbell eyes, sized to properly sink and keep the hook point up
Body: Aunt Lydia's Antron yarn pieces, alternating tan and brown or other combinations
Weed Guard: Optional, but 10- to 12-pound mono loop or stand-offs are OK
Tie on the rubber legs well past the hook bend, so that they all splay outward. Tie on the dumbbell eyes on top of the hook shank, about 1/8 inch back from the hook eye. Then, tie on alternate-color lengths of yarn strips laterally on top of the hook shank, from the

rubber legs up to the dumbbell eyes. Cement each strip to the hook as they are tied. Trim the yarn to the shape of a crab carapace, whip finish and cement. This pattern is almost the same as shown on page 78 of Reference 3.

Lenny's Tarpon Shrimp*
Originator: Capt. Lenny Moffo
Hook: 2/0 Eagle Claw Billy Pate
Thread: Pink
Tail: 2 Clumps of light tan or pink marabou or Ultra Hair plus 5 to 10 strands of pink or pearl Krystal Flash
Claws: Pair of shell-pink rooster feathers, plus a pair of tan or light ginger rooster hackles and a pair of cree or barred ginger hackle
Body: 2 to 4 tan or light ginger saddle hackles plus light tan chenille
Eyes: Pair of #4 black beads (with hole) and a piece of 60- to 80-pound mono
Using super glue gel, cement the beads to both ends of the mono. Coat the beads and part of the mono with clear epoxy. After the epoxy has set, cut the mono in half and flatten the ends where they will be tied onto the hook, at the same time bending the mono at that point to a 45-degree angle. Tie on the first clump of tan marabou onto the top of the hook shank, at the hook bend. Then tie the Krystal Flash on top of the marabou and tie on the second clump of marabou on top of the Krystal Flash. At about 2/3 the length of the hook shank from the hook eye, tie on first the pair of pink rooster feathers, then the pair of ginger rooster hackles and then the pair of cree hackles. All should be tied to the side, splayed outward and nesting evenly with each other. The cree hackles should cover about 3/4 of the length of the ginger hackles. Tie on the tan saddle hackles and palmer forward about 3/8 of an inch. Wind the thread up on the palmered hackle, to cause the fibers to lay back to the rear. Wind on the mono/bead eyes just forward of the palmered hackle, making sure to keep the mono in the same plane as the hook shank and aiming rearward about 45 degrees. Then tie on and palmer forward another pair of saddle hackles and wind thread rearward to again lay the fibers back. Tie on the chenille and wind forward to the hook eye. Whip finish and cement. This recipe is very similar to that shown on page 78 of Reference 3.
*Favorite Fly of Capt. Lenny Moffo

Lobster Fly
Originator: Whitey Cowen
Hook: 4/0 to 6/0
Tail: Red heavy felt, cut from template
Body: Red felt wrapped over built-up body, rattie optional
Ribs: Gold wire
Eyes: Craft beads, melted onto heavy mono plus dumbell for weight
Beard: Red deer hair
Head: Red deer hair
Claws: Red felt, cut from template
Legs: Red rubber bands
Antennae: 4- to 6-inch stripped red turkey quill shafts
Weedguard: 80-pound mono
Tie in tail, dumbell and weedguard at hook bend. Wrap underbody to shape with heavy thread or alternate material. Tie in gold wire at hook bend. Wrap body with felt strip, gluing while wrapping. Wrap gold wire over felt body. In turn, tie in mono/craft eyes, head, beard, antennae and claws. Thread rubber legs through the body, trimming to proper length.

Mack Wool
Originator: Bob Popovics
Hook: 6/0 or 7/0 straight eye, filed to a sharp needle tip
Tail: White lamb's wool, plue 2 turquoise and 4 green rooster tail feathers
Throat: Red and white lamb's wool and rainbow Krystal Flash
Collar: Light olive lamb's wool
Head: Dark olive lamb's wool
Eyes: Solid plastic, black pupils over yellow
Tie on the 6 tail feathers on the sides of the hook shank, at the hook bend, with the green on the outside. tie on a clump of the white lamb's wool over and around the tail butts. Mark the outer green feathers with vertical markings using a black marking pen. Tie on the plastic eyes about 1/4 inch behind the hook eye. Tie on first the red Krystal Flash and then the white and red lamb's wool as a throat, behind the plastic eyes. Then tie on small clumps of the light olive lamb's wool for a collar. Just behind the hook eye, in front of the collar, tie on clumps of the dark olive lamb's wool for the head. Whip finish and cement. Add 3 light coats of epoxy to the head, to preserve its broad shape. This recipe is identical to the pattern shown on page 79 of Reference 2.

Mangrove Minnow
Originator: Unknown
Hook: #6 to 2/0, long shank
Thread: White and black flat waxed nylon
Body: Lead fuse wire and thread
Wing: White, chartreuse and olive bucktail, 5 to 7 strands of peacock herl, silver and gold Krystal Flash and gold Flashabou
Head: Thread
Eyes: Chartreuse or yellow Mylar Prizmatic eyes
Using pliers, bend the hook at a point about 1/4 inch from the hook eye, upward and away from the hook gap. Tie on a piece of lead wire and wrap it from the hook bend to the recently-made bend. Cover it with black thread and cement. Wind the thread up to the hook eye and invert the hook in the vise. On top of the hook shank, just behind the hook eye, tie in a small clump of white bucktail and some silver Krystal Flash. While tying on successive materials, build up a sharply-angled base, so that the fibers will cover and protect the hook point. Tie on a clump of chartreuse bucktail and gold Krystal Flash, slightly shorter than the white bucktail. Then add a slightly longer layer of olive bucktail topped with gold Flashabou. Add the peacock herl topping. Build a white thread head and then add a multi-turn black thread stripe in the middle of the head. Or, apply Mylar stick-on eyes. Whip finish and cement. For extra durability, coat the head with 5-minute epoxy, and add a drop of head cement in the wing fiber base, to help to keep the fly's high profile. This recipe is the same as shown on pages 68-69 in the December 1999 Issue of *Florida Sportsman* magazine.

Matt's 40*
Originator: Capt. Matt Hoover
Hook: #1 to 1/0, 34007 Mustad
Thread: Black Danville, flat waxed nylon
Tail: 4 white neck hackles
Body: White & olive marabou
Topping: Peacock herl
Eyes: Prism stick-ons
Head: 5-minute clear epoxy
All of the material is tied in at the bend of the hook. Tie in one shock of white marabou on each side of the bend. Then tie one shock of olive marabou on top. Tie in 2 white neck hackles on each side, with the feather

tips curved inward. Make sure that the tips of the feathers extend beyond the rest of the dressing. Next, tie in about 10 strands of peacock herl on top. Shape the head with the black thread. Then attach the prism eyes. Add epoxy around the eyes and the head, rotating the fly while the epoxy is setting up.
*Favorite Fly of Capt. Matt Hoover

McCrab
Originator: George Anderson/John Barr/Jim Brungardt
Hook: 1/0 to 3/0 Mustad 34007
Thread: Danville's tan, flat waxed
Body (Carapace): Tan deer or elk body hair
Legs: Tan rubber band segments or Sili-legs
Eyes: Burnt, 40-pound Mason mono, plus additional lead eyes for weighting
Underbody: White hot glue
Clamp hook in vise with hook point on top. Spin deer hair densely on the hook from the bend to just behind the hook eye. Trim the hair flat below the shank, slightly rounded above the shank. Body should be oval-like in overall shape. Body should be about 1.25 inches long and 7/8 inches wide, for a 2/0 hook. Tie in lead eyes on the bottom of the shank, behind the hook eye. Weight of lead depends upon size of fly, density of spun deer hair and desired sink-rate. Apply cement. Apply hot glue to the underbody and glue legs and mono eyes in proper positions. For additional realism, claws made from rubber band material can also be glued into the underbody. (Note: the original pattern calls for ginger variant hackle tips, splayed outward, to simulate claws.) The hook runs laterally through the crab, so that when retrieved the crab moves sideways as it does in nature. Legs and mono eyes should point toward the center of the carapace or perpendicular to the hook shank. Smooth the glue on the bottom to flatten it and fill in the bottom to within 1/8 inch from the body's outer edge. This recipe is esentialy the same as shown on page 11 of Reference 2.

Mini Clouser
Originator: Bob Clouser
Hook: #6
Thread: Chartreuse
Wing: White and chartreuse bucktail, plus pearl Krystal Flash
Eyes: Small silver bead chain
Weedguard: 20-pound double mono
Invert hook in vise (hook and bend up) and tie in bead-chain eyes about 1/8 inch from hook eye, using a figure-8 wrap. Tie on one end of the mono weedguard loops near the hook bend. Tie in first the white bucktail and then 4 strands of Krystal Flash on the side of the bucktail. Then, tie in the chartreuse bucktail on top of the white bucktail. Bucktail should be about twice the length of the hook. Finally, tie on the two ends of the mono weedguard loops, whip finish the head and cement. This recipe is an adaptation of the Clouser Deep Minnow pattern described on page 42 of Reference 2.

Mini Deceiver
Originator: Lefty Kreh
Hook: #6
Thread: Chartreuse
Wing: 6 to 12 white saddle hackles
Gill: 4 strands red Krystal Flash
Collar: White and chartreuse bucktail, plus 12 strands of pearl Krystal Flash
Head: Chartreuse thread with painted white eye and black pupil
Tie in the saddle hackles at the hook bend. Tie in gill

material under hook shank, near hook eye. Tie in white bucktail on bottom and sides and chartreuse bucktail on top for collar. Add pearl Krystal Flash on sides, build up thread head and whip finish. This recipe is an adaptation of the Deceiver pattern shown on page 15 of Reference 1.

Monomoy Flatwing*
Originator: Peter Alves
Hook: #2 - 3/0
Thread: White
Eyes: Stick-on Prizmatic
Body: Pearl Bodi braid
Tail: White bucktail, 2 white saddle hackles plus pearl or silver Flashabou
Collar: White bucktail
Gills: Red Krystal Flash
Overwing: Olive saddle hackle
Tie on a sparse amount of white bucktail at the sides and bottom of the hook shank, at the hook bend. At the same place, tie on first a few strands of Flashabou and then 2 white saddles tied flatwise on top of the hook shank. Tie on the body braid and wrap forward to the hook eye. Tie off, and then tie on the red Krystal Flash (short) under the hook shank as gills. At the same place, tie on some more white bucktail on the sides of the hook shank and then a single olive hackle, flatwise, on top. The olive saddle hackle should include plenty of webby fibers near the butt. Build up a small thread head, whip finish and cement. Attach the stick-on eyes to the thread head and coat with clear epoxy.
*Favorite Fly of Peter Alves

Moriches Mouthful*
Originator: Lefty Kreh
Hook: 2/0 to 4/0
Thread: Flat waxed white
Tail: 10 to 20 very slender white neck hackles, plus 4 to 8 strands of pearl Flashabou
Body/Shoulder/Wing: White bucktail plus pearl Krystal Flash
Beard: 10 - 12 short lengths of red Krystal Flash
Eyes: Stick-ons, gray with black pupils
Tie in the neck hackles at the hook bend, on each side of the hook shank. Also tie in the pearl Flashabou at this point and cement butts. Tie in small clumps of white bucktail on all sides of the hook, starting just forward of the butts of the tail hackles and continuing all the way up to the hook eye. At the same time, tie in 4-6 strands of the Krystal Flash on top of each clump. Invert the fly and tie in the red Krystal Flash at the throat, as a beard. Build up a thread head, whip finish and cement. Thoroughly saturate the head with epoxy, after teasing the fibers to the correct profile. After the epoxy has set, add the stick-on eyes and re-coat the head with another coat of epoxy. Add color or striping as desired with permanent marking pens.
*Favorite Fly of Capt. John Killen

Muddler Minnow (A)
Originator: Dan Gapen
Hook: #6 to 2
Thread: Brown
Tail: Gray-brown hen hackles and strands of gold Flashabou
Body: Gold tinsel or gold braid
Collar and Head: Natural, gray-brown deer hair
Tie on the hen hackles on both sides of the hook shank, at the hook bend. Also, tie on the gold Flashabou on top of the hook shank. Tie on the gold tinsel and wrap forward about 1/2 way up the hook shank. Tie off the tinsel and spin and pack the deer-

hair collar so that the deer-hair fibers flare back past the hook bend. Continue spinning and packing the deer hair up to the hook eye, so that the fibers extend radially from the hook shank. Tie off, whip finish and cement. Trim the head to a rounded blunt shape. This pattern is very similar to the classic pattern developed by Dan Gapen many years ago.

Myglass Minnow
Originator: Unknown
Hook: #2 Tiemco 811S
Thread: White 3/0 monocord
Tail: Small silver Mylar braid and a long white or grizzly hen hackle
Rattle: Small glass rattle
Wing: White bucktail plus pearl and black Krystal Flash
Underwing: White bucktail
Body: Silver Mylar strip and pearl Krystal Flash
Eyes: Painted black on white
Weedguard: 16-pound hard Mason mono loop
Tie on one end of the mono on top of the hook shank, from the hook eye to the hook bend. Trim the hen hackle to an overall length of about 3 inches, cutting all fibers except those needed to simulate a forked tail. Cut off a 3-inch piece of Mylar braid and insert the trimmed hackle so that just the forked tail protrudes. Add a drop of super glue just in front of the tail fork and squeeze the braid with pliers once the hackle is fully inserted, to flatten the braid end in the plane of the tail fork. Coat the glass rattle with clear epoxy and insert it into the other end of the Mylar braid, squeezing it down until it is seated against the flattened portion of the braid. Tie the braid onto the top of the hook shank, from the hook eye to the hook bend. Build up a smooth body profile with thread. Tie on some pearl Krystal Flash at the hook bend and wrap forward about 1/8 inch. Tie off, and tie on first the white bucktail and then the pearl and black Krystal Flash on top of the hook shank. Then add a small clump of white bucktail under the hook shank, at the same place. Wrap the rest of the body forward with a strip of Mylar and tie off at the hook eye. Also, tie off the other end of the mono loop at the hook eye, whip finish and cement. Paint on the eyes and coat with clear epoxy.

Needlefish Zonker
Originator: Unknown
Hook: #4 - 1 Tiemco 811S
Thread: White
Tail/Body: White or silver-gray Zonker strip and 4 - 6 strands of pearl Flashabou
Collar: Cross-cut white or silver-gray Zonker strip
Weedguard: V-style 30- to 40-pound fluorocarbon
Anti-Foul Loop: 30- to 40-pound fluorocarbon
Eyes: Stick-ons, black over white or silver
Tie on the anti-foul loop and the pearl Flashabou at the hook bend. Tie on the Zonker strip at the same place, wrapping it forward about 1/8 inch. Tie on the cross-cut zonker strip over the wrapped strips and wrap forward for about 2 or 3 turns. Build up a thread head at about the middle of the hook shank and taper it forward to the hook eye. Tie on the weedguard and position its legs in place. Whip finish and cement. Attach the eyes at the thread head and coat the entire front half of the fly with 5-minute epoxy.

Night Snook Fly
Originator: Capt. Jim Grace
Hook: #1 to 1/0
Thread: White
Body: None
Tail: None

Weedguard: Stainless steel wire
Wing: About 100 1-inch strands of pearl Flashabou
Divide the Flashabou into three approximately equal bunches. Tie on the first bunch on top, just ahead of the hook bend. Tie on the second bunch in the same fashion, about midway between the first bunch and the hook eye. Tie on the third bunch, just past the hook eye. Tie on the weedguard, build up a small head, tie off and seal with head cement. This pattern recipe is from Reference 1, page 5.

Nix's Crab
Originator: Lew Jewett, Jimmy Nix
Hook: Straight eye, standard length
Thread: Red
Underbody: Lead wire
Head: Deer body hair
Claws: Short grizzly hen hackles
Eyes: Melted monofilament
Legs: Gray rubber hackle
Body: Several sandy dun hackles and four cock ring neck pheasant body feathers
Weedguard: Optional mono weed guard
Wrap the hook shank with lead wire, the amount depending on desired sink rate. Tie down with thread and cement. Tie on 3 lengths of rubber legs on the bottom of the hook shank, at the hook eye, the hook bend and midway. These legs should be tied cross-wise and long. Tie on a small tuft of deer hair at the hook bend so that the fibers will flare outward and beyond the hook bend. Then tie on a pair of grizzly hackles so that they are splayed outward by the deer hair, with their natural curve inward. At the same place, tie on a short piece of heavy monofilament cross-wise, with its ends singed. At the same place, tie on a few sandy dun hackles and palmer forward to just short of the hook eye. Trim these hackle fibers, top and bottom. Tie on the 4 pheasant feathers flat-wise at the hook eye. Build up a small thread head, whip finish and cement. This recipe is the same as shown on page 11 of Reference 2.

Page's Menemsha Minnow
Originator: Page Rogers
Hook: Straight eye, extra-long shank stainless
Thread: Flat waxed nylon
Tail: Clump of white calf tail and silver Flashabou
Body: Prizmatic tape to match shape and coloration of menhaden
Eyes: Press-on Witchcraft Prizmatic
Tie on the tail at the hook bend on top of the hook shank, and then tie on the Flashabou on top, tie off and cement. Attach the lower and upper body tape sections, and paint on gills with a red marking pen. Paint on a lateral line with a black marking pen. Attached stick-on eyes. Coat entire body with a liberal amount of clear 5-minute epoxy.

Page's Sand Eel
Originator: Page Rogers
Hook: Mustad 34011 or Eagle Claw 066SS
Thread: White Danville, flat waxed nylon
Tail: Polar white Fly Fur, fluorescent Day-Glo chartreuse FisHair, lime pearlescent Fly Flash, silver Flashabou and moss green Fly Fur
Body: Pearl Mylar tubing
Eyes: Witchcraft 2 EY, black on silver
Tie all tail materials around the hook shank, just behind the hook eye, so that the materials extend beyond the end of the fly 1 to 2 inches. Slip the Mylar tubing over the fly, from the front and tie down at the hook bend and at the hook eye. Build up a small thread head, whip finish and cement. Color the body with a permanent marker; dark green on top and

light green on the sides. Paint on the gills with a bright red glossy paint. Attach the eyes. Cover the body with 1 or 2 coats of clear epoxy. This recipe is the same as shown on page 84 of Reference 3.

Page's Slim Jim
Originator: Page Rogers
Hook: 2/0 Wright & McGill 66SS
Thread: White
Tail: 4 to 6 long black saddle hackles
Body: Silver Mylar tinsel
Beard: White bucktail
Wing: Black bucktail
Head: Thread
Eyes: Painted white with black pupils
Tie on the black saddles, curved inward, on the top of the hook shank at the start of the hook bend. Tie on some silver Mylar tinsel and wrap the thread forward to the hook eye. Wrap the body with the Mylar tinsel and tie off at the hook eye. Tie on the white bucktail beard under the hook shank, just behind the hook eye. Tie on the black bucktail wing on top of the hook shank, just behind the hook eye. Wing and beard fibers should extend well into the hook bend. Wrap a small thread head, whip finish and cement. Paint on the eyes and coat with a clear cement or epoxy. This recipe is the same as on page 57 of Reference 1.

Page's Worm Fly
Originator: Page Rogers
Hook: #1 Straight eye stainless steel
Thread: Tobacco brown flat waxed nylon
Wing: Fluorescent pink and fluorescent red marabou
Body: Continuation of wing materials plus fluorescent pink chenille and fluorescent red hackle
Head: Thread
Tie on a large tuft of pink marabou on top of the hook shank, at the hook eye. Then tie on a sparser tuft of the red marabou on top. Work the tying thread back to the hook bend and tie on the chenille and the hackle feather. Work the tying thread back to the hook eye. Position the marabou over the top of the hook shank and overwrap the chenille to the hook eye, tying it off. Color the top of the chenille with a dark brown marking pen. Palmer the red hackle ribbing forward over the chenille, tying off at the hook eye. Build up a prominent thread head, whip finish and cement. Cover head with clear epoxy. This recipe is the same as shown on page 151 of Reference 5.

Palolo Worm
Originator: Unknown
Hook: Straight eye, long shank
Thread: Bright orange
Tail: Bright orange calf tail
Body: Fluorescent orange chenille
Head: Tan chenille
Tie on the calf tail at the hook bend so that it extends approximately 1 inch past the hook bend. Tie on and wrap the orange chenille forward to within 1/4 inch from the hook eye. Then tie on and wrap a few turns of the tan chenille. Build up a small thread head, whip finish and cement. This recipe is the same as shown on page 32 of Reference 2.

Patrick's Shrimp
Originator: Patrick Elkins
Hook: #2 Mustad 34011
Thread: Tan 3/0 mono cord
Feelers: 2 slender grizzly hackles and pearl Flashabou
Rattle: Medium glass rattle
Body: Flashabou Minnow Body
Wing: White and brown bucktail plus pearl and gold Krystal Flash and pearl Flashabou

Eyes: Mono with black beads
Wrap the hook shank with thread, from the hook eye to the hook bend. Tie on the grizzly feelers on top of the hook shank. Tie on a very short piece of large-diameter mono at the hook bend, on top of the hook so it is perpendicular to the hook shank. Slip black beads onto the mono ends, glue and trim. Slide the glass rattle into the Minnow Body and unravel about 3/4 inches of the fibers from one end. Tie the Minnow Body down on top of the hook shank just to the rear of the mono eyes, so that the unraveled ends extend beyond the rear of the hook, and place a drop of epoxy in this area. Wrap the thread back to the hook eye. Snug the rattle down to the rear of the Minnow Body and tie the other end down on top of the hook shank, at the hook eye. Trim off the end near the hook eye and invert the hook in the vise. Coat the junction between the Minnow Body and the hook shank with epoxy and allow to set. On top of the hook shank just behind the hook eye, tie on the white bucktail, the pearl Krystal Flash, the brown bucktail, the gold Krystal Flash and the pearl Flashabou, in that order. Wind a small thread head, whip finish and cement.

Pencil Popper
Originator: Unknown
Hook: Straight eye, long shank or kinked style
Tail: 6 to 8 white hackles
Skirt: White hackle
Underbody: Fine, white chenille
Body: Cork or foam, tapered to the rear and cupped (angled down) in the front
Eyes: Yellow with black pupils, stick-ons or painted
Pierce the body with an awl or a long threaded screw, so that the hole enters at the center of the small diameter end and exits at the lower part of the cupped section. Tie on the white hackles at the hook bend, splayed outward and then wrap a few turns of a white hackle to build a skirt. Tie on the chenille, wrap forward and tie off at the hook eye. Coat the chenille with super glue and allow to dry hard. Then recoat with epoxy glue and force the body onto the hook, butting the small diameter end up against the skirt and allowing the hook eye to protrude out the front by about 1/8 inch. Paint the body white, with the front third painted a bright red. Paint on or stick on the eyes and coat the body with clear epoxy. This recipe is very similar to that shown on page 34 of Reference 2.

Peterson's Cinder Worm
Originator: Eric Peterson
Hook: #4 - 1
Thread: Black
Tail: Red marabou and orange Krystal Flash
Body: Red dyed deer body hair
Head: Black or olive dyed deer body hair
Tie on a small amount of Krystal Flash at the hook bend, on top. In the same place, tie on a generous amount of red marabou. Spin and pack the red deer hair forward to about 3/16 inch from the hook eye. The first few turns should be flared back to blend in with the marabou. Spin and pack the black deer hair up to the hook eye. Whip finish and cement. Trim the head and body to a narrow, round shape. This is the same pattern as shown on page 32 of Reference 2.

Pete's Persuader
Originator: Bob Johns
Hook: Straight eye, standard length
Wing: 6 - 10 white and 2 grizzly saddle hackles plus some pearl Krystal Flash
Topping: Half dozen strands of peacock herl

Throat: White rabbit hair, including guard hairs
Collar: Natural cream lamb's wool
Head: Natural cream lamb's wool
Eyes: Solid plastic
Midway between hook eye and hook bend, tie in 3 - 5 white saddle hackles on each side of hook shank. At the same place, tie in a grizzly saddle and some pearl Krystal Flash. Then tie in peacock herl topping and a few more strands of pearl Krystal Flash. Under saddle butts, tie in rabbit fur with guard hairs. Over saddle butts, tie in some lamb's wool. Then spin lamb's wool up to the hook eye, tie off, whip finish and cement. Trim head section only to rounded bullet head shape. Glue and insert eyes into finished head. This pattern shape is the same as on page 74 of Reference 2.

Petrie Shrimp
Originator: Mark Petrie
Hook: #2 Mustad 34011
Antennae: Black rubber strips
Tail: Tan marabou with gold Sparkle Yarn
Body: Medium orange Ice Chenille and tan Furry Foam
Eyes: Burnt 100-pound mono
Weedguard: Mono loop
Tie on one leg of the mono loop weedguard on top of the hook shank. At the hook bend, tie on a short piece of 100-pound mono cross-wise on top of the hook shank. Singe the ends of this mono to form a pair of black eyes. At the same place, tie on a small tuft of gold Sparkle Yarn and a large clump of tan marabou, on top of the hook shank. Also, at the same place, tie on two black rubber strips, a small strip of Furry Foam and a piece of Ice Chenille. Wrap the tying thread forward to the hook eye and wind the Ice Chenille to that point and tie it off. Spiral the thread back about halfway to the mono eyes and bring the Furry Foam forward and tie it down. Continue tying it down in progressively smaller segments toward the hook eye and tie off at the hook eye. Tie on the other end of the mono weedguard loop at the hook eye, whip finish and cement. This recipe is the same as shown on page 84 of Reference 3.

Phantom Mullet*
Originator: Steve Reifsneider
Hook: 3/0 Daiichi
Thread: 3/0 clear mono or white
Tail: Pearl Witchcraft Tape
Body: Medium silver E-Z Body tubing
Shoulder: Pearl Witchcraft Tape
Wing: White yak hair, tan and olive Icelandic goat hair plus pearl Flashabou and lavender Enrico's Sea Fiber
Eyes: Silver 3-D stick-ons
Head: Thread
Slide the E-Z Body onto the hook so that it covers the hook shank from the hook eye to the start of the hook bend. At the hook eye, tie on a clump of white yak hair under and on top of the hook shank. Add 10-18 strands of pearl Flashabou or Mylar Motion Pearl and some lavender Sea Fiber. Then, also on top of the hook shank, tie in a sparse clump of tan goat hair followed by a generous clump of olive goat hair. Cut two feather-shaped shoulder pieces of Witchcraft tape and tie them on the sides, in the same place. Build up a sizable thread head, whip finish and cement. Apply the stick-on eyes on the front edges of the shoulder, and cover the head and eyes with clear epoxy. Finally, cut a tulip-shaped tail section from the Witchcraft tape, insert it in the open end of the E-Z Body tubing and seal the end with Zap-a-Gap.
*Favorite Fly of Chris Goldmark

Phillips' Header*

Originator: Capt. Chris Phillips

Hook: 1/0 Tiemco 800-11S

Thread: White flat waxed nylon

Tail: 6, 4- to 5-inch yellow saddle hackles, 10 strands of gold and red Flashabou and yellow bucktail

Back: Red bucktail

Topping: 8 strands of peacock herl

Head/Overbody: Large natural pearl EZ Body

Eyes: 5/16-inch red holographic eyes

Tie on the saddle hackles at the hook bend and wrap the tying thread up the shank to a point about halfway to the hook eye. Then, tie on a clump of yellow bucktail under the hook shank, a clump of red bucktail on top of the hook shank, with the strands of Flashabou on the sides. Tie the peacock herl over the red bucktail. Slide the EZ Body sleeve over the hook eye and tie the end down onto the hook shank just behind the hook eye. While holding the body and tail in place, roll the EZ Body back over itself, capturing the fly's fibers and keeping them together at the hook bend. Place 2 globs of super glue gel on the backs of the eyes and press them in place on the EZ Body, so that the gel and eyes adhere to the underlying hook shank. Mark the EZ Body as desired with permanent marking pens for gills, stripes, etc. This fly is also effective when tied in a red/white color combination.

*Favorite Fly of Capt. Chris Phillips

Phil's Tarpon Crab

Originator: Capt. Phil O'Bannon

Hook: 4/0 tarpon fly hook

Thread: Clear monocord

Tail: 4 to 6 broad hackles plus some Krystal Flash

Body: Fine deer body hair

Eyes: Long, mono stalk eyes

Wrap the hook shank from hook eye to the hook bend. Tie in hackle tip tails at the hook bend at the side of the hook shank, splayed outward. Add a few strands of Krystal Flash on top. Spin and pack the deer hair onto the hook shank for about 3/4 of its length. Tie on the eyes, extending 90 degrees from the shank, and then spin and pack additional deer hair through and past the eyes. Tie off at the hook eye, whip finish and cement. Trim the deer hair to suit.

Pink Grizzly Tarpon

Originator: Unknown

Hook: 4/0

Thread: Red

Tail: Pink bucktail or calf tail

Wings: 4 grizzly and 2 pink wide neck hackles, plus some pearl Krystal Flash

Collar: 1 grizzly and 1 pink wide hackles

Eyes (Optional): Non-lead dumbbells

Tie on the bucktail tail on top of the hook shank, at the hook bend. Add the Krystal Flash to the tail. Tie in the neck hackles on each side of the hook, at the hook bend. Each side should consist of 3 hackles, 2 grizzly hackles with a pink hackle in between. Hackles should splay outward, tarpon fly style. At the same place, wind a pink and a grizzly hackle together for a dense collar. If weight is needed, tie on weighted dumbbells just forward of the collar. Taper the beak of the fly down to one thread layer over the shank, wind forward to the hook eye, whip finish and cement. Paint eyes on the dumbbells and coat the beak with clear epoxy.

Pink Squid (A)

Originator: Unknown

Hook: 1/0 to 2/0 long shank

Thread: White

Eyes: Large plastic

Tail: 6 to 8 white or pink saddle hackles plus pearl or pink Flashabou

Body: Pearl Crystal Chenille

Collar: White cross-cut rabbit fur

Tie on the saddle hackles and Flashabou at the hook bend. Tie on the Crystal Chenille and wrap forward halfway to the hook eye. Tie off, and then tie on the rabbit fur strip and palmer forward to the hook eye. Tie off, whip finish and cement. Attach the plastic eyes to the rabbit fur with a glob of epoxy.

Pop's Bonefish Bitters (Amber)

Originator: Craig Mathews

Hook: #10 to #6 Mustad 3407, Daiichi 2546, Tiemco 800S

Thread: 6/0 amber

Body: Thread

Body Hackle: Amber Sili-Legs

Tail: Amber Z-lon

Front Hackle: Natural deer hair

Eyes: Gold bead chain

Wrap the straight portion of the hook shank with thread, coat with clear epoxy and allow to dry. Tie on the bead-chain eyes on top of the hook shank, just behind the hook eye. Tie on three sets of Sili-Legs cross-wise under the hook shank at its midpoint. Spread out to simulate crustacean legs and add a drop or two of cement. Tie on a small tuft of Z-lon at the hook bend. Spin and pack deer from the hook bend to the bead-chain eyes. Trim just the front section of the deer hair, to streamline the body. Wrap the tying thread to the hook eye, whip finish and cement. This recipe is the same as on page 86 of Reference 3.

Puff

Originator: Capts. Nat Ragland\Steve Huff

Hook: #2 to 1/0 Mustad 34007

Thread: Tan or brown Danville, flat waxed nylon

Tail: 8 cree or brown neck hackles

Body: Brown or tan chenille

Eyes: Small bead chain

Tie in 4 of the neck hackles splayed outward just forward of the bend of the hook. Then palmer 2 - 4 neck hackles just in front of the splayed hackle. Lay the palmered hackle back "Keys style" by back-winding the thread. Wind the thread forward and attach the bead-chain eyes about 2/3 of the distance along the hook shank. Bring the thread back to the palmered hackle and tie in the chenille. Wind the chenille forward to the hook eye and whip finish the thread.

Quonny Mummy

Originator: Unknown

Hook: #1 Mustad 34007

Thread: Olive mono cord

Tail: 5 strands of olive Flashabou and 4 olive grizzly saddles (2 to 2 1/2 in. long)

Body: Light tan and olive deer body hair

Eyes: Small lead dumbbells

Tie in the dumbbell eyes on top of the hook, about 1/4 inch behind the hook eye. Tie on the Flashabou strands at the top of the hook shank, at the hook bend. At the same place, tie on the 4 olive grizzly saddles on the side of the hook shank. Spin and pack the olive deer hair throughout the body and up to the hook eye, except for one small bunch of tan deer body hair just behind the dumbbell eyes. Whip finish and cement. Trim the deer hair to shape.

Randy's Spoon Fly

Originator: Capt. Randy Hamilton

Hook: 1/0 or 2/0 Gamakatsu SC 15

Thread: 6/0 tan UNI-Thread

Tail: Red fox tail plus slinky olive fibers

Body: Offray Gold Coast #7985628116, 1.5-inch woven craft ribbon

Eyes: Small dumbbells

Weedguard: 22-pound steel Calcutta wire

Place the hook in the vise so that the eye is pointing down to the floor. Tie in the squirrel tail, well past the bend of the hook. Also, tie in 6 to 8 strands of olive slinky fiber. Tie in the dumbbell eyes directly over the tail wraps and move the hook to the normal tying position. Cut about 2.5 inches of the wire and bring the two ends together, forming a teardrop shape. Slide your thumb all the way down the loop until a kink is formed at the end. Kink the wire ends about 1/8 inch from the ends, forming 2 dog-ears. Wrap the tying thread forward and tie in the wire weedguard so that the dog-ears remain extended. Bend the weedguard to the proper position and kink the loop end to fit under the hok point. Bend the dog-ears over the thread wraps with long-nose pliers and then overwrap the dog-ears and the previous wraps. Whip finish the thread at the hook eye and cement. Spray 3-M's M-77 adhesive onto the back of the Offray ribbon and let it cure for 5 minutes. Cut a piece of ribbon long enough to just fit between the hook eye and the dumbbell eyes. Reposition the hook in the vise so that the hook bend and point are on top. Fold the ribbon over the hook shank lengthwise and press the edges together so that the ribbon extends equally above and below the hook shank. Cut the ribbon to a teardrop shape and round all edges. When the ribbon (blade) is positioned so that it is symmetrical, put a thin coat of 2-part clear epoxy on the blade and over onto the hook eye and dumbbell eyes.

Rat Tail

Originator: Steve Shiba

Hook: Mustad 34007/3407, Daiichi 2546 or Tiemco 811S

Tail: Chartreuse, black, white, purple, black/purple, or black/raspberry Rat Tail

Body: Foam, color to match/complement the tail

Eyes: Black on yellow post-type

Tie the Rat Tail onto the middle of the hook shank and cement in place. Shape the foam to a bullet-nose profile and pierce a hole through its center. Wrap the hook shank with a fine chenille and coat with superglue. Allow to dry, and then recoat the hook shank with epoxy and force the body over the front of the hook and back to the tail. Pierce the front of the body for eye sockets, add a drop of epoxy and insert the eye posts. This recipe is the same as shown on page 88 of Reference 3.

Rats Arse

Originator: Harry Koons

Hook: 1/0 to 3/0 Mustad 34007

Tail: 4 to 6 saddle hackles and 8 - 16 strands of Krystal Flash

Body: Rabbit strip

Wing: 4 short and webby saddle hackles and 8 strands of holographic tinsel

Eyes: Lead dumbbells

Head: Thread, plus epoxy and glitter

Tie on the dumbbell eyes on top of the hook shank, about 1/4 inch behind the hook eye. Tie on the long saddle hackles and flash material at the hook bend, on the sides of the hook shank. Saddle curvature should be inward. Tie on the rabbit strip on top of the hook shank, from the hook bend to the hook eye. Invert the hook in the vise and tie on the webby saddle hackles on the top of the hook shank, just in front of the dumbbell eyes, veiling the hook point. Build up a thread head, whip finish and cement. Coat the head with 5-minute epoxy, with glitter mixed in. Color of materials at the option of the tier.

Rattle Rouser
Originator: Kirk Dietrich
Hook: 1/0 Mustad 34011
Thread: Red Flymaster Plus
Rattle: Standard glass rattle
Body: Large gold Mylar tubing
Wing: Tan and olive bucktail plus red and gold Flashabou
Eyes: Painted black on yellow

Wrap the entire hook shank from eye to bend with the tying thread. Slip the glass rattle inside the Mylar tubing. Unravel about 3/4 inch of the tubing, and tie it onto the top of the hook shank, at the hook bend. Wrap the tying thread forward to the hook eye. Snug the rattle against the unraveled end of the tubing and tie down the loose end at the hook eye, so that the tubing and rattle are firmly against the top of the hook shank. Trim the remaining tubing ends near the hook eye. Invert the hook in the vise and coat the junction of the hook shank and Mylar tubing with clear epoxy. After the epoxy sets, tie on first the tan bucktail, the red Krystal Flash, the olive bucktail and then the gold Flashabou, on top of the hook shank, at the hook eye. Build up a sizable thread head, whip finish and cement. Paint on the eyes and add a coat of clear epoxy on the head.

Rattle Shrimp
Originator: Unknown
Hook: #1 Mustad 34007
Thread: Clear, fine mono
Tail: Gold Krystal Flash and gold Flashabou
Body: Gold Mylar piping, with glass rattle inside
Eyes: Small lead dumbbell eyes

Tie on the dumbbell eyes on top of the hook shank, at the hook bend. Then tie on the gold Krystal Flash and Flashabou just in back of the dumbbell eyes. Tie on one end of the Mylar piping just in front of the dumbbell eyes, on top of the hook. Insert the glass rattle and tie off the other end of the piping next to the hook eye. Whip finish and cement. Coat piping and hook shank with epoxy to obtain a hard finish.

Rattlin' Rose
Originator: George Rose
Hook: #2 standard length
Thread: Black monocord or equivalent
Body: Large gold Mylar tube plus small worm rattle
Wing: Brown and olive bucktail
Head: Large black, with painted eyes

Invert the hook and place in the vise, point side up. Wrap hook shank with thread and tie in the rattle, on top. Slip the Mylar tubing over the rattle chamber, securing at both ends. Leave about 1/4 inch of the tail-end of the Mylar tubing unraveled, for a tail. Tie in a medium-sized clump of wing fibers, brown over olive, so that the hook point is covered. Build up a head with tying thread, whip finish and cement. Paint on eyes, either white or red with black pupils. Coat painted eyes for extra durability.

Rattling Deceiver
Originator: Lefty Kreh
Hook: Mustad 34011
Thread: Red 3/0 flat waxed nylon
Tail: 6 to 8 olive saddle hackles and pearl or olive Krystal Flash
Beard: Red Krystal Flash or Fly Fur
Body: Thread
Collar: White and olive bucktail plus red Krystal Flash
Rattle: Small plastic rattle

Tie on the saddle hackles on the side of the hook shank with the hackles curving inward, at the start of the hook bend. Also add a few strands of Krystal Flash outside the hackles. Tie the rattle onto the top of the hook shank, from the hook bend forward. Wrap the rattle fully and then saturate the wraps with clear epoxy. In back of the hook eye, tie on a few clumps of white bucktail, to the bottom and sides of the hook shank. At the same place, on top of the hook shank, tie in a few bunches of olive bucktail, Krystal Flash and peacock herl. Wrap a small thread head, whip finish and cement. Eyes are optional.

Ray's Fly
Originator: Ray Bondorew
Hook: Eagle Claw 254NA, 1x short
Body: Silver Mylar yarn
Wing: White, olive and yellow bucktail plus pearlescent Mylar
Topping: 7 to 14 strands of peacock herl

Tie on the Mylar yarn at the hook bend and wrap forward to just short of the hook eye. At the hook eye, tie on first a small clump of white bucktail, then the pearlescent Mylar, and sparse clumps of yellow bucktail and olive bucktail. The white bucktail should be about twice the length of the hook, the yellow bucktail a little longer and the olive bucktail slightly longer. Then tie on the peacock herl topping, which should extend just beyond the wing. This recipe is the same as shown in page 34 of Reference 5.

Razzle Dazzle
Originator: Ken Abrames
Hook: 2/0 to 5/0, Eagle Claw 254NA 1x short
Tail: 1 saddle hackle each of olive, silver doctor blue and yellow, plus 4 white saddlehackles plus 2 strands each of blue, light green, silver, red and gold Mylar
Body: Silver Mylar piping
Throat: Long white bucktail
Wing: 1 olive saddle hackle and 1 short silver doctor blue saddle hackle
Eyes: Jungle cock

At the hook bend, tie in a sparse ring of white bucktail around the hook shank. Then tie on top (flatwing style), in turn, 3 white saddles, gold Mylar, a yellow saddle, red Mylar, a silver doctor blue saddle, silver Mylar, a white saddle, light green Mylar, an olive saddle and blue Mylar. All saddles should be long, and the Mylar strips should extend at least 3/4 inches past the saddles. Tie on and wrap the Mylar piping up to the hook eye. Tie on a single-layer of long white bucktail around the bottom and sides of the hook. Tie on first a long olive saddle and then a short silver doctor blue saddle, flat style on top of the hook shank. Tie in the jungle cock eyes, build up a thread head, whip finish and cement. This fly should be at least 7 inches long.

Red-Hot Rat Tail*
Originator: Capt. David Kreshpane
Hook: 1/0 to 2/0 Tiemco 800S
Thread: White 6/0 flat waxed nylon
Tail: Red and silver Flashabou or Fire Fly and red Rat Tail
Body: Red chenille and a black saddle hackle
Head: Pearl Lite Brite

Tie on an equal number of red and silver Flashabou strands at the hook bend, around the shank. Add a length of Rat Tail at the same place and trim Flashabou and Rat Tail to extend 2 inches beyond the hook end. At the hook bend, tie in the black saddle hackle and the red chenille. Wrap the chenille forward and tie off about 1/8 inch behind the hook eye.

Palmer the black hackle forward to the same point and tie off. Dub on a head of Lite Brite, tie off at the hook eye, whip finish and cement.
*Favorite Fly of Capt. David Kreshpane

Rednose Mudminnow
Originator: Capt. Chuck Scates
Hook: Straight eye, standard length
Wing: White bucktail, green Flashabou, plus 4 medium blue and 4 yellow saddle hackles
Collar: Natural deer body hair
Head: Natural and red deer body hair
Eyes: Hollow plastic

At midpoint of the hook shank, tie on the wing materials. First tie on the white bucktail and then the green Flashabou on top of the hook shank. Then tie on 2 blue followed by 2 yellow saddle hackles on each side of the hook shank. Over the wing butts, tie on some deer body hair so that it will flair over the saddles, surrounding the hook shank. Then, spin and pack the deer hair up to the hook eye, with the last 1/4 inch of hair being red-dyed deer hair. Clip the head and nose to a minnow shape and add the plastic eyes with a dab of Zap-a-Gap or silicone rubber. This fly can also be tied and used successfully with a black nose. This recipe is the same as shown on page 56 of Reference 2.

Rhody Flatwing*
Originator: Bill Peabody
Hook: 1/0 Wright & McGill 254SS
Thread: White or clear mono
Tail: Long white bucktail, 1 long olive saddle feather and 3 strands of gold Flashabou
Body: Braided pearl Mylar or Bill's Bodi Braid
Collar: White bucktail
Wing: Yellow, blue and olive bucktail and 6 strands of pearl or olive Krystal Flash
Topping: 4 to 5 strands of peacock herl
Head: White thread

At the hook bend, tie on a sparse clump of white bucktail on top, over which is the olive saddle, tied flat, and the gold Flashabou. Tie on the Bodi Braid and wrap forward to within 1/8 inch of hook eye. Tie on a sparse clump of short white bucktail around the hook shank, just behind the hook eye. Tie in a sparse mixture of yellow and blue bucktail on top, just behind the hook eye, followed by a covering layer of olive bucktail and the Krystal Flash. Add the peacock herl topping, build up a small thread head, whip finish and cement. This recipe is quite similar to the one shown on page 56 of Reference 2.
*Favorite Fly of Capt. Eric Thomas

Ribbon Crab
Originator: Capt. Lenny Moffo
Hook: #4 to 1/0 Mustad 34007
Thread: Brown 3/0 monocord
Weight: Lead dumbbells
Tail: Brown bucktail and 2 brown-dyed grizzly hackles
Body Shell: Olive dressmaker's ribbon
Eyes: Artificial flower stamens
Legs: Rubber latex pieces
Belly: White acrylic paint

Wrap the hook shank with the tying thread and then tie in the bucktail well into the hook bend, keeping the fly's hook point riding upward. Tie in the brown-dyed grizzly hackle on each side of the bucktail, the hackle points splayed outward. Wrap the thread to the middle of the hook shank and tie on the lead dumbbell, which has already been flattened with heavy-duty pliers. Tie off the thread and cut it off. Spray a section of the olive ribbon with clear lacquer. When dry, cut with scissors to an appropriate carapace shape and glue it with a glue gun onto the bottom of the hook, opposite the dumbbell eyes. Cut crab legs and claws to shape and tie an overhand knot in each, to set them in a bent position. Use the glue gun to glue the legs and claws in place, on the same side as the dumbbell eyes. Set the flower stamen eyes between the large claws and glue in place. Coat the dumbbell eye-side of the body with 5-minute epoxy, smooth to a convex shape and allow to set. Paint the convex side of the body with white acrylic paint and after dry, coat the entire body, both sides with clear epoxy. Color legs and claws as desired with permanent markers.

Ridgeway's Food Fly
Originator: Capt. Adam Ridgeway
Hook: #4 Mustad 34007
Thread: Brown flat waxed nylon
Tail: 2 feathers of sand grizzly marabou and 4 strands of root beer Krystal Flash
Body: Root beer Estaz or Estaz Grande and brown grizzly hackle
Eyes: 5/32 to 7/32 lead dumbbells
At the hook bend on the side of the hook shank, tie on the marabou feathers, leaving about 1 to 1 1/4 inches of feather extended beyond the hook. The feathers should be in line with the hook shank. Add the Krystal Flash to each side, in the same place. Over the feather butts, tie in first the brown hackle and then tie in the Estaz in front of the butts. Wrap the thread forward to the hook eye and then tie in the dumbbell eyes on top of the hook shank, about 1/8 inch behind the hook eye. Wrap the Estaz forward and tie in behind the dumbbell eyes. Palmer the brown hackle forward and tie off at the same place. Wrap the thread forward over the dumbbell eyes, build a small head, whip finish and cement. Tease Estaz strands out from under the palmered hackle to create a full body. Trim the hackle and Estaz on top of the fly (opposite the hook point).

Roccus Rattle*
Originator: Capt. Bill Strakele
Hook: 2/0 to 3/0 Mustad 3407
Thread: 3/0 flat waxed tan
Tail: 8 white saddle hackles (5 - 6 inches long) plus 8 strands of pearl Krystal Flash and 8 strands of pearl Flashabou
Collar: Crosscut tan rabbit fur
Head: white thread and pearl Krystal Flash
Rattle: Kadco rattle
Eyes: 7/32 molded silver Witchcraft
Wind a bed of thread on the hook shank from the hook eye to the hook bend. Tie 4 saddles on each side of the hook shank, at the hook bend, so that the feathers splay outward. Tie in 4 strands each of Krystal Flash and Flashabou over the saddles and cement butts firmly in place. Trim/taper one end of the rattle with a razor blade and tie the rattle onto the top of the hook shank, leaving a 1/4-inch gap between the tapered end and the hook eye. Trim a small piece of wood (part of a dental plaque remover works fine) with a razor blade and insert as a tapered filler between the hook eye and the rattle, tying it on the hook shank with thread. Lock the rattle and the filler piece to the hook shank with a few drops of ZAP. Glue in one end of the rabbit fur at the rattle's midpoint with a drop of ZAP, palmer the rabbit strip forward and tie off at the hook eye. Build up a thread head, wrap with a single strand of Krystal Flash, whip finish and cement. Attach the eyes to the thread head and then coat the head with a thin layer of clear epoxy, being careful to just cover the edges of the eyes

with epoxy.
*Favorite Fly of Capt. Bill Strakele

Roccus Rattle (A)
Originator: Capt. Bill Strakele
Hook: 2/0 to 3/0 Mustad 3407
Thread: 3/0 flat waxed tan
Tail: 8 white saddle hackles (5 - 6 inches long) plus 8 strands of gold Krystal Flash and 8 strands of pearl Flashabou
Collar: Crosscut white rabbit fur
Head: White thread and gold Krystal Flash
Rattle: Kadco rattle
Eyes: 7/32 molded silver Witchcraft
Wind a bed of thread on the hook shank from the hook eye to the hook bend. Tie 4 saddles on each side of the hook shank, at the hook bend, so that the feathers splay outward. Tie in 4 strands each of Krystal Flash and Flashabou over the saddles and cement butts firmly in place. Trim/taper one end of the rattle with a razor blade and tie the rattle onto the top of the hook shank, leaving a 1/4-inch gap between the tapered end and the hook eye. Trim a small piece of wood (part of a dental plaque remover works fine) with a razor blade and insert as a tapered filler between the hook eye and the rattle, tying it on the hook shank with thread. Lock the rattle and the filler piece to the hook shank with a few drops of ZAP. Glue in one end of the rabbit fur at the rattle's midpoint with a drop of ZAP, palmer the rabbit strip forward and tie off at the hook eye. Build up a thread head, wrap with a single strand of Krystal Flash, whip finish and cement. Attach the eyes to the thread head and then coat the head with a thin layer of clear epoxy, being careful to just cover the edges of the eyes with epoxy.

Roccus Rattle (B)
Originator: Capt. Bill Strakele
Hook: 2/0 to 3/0 Mustad 3407
Thread: 3/0 flat waxed tan
Tail: 8 white saddle hackles (5 - 6 inches long) plus 8 strands of root beer Krystal Flash and 8 strands of pearl Flashabou
Collar: Crosscut olive rabbit fur
Head: White thread and root beer Krystal Flash
Rattle: Kadco rattle
Eyes: 7/32 molded silver Witchcraft
Wind a bed of thread on the hook shank from the hook eye to the hook bend. Tie 4 saddles on each side of the hook shank, at the hook bend, so that the feathers splay outward. Tie in 4 strands each of Krystal Flash and Flashabou over the saddles and cement butts firmly in place. Trim/taper one end of the rattle with a razor blade and tie the rattle onto the top of the hook shank, leaving a 1/4-inch gap between the tapered end and the hook eye. Trim a small piece of wood (part of a dental plaque remover works fine) with a razor blade and insert as a tapered filler between the hook eye and the rattle, tying it on the hook shank with thread. Lock the rattle and the filler piece to the hook shank with a few drops of ZAP. Glue in one end of the rabbit fur at the rattle's midpoint with a drop of ZAP, palmer the rabbit strip forward and tie off at the hook eye. Build up a thread head, wrap with a single strand of Krystal Flash, whip finish and cement. Attach the eyes to the thread head and then coat the head with a thin layer of clear epoxy, being careful to just cover the edges of the eyes with epoxy.

Roccus Rattle (C)
Originator: Capt. Bill Strakele
Hook: 2/0 to 3/0 Mustad 3407

Thread: 3/0 flat waxed tan
Tail: 8 white saddle hackles (5 - 6 inches long) plus 8 strands of rainbow Krystal Flash and 8 strands of blue Flashabou
Collar: Crosscut blue rabbit fur
Head: White thread and rainbow Krystal Flash
Rattle: Kadco rattle
Eyes: 7/32 molded silver Witchcraft
Wind a bed of thread on the hook shank from the hook eye to the hook bend. Tie 4 saddles on each side of the hook shank, at the hook bend, so that the feathers splay outward. Tie in 4 strands each of Krystal Flash and Flashabou over the saddles and cement butts firmly in place. Trim/taper one end of the rattle with a razor blade and tie the rattle onto the top of the hook shank, leaving a 1/4-inch gap between the tapered end and the hook eye. Trim a small piece of wood (part of a dental plaque remover works fine) with a razor blade and insert as a tapered filler between the hook eye and the rattle, tying it on the hook shank with thread. Lock the rattle and the filler piece to the hook shank with a few drops of ZAP. Glue in one end of the rabbit fur at the rattle's midpoint with a drop of ZAP, palmer the rabbit strip forward and tie off at the hook eye. Build up a thread head, wrap with a single strand of Krystal Flash, whip finish and cement. Attach the eyes to the thread head and then coat the head with a thin layer of clear epoxy, being careful to just cover the edges of the eyes with epoxy.

Rosario's Minnow
Originator: Rosario Martinez
Hook: #2 Mustad 3011
Thread: Light green 3/0 monocord
Body: Large light Flexi Cord
Eyes: Stick-ons, silver with black pupils
Cut a piece of Flexi Cord about twice as long as the hook length. Pinch down one end and slip it over the hook eye, tying it down next to the hook eye. Tie off the thread and cement. Roll the Flexi Cord over on itself and cut a slot in its lower edge so that it will slide past the hook point/bend and extend beyond the end of the hook. Tightly tie down the Flexi Cord about 1/4 inch past the hook end and unravel the end fibers. Cut off the fibers to the shape of a tail. Squeeze the fly down to a high, narrow profile and lightly coat with clear epoxy to maintain its shape, to seal the slot in the lower part and to lock the material to the hook. Add the stick-on eyes, use permanent markers to add prey markings and finish with another light coat of clear epoxy.

Royal Anchovy
Originator: Bob Lindquist
Hook: #6 - 2 Gamakatsu SL11-3H or equivalent
Tail: White arctic fox fibers, light pink (not cerise) and chartreuse marabou, and pearl Glimmer
Underbody: Lead tape
Overbody: Bill's Bodi Braid
Topping: Dozen fibers of blue bucktail
Eyes: Stick-ons or plastic
Tie on the arctic fox tail at the hook bend, on top of the hook shank. Tie on pearl Glimmer to surround the fox tail. Tie on light pink marabou on top, an amount approximately equal to 1/3 of the arctic fox. Then add a similar amount of chartreuse marabou on top of the pink. Cement and tie on a piece of lead tape from the tail butts to the hook eye, trimmed to the shape of an anchovy. Tie in a piece of pearl Bill's Bodi Braid at the tail and wrap forward over the lead to the hook eye. Tie on about a dozen fibers of blue bucktail on top of the hook shank just behind the hook eye. Trim the ends, whip finish and cement. Then coat the

body with clear epoxy, keeping the blue topping together over the body until the epoxy sets. Attach the eyes and add another coat of clear epoxy. This recipe is the same as featured in the Fall 1999 issue of *Fly Tyer* magazine.

Sand Eel
Originator: Lou Tabory
Hook: 1/0 Wright & McGill 66SS
Thread: White 2/0 nylon
Wing: White bucktail and peacock herl
Body: Continuation of wing materials
Overbody: Clear vinyl or piece of zip-lock bag material
Tie on the white bucktail just behind the hook eye and then tie on a few strands of peacock herl over that. Work the tying thread back to the hook bend and tie on a strip of clear vinyl. Wrap the tying thread back again to the hook eye. Lay the wing materials down on top of the hook shank, making sure that the bucktail and herl maintain their same relative positions. Wrap the vinyl strip forward over the body, tie off at the hook eye, whip finish and cement. Coat the body with clear vinyl cement. This recipe is very similar to that shown on page 58 of Reference 2.

Sand Eel Fly*
Originator: Unknown
Hook: #4 or larger 7766
Tail and Underbody: Ice Chenille and Rainy's Float Foam (parachute posts)
Body: Corsair tubing, 3/8-inch diameter x 3 1/2 to 4 inches long when stretched
Body Marking: Lime peel, chartreuse and brown Prismacolor marking pens
Eyes: #2 silver Witchcraft
Pull a 4- to 5-inch piece of Ice Chenille through the tubing (with a v-wire or tiny loop) so that about 1/2 inch sticks out from either end. Poke a small hole on one side of the tubing, at its midpoint, and slide the tubing over the hook eye until the hole is well past the start of the bend of the hook. Use tweezers or a bodkin to pack a few pieces of Float Foam into the belly of the tubing, between the underside of the hook shank and the inner surface of the tubing. Attach the tying thread behind the hook eye, squeeze the tubing and chenille down to the hook shank and wrap over to secure in place. Cut off excess pieces of tubing and chenille from near the hook eye, build a small thread head, whip finish and cement. Pull the tubing/chenille from the tail end and cut off at the appropriate length and diameter. Tie down the tubing about 1/4 inch from the tail end and trim the excess tubing so that the extended chenille forms the tail end. Cement the tail tie-down area. Color the fly as desired with the marking pens and add eyes to the head. Coat the head with head cement or clear epoxy.
*Favorite Fly of Cooper Gilkes

Sar-Mul-Mac
Originator: Dan Blanton
Hook: 3/0 TMC 811S
Thread: White, single-strand nylon floss
Throat: White bucktail
Wing: 6 white saddle hackles, silver Flashabou, royal blue bucktail, and chartreuse Krystal Flash
Topping: 10 strands of peacock herl
Eyes: Solid plastic, 7 mm amber
Head: White chenille
Gills: Red chenille
Tie on the plastic eyes, about 1/4 inch from the hook eye. To the rear of the plastic eyes, tie on the white bucktail throat on the sides and bottom of the hook shank. Then tie on the white saddle hackles on top of the hook shank and then the blue bucktail over the

saddles. Tie on a dozen strands of silver Flashabou on each side and the chartreuse Krystal Flash on the top. Then, tie on the peacock herl topping, leaving about an inch and a half of the butts extended forward. Cement the wraps at this point very heavily. Wrap on a turn or two of the red chenille about midway between the hook eye and hook bend. Tie off and then tie on the white chenille, wrapping forward around the eyes to shape the head. Tie off and whip finish at the hook eye and cement. This recipe is similar to the pattern on page 69 of Reference 2.

Scates' Shrimp*
Originator: Chuck Scates
Hook: Straight eye, standard length
Thread: Yellow
Weedguard: Stiff monofilament
Antennae and Mouth: Yellow bucktail and natural deer body hair
Eyes: Melted monofilament, painted black or red
Head and Abdomen: Yellow chenille
Legs: Black hackle
Shellback: Yellow Krystal Flash
Tail: Yellow Krystal Flash butts
Tie on one end of the mono weedguard over the top of the hook shank. Tie in the monofilament eyes at the hook bend. Tie in a few strands of yellow bucktail and a small clump of deer body hair at the end of the hook, halfway around the bend. Also, tie in the yellow Krystal Flash and the yellow chenille at this point. Wrap the chenille just past the mono eyes and tie in the black hackle feather. Continue wrapping the chenille to a point just short of the hook eye and tie it off. Palmer the black hackle through the chenille and also tie off at the head. Trim the black hackle fibers at the top and tie the other end of the mono weedguard loop under the hook shank close to the hook eye. Bring the yellow Krystal Flash shellback fibers forward over the top of the fly and tie off in back of the hook eye. Allow some of the yellow fibers to extend downward to act as the tail, before cutting. Build up the head with thread, whip finish and cement. Paint the mono eyes black or red. This pattern, also commonly tied in red and fluorescent white, is the same as shown on page 19 of Reference 2.
*Favorite Fly of Capt. Sally Moffett

Sea Serpent
Originator: Chris Windham
Hook: #4 to 1/0 Mustad 3407
Thread: Black or cream nylon
Tail and Body: Black or chartreuse rabbit strip
Body Collar and Head: Red or white deer body hair
Use the first set of colors for a black/red serpent and the second set for a chartreuse/white serpent. Tie a rabbit strip on top of the hook shank, at the start of the hook bend. Then, spin and pack the deer body hair the rest of the way to the hook eye. Whip finish and cement. Trim the deer hair to an appropriate shape, leaving the rear fibers splayed back over the rear of the hook and leaving a dorsal-like projection on top. This recipe is the same as shown on page 98 of Reference 3.

Seaducer
Originator: Homer Rhodes and Chico Fernandez
Hook: Straight eye, standard length
Wing: 4 white saddle hackles
Collar: Orange and white saddle hackles with stiff fibers
Tie on the wing hackles on each side, splayed outward. Tie on one white saddle hackle, palmering forward about 1/3 of the hook shank. Repeat with the orange saddle. Repeat again with another white

saddle hackle, tie off at head, whip finish and cement. This recipe is the same as on page 60 of Reference 2.

Seaducer (A)
Originator: Homer Rhodes/Chico Fernandez
Hook: #4 - 2/0
Thread: 2/0 nylon in red, chartreuse or white
Tail: 6 soft and straight Chinese neck feathers (white, chartreuse or yellow), plus white calf tail and several strands of pearl Krystal Flash
Body: Palmered grizzly saddle hackle or other color matching the tail feathers
Beard: Iridescent red Krystal Flash
Eyes: Very small to medium lead dumbbells
Weedguard: 20-pound hard mono loop
Tie in the dumbbell eyes on top of the hook shank, about 1/8 inch from the rear of the hook eye. Tie on one end of the mono weedguard, on top of the hook shank, from the dumbbell eyes to the hook bend. Tie in the calf tail at the hook bend, on top and sides of hook shank. Tie on the strands of Krystal Flash on top of the hook shank, extending about a hook's length beyond the end of the hook. Tie in the Chinese neck hackles to each side of the hook shank, so that they extend another hook's length beyond the Krystal Flash fibers. Tie the large saddle hackle at the hook bend and palmer up to the edge of the dumbbell eyes. Tie on the iridescent red beard under the hook shank, so that it extends just to the hook point. Tie on the other end of the mono weedguard loop just to the rear of the hook eye. Build up a thread head, whip finish and cement. This recipe is a weighted variation of the pattern shown on page 60 of Reference 2.

Seaducer (B)
Originator: Homer Rhodes/Chico Fernandez
Hook: #2 to 4/0 Mustad 34007
Thread: Danville's red, flat waxed
Tail: 8 to 12 supple, yellow saddle hackles plus 6-10 narrow silver Mylar strips
Body: 2 to 4 webby, yellow saddle hackles
Head: 1 webby, red saddle hackle
Wrap hook shank with thread. At the start of the hook bend, tie in yellow saddle hackles on each side, splayed outward, so that they extend about two hook shank lengths beyond the bend. Add a drop of cement to wraps. Tie in the Mylar strips on each side, parallel to the saddle stems. Tie in the webby saddles over the tail stems and palmer them forward about two-thirds the length of the hook shank. Tie in the webby red saddle hackle, palmer forward and tie off. Add a drop or two of cement. This pattern is a variation of the pattern on page 8 of Reference 1.

Seaducer (C)
Originators: Homer Rhodes and Chico Fernandez
Hook: #4 - 1 Mustad 3407
Wing: 4 orange saddle hackles plus gold and copper Flashabou
Collar: Orange and orange saddle hackles with stiff fibers
Tie on the wing hackles on each side, splayed outward. Then tie on the Flashabou on top of the hook shank. Tie on one brown saddle hackle, palmering forward about 1/3 of the hook shank. Repeat with the orange saddle. Repeat again with another brown saddle hackle, tie off at head, whip finish and cement. This recipe is very similar to that shown on page 60 of Reference 2.

Seafoam Popper
Originator: A.J. Hand
Hook: #1 to 2/0, Eagle Claw 2044-SS with kinked shaft
Thread: White

Tail: Chartreuse and white bucktail, plus pearl
Krystal Flash
Body: Chartreuse closed-cell foam
Eyes: Stick-ons or doll eyes

Tie on the bucktail and Krystal Flash at the hook bend, around the shank. Form the foam body with sandpaper, grinding tool. etc. or buy stock parts. Cup the front face, so it will capture air bubbles while being stripped. Use an awl to pierce a hole in the body from the center of the tapered rear to the lower portion of the cupped face. Coat the hook shank generously with epoxy and slide on the body up to and slightly over the tails butt wraps, stroking away excess epoxy as it's forced out the rear of the body. Epoxy the eyes in place and lightly coat with a drop of epoxy. This is a standard pattern originally developed by A.J. Hand and now successfully used in many color combinations, especially yellow/white, olive/white, red/white, and black/white. This recipe is essentially the same as on page 98 of Reference 3.

Sedotti's Slammer

Originator: Mark Sedotti
Hook: 3/0 Tiemco 800S
Thread: White
Weight: 0.030-inch lead wire plus lead keel
Tail: 2 pairs of white schlappen feathers
Midfly: White bucktail plus pink Krystal Flash and
silver Flashabou
Sides: White bucktail
Back: Peacock herl
Head: Olive and white bucktail
Eyes: 10 mm doll eyes

Wrap the hook shank with the lead wire and then tie in a lead keel. Tie in the schlappen feathers at the hook bend. At the midpoint of the hook, tie in a clump of white bucktail on both the top and bottom of the hook shank. In the same spots, tie in the Krystal Flash and Flashabou. Tie on the peacock herl back just to the rear of the hook eye. Tie on the olive bucktail on top of the herl, and then tie on clumps of white bucktail on the sides and bottom of the hook shank. Build up a small thread head, whip finish and cement. Glue on the eyes. This recipe is the same as described on page 148 of Reference 4.

Shineabou Shad

Originator: Jimmy Nix
Hook: #4 to 1/0 Mustad 34011 or equivalent
Underbody: Silver-gray Antron dubbing
Overbody: Fluorescent light gray marabou plus several
strands of pearl and silver Krystal Flash, 6 to 8
strands of peacock herl and 2 mallard flank feathers
Gills: Fluff of red saddle hackle
Head: Gray deer hair or wool (the latter for a sinking
pattern)
Eyes: Plastic doll eyes or painted dumbbells (latter for
sinking pattern)

Wrap the Antron dubbing over the rear 2/3 of the hook shank. Just in front of the dubbing, tie on the marabou feathers surrounding the underbody, so that the fibers extend one shank's length beyond the bend. Fasten the Krystal Flash to each side and the herl strips on top. Then tie on the flank feather to each side. Tie on the eyes near the hook eye and spin/pack the deer hair through and over the eyes to the hook eye. Whip finish and cement. Trim the body and head to a shad shape. This recipe is the same as shown on page 117 of Reference 5.

Slider

Originator: Larry Dahlberg
Hook: #1 - 2
Thread: Red

Tail: Tan marabou, 2 grizzly saddle hackles and gold
Krystal Flash
Body: Deer body hair
Weedguard: 20-pound double mono loop

Tie on the marabou, on the rear 1/3 of the hook shank, with 2 strands of Krystal Flash on each side. Then tie on the grizzly saddle hackles, one each side, splayed out. Spin on deer hair loosely, up to within 1/8 inch from the hook eye. Whip finish each hair section and add a drop of glue. Do a final whip finish, add cement and trim deer hair to desired shape. Loosely packed deer hair allows the fly to ride just under the water surface, making it more accessible to redfish. This recipe is an adaptation of Larry Dahlberg's Dahlberg Diver, described on page 43 of Reference 2.

Snapping Shrimp

Originator: Chico Fernandez
Hook: #4 -#1, Mustad 34007 or equivalent
Thread: Black
Butt: Orange yarn, dubbing or chenille
Body: Tan, brown or root beer dubbing or chenille
Wing: Brown Craft Fur or FisHair and brown or pearl
Krystal Flash
Head: Black

Invert the hook in the vise so that the point is above the hook shank. Tie in the black tying thread well above the hook bend and tie on a short length of orange chenille. Wrap a few turns and tie off. Then tie on a piece of tan chenille and wrap forward to within 1/8 inch of the hook eye. Tie off and tie in the pearl Krystal Flash and the Craft Fur, both extending at least one inch beyond the end of the hook. Build up a small thread head, whip finish and cement. This recipe is the same as on page 20 of Reference 2.

Sparse Chartreuse Clouser

Originator: Bob Clouser
Hook: #2 Mustad 34007 or Eagle Claw 413
Thread: Chartreuse flat waxed nylon
Eyes: Small bead-chain eyes
Throat: Chartreuse bucktail
Wing: Chartreuse bucktail and 10 strands of gold
Flashabou

Tie on the bead-chain eyes on top of the hook shank, about 1/8 inch behind the hook eye. Tie on a sparse throat of bucktail fore and aft of the bead-chain eyes. Invert the hook in the vise and tie on the Flashabou (about 1/2 inch longer than the bucktail) in front of the bead-chain eyes, on top of the hook shank. In the same place, tie on a sparse clump of chartreuse bucktail, whip finish and cement.

Squid Fly

Originator: Unknown
Hook: 1/0 to 3/0 Mustad 34011
Thread: White
Tail: 100-pound mono and 8 long white saddle
hackles
Body: Pearl Ice Chenille
Collar: White Polar Fibre
Eyes: 5/16 inch, red 3-D eyes

Tie the 8 saddles to a 2-inch piece of the mono, so that all hackles are splayed outward in a circular pattern. Trim off any unnecessary mono from the short end. Tie the mono with saddles onto the top of the hook shank, so that the saddle butts extend just beyond the bend of the hook. Glue the 3-D eyes to the sides of the hook shank directly over the hook point, using either hot glue or Zap-a-Gap. Tie on the ice chenille at the hook bend, over the mono junction, and wrap the length of the hook 3 times, tying it off at the hook eye. Tie on 2 clumps of Polar Fibre just behind the hook

eye, one at the top and one at the bottom of the hook shank. Build a small thread head, whip finish and cement.

Stick Candy

Originator: Bob Popovics
Hook: Straight eye, long shank
Thread: White
Underbody: Silver Mylar tinsel
Wing: White and gray Ultra Hair, plus sparse silver
Mylar
Body: Epoxy
Eyes: Stick-on, silver Prizmatic eyes with black pupils
Gills and Mouth: Painted with red marking pen

Wrap silver Mylar tinsel over the hook shank, ending with thread near hook eye. Tie on a bunch of White Ultra Hair at the head, over which a bunch of gray Ultra Hair is also tied. Add a sparse amount of silver Mylar to each side and loosely wrap to form a cylindrical body from hook eye to bend. Add epoxy to solidify shape. Stick on eyes and paint the gills and mouth with a red marking pen. Add a final light coat of epoxy over the body, eyes and mouth. This recipe is from page 63 of Reference 2.

Stir Fry

Originator: Bill & Kate Howe
Hook: #6 to 2/0 Mustad 34007/3407, Eagle Claw
254/354, Tiemco 800S/811S, Pate or Owner SSW
Thread: White
Wing: Polar pearl Lite Brite; red crinkle nylon; white
Ocean Hair; smoke, olive and black Ultra Hair;
peacock Krystal Flash; and silver Flashabou
Head: Thread, marked with black marker and coated
with Hot Stuff Special T Glue and Jolly Glaze
Eyes: Stick-on Prizmatic eyes

Tie on the wing to the rear of the hook eye, applying the materials in the order listed to simulate a baitfish coloration. Wind a thread head, whip finish and cement. Color the head with markers as desired. Add the glue and accelerator to the front of the fly, to maintain wing fibers in the proper position and keep a relatively high profile. After the glue sets, add the eyes and coat with Jolly Glaze. This recipe is the same as shown on page 104 of Reference 3.

Surf Candy

Originator: Bob Popovics
Hook: Straight eye, standard length
Thread: White
Extended Tail: Badger hackle, trimmed, epoxied to 30-
pound mono and sheathed inside silver braided
Mylar
Underbody: Braided pearlescent Mylar tubing
Wing/Body: Polar Bear Ultra Hair and gray Ultra Hair
Body and Head: Epoxy-saturated
Eyes: Stick-on Prizmatic eyes
Gills: Painted red with a marking pen

Trim a badger hackle tip to simulate a forked tail and epoxy to length of mono. Insert assembly into silver braided Mylar and cement so it won't unravel. Wrap the pearlescent tubing over the hook shank, from hook eye to bend. At the hook eye, tie on a small bunch of the Polar Bear Ultra Hair, followed by the extended tail assembly, another bunch of Polar Bear Ultra Hair and a final bunch of gray Ultra Hair. Tie off the head and whip finish. Add epoxy to the head/body to form basic shape. Darken top with a magic marker and add Prizmatic eyes. Trim end of wind to blend in with forked tail. Paint on gills and add a final light coat of epoxy over body/head. This recipe is from page 64 of Reference 2.

Surf Candy (A)

Originator: Bob Popovics

Hook: 1/0 Wright & McGill 254SS or Tiemco 800S/811S

Thread: 3/0 monocord of fine mono thread by Larva Lace

Extended Tail: Badger hackle, trimmed, epoxied to 30-pound mono and sheathed inside silver braided Mylar

Underbody: Flat or braided silver Mylar

Wing/Body: White Ultra Hair, light green Ultra Hair and green Flashabou

Body and Head: Epoxy-saturated and mixed with glitter flakes

Eyes: Stick-on Prizmatic eyes

Gills: Painted red with a marking pen

Trim a badger hackle tip to simulate a forked tail and epoxy to length of mono. Insert assembly into silver braided Mylar and cement so it won't unravel. Attach the tail section to the hook shank and cement the wraps. Wrap the Silver Mylar from the hook eye to the hook bend and back to the hook eye. At the hook eye, tie on small bunches of the white Ultra Hair to each side of the hook shank, at the hook eye, followed by a small bunch of light green Ultra Hair on top. Also add a few strands of green Flashabou on top. Tie off the head and whip finish. Add the glitter-mixed epoxy to the head/body to form basic shape, squeezing the sides to enhance its vertical profile. Darken top with a magic marker and add Prizmatic eyes. Paint on gills and add a final light coat of epoxy over body/head. This recipe is very similar to that shown on page 64 of Reference 2.

Synthetic Clouser

Originator: Bob Clouser

Hook: Straight eye, standard length

Eyes: Lead dumbbells, painted red with black pupils

Throat: White FisHair or Ultra Hair bucktail

Wing: Silver Krystal Flash, silver Flashabou, white FisHair or Ultra Hair, and black, brown or blue FisHair or Ultra Hair

Tie the dumbbell eyes on top of the hook, about 1/4 inch behind the hook eye. Tie on the white synthetic hair, fore and aft of the eyes, so that the length extends about 2-3 hook lengths beyond the end of the hook. Invert the hook in the vise. Tie on first the Krystal Flash and the Flashabou, then the white synthetic hair and then the dark synthetic hair, in front of the dumbbell eyes. The flash material and the synthetic hair should be as long as the white synthetic hair throat, but the dark synthetic hair should extend to just beyond the end of the hook. Tie off, whip finish and cement the head. This recipe is very similar to the pattern shown on page 52 of Reference 2.

Tabory's Slab Fly

Originator: Lou Tabory

Hook: 2/0 to 4/0, straight eye, standard length

Eyes: Pewter dumbbells with plastic pupils, black/yellow

Tail/Wing: 3 or 4 shades of bucktail, pearl Flashabou and peacock herl

Body/Head: White deer body hair

Tie on the dumbbell eyes on top of the hook shank, about midway between the hook eye and the hook bend. Tie on three or four successively darker shades of bucktail on top of the hook shank, between the hook bend and the dumbbell eyes. Overall fly length should be 4 to 8 inches. One popular series of colors is white, yellow, red, and olive. Also tie on the Flashabou and finally the peacock herl. Spin and pack the deer body hair, starting just in front of the tail wrappings, continuing through the dumbbell eyes and ending at the hook eye. Allow the rear fibers to

flare to the rear, blending in with the wing. Whip finish and cement at the hook eye. Trim the front portion of the deer hair to a baitfish profile by somewhat flattening the sides. Attach the colored eyes to the dumbbells and add a drop of clear epoxy to each. This recipe is the same as on page 123 of Reference 6.

Tabory's Slab Side

Originator: Lou Tabory

Hook: #4 to 5/0

Tail: Pink and white bucktail and peacock herl

Head/Shoulder: Spun white deer body hair

Eyes: Lead or glass eyes

Tie on the white bucktail tail so that it extends about 2 hook lengths beyond the end of the hook. Tie on the pink bucktail and then a half dozen strands of peacock herl on top of the white bucktail. Tie on the dumbbell eyes on top of the hook, about one-third of the way from the hook eye to the bend. Spin and pack the deer hair up to, around and past the eyes and tie off at the hook eye. Tie off the thread, whip finish and cement. Trim the deer hair so that the body is slender, but high. This recipe is the same as for the pattern shown on page 58 of Reference 1.

Tabory's Slab Side (A)

Originator: Lou Tabory

Hook: 4/0 Mustad 34007 debarbed

Thread: Plain Kevlar

Tail: Layered long bucktail, green over white

Head/Shoulder: Spun green deer body hair

Eyes: Red dumbbells

Tie on tail material so that it extends about 2 hook lengths beyond the end of the hook. Tie on the dumbbell eyes on top of the hook, about one-third of the way from the hook eye to the bend. Spin and pack the deer hair up to, around and past the eyes and tie off at the hook eye. Tie off the thread, whip finish and cement. Trim the deer hair so that the body is slender, but high. Soak the underside of the body and eyes with super glue so that the fly will ride hook point down. This fly is a variation of the pattern shown on page 58 of Reference 1.

Tabory's Slab Side (B)

Originator: Lou Tabory

Hook: #4 to 5/0

Tail: Blue and white bucktail and peacock herl

Head/Shoulder: Spun white deer body hair

Eyes: Lead or glass eyes

Tie on the white bucktail tail so that it extends about 2 hook lengths beyond the end of the hook. Tie on the blue bucktail and then a half dozen strands of peacock herl on top of the white bucktail. Tie on the dumbbell eyes on top of the hook, about one-third of the way from the hook eye to the bend. Spin and pack the deer hair up to, around and past the eyes and tie off at the hook eye. Tie off the thread, whip finish and cement. Trim the deer hair so that the body is slender, but high. This recipe is the same as for the pattern shown on page 58 of Reference 1.

Tabory's Snake Fly

Originator: Lou Tabory

Hook: #4 to 2/0 Mustad 34007 or 34011

Thread: Black

Tail: Black ostrich herl or saddle hackles

Wing: 1 or 2 sections of black marabou and black Krystal Flash

Head: Black dyed deer body hair

Tie on the tail material at the hook bend. Tie on several strands of Krystal Flash just in front of the tail windings. Tie on a pair of marabou feathers on the side of the hook shank, about midway on the hook

shank. Spin and pack the deer hair from just in front of the marabou to the hook eye. Whip finish and cement at the hook eye. Trim the front of the deer hair to obtain a tapered nose and to flatten the underside. Chartreuse, orange or red are other productive colors. Head and hook size determines fly buoyancy and action. For very small flies, use just the marabou for a combination wing and tail. This recipe is the same as shown on page 211 of Reference 7.

Tan Clouser

Originator: Bob Clouser

Hook: #2 - 6 Mustad 34007

Thread: White 6/0 flat waxed nylon

Tag: Krystal Flash

Underbody: Pearl Mylar

Body: Medium clear vinyl rib

Eyes: Lead dumbbell

Wing: Tan craft fur or calf tail

Tie on the dumbbell eyes on the top of the hook shank, about 1/4 inch behind the hook eye. Tie on the Krystal Flash tag at the hook bend; at that point, also tie on first a short length of vinyl rib and a strip of pearl Mylar. Wrap the thread forward to the dumbbell eyes and follow it by wrapping the Mylar strip to that point and tying it off. Wrap the vinyl rib forward also, and tie it off. Tie on a clump of craft fur or calf tail in front of the dumbbells, so that it flares up to and beyond the hook point and bend. Wrap a thread head, whip finish and cement. This recipe is very similar to the recipe shown on page 42 of Reference 2.

Tan Turneffe Crab

Originator: Craig Mathews

Hook: #8 - 4 Mustad 3407, Daiichi 2546 or Tiemco 800S

Thread: Tan 6/0

Underbody: Lead strips or wire wraps

Body: Tan Furry Foam

Legs: Tan round rubber

Wing: Natural deer hair

Eyes: Gold bead chain

Wind on the lead for appropriate weighting and cement in place. Keep frontal profile as flat as practical. Cut 2 pieces of Furry Foam simulating the outline of a crab carapace. Glue the lower piece onto the underside of the hook shank so that about a 1/8 inch gap remains between the hook eye and the front edge of the carapace. Put more glue on the inner surface of this body piece and lay in 6 round rubber legs for crab legs. Apply the upper piece of Furry Foam and press to glue in place. Spin and pack a few turns of deer body hair up to the hook eye, whip finish and cement. Mark the legs with black permanent marker. Trim the deer hair head, leaving many longer fibers extending over the Furry Foam carapace. This recipe is very similar to that shown on page 110 of Reference 3.

Tan/White Clouser

Originator: Bob Clouser

Hook: #8 - 6 Tiemco 811S

Thread: Tan

Wing: Tan/white bucktail, pearl Flashabou and root beer Krystal Flash

Eyes: Extra-small silver bead-chain

Tie on the bead-chain eyes on top of the hook shank, about 1/8 inch behind the hook eye. Invert the hook in the vise and tie on a large clump of white bucktail on top of the hook shank, just behind the hook eye. Over this, tie in a large clump of tan bucktail followed by some pearl Flashabou plus 3 - 4 strands of the root beer Krystal Flash. Build up a small thread head, whip finish and cement. To imitate a bay anchovy, this fly should be fairly deep-bodied.

Tarpon Crab
Originator: Tim Borski
Tail (Claws): Tan calf tail, 2 grizzly saddle hackles, 4 furnace saddle hackles and orange Krystal Flash
Body: Natural deer body hair
Eyes: Extended natural glass taxidermy eyes
Legs: Long, soft brown saddle hackle
Tie in a bunch of calf tail at the hook bend, over which are tied several strands of the Krystal Flash. Then tie in 3 saddle hackles on each side, splayed outward. The 3 saddle hackles each consists of a grizzly saddle with a furnace saddle on each side. Tie in the taxidermy eyes, extending along the sides of the claws. Tie in the long saddle hackle and then spin and pack the deer-hair body up to the hook eye. Trim the deer hair to shape and wind the long brown hackle through the body up to the hook eye. Tie off, whip finish and add cement. This recipe is from page 13 of Reference 2.

Texas Tout Fly*
Originator: Capt. Chuck Uzzle
Hook: #4 Mustad 34011
Thread: 6/0 nylon
Tail: Marabou
Body: Large Ice Chenille
Eyes: 3/16 inch Wapsi Cyclops Eye
Place Cyclops Eye on the hook and push to the hook eye. Wrap thread to lock eye in the right position. Cover the hook shank with thread from the eye to the start of the hook bend. Tie on a clump of marabou on top of the hook, at the start of the hook bend. Tie on a piece of Ice Chenille on top of the butt wraps of the marabou and wrap the tying thread forward to the eye. Wrap the Ice Chenille forward and tie off at the eye. Whip finish and cement the head and eye. Various color choices can be used, but it seems best to have a significant contrast in colors between the marabou and the Ice Chenille.
*Favorite Fly of Capt. Chuck Uzzle

Tricolor Clouser
Originator: Bob Clouser
Hook: #2 Mustad 34007
Tying Thread: Danville flat waxed chartreuse green
Length: 1.5 inches Approx.
Tail: Pearlescent green Krystal Flash
Wing: White and green Bucktail
Weedguard: 16-pound Mason (Optional) monofilament
Eyes: Lead or brass, size dependent on water depth
Starting with the hook shank up, wrap the shank 3/4 of the distance from the hook bend to the eye with thread. Tie in eyes on top of shank, about 1/4 inch back from hook eye. On the same side of the shank, in front of the eyes, tie in some white bucktail, wrapping back to the eyes. Turning hook over, tie in 6 lengths of the Krystal Flash, also in front of the eyes. On top of the flash, tie in some light green bucktail, using about half of the material used for the white bucktail. Then tie in an equal amount of darker green bucktail over the light green bucktail. Whip finish and cement the head. This recipe is a variant of the Clouser Deep Minnow on page 42 of Reference 2.

Ultra Shrimp
Originator: Bob Popovics
Hook: #1 - 1/0 straight eye, standard length
Thread: Clear mono or tan nylon
Underbody: Tan thread
Forelegs: Tan Ultra Hair or Super Hair
Body: Tan Ultra Hair or Super Hair, gold Krystal Flash
Antennae: A few fibers of tan Ultra Hair or Super Hair
Eyes: Melted monofilament
Legs: Light ginger or badger hackle
Tail: Tan Ultra Hair or Super Hair

Back: Ultra Hair or Super Hair
Tie in ginger hackle at hook bend and wrap hook shank with thread, ending near hook eye. Palmer the ginger hackle down to the hook eye and tie off. Trim hackle flat on top. Tie in mono eyes, extending back and upwards. Tie bunch of Ultra Hair on top of hook, extending well beyond both hook eye and hook bend, with thread ending up at hook bend. Divert small group of hair fibers pointing downward as forelegs. Point the remainder of the fibers upward, surrounding the mono eyes. Leaving a small group of Ultra Hair fibers to form the tail, pull the remaining fibers toward the eyes and tie off. Trim the Ultra Hair so that a few fibers are extending forward like antennae, the rest trimmed to a point past the eyes. Also trim the forelegs and tail to proper proportions. Add epoxy to the back and body to keep its shape. This recipe is from page 21 of Reference 2.

Ultra Shrimp (A)
Originator: Bob Popovics
Hook: Straight eye, standard length
Thread: Clear mono
Underbody: Tan thread
Forelegs: Tan Ultra Hair or Super Hair
Body: Tan Ultra Hair or Super Hair, gold Krystal Flash
Antennae: A few fibers of tan Ultra Hair or Super Hair
Eyes: Melted monofilament
Legs: Light ginger or tan hackle
Tail: Tan Ultra Hair or Super Hair
Back: Ultra Hair or Super Hair
Tie in ginger hackle at hook bend and wrap hook shank with thread, ending near hook eye. Palmer the ginger hackle down to the hook eye and tie off. Trim hackle flat on top. Tie in mono eyes, extending back and upwards. Also tie in bunch of gold Krystal Flash over eyes. Tie bunch of Ultra Hair on top of hook, extending well beyond both hook eye and hook bend, with thread ending up at hook bend. Divert small group of hair fibers pointing downward as forelegs. Point the remainder of the fibers upward, surrounding the mono eyes. Leaving a small group of Ultra Hair fibers to form the tail, pull the remaining fibers toward the eyes and tie off. Trim the Ultra Hair so that a few fibers are extending forward like antennae, the rest trimmed to a point past the eyes. Also trim the forelegs and tail to proper proportions. Add epoxy to the back and body to keep its shape. This recipe is similar to the pattern on page 21 of Reference 2.

Utility Minnow
Originator: Capt. Lenny Moffo
Hook: 1/0 Gamakatsu SC15
Thread: Chartreuse 3/0 monocord
Tail: Chartreuse over white bucktail plus gold Flashabou
Body Accent: 2 bronze-dyed grizzly hackles
Wing: Chartreuse over white bucktail
Topping: 4 strands of peacock herl
Throat: Short tips of white bucktail
Head: Flat waxed 3/0 orange thread
Eyes: Witchcraft Stick-ons
Wrap hook shank with thread and tie on a small clump of white bucktail at hook bend. Then tie in 3 or 4 strands of Flashabou followed by a small clump of chartreuse bucktail at the same place. Halfway forward to hook eye, tie in grizzly hackles on sides of hook shank. Tie in a small, short clump of white bucktail on hook shank bottom just to the rear of hook eye, as a throat. Then tie in white and then chartreuse bucktail on top of hook shank and add peacock herl. Switch to an orange tying thread and form fly head, whip finish and cement. Glue on the decal-type eyes and, when dry, cover the entire head with clear epoxy.

Variegated Clouser
Originator: Bob Clouser
Hook: #6 Tiemco 811S
Thread: White
Wing: Light aqua/white bucktail and pearl Flashabou
Eyes: Silver bead chain
Weedguard: V-style 20-pound fluorocarbon
Tie on extra-small bead-chain eyes on the top of the hook shank, about 1/8-inch from the hook eye. Invert the hook in the vise and tie on the white bucktail on top of the hook shank, just in back of the hook eye. Tie in the pearl Flashabou and then the light aqua bucktail at the same location. Tie on the weedguard, whip finish and cement. Using an olive permanent marker, create vertical banding on the bucktail to imitate sheepshead markings. Overall fly appearance should be short and chunky.

Wagtail Deceiver
Originator: Lefty Kreh, Barry Clemson
Hook: 3/0 to 5/0
Thread: White flat waxed nylon
Tail: 10 white saddle hackles, braided Mylar tubing and 10 strands of silver Flashabou
Body: 10 strands of pearl Flashabou
Collar: White bucktail
Wing: White and light blue bucktail
Eyes: Stick-on Prizmatic eyes
Glue and wrap 5 saddle hackles into one end of a piece of Mylar tubing (core left in). Tie in the other end onto the top of the hook shank, at the hook bend. Tie 5 more saddle hackles at the hook bend, Deceiver style, plus 10 strands of silver Flashabou (1/2 the length of the saddles). Tie in 10 strands of the pearl Flashabou around the hook shank at mid-body. Tie in a collar of white bucktail under the hook shank, just behind the hook eye. Then tie in a clump of white bucktail, followed by a clump of light blue bucktail, on top of the hook shank. Build a thread head, whip finish and cement. Add the Prizmatic eyes with a drop of Goop.

Walter's Minnow
Originator: Walter Fondren
Hook: #2 Mustad 34011
Thread: Clear mono
Tail: 12 strands of pearl Flashabou
Body: Small pearl Mylar tubing
Overbody: Length of clear luggage tag cord
Eyes: Painted black on white
Slip the Mylar tubing onto the hook shank from the hook-point end. Tie it off at the tail well down into the hook bend. Tie on the Flashabou tail fibers at the same point. Tie on the luggage tag cord at the same point and wrap the tying thread forward over the Mylar tubing. Tie off the tubing at the hook eye and tie off the luggage tag cord at the same place, trimming off the excess material. Build a small thread head, whip finish and cement. Paint on the eyes and coat with clear epoxy.

Walter's Shrimp
Originator: Walter Fondren
Hook: #4 Mustad 3011
Thread: White flat waxed nylon
Feelers: Pearl Kinky Fiber, pearl Fluorofibre and pearl Flashabou
Antennae: 2 black lengths of Supreme Hair
Body: Pearl Flashabou dubbing
Overbody: Clear luggage tag cord
Eyes: Medium mono with black beads
Weedguard: 16-pound mono loop
On top of the hook shank, tie on one end of the mono weedguard loop, from the hook eye to the hook bend. On top of the hook shank, well into the hook bend, tie on a mixture of the Kinky Fiber, Fluorofibre and

Flashabou. Then tie on the 2 antennae. On top of these wraps, tie on a short piece of mono, perpendicular to the hook shank, add the black beads, cement and trim. Work the tying thread back to the hook eye and dub a Flashabou body back to and around the mono eyes, generally increasing body diameter toward the rear. Cut a piece of luggage tag cord about 1 1/4 inches long. Clip one end of the luggage tag cord to a very shallow angle and gradually shave or slice one edge, reducing its thickness by about one half at the other end. The resultant flat edge should start on the side opposite the pointed end of the cord. Put a strip of super glue gel on this flat edge and place the cord on top of the dubbed body. Work the tying thread back to the hook eye in 1/8-inch-wide spirals, tying the cord securely to the body and creating a segmented back profile. Tie off and trim the end of the cord, tie off the loose end of the weedguard loop, make a small thread head, whip finish and cement.

White/Red/Grizzly Whistler
Originator: Dan Blanton
Hook: 1/0 to 6/0 Mustad 9175 or 34007, or Wright & McGill 254 CAT
Wing: White bucktail and 4 wide grizzly neck feathers
Body: Medium red chenille
Collar: 3 large webby red hackle feathers
Head: Built up with thread
Eyes: Silver bead chain or lead dumbbells
Tie on a full clump of the bucktail around the hook shank at the hook bend. Add 2 grizzly feathers to each side, each pair splayed up and down. Cement the butt ends generously. Wind the chenille body forward about 2 turns and tie off. Then palmer the 3 hackle feathers forward to within 1/4 inch of the hook eye. Tie on the eyes just behind the hook eye, whip finish and cement. This recipe is the same as shown on page 29 of Reference 1.

White Water Witch
Originator: Ray Smith
Hook: Straight eye, standard or long shank
Thread: Black
Tail: Black bucktail or FisHair
Body: Silver braided Mylar
Wing: Black bucktail or FisHair
Throat: Red bucktail
Head: Thread
Tie on a sparse clump of black bucktail on top of the hook shank, at the hook bend, extending about 3 inches beyond the end of the hook. Tie on and wrap forward the braided Mylar body up to the hook eye. Tie on a sparse throat of red bucktail under the hook shank, just in front of the hook eye. Tie on another sparse clump of black bucktail on the top of the hook, just in back of the hook eye. The ends of this clump should extend about 1 1/2 inches beyond the end of the hook. Build up a thread head, whip finish and cement. This recipe is identical to the one shown on page 67 of Reference 2.

Whitlock's Matuka Sculpin
Originator: Dave Whitlock
Hook: Up to 4/0 Tiemco 811S or equivalent
Thread: Yellow Danville single-strand unwaxed floss
Underbody: Loop of Mason monofilament (same diameter as hook wire) and lead wire
Overbody: Cream fuzzy wool or Mohair yarn
Cheek: Red Antron yarn
Wings: 4 to 8 wide grizzly or cree saddle hackles dyed or colored tan and olive
Pectoral Fins: Cock pheasant flank feathers
Head: Cream, olive, black and golden brown deer body hair
Rib: Fine stainless steel wire
Eyes: Wapsi dolls eyes

Weedguard: Optional monofilament
Tie on the monofilament on each side of the hook shank, loop to the rear. Cement with Zap-a-Gap and wrap with lead wire. Tie on the stainless steel wire at the hook bend and then dub on the yarn over the rear 2/3 of the hook shank, and add in front several turns of the red Antron to simulate gills. Tie on the saddle hackles on top, to the rear of the hook eye, and then bind them down, Matuka-style, with the stainless steel wire. Tie on the pheasant flank feathers just in front of the cheek, concave sides turned out. Spin and pack the deer body hair up to the hook eye, whip finish and cement. Trim the deer hair to a sculpin shape and cut out small recesses for the eyes. Place a drop of Goop into the eye sockets and insert the eyes. This recipe is the same as shown in Reference 5.

Woolhead Finger Mullet
Originator: Unknown
Hook: 1/0 to 2/0 Mustad 34011 or equivalent
Thread: Silver or gray flat waxed nylon
Body: Pearl Estaz or Crystal Chenille
Overwing: Craft Fur, Sea Fibers or equivalent and 2 tan grizzly hackle tips
Throat: Red marabou
Head: Light yellow wool dubbing
Eyes: Stick-ons, silver with black pupils
Tie in the pearl Estaz at the bend of the hook, wrap to the middle of the shank and tie off. Tie in a clump of the craft fur, allowing it to cover the Estaz and to extend an inch or so beyond the hook bend. In the same area, tie in the hackle tips on the lower sides of the hook shank. Then tie in the red marabou throat and dub on a thick wool head. Whip finish and cement. Place a drop of super glue gel on each side of the head and attach the stick-on eyes.

Woolhead Mullet
Originator: Unknown
Hook: Straight eye, standard length, up to 4/0
Thread: White Danville flat waxed nylon
Wing: White bucktail, 6-10 white saddle hackles
Collar: White lamb's wool
Head: White lamb's wool
Eyes: Stick-on Prizmatic
Tie on a clump of bucktail around the hook shank, at the hook bend. Tie on the saddles on the sides and top of the hook, with feathers curving inward. Spin, wrap and pack the lamb's wool from the hook bend to the hook eye. Whip finish and cement. Trim the wool to a tapered bullet nose so that its shape blends in with the wing. Attach eyes and lock in with a drop or two of epoxy. Mark up the head and feathers as desired with waterproof felt markers, to simulate mullet features. This pattern is very similar to the pattern on page 40 of Reference 2.

Woolly Bugger Express*
Originator: Unknown
Hook: Debarbed #2, Mustad 34011
Thread: 6/0 black on body, red on head
Tail: Black marabou
Body: Large black ice chenille
Rib: Black saddle hackle
Tie on a clump of black marabou with black thread on the hook, at the hook bend. At the same place, tie on a long black saddle hackle and the ice chenille. Wind the chenille forward and tie off at the hook eye. Palmer the black hackle through the chenille and tie off at the hook eye. Tie off the black thread with red thread and build up a small head. Tie off, whip finish and cement the head. This pattern is a variant of the classical Woolly Bugger tied and fished all over the world.
*Favorite Fly of Capt. Larry Kennedy

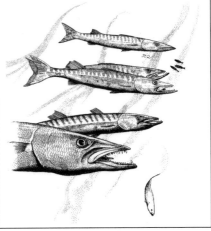